Riots and Community Politics in England and Wales 1790–1810

Riots and Community Politics in England and Wales 1790–1810

John Bohstedt

Harvard University Press
Cambridge, Massachusetts
London, England
1983

Publication of this book has been aided by a grant
from the Andrew W. Mellon Foundation

Library of Congress Cataloging in Publication Data

Bohstedt, John, 1943–
Riots and community politics in England and Wales, 1790–1810.

Includes bibliographical references and index.
1. Riots—England—History—18th century.
2. Riots—Wales—History—18th century.
3. Local government—England—History—18th century.
4. Local government—Wales—History—18th century.
I. Title.
HV6485.G72E53 1983   322.4′4′0942   82–15480
ISBN 0–674–77120–6

To Jinx

Acknowledgments

Many people have helped me on my way. My mentors, R. R. "Pat" Cone, Robert Flick, Eric C. Kollman, and David S. Landes, infected me with their own love of disciplined inquiry, argument, and imagination. The pioneering works of E. J. Hobsbawm, George Rudé, E. P. Thompson, and Charles Tilly provided the direct inspiration and examples for this study; all four scholars have also generously taken the time to comment on my work at various stages.

I owe a great deal to the cheerful competence and energy of the staffs of the Public Record Office, the Devon County Record Office, the Exeter City Record Office, the Exeter City Library, the Lancashire Record Office, the Lincolnshire Record Office, the Birmingham Central Reference Library, the Oxfordshire Record Office, the Staffordshire Record Office, the Warwickshire Record Office, the University of Nottingham Manuscripts Division, the Beinecke Library of Yale University, the Widener Library of Harvard University, particularly the Government Documents Division, and the Interlibrary Loan Services of both the Widener Library and the James Hoskins Library of the University of Tennessee. I especially thank Mr. P. A. Kennedy, Esq., County Archivist for Devon, for his hearty encouragement and for guiding me to the valuable Clifford Papers at Ugbrooke House. Quotations from Crown-copyright records in the Public Record Office appear by permission of the Controller of Her Majesty's Stationery Office, while quotations from Crown-copyright records among the Fortescue lieutenancy papers in the Devon County Record Office appear by permission of the Keeper of the Public Records. I am very grateful to Lord Clifford for allowing me to consult papers in his possession.

My research and writing was supported by fellowships from the Danforth Foundation and the Frank Knox Memorial, by a grant from the British Social Science Research Council, by a Summer Stipend from the National Endowment for the Humanities, by grants from research funds administered by the Harvard Graduate Society, and by a year's leave from teaching duties granted by the President and Fellows of Harvard College, for all of which I am deeply grateful.

At the University of Tennessee, my colleagues Sarah R. Blanshei, LeRoy P. Graf, and Paul J. Pinckney adjusted teaching schedules and otherwise supported my writing in substantial ways. I must thank a number of people who gave a great deal of care to the typing of an often difficult manuscript, particularly Sarah Center, Jan Doyle, Laura McCabe, Debra Pierce, Linda S. Watson, and Dorothy Wilkerson. My friends and colleagues, Sarah R. Blanshei, Andrew Charlesworth, Cliff Honicker, David S. Landes, H. J. Hanham, Wallace T. MacCaffrey, Paul J. Pinckney, Roy Rosenzweig, and Charles Tilly, read part or all of the manuscript and commented upon it, and their efforts to help clarify the argument have been enormously helpful. Aida D. Donald gave me wise counsel and encouragement at decisive moments as I prepared the manuscript, while Rose M. Udics edited it with great care and sorted out many syntactical tangles. Wynne L. Brown created first-rate maps and graphs. Phylis and Phil Morrison generously made a place for me in their home, a place of rich excitement and caring. It provided me ideal surroundings in which to put the finishing touches on the manuscript. My family, Jinx, Rachel, and Jake, have helped at every stage from gathering materials to proofreading. Their unflagging support has sustained me through many days and nights.

Knoxville, Tennessee

January 1983

Contents

1

The Politics of Riot

A play is only a moment, but to create
that moment you have to write a whole play.

—Thomas Babe, 1980

Seventeen ninety-five was a year of desperation for the common
people of England. The harvest of 1794 had failed. As stocks of
food ran out, prices rose, gradually in the spring, and then ever
faster, until in August they reached levels unknown to living
memory.

At Barrow-upon-Soar near Leicester that summer, hunger grew
acute. Neighboring farmers preferred to send their grain to larger
towns nearby instead of selling it in the village, and the poor
worried aloud that "every bit of bread which they eat...would be
their last" and grimly vowed "not to suffer any more grain, *grown
in their Parish*, to pass through the village."[1]

Just after midnight on Thursday, August 6, the noise of two
wagons of wheat rumbling through the village electrified people.[2]
Several young men ran across the fields to intercept the wagons at
the next hamlet. They drove them back to the parish church at
Barrow, where a crowd of several dozen stacked the sacks of wheat
against the churchyard wall. Later, they moved them to the church
belfry, to "secure [them] from depredation," then rang the church
bells to summon the neighborhood. Delegates from the three
"coalesced" villages of Barrow, Sileby, and Quorn went to the
nearest magistrate, a Reverend Mr. Storer, "to solicit [his] friendly
interference." He feared he could be of little service but said he
would come down presently to "settle with the Parish Officers."

Shortly after daybreak, the first of several bargains was struck.
The owner of the wheat, a baker from Leicester, arrived at Barrow
to see what had become of his grain. He was met on the road by
two graziers of Barrow, who persuaded him to let the poor have

the wheat at a reduced price if the parish would make up the difference. Accordingly, the wheat at the church was divided among the three villages, and part of it was sent to the mill to be ground.

At noon, however, the local equilibrium was shattered by the intrusion of outsiders. The Leicester Yeomanry, volunteer cavalry, rode into Barrow led by another of the county magistrates. Perhaps the baker had had a change of heart. Perhaps the Yeomanry had been set in motion by the inital alarm, for they had been called out that morning, they later reported, "to quell a riot...of a very serious nature at Barrow." No doubt these amateur guardians of property and order were tired and tense, for they had been out the three previous days dealing with riots at Leicester and Shepshed. Justice Storer met the cavalry just outside Barrow. He assured them, a bit defensively, that the grain was lodged in the church and that he had warned the people of the peril they courted by their unlawful seizure. He and the outsiders agreed that the wheat would be restored to its owner, who would then sell the grain to the villagers "to do away in some measure the crime of stealing." The cavalry said later that, as they rode into the village, they had passed public houses that seemed filled with "disorderly men mostly armed with clubs" who rained fierce threats and contempt upon them.

The arrival of the cavalry multiplied the crowd at the church-yard. Some villagers were drawn by simple curiosity, some came "to protect the corn which by a union of plausible circumstances, they had unfortunately been led to consider as their own." The villagers and the cavalry wrangled furiously, for the cavalry treated the seizure of the grain as "nothing short of robbery" and insisted it be restored to the owner. The crowd rejected that claim as "unjust, after...it had been so legally bargained for." They declared "they would rather lose their lives on the spot than part with any of it." According to the cavalry, the frantic and insulting mob shook clubs in the troopers' faces and threatened to tear their hearts out and to join the Leicester mob and plunder the banks. The Riot Act was read, and the people were warned that the cavalry's weapons were loaded. At length a compromise was struck, and the wheat was divided between the villages and Leicester.

But tempers still simmered. As the wagon for Leicester moved off, a volley of stones, brickbats, and clubs flew at the cavalrymen who first fired into the air. But then they thought they heard shots from the crowd, so they fired into it. Two men fell dead in the churchyard, shot through the head, and another was mortally wounded. At least six other persons were also shot. The cavalry chased the people through the streets of the village until only the wounded and dead remained in sight. Then the Yeomanry reformed and escorted the wagon out of town. The people later reported that the stones had been thrown by some intemperate "women in no respect connected with the people in the churchyard." Two of those killed had large families. The incident entered local tradition as the "Barrow butchery."[3]

The riot at Barrow was atypical only in its tragic climax: fatalities were rare in the riots of this period.[4] The shootings seem to have resulted from the clash of conflicting perceptions of legitimacy and property: parochial right versus the rectitude of the propertied Yeomanry, the immediate survival of the villagers versus the wider security of commerce.[5] That tension was heightened by hunger and fatigue, and it reached flash point when bargaining failed to bridge the gaps in sympathy.

In other respects the Barrow episode epitomizes the local political bargaining so characteristic of the riots of this period. Most significant, the rioters deliberately made their interception of the grain a *public* act. They seized the high ground politically—and even literally, for the churchyard where the crowd stood was four feet above the road where the cavalry stood, and that not only "equalized" them physically but also added to the Yeomanry's anxiety. The crowd *appropriated* the public center of the parish, the church, to underscore and perhaps to "sanctify" the legitimacy of their actions. They immediately tried to activate local authority and to call out the rest of the community as coadjutors and mediators. By maintaining discipline, by physically securing the wheat, and by negotiating carefully, they tried to minimize the dangers of dissension, pillage, moral disintegration, and legal liability. By drawing in other members of the community the rioters transformed their formally illegal seizure into a public act rendered intelligible and tolerable by the mutual familiarity of the parties (rioters, magistrates, and middle-rank mediators), and by the familiarity of their actions, claims, and roles. But if a fragile consensus was viable in the local environment, it withered in the harsh light of external definitions of property, order, and force.

Riots were quintessentially local politics. Mobs typically mustered groups of people who shared a praxis of common experience and perception. And rioters had to reckon with local magistrates and gentlemen with whom they might have a variety of political and social ties. These "horizontal" and "vertical" social networks—the framework of community politics—shaped the form and frequency of collective violence at two levels. Immediately, at the moment of forceful confrontation, the structure and dynamics of community politics shaped the interaction between crowds, targets, and authorities. At one remove, both before and after a riot, community politics determined the attitudes and actions of rioters and authorities: their prior calculations and preparations; their response to riot including the magistrates' efforts at remedy and repression; and their assessments entered in the ledger of local memory. Was the riot a "success" or was it an atrocity? Which judgment would be consulted at the next crisis?

By *riot* I mean an incident in which a crowd of fifty or more people acted in hostile fashion to damage or seize property, to attack persons physically, or to coerce individuals to perform or desist from some immediate action. That definition is a functional rather then legal one. The criterion of crowd size is somewhat arbitrary. The common law regarded a riot as a violent and cooperative action by three or more people. The Riot Act of 1715 specified that if twelve or more people remained assembled an hour after the Riot Act proclamation had commanded them to disperse, they were guilty of a felony. I have used a larger number on the assumption that crowds of such size acted upon "public," that is, social, motives and interests and not merely on "private" familial or individual interests. The criterion of physical attack, damage, or coercion distinguishes riot from mere "protest," for indeed, riots produced a tangible result and usually required some magisterial response, whether remedy or repression.

The word *community* in this book does not imply any rosy assumptions about membership, communality, or mutual benevolence between rulers and ruled. By communities I mean simply towns and villages that had some geographical unity and that typically had more or less objective institutional identities marked by parish and township boundaries, local governments, markets, and so on. The degree of cohesion they possessed and its relationship to riots is one of the central questions to be explored in this book.

I use the word *politics* in two senses in this study. Sometimes I mean local or national *institutions* of government and the conflicts connected with them, such as election riots or ideological warfare between Reformers and "Church and King" loyalists. But much more often I mean a more informal kind of social politics or bargaining, and in this book I try to show that riot was a kind of informal give-and-take that shared several characteristics of institutional politics. Riots were social politics in the sense that they tested rioters' and magistrates' resources of force and persuasion, affected the policies of local authorities and the distribution of goods and social burdens, and took place within calculable conventions, which I call the "protocol of riot." They did not normally challenge the arrangement of local power; riots were "extra-institutional" rather than anti-institutional, a distinction Pauline Maier makes in *From Resistance to Revolution* (1972). But neither were riots a *functional* confirmation of the social and political status quo. For riots were direct contests of coercion, their outcomes were uncertain, and they were certainly not approved by the authorities. Hence riots were a *constituent* element in the local physiology of power and conflict.

Riots were doubtless the most common form of popular political action in this period. The episode at Barrow was only one of more than a thousand riots in England and Wales between 1790 and 1810, the generation before the Luddites.[6] Indeed, riot was so familiar that its frequency did not shake the confidence, not to say complacency, of either national or local authorities. To be sure, the government of the day could hardly ignore clamorous hunger; in the dearth of 1795, for example, the government purchased grain on the Continent and apportioned it among the ports for distribution. Parliamentary committees investigated the causes of high prices, and in 1795 and 1801 the government even conducted the first censuses of agricultural production. The Privy Council piously resolved to give up fine white bread and recommended that its local counterparts follow suit.[7] "Let them eat coarse bread" was a telling English inversion of "Let them eat cake." In the most disturbed years, the government issued royal proclamations and circular letters condemning rioting, and it routinely dispatched military detachments to back up local peace keepers. But only once was a Special Commission created, when militiamen rioted in the spring of 1795.[8] Local magistrates were even busier administering doses of conciliation, relief, and repression. But their initial alarm generally faded quickly, when they recognized the rioters as members of their own community. Both local and national officials reacted much more vehemently to the merest rumor of Jacobin activity; they felt much more threatened by what they called its "system" (meaning both organized conspiracy and penetrating criticism of the social system) than by the familiar *fact* of riotous violence.[9]

Why were riots so common as to be commonplace? How can the complex patterns of interaction in riots like the one at Barrow be explained? Eighteenth-century English common people were accustomed to acting collectively, publicly, and forcefully. The society could be portrayed (and was, by William Hogarth) as "crowds, crowds everywhere": crowds in the marketplace and at harvest home; crowds fired by Wesleyan field preachers, by prophets like Joanna Southcott and Richard Brothers, or by the open-air rhetoric of the London Corresponding Society; crowds celebrating electoral largesse or exercising the heckler's franchise; crowds at countless community rituals like the hobbyhorse or "throwing the hood"; crowds along the road to the gallows at Tyburn; crowds at fairs, bull baitings, boxing matches, and balloon exhibitions; crowds, not passive "audiences," at theaters; crowds at football or hurling or snowballing. Even the dissolution of a marriage might be solemnized by a crowd, in the public ritual of popular divorce known as a "wife sale," at which a wife would be led to the marketplace in a halter and "auctioned" to a new partner. The proceeds would often be spent at the nearest public house for a toast to the new alliance.[10]

Three elements of such popular spectacles are significant here. First, the crowds followed rough conventions of behavior ranging from the cathartic ceremony and spectacle surrounding hangings at Tyburn to precise gleaning customs in the harvested fields. Second, such occasions had specific social functions and sometimes underlined the contingent nature of social hierarchy. For example, the good-natured but inexorable extortion of drink money, so often a part of folk celebrations, both overturned rank and authority for a moment and forcibly reminded the rich of their material obligations to the poor. And third, many of these gatherings set the authorities on edge—this period witnessed a marked intensification of the campaign to suppress popular amusements.[11] Thus in many ways crowds were "embryos" of riots.

The tradition of riot was fed not only by luxuriant crowd-life but also by the habitual resort to force by smaller groups in countless episodes. Riotous assault must have been one of the most frequent offenses, after theft, before the courts.[12] No doubt most of these assaults were simple personal quarrels, but the legal formulas of the bills of indictment are opaque and tantalizing. For instance, three laborers of Potterne, Wiltshire, were charged with "wickedly, maliciously and violently" stoning the widow Sarah Reed, "wounding her all over her body."[13] Did they accuse her of being a witch, a scold, or a madam? Or was this mindless hooliganism? One cannot know. The motives are more obvious when small groups attacked sheriffs' bailiffs, tithing men, tax collectors, or excise men in the execution of their duties. The hapless parish constable who impounded heifers, pigs, and horses, or arrested neighbors accused of misdemeanors, might well find his quarry violently rescued from him.[14] Besides riotous rescues and assaults, the courts also frequently heard cases of "forcible entry": the aggressors were charged with riotously entering a house or close, dispossessing the owner of it, and destroying property, often walls or hedges. These incidents may have been attempts to settle, by force or litigation, property disputes between families or small groups. The violence of small groups differed from that of riots primarily in size and scope, and therefore in political significance, but small incidents sometimes had wider social implications. At Witney in Oxfordshire a dozen people rescued six girls from the constable and overseers; these poor, "chargeable" children were being taken as parish apprentices to a cotton spinner in Warwickshire.[15] Almost any brawl or rescue could, and sometimes did, escalate to become a riot.

Nonviolent "demonstrations" were yet another cousin of riots. Frequently, crowds called on magistrates for aid, or paraded through the marketplace in hard times with a "mourning loaf" draped in black, or picketed in a strike, or staged political rallies. These demonstrations might serve as premonitions of riot unless remedial action were taken, or they might attempt to "borrow" force and effect from a riot in a nearby town. But common law distinguished between riot and riotous or unlawful assembly. "When three or more persons shall assemble together with an intent mutually to assist one another against any who shall oppose them in the execution of some enterprise of a private nature with force or violence against the peace, or to the manifest terror of the people, whether the act intended is lawful or unlawful, if the intent only is proven it shall be unlawful assembly; if they execute their intention it is riot."[16] The distinction between assembly and riot, between intent and execution, is precisely the difference between the political effectiveness of mere supplication on the one hand and of direct action on the other. Demonstrations were unlikely to be effective unless connected in time or space with riots that reinforced their claims. Violence compelled response from above. Riots were political "trials by ordeal," not merely unilateral *protest* or "functional dialogue."[17] Moreover, although people could be prosecuted for riotous assembly, the "protocol of riot" reserved most prosecutions for incidents in which actual violence—and hence damage or power—was at issue. Violence was a defining characteristic of riot with political and legal significance.

Finally, some of the crucial elements of riot appeared in almost pure form in rituals of community censure known generically as "rough music," or *charivari*.[18] A contemporary description conveys the essence of the form:

> About 1790 one of the members of the Camden Society witnessed a procession of villagers on their way to the house of a neighboring farmer, in the parish of Hurst [Berkshire] who was said to have beaten his wife. The serenaders, consisting of all ages and denominations, were well supplied with kettles, tin cans, cover-lids, hand-bells, pokers and tongs, and cows' horns, and drawing up in front of the farm, commenced a most horrible din, showing at least that the ceremony was known by the name of rough music? After some time, the party quietly dispersed, apparently quite satisfied with the measure of punishment inflicted by them on the delinquent.[19]

The ceremonies might also include a dramatic reenactment of the offense and the burning of an effigy. The censors made clear to all the nature of the transgression. At Cropthorne, Worcestershire, a group of men cried out "Horns!" and "Cuckold Horns!" at the house of Samuel and Ann Bagshaw, and sang,

> I am a Farmer's son born in another country
> And now my wife has made me a cuckold for to be,

and

> With his pack on his back and his horns on his head as you may tell, the Devil for them has a corner in hell.[20]

On occasion, censure led to physical assault.[21]

The targets of such censure were frequently those who had violated communal sexual or family norms. But "rough music" was also employed against "public enemies," especially against strikebreakers. For example, the shag weavers of Banbury had formed a strong labor organization in the early 1790s. In 1793 one of the members incurred the odium of his colleagues by resuming work during a strike over apprenticeship regulations. "Yesterday [the shag weavers] met in this place [Banbury] and a body of about two hundred paraded the streets with martial music and then proceeded to a place two miles distant, the residence of the man so working and violently took his piece of shag from the loom and triumphantly returned two and two, with each a green bough on his hat, one of them bearing the shag mounted on an ass preceding the rest with fifes playing...in spite of every endeavor to resist they marched and in triumph laid the shag at the door of the master to whom it belonged." The combination of tight organization and ritual punishment exemplifies the mixture of forward-looking and traditional elements in labor movements of this period.[22]

Unpopular officials were also communally chastised by *charivari* or by a closely related practice, burning in effigy, better known because of some of its famous targets. In the winter of 1792–93, Tom Paine's effigy appeared in countless local rituals that echoed the opening guns of the government's campaign against radicalism. But Paine was only the leading light. A minister of Handsworth, a spinster of Creech St. Michael (Somerset), a prominent Quaker miller of Dartford, a bishop of Rochester, a county magistrate of the West Riding, and several tax officials all suffered local ignominy. Conversely, the populace often acclaimed its favorites by carrying a victorious parliamentary candidate around the market square in a chair, a practice called "chairing" (see Hogarth's painting "Chairing the Member," 1754), or even more dramatically, by unhitching a popular figure's carriage from the horses and pulling it into town. Sir Francis Burdett had to suffer this adulation despite his distaste for it.[23]

"Rough music" was not frivolous. Besides causing occasional serious assault, humiliation by "rough music" was meant to be complete and lasting. "The person who has been thus treated, seldom recovers his honour in the opinion of his neighbors."[24] E. P. Thompson argues that "the purpose of *charivari*, particularly when it was repeated night after night, was precisely to chase the victim (or victims) from the neighborhood 'with drums and trumpets.'"[25]

The authorities certainly did not take such customs lightly. They tried to appropriate the force of community censure by using the pillory as punishment, but that intention could backfire when crowds rejected the official line. The Jacobins John Frost in 1793 and Daniel Eaton in 1812 were applauded and adored by London crowds when they stood in the pillory in punishment for seditious offenses. The ritual of political theater and "participatory" punishment ceased to be a usable weapon when the intended audience turned it into a mockery or even a triumphant reversal of its meaning. The public processional to the Tyburn gallows was abolished in 1783, and the pillory in 1816, on just such grounds.[26]

Meanwhile, what could not be abolished could be severely

punished. In 1793 seven people convicted of carrying a man on a stang (rail), in a northern variant of rough music, were sentenced to be imprisoned for two years in the Durham Gaol and to find sureties for their good behavior for three years. Other censors received sentences ranging from six weeks to one year.[27]

It has been said that the Rebecca Riots, which took place in Wales between 1839 and 1843, "were an extension of the practice of the *ceffyl pren*," the Welsh variant of *charivari*.[28] Indeed, riots in general were a close relative of "rough music." In both forms the community was typically defending its integrity.[29] The regulation of morality tended to call for symbolic and psychological coercion, while the typically concrete objectives of riot required direct physical action. But the essential ingredients of "rough music"— righteous indignation and punishment for transgression of public norms—were central elements of riot. Both riot and "rough music" resembled the exorcism of a personified evil, although the direct action of a riot was anything but magical. Moreover, the use of sensory symbols and ritual in both forms strongly suggests a basis of shared experience and social ties underlying those common meanings. Indeed, that ritual, and more generally the public character of both riots and "rough music," seem to have provided and symbolized limits to violence that were only rarely exceeded.[30]

On such a social stage, crowded by popular spectacles, brawls, and processions, riots stand out as at once the most social and most violent, which is to say the most political, episodes. Why did people riot? What were the "causes" of riot? The ambiguities in the second question suggest some serious problems in current scholarship.

In the past thirty years, our understanding of riots has been tremendously advanced by a rich stream of impressionistic studies. Historians have chosen to analyze riots that were especially conspicuous in one way or another: food riots, because they were numerous and clustered; individual urban riots, because they were unusually violent and connected with national political *causes célèbres* like those of John Wilkes, Lord George Gordon, and Joseph Priestley; machine breaking and "Church and King" riots, because they were stations on the evolutionary path of working-class radicalism and the labor movement; or waves of riots that provoked national alarm, like those led by Ned Ludd, Captain Swing, and Rebecca.[31]

These works have created the prevailing scholarly consensus

that riots were rational responses to real grievances rather than unfocused outbursts of crowd madness. That is, they have generally found that rioters acted on intelligible grievances, used appropriately disciplined tactics aimed at relevant targets, and avoided gratuitous violence. I agree that many riots were "rational" in that sense. The analysis of riots as "rational responses" has been a valuable antidote to earlier, primitive theories that riots were the work of an antisocial "riff-raff" or that they resulted from the breakdown of social restraints. But the "rational response" interpretation is not a *sufficient* explanation, for it suggests that the rioters' "rationality" was a function of innate human nature rather than the product of historical factors.[32] A new, indiscriminate orthodoxy threatens to replace the "bad" old syndrome of crowd "madness" with a "good" new stereotype of plebeian rationality. No wonder R. C. Cobb protests, "Professor Rudé's crowd is somehow altogether too respectable."[33]

The problem is only partly solved if we explain rioters' rationality as the product of a legitimizing and directing ideology. By *ideology* I mean a historically rooted, descriptive and normative mental map of both the way the world works and the way the world should work. E. P. Thompson has reconstructed one important ideology, the "moral economy" of eighteenth-century bread rioters, which asserted that food merchants had no right to windfall profits at their neighbors' expense in times of scarcity and thus justified market regulation by magistrates and mobs.[34] But the reconstruction of the crowds' ideology cannot explain why some people *acted* on that ideology and others did not.

For indeed, the deeper methodological weaknesses in the "rational response" interpretation of riots are twofold. First, because the approach is selective and unsystematic, the interpretation of riots as "rational responses" to real grievances cannot explain the *incidence* of riots, for it cannot be tested in negative as well as positive instances, that is, in instances in which real grievances did *not* produce riots. Second, the assumptions underlying the "rational response" theory do not explain why crowds acted as crowds, for they seem to assume that the grievance *created* the riotous crowd.

The problem of the incidence of riots can best be analyzed by collecting a systematic sample of riots to determine when, where, and over what issues crowds typically acted violently. It seemed preferable to me to answer those questions by allowing crowds to "vote with their feet," by gathering an objective sample of all riots rather than selecting events of particular interest to contemporary observers or to later historians. On the basis of my definition of a riot I compiled a "national sample" consisting of all riots reported in two kinds of sources between 1790 and 1810: newspapers and the general Domestic Correspondence file of the papers of the Home Office (H.O. 42), the governmental department most directly responsible for peace keeping.

The time period of my study is not defined by dates of historical significance, although between 1790 and 1810 English society did experience many historically important pressures from the wars with France, food scarcities, and political and industrial changes. But those events are of subordinate interest here, and I tried rather to choose an arbitrary, but representative, slice of the society's life. Moreover, I stopped short of a full discussion of Luddism, since those riots, which began in 1811, have already been extensively analyzed.

In order to collect a relatively unbiased sample, I used two sets of contemporary records that reflected official and public observation and thought. H.O. 42 files consist of letters to the Home Office from local magistrates and other citizens and some copies of Home Office replies. Although the letters in H.O. 42 frequently asked the Home Office to send troops or to take some other action, such as sending relief food shipments, they might simply report riots, or threatening letters, or seditious activity without requesting any action by the Home Office. They were usually eyewitness accounts by the magistrate on the spot. While they naturally expressed concern or alarm, the magistrates' attitude toward "mobs" was generally matter-of-fact. Magistrates did not typically assume that rioters were criminal scum or insurrectionaries, nor did they seem to distort or prejudge their description of rioters' behavior.

Newspapers provided an independent set of observations of the period. Late eighteenth-century newspapers contained not only national news of war and politics but also many items of local concern and simple human interest. Alongside reports of the social activities of ladies and gentlemen were accounts of storms, grisly accidents, freaks of nature, murder and adultery, and riots. In short, while riots might be reported because they were of general public concern, owing to their intensity, or their political or social implications, or because they had cumulative significance, in food crises for instance, they were often reported simply as events of human interest.

I collected reports from two national newspapers for the entire period. For most of the period, those newspapers were *The Observer* (a London weekly) and the *Morning Chronicle* (a London daily). For particular periods in the 1790s in which either or both of those newspapers were not available to me, I substituted *The Times* or the *London Chronicle*, or both. Finally, to round out the sample, I used the annual chronologies of events printed in the *Annual Register*, which of course often summarized newspaper stories.

Hence, all 617 riots reported in one of these four sources (H.O. 42, two newspapers, and the *Annual Register*) composed my "national sample" and form the basis for my quantitative statements about the incidence of riots, the number of fatalities, and so on. While the reports themselves do not seem to contain serious distortions of the rioters' actions or possible motives, obviously any selection of social sources contains some biases.

London riots are almost certainly overrepresented in my sample, because I used London newspapers, although riots in London seem to be underrepresented in the Home Office files. That bias can be controlled by separating London riots from the body of the national sample and treating the national sample as two samples: of London and of provincial riots. However, outside London, the sample does not seem to have a systematic geographic distortion. These national newspapers did report news from all over the nation—the Home Counties, for instance, were not particularly favored—especially because they relied upon the provincial press as much as upon correspondents for their news. No obvious geographical "black holes" seem to exist.

Could there have been remote rural areas in which unreported rioting took place? Possibly. But my definition of riot as crowd violence makes it unlikely, for such incidents usually attracted notice or required some administrative response (though doubtless familiar rituals like "rough music" or violent fights between factions and intervillage contests might have gone unnoticed). However, the reliability of the national sample on this score is supported not only by the reports on events in remote rural villages in both the newspapers and the Home Office correspondence but also by other evidence: I searched many Quarter Sessions records, and for the years of scarcity, 1795–1796 and 1800–1801, I read many other newspapers, including many provincial newspapers, without encountering a significant number of additional rural riots. Those few rural riots that were reported in the national sources do indeed seem exceptional in several ways (see Chapter 8).

A more serious and genuine bias in the Home Office papers

may have misled historians into exaggerating the predominance of food, labor, and political riots. Riots involving military forces—recruiting riots and civilian-military brawls—were often reported to and handled by the War Office, Horseguards (the office of the Commander-in-Chief), or the Admiralty. Hence the relevant correspondence is in their archives rather than in the Home Office files. Newspaper reports help to correct this bias, but my national sample probably does underestimate the number of riots related to the military.

Table 1 breaks down the national sample of riots by the issues manifested in the crowds' behavior. Now, at the elementary level of the "rational response," this profile answers the question of why people rioted: there were plenty of provocations. Harvest failures in 1794–1795 and 1799–1800 led to food scarcities and high prices that provoked hundreds of riots in which crowds lowered prices or seized food shipments. A third scarcity began in 1810, and food rioting flowed into Luddism. The wars against

Table 1. Issues provoking riots in England and Wales, 1790–1810.

	London		Provinces		Total	
Issues	Riots	%	Riots	%	Riots	%
Food	5	4.1%	237.0	48.0%	242.0	39.2%
Labor	6	4.9	38.5	7.8	44.5	7.2
Military	31	25.2	102.5	20.7	133.5	21.6
Political/ideological	17	13.8	46.0	9.3	63.0	10.2
Brawls	20	16.3	14.0	2.8	34.0	5.5
Miscellaneous	43	35.0	46.0	9.3	89.0	14.4
Unknown	1	0.8	10.0	2.0	11.0	1.8
Total	123	100.1	494.0	99.9	617.0	99.9

Sources: All riots reported in either the *London Observer*, the *Morning Chronicle*, the *Annual Register*, or files of the Home Office (H.O. 42).

Note: Categories of issues include the following sorts of riots (groups of more than 10 riots have the number of riots in parentheses; fractions refer to riots about more than one issue). *Food:* food prices (154.5), food shipment (53.5), miscellaneous (13), unknown food issue (21). *Labor:* wages (36), machinery, strike enforcement. *Military:* recruiting (53.5, of which impressment = 34), mutinies (22), civilian-military brawls (31), and others. *Political/ideological:* "Church and King" riots (11), local and parlamentary elections (20), illuminations (attacks on people who did not illuminate their windows during celebrations of military victories), religious ideology, and others. *Brawls:* Irish versus Irish, Irish versus non-Irish, other ethnic, town-gown, and other. *Miscellaneous:* enclosures, smuggling, theater, rescues not connected with other riots (17), attacks on unpopular individuals (29; 21 in London), resistance to officials (12), tollgates, other.

Revolutionary and Napoleonic France between 1793 and 1815 strained Britain's politics and its economy. In particular, wartime demands for manpower aroused popular resistance to press gangs, "crimps" (recruiters for profit), and militia balloting (see Chapter 8). Military mobilization also resulted in mutinies and in brawls between civilians and soldiers. Together, food scarcities and military frictions provoked nearly three-fifths of the riots in this period. Political and industrial conflicts were the most important remaining incidents. Whig mobs battled Tory mobs in the streets of populous boroughs in time-honored electoral rituals. Supporters of "Church and King" attacked Jacobins and Dissenters as part of the national mobilization of loyalism in the 1790s. Labor disputes also led to several dozen riots. Immediate trade and price fluctuations, emerging labor scarcities and surpluses, and ultimately, industrial growth and technological change provoked wage claims by seamen, cotton spinners, and farm laborers, and machine breaking by vulnerable weavers and wool combers.[35]

The profile of issues in Table 1 suggests some minor revisions in current views of the relative weight of different grievances. Food riots are not quite so prominent as hitherto believed, primarily because the steady incidence of other riots has been underestimated.[36] Labor and political riots were not so numerous as their place in historiography would suggest. It is not surprising that military issues were so prominent in wartime. But the number of "miscellaneous" riots does suggest a sizable field of unexplored terrain.

More important, this national sample permits the "rational response" theory of riots to be tested more rigorously. And testing reveals that "real" grievances did not produce riots as regularly and inevitably as the "rational response" explanation would predict. For instance, although the parliamentary enclosure movement reached its peak during the war, and although enclosures undeniably hurt the poor, only six riots were over enclosures.[37] But the best illustration of the weakness of the "rational response" interpretation is the complex relationship between high food prices and the incidence of riots. At first glance that relationship seems simple and direct. In an age when more than half a laborer's family budget was spent on food and more than a quarter on bread, harvest failure and soaring bread prices threatened immediate catastrophe to many family economies. Hardship was multiplied by the severe impact of harvest failure on incomes, farm profits, consumer demand for industrial goods, and hence on employment.[38] Moreover, it has frequently been argued that in a "preindustrial" age, food prices provided the most common and compelling motives for collective action, when labor and political organization was still relatively primitive.[39] Hence it is not surprising that food scarcity was the manifest issue in nearly half the riots in this period. More generally, economic hardship has traditionally been historians' favorite explanation of popular unrest.[40] William Cobbett's famous declaration, "I defy you to agitate a man on a full stomach," has too frequently been converted to the axiom that hungry men rebel.

However, it has become increasingly doubtful whether hardship alone can explain collective violence. E. P. Thompson has attacked the "spasmodic" version of popular history that had treated food riots as elementary "rebellions of the belly." He reconstructs the "moral economy" of food rioters, a rich ideological fabric woven from traditions of official market regulation and normative beliefs that food producers and dealers should serve a communal need, especially local need, and should be guided by the "just price" rather than by the impersonal dictates of supply and demand—and the pursuit of individual profit. As valuable as that ideological reconstruction is, Thompson's argument is really a more sophisticated version of the "rational response" theory: cause (hunger) and effect (riot) remain, but the intermediate cultural formation, the "moral economy," legitimizes and shapes the response. Thompson accepts as "a self-evident truth" that "people protest when they are hungry." "Having granted that the primary stimulus of 'distress' is present," he argues that the "spasmodic" interpretation concludes investigation where it ought to begin: "being hungry...what do people do?"[41] The concept of the "moral economy" adds flesh to the bones of a skeletal view of "economic man" more than it alters his physiology.

But the empirical, causal links between hardship and collective violence are even weaker than critics have suggested. Many have pointed out that food riots did not always occur at the moments of most severe hardship but that recognition has not aroused sufficient agnosticism.[42] Figure 1 compares the incidence of riots in my national sample with fluctuations in wheat prices. Quite clearly, rioting reached peaks in 1795 and 1800, years of high food prices. But in both crises, still higher prices in the following year coincided with sharp drops in the incidence of rioting. Some historians have continued to insist upon simple economic causation by suggesting that it was the steepness or suddenness of the price rise, rather than its absolute level, that touched off rioting. That may well be.[43] But sharp rises in 1798–1799, 1804–1805, and 1808–1809 coin-

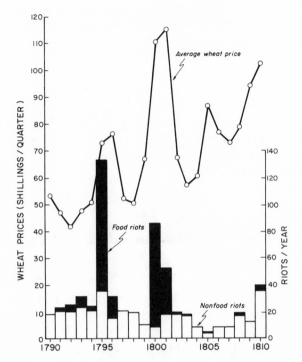

Figure 1. Riots and prices in England and Wales, 1790–1810 (see note 46).

cided with *decreases* in the incidence of rioting, while the dearth of 1810 was not nearly so riotous as the earlier crises.

Even in the short run, rioters did not march to the beat of the economic pulse. Figures 2 and 3 compare wheat prices and riots in 1794–1796 and 1799–1801. Once again, neither the absolute level of price increases nor their sharpness seems to account for the timing of riots. Only the riots in the summer of 1795 correspond to the price curve. On the other hand, dozens of riots took place in the spring of 1795, in reaction to a pronounced but gradual rise in the price of wheat. These riots may well have been reactions to the expiration of relief programs, which had shielded the poor through a very hard winter.[44]

Conversely, a much sharper rise in prices in the last half of 1799 and the first half of 1800 failed to ignite a wave of violence. In that year, the major explosion came in September, when prices had dropped by more than 40 shillings from the peak before the harvest and then had rebounded upward by 10 to 15 shillings. People rioted because they felt betrayed. Before the harvest, the apparent abundance of the grain standing in the fields had promised a

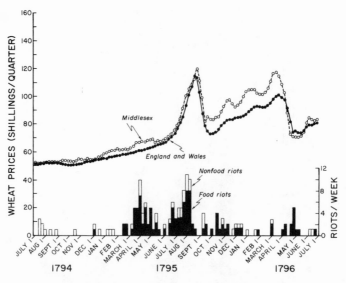

Figure 2. Riots and prices in England and Wales, 1794–1796 (weekly averages for wheat prices from the *London Gazette*).

plentiful crop, and prices had fallen sharply as the harvest neared. But closer examination of the wheat revealed that the grains were hollow and light. That discovery sent prices back up. Consumers still believed the harvest to have been a good one, and so they were doubly outraged at the idea of "starving in the midst of plenty."[45] The rumblings in the body politic welled up from felt injustice as much as from hunger.

Statistical analysis provides a more precise measure of the relationship between prices and riots. The results are revealing. There is no significant relationship between all riots and wheat prices.[46] Hence it does not seem possible to claim that food prices were some sort of underlying general cause of collective violence in this period. Indeed, a slight majority of the riots in this period were triggered by noneconomic causes.[47] The only statistically significant relationship is that between food riots and wheat prices.[48] Of course, food rioters themselves demonstrated by their claims and actions that they were protesting high prices, but that is hardly the end of the story. The statistical relationship, while significant, is not strong. The standard measure, the square of the correlation coefficient, suggests that only about 17 percent of the variance in food riots was associated with wheat price levels. Moreover, in the periods of dearth from 1794 to 1796 and 1799 to 1801, no significant

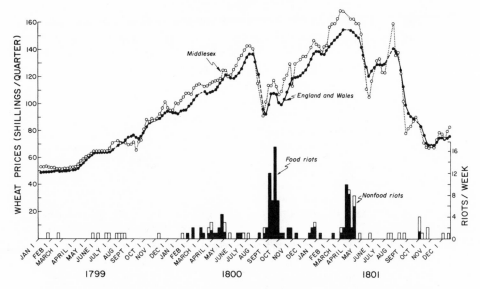

Figure 3. Riots and prices in England and Wales, 1799–1801 (weekly averages for wheat prices from the *London Gazette*).

statistical relationship existed between weekly price fluctuations and the frequency of food riots.[49]

In general, the chronological relationship between food prices and riots was probably complicated by at least three general factors. First, the inflation of the 1790s dulled potential outrage in the following decade. Second, the war against Napoleon was much more popular than that against Revolutionary France.[50] Both radical political criticism of the government and resistance to recruiting receded, and, of course, repression had dissolved Jacobin organizations. Political animus thus did not aggravate hardship as much as it had before 1802. Third, in the short run, both relief and repression in response to the initial waves of rioting in 1795 and 1800 may account for the decline in violence even while prices continued to rise.[51] In the longer run, expenditures for relief increased sharply after 1795, faster than the population increased, both in counties that did and did not employ the "Speenhamland system" of pegging relief scales to food prices.[52] That relief probably softened the impact of high prices on consumers. In sum, local and national politics were a decisive intervening variable between market fluctuations and crowd action.

But food riots were geographically as well as chronologically "idiosyncratic." The biggest anomaly was London. The capital was rarely disturbed by food riots, although it contained one-tenth of the nation's population and although it witnessed well over one hundred riots over other issues (see Table 1). Yet London's prices fluctuated as sharply as those of other English markets (see Figures 2 and 3; Middlesex prices stand in for London's).

Outside London, prices were an even worse predictor of riot. Figures 4 and 5 display the price behavior for the three most riotous and three least riotous counties in 1795–1796. Prices behaved very similarly in these two sets of counties, but consumers did not. Nor, once more, did riots in the riotous counties always take place at the "predicted" breaks in the price curve. This demonstration, which could be repeated for 1800–1801, illustrates the inadequacy not only of economic motivation as an explanation for riot, but also that of ideologies like the "moral economy" or radicalism. General motivations, whether hardship or ideology, are not sufficient explanations for the incidence of collective action. They must be anchored in the local social frameworks that

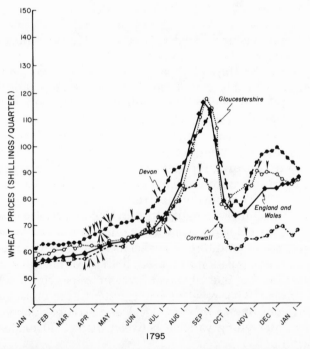

Figure 4. Weekly wheat prices (from the *London Gazette*) and riots in the three most riotous counties, 1795: Devon (14 riots), Cornwall (7 riots), and Gloucestershire (6 riots). Arrows indicate riots.

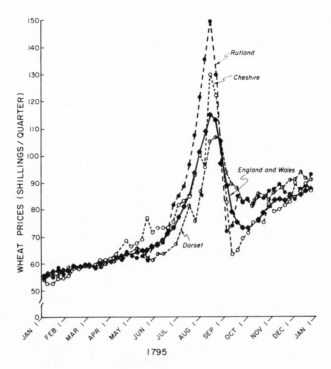

Figure 5. Weekly wheat prices (from the *London Gazette*) in three counties having no food riots in 1795.

supported (or failed to support) such ideology and promoted (or blocked) its translation into collective action. For why did the "moral economy" promote riots as the social response to dearth in some places—in small market towns, for instance—but not in others—in London and in the agrarian countryside?[53]

Besides failing to account for the chronological and geographical incidence of riots, the "rational response" explanation of riots does not explain why crowds acted as crowds. It assumes that tensions accumulated in *individual* minds until a critical state was reached and, presumably, like-minded individuals joined in riot.[54] But genuinely *collective* action must not be taken for granted. William Reddy has said it well: "What must be characterized is the community base that made coherent action possible, a sense of membership that stands in a prior relationship to the motives of individuals...For such coherence to be possible when no agency or organization is directing events, it is necessary that the participants have shared expectations of each other."[55]

Misery may love company, but it does not necessarily create the complex cohesion and discipline of a crowd like that at Barrow. It may just as well, or more easily, create atomistic contention or apathetic despair, poles apart from a binding consensus.[56] The Barrow rioters did not simply act spontaneously but carried out a series of complex, self-conscious, collective actions sensitive not only to their fellow villagers but also to the local magistrate, middling mediators,[57] and the owner of the grain. They coordinated collective action toward a positive goal.

In short, the actors in riots were, in the first instance, crowds, not individuals, and at Barrow, the organism within which the riot occurred was not merely the crowd but the whole community, which transacted the "classic," marketplace kind of bargaining, at least until the alien Yeomanry arrived. The questions become not simply how tensions accumulated, or what cultural traditions led to riot, but which kinds of groups were capable of taking *action* on grievances that were "infinitely" widespread but that led to violence only in finite instances and in patterned ways. What kinds of groups and what kinds of communities produced what sorts of riots?

The Barrow riot strongly suggests that riots were local "social politics," that is, informal tests of power and policy shaped by local social relationships. That suggestion is borne out by three important characteristics of the "issues" manifested in the riots classified in Table 1. First, the issue was typically an external threat to a community; it tended to unite a community rather than to polarize it. Farmers and food dealers who "selfishly" raised prices in time of scarcity risked alienating their normal customers, the great majority of nonagrarian townspeople. That was all the more true if the suppliers served distant markets, because "exportation" of food from the neighborhood was considered a menace to local welfare. A Devon miller who supplied the navy with ship's biscuit reported that he had been attacked because of "an Idea that ive done much injury to the community."[58] Press gangs, recruiting parties, or crimps, and soldiers on the march (or on the make, who snatched a farmer's chickens or his daughter) were also obvious physical menaces to communities and London neighborhoods. Likewise, individual entrepreneurs could be cast as aggressors against a community's livelihood when they cut wages or introduced labor-saving machinery, especially where one industry dominated a town or neighborhood.[59]

Such provocations not only galvanized "the lower orders"— the artisans and laborers, men and women, of the community—

into collective defense, but also evoked a sympathetic response from members of the "middling" ranks, like the graziers and other mediators at Barrow. These "allies" of the crowd might be motivated by humanitarianism, a desire for social peace, or self-interest, for they joined in loud complaints against high prices and taxes and sometimes oranized boycotts or ad hoc committees to bring pressure upon merchants.[60] The middle class could also turn hostile if press gangs harassed men of standing in the community or menaced indispensable employees.[61] Riotous opposition to new textile machinery in Wiltshire in 1802 found widespread support, in part because smaller manufacturers were unwilling or unable to make technical innovations,[62] and perhaps also because replacing the many well-paid shearmen with machines would have reper-cussions on shopkeepers, landlords, and local payers of poor rates (the local taxes that financed relief payments to the poor, or poor relief).

The point is that the physically or perceptually alien threats that provoked riots did not create crowds from simple "pools" of individuals; they mobilized networks of people and relationships that already existed—networks of kinship and camaraderie, in work, play, marketing, worship, or neighborhood, as well as institutional networks, such as political and labor "combinations," friendly societies (local mutual-relief clubs), Volunteer Corps, and so on. Such informal and formal memberships helped to create habits of collaboration that made collective violence practicable. Common understandings among peers informed the rioters' judg-ments and tactics. Face-to-face familiarity bound violence into safe forms, and so, by limiting the legal, physical, and moral risks of riot, helped nurture a tradition of disciplined violence. At the same time, in such dense communities the common people's estab-lished, predictable, "vertical" relationships with local figures of authority (authority based both on wealth and patronage and upon formal legal power and responsibility) were crucial factors that shaped not only the immediate public confrontations of mobs and magistrates in the streets, but also the "secondary" stages of crisis, when magistrates and gentlemen brought pressure to bear on food merchants, press gangs, and even ministers of government. In short, a community dealt with an alien threat to its common welfare by mobilizing its political relationships—both "horizontal" and "vertical"—and riot was often the decisive motivating center of that mobilization.

Political riots—election contests and "Church and King" riots—were different. Rather than mobilizing a community against an external threat, they typically split a community internally along vertical fissures. To be sure, the "Church and King" riots in Birmingham, Manchester, and Nottingham implicated existing political and social networks in these towns.[63] And sometimes an election riot might involve defense of local interests against outsiders. For example, between 1804 and 1806 three elections were held at Knaresborough, a "pocket borough" controlled by the Duke of Devonshire, and on these occasions townspeople rioted against the duke's cutbacks of election expenditures in the town, against his use of his distant tenants and friends to act as Knaresborough's electors, and against his importing special constables and cavalry to enforce his wishes.[64] Attacks on Dissenters, radicals, or "miscreants" who failed to illuminate their windows during a victory celebration could be construed as communal punishment of nonconformity. Perhaps the Paine burnings of 1792–1793 were an intermediate link between such political riots and the wider custom of "rough music." But more generally, political conflict almost by definition divided a community internally into socially heterogeneous parties of roughly equal social standing. Perhaps that is why political violence was relatively rare by contrast with other kinds of riot, for the complexities of overlapping ties between factions would tend to reduce violence.[65]

If the issues that provoked riots were typically external intrusions, they were, secondly, concrete and immediate threats. Riot was not merely protest, but violent direct action to promote specific and tangible relief. Forced sales of food, interceptions of grain shipments, expulsion of military recruiting and impressment parties, and "collective bargaining by riot" in industrial conflicts were clear examples of direct action that might both gain on-the-spot relief and also goad the gentry into taking more lasting measures to defend popular welfare.[66] Rioters practiced "the art of the possible." People were unlikely to take the risks of collective violence unless success was within reach—and for eighteenth-century crowds, that meant physical reach.

Once again, political riots were an exception. "Church and King" riots might succeed in injuring or temporarily driving unpopular figures out of public life,[67] but when riots were too blatantly "successful" in determining the outcome of an election, it was *ipso facto* likely to be overturned by Parliament.[68] More generally, wider political objectives were beyond the reach of physical violence. Very few pieces of legislation were blocked or amended in the eighteenth century because of riotous resistance to them.[69] Significantly, most radical Reformers avoided violence. The London Corresponding Society spelled out its policy quite emphatically in 1794 in a pamphlet entitled *Reformers No Rioters:* "riots, tumult, and violence are not the fit means of obtaining redress of grievances."[70] Radicals sought to take the high road, to appeal to right and reason rather than to force. They were squeamish about violence, and they could not afford the drastic legal and political liabilities that would grow if they added violence to radicalism.[71] Finally, insurrection was obviously futile, especially by contrast with riot that did work so well within local political contexts.

Third, although the issues in riots were "concrete," they were nevertheless legally, politically, or ethically ambiguous. For example, although the old statutes against common food-wholesaling practices (forestalling, regrating, and engrossing) had been repealed by 1791, the lord chief justice was still ready to encourage prosecution under common law for such offenses. Many local authorities needed no such encouragement.[72] Nor were property rights absolute, despite the Home Secretary's injunctions to local magistrates to protect them. Attacks on fixed capital (mills or houses) or industrial property (machinery, cloth, and, stretching the category, sheep), often incurred heavy penalties.[73] But rioters who seized food or lowered prices usually received more lenient treatment—apparently property rights in foodstuffs were still considered negotiable by many local authorities. The Assize of Bread, still enforced but falling into disuse, epitomizes this ambiguity.[74] Aspects of military recruiting were also open to dispute. There was still room for debate over the central issue of impressment, liability for service and exemption. "Persons using the sea" were liable; "gentlemen" and harvesters, among others were exempt. The flexibility of such categories provided ample occasions for disputes that could lead to violence.[75] "Crimping" (recruiting for profit) was another tangled practice. By 1795, market pressures on the price and supply of men often made crimping tantamount to kidnapping.[76] Collective bargaining was certainly problematic. The common law and, after 1799, general statutes, proscribed labor combinations (more or less informal "unions") to raise wages, but erratic enforcement made the future of any individual combination uncertain and therefore a matter for careful calculation. Ancient laws regulating apprenticeship and machinery were still on the books, even if they had not been enforced for decades.[77]

Such ambiguities meant that rioters were usually able to justify their "illegal" actions by appealing to venerable principles and ideological fragments shared by many other members of their community, even though those principles were undergoing controversy and change. That ideological conflict, as well as the breadth and force of communal interests, required magistrates to find a politic compromise to restore equilibrium, not simply to enforce the law mechanically.[78] Conversely, where little or no legal or social ambiguity existed, such as in cases of parliamentary enclosure, riots were likely to be futile, since rioters could expect only unmitigated opposition from the magistrates.

The alien, concrete, and ambiguous nature of these threats to plebeian welfare created the possibility of local political bargaining. But whether, and what kind of, riotous transactions would take place depended upon community politics. Riots were most likely to occur, and to occur most coherently, when certain kinds of threats impinged upon groups of common people accustomed to collective action and belief, when and where the prospects from "taking arms against a sea of troubles" might reasonably outweigh the risks, and where rioters might be able to appeal to the magistrates for neutrality, mediation, or active aid. Hence riots were community politics. They shaped local policy and distributive justice. They tested all the ingredients of horizontal and vertical political cohesion: tradition, law, force, ideology, patronage, persuasion, and interest. And for just that reason, the determining framework of community politics extended outward from the actual moment of violence. The possible outcomes of riot—the gains and costs—were estimated by both rioters and magistrates on the basis of both their existing relationships and the hard-earned "traditions" established by earlier conflicts. Those calculations and legacies thus determined the form and incidence of riots.

Hence, the relationships between riots and community politics must be explored not by "impressionistic" national surveys or isolated local studies, but by systematic comparisons of different kinds of communities having different experience with riots. Indeed, the relationships between riots and communities formed a spectrum. At one extreme stood Manchester, where rapid urbanization had swamped older social networks and older forms of riot, and where newer, more "artificial" forms of popular mobilization began to emerge. At the other extreme lay rural agrarian England, little disturbed by riot, perhaps because horizontal networks among the common people were too sparse and vertical relationships with the local authorities were too tight to permit effective collective action. The center of the spectrum was marked out by the small towns of Devon, whose dense and stable social networks furnished the optimum milieu for the "classic" tradition of riots: riots that were frequent, disciplined, and successful.

2

Devon's Classic Food Riots

Money prices are the product of conflicts of interest
and of compromises; they thus result from power constellations.

—Max Weber, *Economy and Society*

To steer between the two and do justice to both
is the arduous and difficult task.

—Lord John Rolle, December 28, 1800

At the end of the eighteenth century, Devon was one of the most riotous counties in England (*riotous* means riots per ten thousand people in 1801).[1] Devon's food riots epitomized eighteenth-century English riot: classic episodes of orderly disorder, they stood midway in form and style between the "quiet" of rural fastnesses like Rutland and wild scenes in industrial boom towns like Manchester and Birmingham. Differences in the form and frequency of riot reflect differences in local social relations—differences that were accentuated by the Industrial Revolution. Devon witnessed forty-three food riots in 1795–1796 and 1800–1801, following successive harvest failures in 1794–1795 and 1799–1800. These riots were remarkable for their discipline. Devon's rioters seemed to observe a rough "protocol of riot" that drew upon traditional tactics and current calculations of how different magistrates might respond.

Devonians followed two classic forms of riot: the "taxation populaire," or price-fixing riot, and the forcible requisition, in which the townspeople trooped out into the countryside to "regulate" the farmers. In 1795, the "standard" riot consisted of crowds' forcing food vendors to sell their provisions on the spot at reduced prices. Exeter crowds set the example in the first riots of that spring. On Wednesday, March 25, a market day, forty or fifty people assembled in the populous suburb of St. Thomas, across the Exe River from Exeter, and "took possession" of some wheat and potatoes. These they forced the farmers to sell at 7s. 6d. a bushel and 8d. a peck, respectively; the farmers had asked 9s. 6d.

and 10d. On the morning of the next market day, Friday, a crowd of hundreds of women seized potatoes in the Exeter potato market and sold them at 6d. a peck, until the mayor intervened to set a compromise price of 8d. That afternoon a crowd seized all the corn (meaning all cereal grain, in British usage) in the corn market, and the magistrates again intervened to set a compromise price of 8s. At noon on Saturday, a "very considerable" crowd went out on Long Down, two miles west of Exeter, and confiscated forty bushels of a farmer's wheat on its way to the miller at nearby Ide. They fixed the price themselves and bought the wheat at 7s. 8d. per bushel. It was reported that the poor threatened to repeat their regulation of prices if conditions did not improve. No visionaries, these rioters; their prices were simply those of the previous year.[2] Other price-fixing riots took place in the next few days at nearby towns. In Honiton and Topsham, the rioters sold butter and potatoes "at a moderate price" and then "departed quietly."[3]

In 1801 rioters more often fixed prices in the farmyard than in the marketplace. Typically, rioters would assemble in the market towns and then march out into the countryside to force neighboring farmers to sign "contracts" to bring their grain to market at reduced prices. Such crowds embarked from many towns, among them Exeter, Newton, Sandford, Dartmouth, Brixham, Crediton, Ashburton, Sheepwash, Bideford, Colyton, Uffculme, and Modbury (see Figure 6).[4] The rioting in Totnes richly illustrates this type of community mobilization. Totnes was an ancient, middle-sized parliamentary borough with a population in 1801 of about 2,500. It served both as a corn market for its area and as the center for trade in long ells, a kind of woolen cloth, the weavers of which lived in the villages nearby. On the evening of Tuesday, March 31, a clamoring mob of hundreds of people descended on the house of farmer Henry Penney, in the parish of Harburton, just outside Totnes. They pounded on his door and demanded that he sign a paper agreeing to market his produce at fixed prices: wheat at 10s. 6d., barley at 5s. 3d. per bushel, butter at 1s. per pound, and potatoes at 10d. per peck. Again, these prices were compromises.[5] Penney hesitated to come to the door, but when one of the mob cried out, "Bring the halter! Bring the halter!" (implying that he would be hanged), Penney yielded and came to a kitchen window to sign.

Penney began to recognize familiar figures in the crowd. One of the voices, he knew, belonged to Hulse Ley, a currier of Totnes, and when he lit a candle, he recognized Browse Trist, a master cabinetmaker and upholsterer of the town. Trist called out,

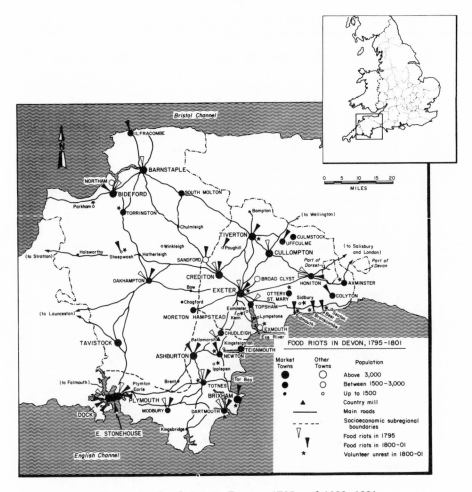

Figure 6. Food riots in Devon, 1795 and 1800–1801.

"Hanaford!" and then, "Clerk!" and a young man brought forward the paper. He refused to identify himself, saying, "No matter what my name is, there is the paper for you to sign!" While Penney signed, many of the crowd cried, "Damn such signing, hang all together and that will be the best signing!" Trist silenced them with, "Hold your tongues, you vary from what we agreed on this morning."

Trist asked Penney what corn or potatoes he had to sell. Penney replied that he had no wheat or potatoes, but he might have some barley. He would know in a month, after he had sown his field. Trist ordered "that he should send word to him, Browse Trist, as soon as he knew." Some impatient members of the crowd cried out "they would wait only three weeks and swore they would be damned if they did not come again in three weeks." But Trist called out, "All signed, all well, move on, my lads." A shower of stones cascaded against the windows as the crowd moved off to make similar demands on other farmers.[6]

Such tactics were not new, but the Totnes crowds in 1801 aimed at a more sophisticated and comprehensive control of local markets than had been achieved by the forced sales of 1795.[7] The day after the visit to the farmers, James Harrison, one of "the principal corn merchants and millers of Totnes," was confronted by a dozen people, several of whom he recognized. He refused to sign their agreement and showed them records of his purchases of foreign corn at prices twice those of the popular maximum.[8]

Before long, parallel committees emerged from the community's mobilization. The mayor convened a meeting at the guildhall on April 2, and the townspeople resolved to publish a handbill asking the farmers to supply the market and assuring them protection against disorder. The meeting instructed a committee of "seven respectable persons to attend the market and see that good order and rule was...kept."[9]

On Friday, April 3, a second "popular," committee published its interpretation of the week's events:

> A numerous body composed of the inhabitants of Totnes, Bridgeton and its vicinity, urged by extreme want of the common necessaries of life, having in a peaceable and orderly manner assembled to claim humanity of the farmers, millers, etc., acknowledge to have received from all promises to prevent an approaching famine which has so long disturbed the publick tranquility, by bringing regularly to market bread, corn, etc. in proportion to the quantity they possess.
>
> We the undersigned being the committee appointed by the people think it highly requisite to declare that we will to the utmost in our power protect persons and property from the least outrage.
>
> N.B. The better to prevent confusion women are required not to attend the corn market.[10]

The nine signers included several members of the crowds who had forced their contracts upon the farmers.

The work of these two committees converged the next day at

the weekly corn market. Hanaford, "clerk" of the mob and a member of the popular committee, presented merchant Harrison with another copy of the agreement he had rejected on Wednesday. But this time four members of the "gentlemen's committee" appointed by the mayor, including two aldermen of the borough and a militia captain, forced Harrison to sign. They insisted that if he did not, they "would as long as they lived ascribe and impute to his obstinacy all the blood that should be spilt," and all the destruction that renewed rioting would bring.[11]

Market regulation in Totnes succeeded, at least for a time. The price of wheat at Totnes for the week of the riots (April 4) was 167s. 8d. per quarter ton (8 bushels), or just under 21s. per bushel. After the riots, the next reported price (April 25) was 86s. 8d., then 96s. (May 2), then 119s. 8d. (May 9), and finally 160s. (May 16).[12] Obviously the crowd's control over the markets was limited to local and direct action. At least one Totnes corn dealer was taken aback by "the most strange revolution in this county in the price of bread," and he decided to ship as much flour to London as possible.[13] But even while the crowd's influence ebbed, more lasting remedies for scarcity were being set in train by the authorities.

Both these riots at Exeter and Totnes illustrate the workings of community politics in the immediate interaction of rioters, targets, and magistrates in conflicts over food prices. The complexity of that interaction suggests that no simple mechanical explanation of riots will serve. For instance the riots cannot be interpreted as a spasmodic, reflex reaction to high prices. The surprisingly long-range plans of the Totnes crowds—when they warned farmer Penney they would return in three weeks rather than seizing his grain on the spot—testify to that.

Devon was not more riotous than other counties because of higher prices or sharper increases, nor did the timing of its riots follow the price curves (see Figures 7 and 8). In 1795–1796 its wheat prices remained within 10–15 percent of the English average, and barley, the mainstay of Devon's workers' diets, was actually cheaper there than in the rest of the country (except for two weeks in April 1796).[14] Rioting spread through south and east Devon in the spring of 1795 before any very sharp rise in prices had taken place; conversely, Devon was quiet when the rest of England protested the price peaks of August and the following winter. Likewise, in the summer of 1800, Devon's grain prices rose sharply to levels slightly higher than the national averages, but the county was almost undisturbed by riots during September when the rest

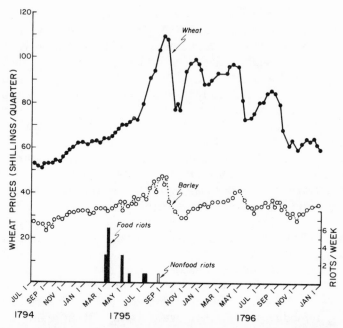

Figure 7.   Weekly prices and riots in Devon, 1794–1796 (prices from the *London Gazette*).

of the country was most agitated. Then Devon reaped the benefits and dangers of a better than average harvest, for lower wheat and barley prices prevailed from September through January, 1801, and prices were actually lower there than in the county's normal supply areas along the Channel coast.[15] That may have strained Devon's own winter supplies, for both Devon's producers and the county's external suppliers sent their grain to better markets elsewhere. In March, both wheat and barley prices in Devon snapped back above the national average. The riots of that month certainly protested high prices. But other counties had even higher prices, yet fewer riots. Although the rioters' actions were unquestionably directed at lowering high prices, their chronological idiosyncrasy prevents us from interpreting them simply as climactic reactions to accumulating hardship (see Figures 7 and 8).

Indeed, these two periods of crisis seem to have had different impacts on the people of Devon. After the harvest failure of 1794, prices rose suddenly and aggravated one of the severest winters in memory and a cold and rainy spring. In 1800–1801, on the other hand, the crisis was not so sudden. By the time of the rioting, prices had been rising for almost two years. Perhaps five years of

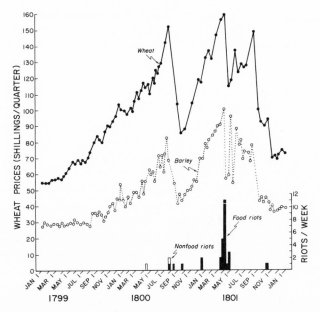

Figure 8. Weekly prices and riots in Devon, 1799–1801 (prices from the *London Gazette*).

steady inflation, together with improving money wages, had dulled the psychological impact of high food prices. The demographic effects were also different: the crisis of 1795 contributed to a sharp increase in the number of burials; that of 1800–1801 was reflected in decreases in the "voluntary" rates of marriages and conceptions in 1801. Moreover, fragments of evidence suggest that by 1801 dearth was forcing workers to part with their savings.[16] In short, the crisis of 1795 seemed to pose a more direct threat to physical survival, while that of 1801 undermined economic security, including that needed for family formation. These different demographic consequences may explain the apparent shift in riot leadership from laborers and women in 1795 to artisans in 1801, and the shift in riot tactics from immediate forced sales in the marketplace in 1795 to the more sophisticated control of prices by "contract" in 1801. Even from a narrowly economic viewpoint, then, Devon's riots were not simple "rebellions of the belly."[17]

Nor were these riots simply outbursts of lawlessness permitted by the weakness of the forces of order. "Classic" riots like those in Devon marked the borderline between crime and routine social politics. Riot, property damage, and seizure of food were formally illegal, and rioters might be punished accordingly—riots were not merely "functional" protests. But when magistrates prosecuted and sentenced rioters, they had to exercise far more careful political discretion than when they dealt with "simple" individual crimes like sheep stealing. For their part, rioters adhered to the "protocol of riot" by avoiding provocative excesses. For if a house or mill were pulled down, rioters would be liable for capital punishment. All members of a crowd could be capitally liable for individual acts of breaking and entering, theft, and, presumably, serious assault.[18] No unruly individuals could be allowed to endanger their comrades.

And so, although magistrates sometimes mediated between rioters and their targets, more often restraint came from members of the crowd, as it had at Totnes. Devon's rioters almost never seized food without paying for it. At Brixham and at Plymouth in 1801, when individuals grabbed a flitch of bacon or a sack of potatoes, the crowds made them restore it to the owners, and then publicly humiliated the offenders. Price-fixing crowds would sometimes seal a farmer's contract with a triumphant shower of stones against his windows, but their leaders prevented more serious damage or abuse. When a Modbury crowd threatened to hang the Reverend Mr. Stackhouse if he did not sign an agreement, their leader "called them away, as losing time." At Totnes, Dartmouth, and Brixham in 1801, the leadership of tradesmen was believed to have restrained the crowds.[19] The "protocol of riot" was sanctioned most obviously by legal consequences, but it also seems likely that rioters wanted to keep to the high ground morally, and also to avoid antagonizing the magistrates, in view of their power over relief.

Nor, finally, can the riots be explained in terms of some abnormal psychological transformations, some "herd instinct" or "collective mind" or hypnosis by the leader, as Gustave Le Bon and his successors have argued.[20] The action of the Devon rioters do not suggest any special transformation of their mental states, such as the loss of their individual identities or critical faculties. On the contrary, rioters acted quite publicly, they appealed to common principles, and their actions were firmly grounded in their social identities and relationships.

Indeed, it is just that public assertiveness that marks riot as community politics and distinguishes it from individual crime, anonymous threatening letters, and supplication by petition. Rioters did not seek the shelter of anonymity. They usually acted in broad daylight, and, as the riot in 1795 at Exeter shows, they did not shrink from confrontations with magistrates. Even when rioters acted at night, as they did at Totnes, they did not try to conceal their identities, and magistrates and victims had little trouble identifying at least the leading spirits. The public assertiveness and the success of Devon's riots contrast with the rage of impotence expressed in anonymous forms of social "blasphemy," such as threatening letters, arson, and sabotage.[21]

What needs investigation is not the dark recesses of some collective subconscious but rather the public mentalities and memberships rioters brought to the crisis. The rioters' mentality is a question of ideology—not abnormal psychology—of the historically developed "filters" and norms that shaped the collective perceptions of crisis in such a way as to focus and enable collective action. E. P. Thompson has brilliantly reconstructed the "moral economy" of English crowds, the legitimizing notions and traditions of action that justified and shaped food riots. The chief principles of that "moral economy" were that the food trade must be governed by community need, not selfish profit motives; hence, food dealers should ask only the "just price," not a market price inflated by scarcity; and the local community should have first claim on the food grown in its fields, even though a distant city might offer a better price. These principles had much in common with the magistrates' ideology of paternalism. But paternalism was supposed to be realized in the magistrates' regulation of the markets, while the "moral economy" took concrete shape in riot. Thompson's synthesis suggests that the "moral economy" was a "selective reconstruction" of the tradition of paternalism, and that rioters felt their actions were legitimate because their principles were derived from paternalism and the tradition of official market regulation.[22]

Were rioters guided by such an ideology as the "moral economy?" The answer must be inferred from their actions, for we have rarely recovered their words and thoughts (though Thompson has made much use of sympathetic pamphleteers and anonymous letters). The Devon rioters' behavior in regulating prices and intercepting food in transit certainly do furnish evidence that a "moral economy" helped justify crowd action. The rioters also acted in a climate of public opinion suffused with ideological condemnation of profiteers. The press often repeated the hackneyed outcry against the ancient villains of the wholesale trade—forestallers, regraters, and engrossers—middlemen who bought grain, usually outside the public markets, in order to sell it again, normally at a profit. At Exeter in 1795, "every person seems to complain loudly," and "those miscreants, the Forestallers," were particularly singled out for blame. And in 1801 the public's support for the lord chief justice, Lord Kenyon, who had reiterated the old prohibitions at the famous Rusby trial the previous July, helped feed "the general conversation of the Country-Towns [that] received a tone most hostile to the farmers."[23] Of course such public opinion encouraged food rioting, while it also supported parallel regulation of the markets by the magistrates.

But it seems doubtful that rioters derived their sense of *legitimacy* from either tradition or paternalism. Their justifications were neither "backward-looking" nor deferential; rather, rioters generally appealed to self-evident need. They would call out, "We are starving alive," or, "It is a hard matter to starve."[24] The Exeter crowd stated their dilemma quite straightforwardly: they "only said that if they were to suffer, they might as well be hung as starved, and they would run the risk of making their situation better, for worse could not be."[25]

Whether the rioters were literally starving or were only dramatizing their hardship, they did not *act* desperately. The Exeter and Totnes crowds sought a negotiated compromise, not charity or outright seizure of the food. After a price-fixing episode at Honiton, a gentleman was warned that "none...wishes to oppress the farmer more than another but to fix the medium between two extremes so as the prices shall not be too high or too low."

At Exmouth, "the people" made their case to an emergency meeting of gentlemen and farmers, saying, "Give us whatever quantity the stock in hand will afford, at a price by which we can attain it and we shall be satisfied."[26]

This pragmatism, however, must not be mistaken for coolly detached reason, for the hunger and moral outrage that moved crowds was unmistakable. Rioters were certainly angry when they threatened to hang farmers and gentlemen, even if they were only bluffing. The common people were angry at "the Bakers and Farmers wicked monopoly," at "the Damnation Farmers who were determined to starve them all to Death," and they held their "betters" responsible for remedial action and demanded redress.[27] Some months before the Modbury riot in 1801, one of the crowd leaders chastised an attorney for the high price of corn, saying, "You are a Man of Property and by God at your Peril get corn cheaper." When the attorney asked why he had been singled out, the man replied, "I mean all of the Gent[lemen] of Modbury."[28] So riot could be motivated by a mixture of anger and deliberate calculation, just as conventional politics were and are.

And sometimes the rioters' pragmatic moderation was embellished by dramatic gestures that were a kind of "counter-theater" to the pretensions of the gentry. The leader of the Modbury rioters styled himself "General Bonaparte"; Browse Trist of Totnes led the mobs as "provost marshall," and wore a cocked hat and powdered wig. At Bellamarsh, the crowd carried two flags, a white one "for an avowal of French principles," and a red one signifying that they would spill their blood in support of such principles." At Dock the rioters celebrated their triumph with a noisy march around the town and called their victory a day "big with Wonder and Astonishment." A farm workers' broadside at Crediton pulled out all the stops, invoking natural justice, reciprocal obligations, and threats of insurrection and apocalypse.[29] There was little deference in it.

The self-assertive pragmatism of Devon's rioters was powerfully summed up in a revealing confrontation at Brixham. A gentleman asked the crowd "why they had not thought it more proper, to appeal to the Govern[t] and Laws of the Country for any address [sic] of Grievances than take the Law into their own Hands as they appeared to have done." They replied that they were following the example of the price regulation at Dartmouth, and some of "the common men" added "that Government had been applied to, long enough and nothing was done for them therefore it was time they sho[d] do something for themselves to keep their families from starving."[30] That homely philosophy was neither archaic nor deferential; what rioters took from tradition was less a sense of legitimacy than conventions of effective action. Those conventions and that effectiveness rested upon the local political framework.

Devon's food riots were both frequent and disciplined because they arose within communities where dense, stable social networks supported common understandings of the nature of and remedies for crisis. Rioters were well-established members of their communities. In almost every case, court indictments gave the parish where the riot took place as the rioter's residence.[31] No doubt such addresses often merely served as a convenience for the justices' clerks who filled out the indictments (just as "labourer" was used, sometimes inaccurately, as a catchall occupation). To be sure, one of the Modbury rioters, Hole, was said to be "an Exeter man"; another, Truscott, was a discharged seaman. But at least four of the six leaders of the 1801 riot in Modbury had been born there and were family men in their thirties and forties. Under the pervasive Settlement Laws, which required verifiable residence as a condition for poor relief, these rioters were "card-carrying" members of their communities.[32]

Moreover, rioters were respectable artisans and laborers, not marginal, dependent, and transient paupers.[33] In 1801 seventeen of the thirty known rioters were men of identifiable trades: four shoemakers, two weavers, a shipwright, blacksmith, master cabinetmaker-upholsterer, hellier (tiler or slater of roofs), stay maker, seaman, butcher, shopkeeper, schoolmaster, carpenter, and currier, together with ten "labourers," two teen-aged girls, and a mariner's wife. In 1795, a substantial minority of the arrested rioters comprised a "yeoman," two weavers, a wool comber, a blacksmith, a thatcher, and a cordwainer (shoemaker), along with thirteen "labourers" and four women.[34] In 1795 in Exeter, it is said, shopkeepers joined the rioters. "Tradesmen" were alleged to have guided several crowds in 1801, at times restraining them, at times instigating them, from behind the scenes. The Dartmouth resolutions (below) were said to be the work of "a body of Tradesmen headed by a few artful and cunning men."[35]

At Brixham, the crowd deliberately conscripted leaders who would lend both status and discipline to their enterprise. The Brixham crowd of Volunteers, Sea Fencibles, and others gathered at the house of George Sanders, a butcher and a captain of the Brixham Volunteers. They insisted that Sanders go with them to force the farmers to sign an agreement similar to one imposed at nearby Dartmouth and threatened to pull down his house if he would not go with them. Sanders and two of his fellow officers, Peter Pridham, a shopkeeper, and William Collier, a schoolmaster, reluctantly agreed to lead the crowd when they promised them "they would be guilty of no outrage or Violence to any person." Many respectable inhabitants also urged Sanders and Pridham to go with the mob. The officers hoped to use their "United Influence in preventing Confusion and Outrage," and added that "two constables went with us for the same reason." The Brixham crowd was certainly not deferential to these officers. They seemed to want leaders who could articulate the crowd's demands, and indeed Pridham and Sanders did forcefully advise the farmers to yield to the popular pressure.[36] But no doubt they also wanted "respectable" leadership to give coherence and hence greater effect to their effort, and perhaps also to symbolize their representation of the community and to lessen the risk of punishment.

Several leaders of the price regulation at Totnes were also men of solid standing in the town. A Robert Tippett and a John Wheeler both led the crowd that coerced farmer Richard Palk and signed the declaration of the people's committee: Tippett occupied the Bear Inn, assessed for the land tax at 12s. 6d., and two fields assessed at 16s. 6d. and 17s.; Wheeler occupied a house assessed at 12s. 1d. The people's committee also included William Hernaman, a shoemaker and occupier of a house assessed at 16s. 4d., "the young [William] Gibbs," apparently the son of a William Gibbs who owned a small orchard and rented a house assessed at £1 1s. 3d., and Richard Andrews, a borough constable. Browse Trist, the self-appointed "provost marshall" of the crowd, was also a master craftsman and namesake of Totnes's Member of Parliament for the period 1754–1763.[37]

The Modbury and Bellamarsh riots also had "respectable" leaders. One of the Bellamarsh leaders, Thomas Campion, aged thirty, was born at Ilsington of poor parents. A blacksmith like his father, Campion had been brought up in "the strictest rules of sobriety, honesty, and industry," and before the riot, he "was approved of by all who had any connections with him. He was, by his peculiar industry, the principal means of providing a comfortable subsistence for his aged parents, who, through infirmities were incapable of providing for themselves." Many "persons of respectability" appealed for the reduction of Campion's sentence.[38] John Cove, aged forty-nine, was a householder in Modbury and a successful shoemaker in 1801 when he joined a job to regulate the farmers. He was active enough to be one of the six men prosecuted for that riot, and he served a month's jail sentence. But that did not make him a social leper. For several years before the riots, he had sold some thirty pounds' worth of shoes to the parish annually for distribution to the poor, and he continued to sell great quantities of shoes to the parish overseers for at least two years after the riot.[39] He is buried near another convicted rioter in the shadow of the parish church, but apparently not in the shadows of community ostracism.

Seldom were rioters among the poorest members of the community, and very rarely did witnesses describe rioters as "the poor." For instance, the wives and relatives of the laboring poor in Honiton assembled in 1800 to ask relief from the portreeve, but they did not take violent action. The only reference to actual rioting by "the poor" comes from a general account in the *London Courier* in 1795. And in 1801, the gentry tried to restore order by guaranteeing that emergency relief would reach the strata of normally "independent" commoners. John Cholwich, chairman of the Quarter Sessions, described measures in Tiverton to relieve "the poor" but added that "the present complainants were of a very different description." One of the leading gentlemen of east Devon, James Coleridge, urged the Sidmouth vestry "to take into consideration the distress of the inhabitants who are just above ye class of paupers." And, as I will show, the county's relief program was specifically designed to aid (and forestall) potential rioters without stigmatizing them as paupers. Even the relatively prosperous Modbury shoemaker John Cove received casual (intermittent) relief (three shillings a week from April to July 1800, and two shillings a week from January through March 1801); his fellow rioter Richard Shepherd received regular out-relief (relief paid to people not living in the poorhouse) of between three and four shillings a week from May 1800 to February 1801. None of the other Modbury rioters appeared on the poor pay lists.[40]

The important "political" distinction is not between poverty and respectability, for no such line could be drawn with any finality for the working classes of the society. The "respectable" artisans and laborers were certainly poor enough to be vulnerable to the personal catastrophe of famine: James Coleridge in 1801 knew "several industrious men who are gradually sinking the hard earnings of many years, and have as yet suffered patiently."[41] But it does seem reasonable to infer that, much more than paupers, they were able to fend off the kind of social control that might be exerted through charity and the poor law, and perhaps also through casual employment. An authority on the Settlement Laws of this period concludes, "The essence of the matter was that paupers were not allowed to think of themselves as citizens. They were like nomads whose one desire was to be left alone."[42]

The resilience of the rioters contrasts strikingly with that description. Clearly they did think of themselves as citizens with rights and claims. They were members rather than wards of their communities. Morally, they had enough stake in an orderly society and enough pride in the legitimacy of their claims to prevent theft or wanton brutality during a riot. Politically, they could speak for their communities and command the attention of the magistrates. But besides their social status as individuals, the rioters drew both leverage and coherence (of perception and action) from the networks that they carried into riot.

The assertive, pragmatic ideology of Devon's rioters and their observance of a "protocol of riot" were rooted in a social cohesion that both enabled and constrained effective collective action. For one thing, Devon's riotous towns were generally small and stable enough to foster intimate social relations. Outside greater Plymouth, five out of six riots took place in towns with populations in 1801 between a thousand and sixty-five hundred. Moreover, these towns were growing only very slowly. Of the twenty-four riotous towns, fully twenty-one increased by less than 10 percent between the censuses of 1801 and 1811.[43] The stability of these communities meant that rioters, magistrates, and victims acted in a milieu of face-to-face familiarity. It was possible to speak of "the young Gibbs," or "one Cove, an elderly man, a widower and shoemaker," or a tenant who "rents from me at £8 a year," or "Hole a weaver, [who] works with Hornwell the overseer."[44] That stable intimacy also meant that the lives of the townspeople were knit together by routine social intercourse: kinship, work, trade, recreation, and folk rituals.[45]

Not the least of these traditions was that of food rioting. Many Devonians could remember the last major food crisis in 1766, when crowds had risen in Exeter, Honiton, and many of the other riotous towns to force reductions in prices and to attack mills and warehouses.[46] That successful experience certainly provided a stock of tactics, oral traditions, and possibly of consultants, from which later rioters could draw. Not surprisingly, among parishes of more than fifteen hundred inhabitants, most of the towns that rioted in 1795 did so again in 1800–1801, while most of the parishes that were quiet in 1795 remained so five years later.[47] Such local traditions of rioting raise all the more sharply the question of what kinds of social networks sustained them.

Far from being agrarian conflicts, food riots pitted town against country. The size and market roles of the towns and the occupations of their inhabitants set off riotous towns sharply enough from their hinterlands to focus grievances on neighboring farmers. Four out of five of Devon's food riots occurred in towns with populations of fifteen hundred or more; only eight riots occurred in smaller towns, and some four hundred rural parishes remained quiet.

Dearth crystallized the normal tension of town-country exchange. Not surprisingly, three-fourths of the riotous towns were market towns, and they accounted for five-sixths of the riots. In the marketplace, consumers dealt with farmers face to face; high prices generated personal antagonism. Those personal relationships made it easier to perceive economic transactions in moral terms; the "moral economy" almost required such a framework. At the same time, buying and selling in the open marketplace was still one of the most central public "rituals" in people's lives, and so marketing built up the consumers' camaraderie and the shared expectations that lay beneath not only the spontaneous forced sales of market-day riots in 1795 but also the more premeditated efforts to control prices in 1801. Moreover, the market towns had long been the places where officials regulated the food trade according to community need, and food rioters continued and extended those traditions.[48] Indeed, those practices may have lasted unusually long in Devon because many of the market towns were incorporated as municipal and parliamentary boroughs with locally "elected" officials.[49]

As the study of marketing practices advances it is increasingly clear that the tradition of direct sales by farmers to consumers in the open marketplace was being replaced by long-distance wholesale trading and transactions in the inns of the market towns, or at the farms themselves, between dealers and farmers who showed only samples of their crops. That trend reached back to perhaps two centuries before the Industrial Revolution. But compared with other counties, Devon still had an unusually high number of small market towns with their public marketplaces, thus providing more natural sites for riot. From this perspective, then, the end of the century was an optimum period for food riot, for Daniel and Samuel Lysons's parochial histories of Devon show clearly that by the first quarter of the nineteenth century many of the small market towns were already dying out.[50] If small market towns were also being extinguished in other counties, it must be one of the chief reasons why food riots declined in frequency in nineteenth-century England.

As it was, however, twenty-one of Devon's thirty-nine market towns witnessed riots, and only half of Devon's forty-two most populous parishes did. The reasons are twofold. First, population: the riotous communities were nearly twice as large as the nonriotous.[51] Second, the contrasts between northwest, south, and east Devon underline the significance of economic and social geography (see Figure 6).[52] Northwest Devon included half the area of the county, and the other two regions a quarter each, but all three regions contained nearly equal numbers of both market towns and populous parishes. In the east and south, for every populous town or market town that remained quiet, two rioted, while in the northwest fewer than one-third of such towns rioted.

Riots occurred predominantly in the south and east because there stocks of corn as well as farmers were accessible to direct control by crowds. The broad crescent running along the Channel coast from Plymouth to Teignmouth comprised the South Hams, a belt of rich, red loam said to be one of the most fertile soils in England, the breadbasket of Devon. There and in the Vale of Exeter, where the "strong loam" continued, farming was more commercially developed, thanks to urban demand, especially from Exeter and Plymouth. Farms were larger, farmers more aggressively entrepreneurial, and middlemen more active.[53] Hence, commerce heightened tensions between local needs and distant demands. Dealers from Exeter and Plymouth were accused of driving up prices in the South Hams in 1800. East Devon, meanwhile, was increasingly pulled into the market orbits of London and Bath, especially for dairy produce—and so at Cullompton in 1795 an anonymous letter and a mob threatened to destroy the dairies that had converted the land from tillage to pasture. Scarcity was further aggravated by "foreign" demands. Crowds attacked large millers in Bellamarsh and Totnes on just such grounds. The great fleets that anchored in Tor Bay for months in 1794 and 1800 carried up the twenty-five thousand extra mouths to feed and drained the region of foodstuffs.[54]

Little wonder that riots multiplied in such a fertile medium. Market towns and ports in the south and east collected and transmitted both economic pressures and news, including riot "news," along dense road and sea networks of trade and travel (see Figure 6). Indeed, eight of Devon's ten important ports had riots, and eight of the ten ports were situated in south and east Devon.[55] In part, the physical flows of foodstuffs through the market towns built up tensions: a wagon of wheat was intercepted and sold out at Newton on its way to Chudleigh, a wagonload of butter at Honiton, perhaps on its way to London, and the people of Sidmouth expressed their "mortification far unparalleled" when they watched local wheat being "purchased under the price [they] had offered and drawn off to some distant parish." In part, these economic networks conducted currents of rumor and example. In 1801 the towns of the South Hams were rumored to "have corresponded with each other and to have mutually agreed to support each other" and to signal the sailors of the Tor Bay fleet to join them; Exeter, "the great volcano," was supposed to have "instructed" Exmouth and Chudleigh; and the Brixham crowd said they followed the Dartmouth people.[56]

By contrast, the quieter northwest was an upland region of clay and gravel soil; the livelihood of the people there was primarily stock raising, with only a little mixed corn and livestock farming in the Taw Valley around Barnstaple. Northwest Devon was only half as densely populated as the south and east,[57] and the market towns and villages were smaller and widely scattered. In short, northwest Devon lacked both the commercial and social density that promoted riots in the south and east. The few riots that did take place in the northwest were isolated in time and place, unlike the chain reactions of the south and east. In addition, the histories of both the parliamentary boroughs and the Volunteer Corps of the north and west leave the impression that the common people were more deferential to their local elites than were people in the south and east, and hence had less of the social autonomy and assertiveness that encouraged riot.

Above all, the distribution of occupations within Devon's communities helped determine whether or not they would riot. No reliable detailed censuses exist for this period, but a crude measure can be derived from the census of 1811: the ratio of "Families chiefly employed in Trade, Manufactures, or Handicraft," to "Families...in Agriculture." A town with a ratio of 2.0 (twice as many trade and manufacturing families as agricultural) was clearly more differentiated from its rural hinterland than a town with a ratio of 0.5 (twice as many agricultural families). The great majority of riots occurred in parishes with a high proportion of nonagricultural employment. That factor distinguishes riotous from nonriotous market towns and riotous "large" parishes from nonriotous "large" parishes, and it reinforces the point that food rioters were town consumers dependent upon the market for food and conscious of a focused sense of grievance against neighboring farmers.[58]

The good-sized towns could more readily muster a "critical mass" of politically autonomous citizens, people not subject to the more immediate controls (employment, poor relief, and pettysessions justice) that the gentry could exert in rural villages.[59] As a rule, food riots did not take place in the rural parishes. Farm laborers got their grain directly from their employers, either at reduced prices or by pilferage: William Marshall, writing in 1796, did not see how Devon's farm workers could support a family without "pillage." Farm laborers on the whole seem to have lacked the supporting social networks that enabled townspeople to riot, for they rarely participated in any riots.[60]

It was not only the social and economic characteristics of townspeople but also in many cases their traditions of collective action that made them formidable rioters. For example, the dockyard artisans at Plymouth Dock had formed a powerful labor combination that spearheaded food riots there in 1801. But the woolen workers were the most prominent group of rioters in Devon. The densely populated towns and villages from Cullompton and Tiverton and Uffculme in the east, down through Exeter and Crediton to Totnes, Ashburton, and Modbury in the south, were centers of Devon's decaying woolen industry. The woolen workers, and particularly the "aristocratic" wool combers, had a militant tradition in east Devon. Tiverton had seen bitter and violent disputes between the gentlemen clothiers and their employees in the first half of the century, and as late as 1793–1794, the wool combers of east Devon had led a campaign against wool-carding machinery.[61] They considered breaking machines but settled instead upon an extensive, and ultimately unsuccessful, drive to petition Parliament for protective legislation. Petitions were sent from the county of Devon and from Devon's towns of Barnstaple, Exeter, Plymouth, Tiverton, Honiton, Ashburton, and Tavistock. The Exeter wool sorters, fullers, combers, and weavers were also well organized in the 1780s and conducted strikes in 1784, 1787, and 1795. Information on the last one is scarce; the incident appears to have been mild. The earlier strikes had involved attacks on mills and cloth in the looms, as well as organized bargaining between the fullers and their employers.[62]

These activities seem to have been an Indian summer of collective militancy for the Devon woolen workers. Their industry had declined from national preeminence in the previous century to a condition of regional stagnation, owing to changes in fashion, the competition of East Anglia and the West Riding, and the calamitous effects of recurrent wars on markets. Only political pressure on the East India Company by Devon's Members of Parliament helped keep the China market open for the dumping of Ashburton and Exeter cloth.[63]

The French wars at the end of the century dealt the coup de grace to the industry, and to the workers' bargaining position. From that time on, great distress was reported. Martin Dunsford observed in 1790 that Tiverton's poor rates had increased mainly because of the "want of constant employ" for the woolen workers. Modbury was full of "decayed manufacturers," while Ashburton had a number of occasionally unemployed "laboring manufacturers over whom some control may be very necessary." And in 1801, employers at Crediton were asked "to employ all idle hands in the weaving line, to prevent their assembling."[64]

Woolen workers, especially the "aristocratic" wool combers, were repeatedly blamed for the tumult in east Devon. A mob of "hundreds" of "woolcombers and weavers entirely" alarmed the farmers and gentlemen of Cullompton for days on end in 1795. One acute observer believed that the wool combers, along with "inferior Tradesmen...& Dissenters," were the directing intelligence behind the crowds, and that their societies ought to be watched by the government. Magistrates suspected that the societies of wool combers, serge makers, and laborers at Cullompton and Tiverton were in contact with their colleagues in Somerset, where rioting was also widespread. The only direct evidence of trade societies' involvement in riots comes from Uffculme in 1801, where "the clubs were and are divided; the riotous part took out money and spent it," but the peaceful members of the wool combers' Apron Society publicly disclaimed any intention of disturbing the peace. Of the fifty-four identifiable rioters in 1795 and 1801, five were wool combers and weavers.[65]

The Devon woolen workers' part in riots appears to be the story of industrialization run backwards, that is, a shift from associational to communal collective action.[66] Strikes gave way to food riots as Devon's woolen industry unraveled. A formerly-powerful organized labor force could no longer stave off industrial disaster, but their militant tradition undoubtedly contributed leaders, experience, and pride to the communal food riots of 1795 and 1801. Together with the other close bonds among Devon rioters, that was no mean legacy.

The local political traditions of many Devon communities also created prime conditions for riot, for those conditions comprised both independent bases for lower-class collective action and ties between plebs and officials sufficient to sustain intelligible bargaining and a protocol of riot. Twenty, or nearly half, of Devon's food riots occurred in ten towns that had the distinction of being boroughs; all but two were municipal boroughs.[67]

Given the antiquity of Devon's parliamentary boroughs, one might expect them to have been "pocket boroughs" tightly controlled by individual patrons, or government boroughs manipulated by means of admiralty or treasury patronage, as were the ancient and corrupt boroughs of neighboring Cornwall, and so to provide little scope for political activity by the common people.[68] However, many of Devon's boroughs had electorates large enough or fractious enough to permit political bargaining and conflict. Ashburton, the only pocket borough to be riotous, was ruled by the Palk family and the Earl of Orford. The Palks were responsible for keeping the Ashburton serge industry alive through their connections with the East India Company and hence the China market. But even at Ashburton the patrons' control was not absolute: perhaps a third of the voters were not fully committed to either the Palks or the earl.[69]

Larger boroughs were even more difficult for patrons to control. At Totnes, a number of would-be patrons competed for alliances with local interests so as to gain the support of some one hundred freemen. Plymouth was an admiralty borough with enough freemen (two hundred) to make a strong, independent party possible, and even occasionally victorious, as it was in 1784 after revenue officers had been disenfranchised. Okehampton's three hundred freeholders and freemen were said to be troublesome to the borough patrons, and as late as 1790, rival officials reported conflicting election results. Exeter's electorate of fifteen hundred freemen enabled the Dissenters to sustain a party in opposition to the Anglican corporation. And at the 1790 election, James Buller spent a lot of money "quilling" (treating?) the electors, successfully as it turned out. Barnstaple and Honiton, with three hundred fifty and seven hundred electors, respectively, were renowned for their venality. In both towns, lower-class voters had banded together to sell their combined votes to the highest bidder. Tiverton was a closed corporation borough with a Dissenting opposition and a turbulent industrial history. Townspeople could remember the riots of 1746, when the woolen workers had tried to install Charles Baring as successor to Oliver Peard as patron of the local industry. Hundreds of townspeople had signed a petition in 1782 calling for a wider franchise in the borough. The cantankerous history of these boroughs provided their citizens with experience in collective action and probably with leaders, both of which might contribute to the cohesion of the crowds in food riots.[70]

At the same time, the patronage networks of these boroughs probably brought local officials and the common people into closer, mutually profitable relationships. For instance, manipulation of the ancient borough charities, as well as private largesse, gave the municipal elite some leverage over potential rioters and their poor relatives.[71] At Exeter, the Corporate Charities of the Weavers and Fullers Company sponsored apprenticeships, a school, and annual doles to dozens of ordinary freemen. The mayors and justices of these boroughs were generally not so socially distant from the townspeople as were the country gentlemen. The town corporations that supplied the justices were predominantly middle-class men—merchants, tradesmen, and professionals—as well as gentlemen and clerics.[72]

Riot itself enforced a rough "responsibility" upon these municipal "ministries," a waning "paternalism" that was merely thinly disguised self-preservation. *After* the Plymouth riot of 1795, for instance, the mayor and magistrates issued handbills to warn that "forestallers and hucksters would be punished." Exeter magistrates tightened market regulations to give individual consumers precedence over "hucksters," and more than a dozen vendors were indicted at the city Quarter Sessions for violations or for forestalling and engrossing in 1795–1796 and 1800–1801.[73] The Exeter magistrates answered the riot of 1795 by searching the inns and public houses around the market, seizing and distributing "great quantities of butter...secreted there" for shipment to distant markets. Likewise, at Honiton the portreeve answered the complaints of a crowd of poor women by conducting a search of the inns around the marketplace. The officials found only three sacks of potatoes, which were added to the parish stocks for sale at reduced prices.[74]

It was in the borough towns that officials negotiated with the crowds—in what seems like an extension of the patronage demanded and proffered on other occasions. The patrons who stood behind the parliamentary and municipal boroughs of course contributed liberally to the relief of the poor in times of crisis.[75] A friend of the borough's Member of Parliament prevented a riot at Ashburton by subsidizing low potato prices out of his own pocket, and he asked the Member "to interest [him]self with the Lords of the Admiralty" so that some of the hundreds of burdensome French prisoners would be sent elsewhere, or there would be a riot. At Tiverton the borough magistrates held meetings to hear the complaints of the poor; at Plymouth and Exeter, mayors and gentlemen intervened between crowds and their targets.[76] At Dartmouth and Bideford the crowds called upon the mayors to sanction their price agreements, and the mayors subsequently brought the farmers into the communal settlement.[77] Local authorities could hardly afford to fly in the face of public opinion expressed as forcefully as riot, particularly when towns such as Totnes and Dartmouth were parliamentary boroughs, and perhaps it was in deference to this reciprocal connection between patronage and local opinion that very few rioters in these boroughs were prosecuted despite the boroughs' turbulence.[78]

Of course patronage was double-edged—it implied possibilities of control as well as protection. It was suggested to the lord lieutenant that the fishermen of Brixham should be warned that their "protections" (from impressment) might be revoked if they were found rioting. He lamented that the dockyard workers were out of control since patronage was controlled by the Navy Board instead of by local officials. And the insubordination of the Brixham Volunteers was blamed upon the inadequate social status of their commander who, as a tavern keeper and post office official, lacked "the influence or manner" that might have prevented his men from rioting.[79]

The most important networks that knit rioters together were the local Volunteer Corps. The Volunteers were organized from 1794 onward as part-time auxiliaries to the militia. It has been argued that the government promoted the Volunteers partly as a means of actively enlisting the common people in the political crusade against Jacobinism. But the evidence suggests that Devon's gentry established the Volunteers chiefly to carry out the traditional militia tasks of controlling riots and defending against invasions. At the same time, gentlemen cherished their own visible roles at the head of such a colorful military embodiment of social hierarchy and paternalism.[80]

Yet, as a police force, the Volunteers were a bad bargain. In 1795, the Tavistock Volunteers were credited with preventing tumult, but the Honiton Volunteers dismissed ten members who had failed to appear when called out against rioters. From Cullompton a terrified correspondent wrote that the Volunteers were "almost all. . . of the lowest class [of] this town and who do not seem to regard in the least let the mob do what they will." In 1797 the Teignmouth Volunteers refused to promise that they would act against riots, and many of them resolved at a public house that they would fix prices at the Newton market. As prices soared again in 1800, the Volunteer Corps throughout Devon provided nuclei and a county network for riot. At the Bull Inn in Axminister an angry tirade by one of the town's original Volunteers prefigured their role in later riots. John Liddon, a dyer, cried out "that he could not get a peck of wheat for half a crown. That the Damnation Farmers were determined to starve them all to Death. That they took the advantage of the Volunteers, and would not bring their corn to market, and if the people rose, which he knew they would soon for that they could not bear it much longer, and Capn Tucker [commander of the Axminster Volunteers] ordered him to fire, he would fire, and he knew exactly where to place the Ball."[81] In December, several "charter members" of the Exeter Volunteers turned in their arms, saying they "would not protect the Farmers." Handbills in east Devon urged the Volunteers "to consider the conduct of the farmers and to sign a paper to be true to the cause." The Sidmouth Volunteers petitioned the magistrates to help regulate the markets. A Sidbury Volunteer declared that a miller "should be hung up at his own door." At Branscombe and at Seaton and Beer, Volunteers led or joined mobs to fix prices.[82]

When the Devon rioting reached its climax in the early spring of 1801, Volunteers led many of the crowds and refused to suppress others. At Exeter, forty uniformed Volunteers joined in the regulation of the farmers. The Newton Volunteers were reported "to a man...[to] have given in their arms and joined the banditry," and the Totnes Volunteers had joined similar actions "to obtain corn." The Dartmouth Volunteer Artillery Company warned their commander they would act against invasion, but not against riot: "No, not to starve our own families...We have committed no outrage, we only mean to compel the farmers to sell their articles at a moderate price."[83]

In large part, the behavior of the Volunteers arose from their social position. The Volunteers were plebeian weekend foot soldiers drawn from precisely the same ranks of artisans and laborers as the members of riotous crowds (unlike their counterparts, the mounted Yeomanry, who were farmers and middle-class men capable of providing their own horses).[84] When the famine threatened, the Volunteers' bellies, their neighbors, and no doubt their wives told them they were consumers first and guardians of the peace a distant second.

Their brief history had already hinted that they would confound the gentry's hopes for a bargain-rate police force. Many joined for reasons besides those of patriotism and local defense— pay, exemption from the militia ballot, and the camaraderie of drill and field days that blossomed afterward at the public house.[85] The Volunteers must also have enjoyed the pageantry of their resplendent uniforms and basked in the social esteem bestowed on them in ceremonies when local gentlemen's wives presented them their colors. For these were emblems of the vital constitutional and social role assigned them by local and national authorities.

But their peculiar constitution gave that imprimatur a significant twist. For the local Volunteer Corps adopted their own regulations. They were under formal military discipline only when called out by the crown, the lord lieutenant, or the sheriff; otherwise, they functioned legally as a voluntary association. They also elected their own officers. In most cases, that meant simply pro forma ratification of choices made by the gentlemen who sponsored the corps. But sometimes the rank and file acted more autonomously, electing commanding officers of less than genteel status—a butcher at Cullompton, a tavern keeper at Brixham, tradesmen in some of the Exeter corps.[86] The gentry were nauseated at the thought of admitting such social inferiors to the company of officers and gentlemen, but they dared not risk impugning the loyalty of the Volunteers by rejecting their choices.[87] At Exeter and Teignmouth, the Volunteer Corps even asserted their right to remove unpopular officers, while some corps adopted rules more like those of a club than a military unit, rules for fining tardy officers, arbitrating disputes by committee, or blackballing candidates for membership. No wonder Colonel (later Lord) Rolle snorted that it was "very improper to allow the Volunteers to nominate their own officers—it is too much like the French."[88]

And so, beyond their actual leadership of food riots, the Volunteers' behavior epitomized the failure of old-fashioned paternalism (or new-fangled political mobilization) to stifle social conflict. For, the incipient social autonomy of the Volunteers and their experience in acting together were important sources for the collective solidarity of the crowds. Lord Clifford expressed the chagrin of the gentry: "An unfortunate distinction has taken place in the minds of many Volunteers. They fancy they have complied with their oath of allegiance when they declare that they will fight for their King and Country against the Common Enemy, but think they have a right to withhold their assistance when called upon to support the Civil Magistrate in the execution of what they disapprove—if Men in arms are permitted to reason on the propriety of the Laws our boasted liberty is at an End."[89]

Many networks—markets, industry, political factions, and Volunteer Corps—contributed to the "horizontal" solidarity of the crowds, and hence to their capacity to act collectively with purpose and restraint. Most of these networks also connected common people and local authorities "vertically," in reciprocal relationships which entailed explicit or implicit bargaining to adjust conflicting interests and establish a rough equilibrium within the necessities of coexistence. In that context, plebeian political autonomy fell midway between deference to and outright defiance of authority. On the level of immediate confrontation, food riot was simply the most dramatic mobilization of these networks.

Food riots also triggered wider community mobilizations by prompting the gentry to bring their political, social, and economic leverage to bear not only on the crowds, to restore order, but also on farmers and dealers, to compel them to contribute to community equilibrium. The gentry's responses were critical influences upon the rioters' behavior, for the rioters implicitly adjusted their actions on the basis of both past experience and current anticipations of those responses.[90] Moreover, the gentry's relief efforts at both the local and the county level were an important achievement of the riots, and they may well have been an indirect objective of the rioters. In sum, rioters could anticipate that magistrates would observe the "protocol of riot." Hence the rioters' actions cannot really be understood outside the "vertical" political frameworks of the local communities and the county.

In local communities riots inspired the elite to drag the old market regulation machinery out of mothballs and to encourage the farmers to contribute to social equilibrium by lowering prices. In the larger towns, officials published impersonal and open-ended appeals. At Plymouth, the mayor asked farmers to sell their commodities at a reasonable price, and fifteen gentlemen called upon farmers to reduce their prices to preclude the "dreadful necessity" of using military force and to prevent the growth of political disaffection. In the neighborhood of Exeter eleven farmers asked suppliers to meet to agree on quotas and prices for the market. The Recorder of Exeter recommended that both buyers and sellers of provisions follow "their respective lines of duty." At Tiverton, neighboring farmers agreed to supply the borough relief committee with corn.[91]

In medium-sized towns, crowd action was translated more directly into community compromise. At Bideford, for example, the magistrates promised a clamoring crowd of a thousand that they would try to persuade the farmers to lower their prices. That persuasion and popular pressure did bring lower prices at the next market, though they also helped dry up supplies.[92] At Dartmouth, when threats failed to disperse a crowd, the mayor promised to persuade the farmers to market their corn, and did so. Nevertheless, for several days, crowds led by tradesmen and Volunteers continued to force price contracts upon the farmers in the neighborhood. The mayor then summoned the principal inhabitants of the town to meet, and they appointed a "General Committee . . . for regulating the market," which tried to regain control of events. They published a set of resolutions setting maximum prices for grain, butter, and potatoes and suggesting that no one buy more than a week's supply for his family. They thanked the "tradesmen and others of [the] borough for their well-regulated behavior and proper conduct on their application to the farmers of the adjacent parishes to supply the market," and they also thanked the "gentlemen farmers for their ready compliance in attending to the representations of the tradesmen and others." The mayor later claimed that the prices were only suggestions, but clearly they were meant to be stronger than that. Rumor had it that if farmers did not bring in their grain, they would be summoned to the Dartmouth committee to explain why.[93]

Meanwhile, in nearby Brixham, high food prices had caused great suffering among "all ranks." The fishermen and Volunteers vowed to follow the example of neighboring towns and visit the farmers. Two of the Volunteer officers then consulted Philip Gillard, "one of the principal Gentlemen Farmers" of the parish, and together they decided to call a vestry meeting that afternoon. Most of the farmers of the neighborhood attended and agreed to sell their corn at the Dartmouth prices. Peter Pridham, a shop-keeper and ensign in the Volunteers, produced a copy of the Dartmouth prices. Gillard asked him to go to Dartmouth to get a copy of the Dartmouth resolutions, "attested by some respectable persons," which he would then be willing to sign. Pridham replied that they "might as well settle it now, for he supposed bring what paper they would tomorrow [the farmers] should be obliged to sign it."[94] He was right. The next day the crowd took the paper to the farmers, having pressed Pridham and two other Volunteer officers into service as spokesmen. Gillard signed the document, apparently not greatly minding that it was brought by a mob rather than a delegation from the vestry. Some of the other victims who had not been parties to the vestry meeting were terrified, but most of them, including "the most intelligent and reputable inhabitants of the parish," later refused to press charges, since peace and quiet had returned, the hungry motives of the crowd were well understood, some had expressed contrition, and the members of the crowd were not "republicans."[95]

I have already shown how the Totnes crowd's requisitions inspired a town meeting and how the mayor's "respectable" committee, to its later chagrin, forced the merchant Harrison to sign the crowd's agreement. Another local merchant complained that "all the principal people seem to hold with the rabble and no person acts against them."[96]

The transactions at Dartmouth, Brixham, and Totnes were only the most elaborate episodes in which communities reached compromises under pressure of riot. At Exmouth "the gentlemen and farmers met and the people waited their decision." The meeting refused to fix a compulsory price, but the farmers agreed to supply food to the people at reduced prices. That satisfied them. At Ottery a leading gentleman hoped "to prevail on [the] farmers to come forward in a reasonable way to preserve the quiet of the place." An anxious parish meeting at Uffculme reached agreement on price reductions while a mob was actually approaching, and the solution was literally held out to the mob. At Newton Abbot, the farmers also met with the magistrates after a riot and agreed to reduce their prices. They acted under compulsion, but they said they could afford the prices agreed upon. Agreements were made in other parishes, too, most of them direct responses to riots in the neighborhood.[97]

Of course these actions recognized that social peace was more important than absolute property rights or, rather, profit rights. But there was little rhetorical bombast about either order or paternalism. Although the officials promised determined efforts to preserve order, they did not condemn the rioters.And although they were quite willing to make the farmers do their duty, they could hardly afford to antagonize them with moralistic condemnations. Their actions did not really *legitimize* the illegal violence that had taken place; on the contrary, by translating the rioters' direct action into community consensus, they committed a euphemism in act. They were not simply restoring peace ad hoc; they were grasping the nettle of disorder and extracting its moral and political core. In that sense, the communal conciliation derived its moral force from the rioters' undeniable claims, rather than vice versa.[98]

These communal settlements were an important part of the rioters' success, and that success is a necessary part of the explanation of the frequency and form of Devon's riots. Riot would have been neither so frequent nor so orderly had there been no payoff.[99] Immediately, a day's regulation of the market was no small matter—at standard contemporary estimates of consumption of eight bushels per person per year, each bushel of grain gained might feed a family of four for two weeks. Even the forced contracts of 1801 sometimes worked. At Exeter and Crediton the fear of further riots induced farmers to supply the markets. Furthermore, officials published several declarations stating that the forced agreements were void—implying that they had once been operative. At Totnes and Dartmouth, the agreements were enforced for a short while, keeping prices low at Totnes for a month after the rioting.[100]

More generally, the rioters' attempts to control prices had mixed results in the weeks that followed a riot. The six market towns that reported to the government inspector of corn returns did not experience a sustained reduction in food prices in either 1795 or 1801, though rioting may have checked a rising curve. Several towns reported that "the people have nearly ruined the markets."[101] The sclerosis of the supply arteries marked the limit of what rioters could hope to achieve directly. Merchants shipped their corn away from the disturbed districts, or cancelled importation orders.[102] But in the smaller communities, the farmers' agreements held up long enough to merge with comprehensive relief programs, the ultimate achievement of the rioters.

If price reductions and relief programs were benefits rioters might hope to gain, they had also to reckon with costs, including physical repression. In fact, force was rarely used against Devon's rioters, and local politics is the reason. Historians have sometimes explained the frequency of eighteenth-century riots as a consequence of the weakness of local "police" institutions.[103] That is too mechanical (and modernist) an explanation, for it begs the questions of when and how riot ceased to be tolerated. As Jerome Skolnick points out, "Order, like violence, is politically defined."[104] One might better reverse the argument and say that police remained weak as long as riots could be tolerated. As long as traditional networks could restrain riots and restore equilibrium, few gentlemen perceived a need to shoulder the administrative and financial burdens of a stronger police force.[105] In this period, the use of force against rioters was hardly a matter of mechanical law enforcement, but rather was shot through with political considerations. The Riot Act proclamation, the ritual threat of force, was apparently too severe to be useful in Devon or elsewhere in England. It was read only three times in Devon in these forty-three riots, two of those being in Plymouth Dock.[106] Professional police forces were virtually nonexistent. The unpaid parish constables were subject to exactly the same sort of pressures as the Volunteers, and like them, more frequently collaborated with crowds than opposed them. Special constables, though usually recruited from the reliable middle class, also defaulted sometimes. In a few instances, particularly in the larger towns, they helped the magistrates to disperse a crowd peacefully or to patrol after a riot.[107] Smaller towns found it difficult to recruit reliable special constables. Magistrates at Sheepwash discovered that ten specially recommended men from a neighboring parish refused to swear to act against rioters with whom they sympathized, and at Newton, a gentleman complained that two respectable men "acting as [special?] constables" had seized two of his father's tenants and threatened to take them before the justice if they did not fulfill the people's contract.[108]

Plenty of military force was available to the magistrates, but they did not use it. For reasons already made clear, the Volunteers were used only five times against rioters, with very poor results.[109] The Yeomanry were used sparingly for opposite reasons. These gentlemen of property and their tenants had good reasons to be reliable guardians of order—too good, for they were probably considered too partisan and too provocative by local officials who might have called them out. And at Newton, the Yeomanry declined to act against the rioting Volunteers, "men trained in the use of arms."[110]

But Devon's strategic location ensured that many other military units were available. In 1795, the Royal Cornish Militia helped to disperse crowds and arrest rioters with little incident at Crediton and Bellamarsh.[111] But nearby forces were not called to the riots either at Plymouth or at Exeter, where the Twenty-fifth Light Dragoons were stationed. Of course, the spring of 1795 had witnessed a whole chain of food riots led by hungry militia men, including the incidents at Plymouth and Dock. And more than once, the troops themselves had created pandemonium in Devon's towns. Hence as a burden on local order as well as on food supplies, troops were often unwelcome guests.[112] Their shaky record may help to account for the magistrates' reluctance to call upon them, but the political dilemmas of the resort to force were a more important reason. At the peak of the rioting in 1801, nearly 5,000 troops were stationed in Devon, in at least four districts where riots took place—at Exeter (1,374 troops), Plymouth (2,777), Berry Head near Brixham (508), and Exmouth (261)—but the only forcible use of troops against crowds took place in Plymouth and Plymouth Dock at the end of March.[113]

Greater Plymouth is the exception that proves several rules about order and disorder in Devon. The borough of Plymouth and its twin, Plymouth Dock, were by far the most rapidly growing towns in Devon, thanks to their great government dockyard. Dock was a particularly unruly town. Sailors were paid off there. They caroused in the streets, spending their pay and time as furiously as possible. They were regularly bilked by shopkeepers who sold them shoddy goods. The dockyard workers were a powerful force in the town, exceedingly well paid, protected from local controls by far-away government patronage, and united by a tightly oranized work hierarchy in the physical enclave of the yard. In

1801 their combination united with those at the other royal dockyards along the south coast to demand pay increases. Two county magistrates had jurisdiction, but not authority, over this boom town of twenty-three thousand. One of them was a new magistrate, both were under a cloud for manipulating public house licenses, and the dockyard commissioner refused to cooperate with them.[114]

In short, because greater Plymouth was a large, booming, urban conglomerate in which traditional networks had begun to dissolve, crowd action and political "bargaining" were less orderly there than in Devon's more compact and stable towns. Food riots degenerated into unruly destruction of property and theft of food.[115] Although the authorities twice used military force against rioters, the magistrates suffered an utter fiasco in 1801 that helps to demonstrate why troops were not deployed more often. On March 30 at Plymouth and on the 31st at Dock, riots began with forced sales in the marketplaces. But toward late afternoon the Plymouth crowd began to seize bread and meat, "paying anything or nothing for it." Parties of the Surrey militia charged and dispersed them.[116] At Dock the following day, the crowd went from the marketplace to the bakers' shops, "obtained their bread at half price, broke their windows and became extremely riotous." The magistrates read the Riot Act, and when the crowd refused to disperse, the dragoons cleared the streets with a cavalry charge and wounded several rioters. Rumors, later proved false, spread that a rioter had been killed.

The magistrates arrested several rioters and took two to the guardhouse for examination. Late in the afternoon a vast crowd of dockyard men marched up to the guardhouse to demand the release of the prisoners, one of whom was their workmate. The crowd was surrounded on four sides of the square by an imposing array of cavalry, militia, and Volunteers, together with four artillery pieces that had been loaded with canister and grapeshot before the eyes of the crowd. But the dockyard men were unimpressed by either magistrates' warnings or menacing guns, and they stood fast. The magistrates released one prisoner, then the other.[117]

The magistrates said they could not bear to use their drastic weapons, for, as they said, "Had we proceeded to such coercive measures as their lawless conduct merited, the most dreadful consequences must have ensued, and many hundreds must have fallen." Local editorial opinion split. The *Exeter Flying Post* believed such a surrender would lead to further trouble. The *Sherbourne and*

Yeovil Mercury, however, commended the magistrates: "The whole conduct of the Magistrates, which happily prevented the lives of hundreds from being taken away, and preserved the peace of one of the first mercantile towns in England, has been considered by the public as highly meritorious."[118] The *Mercury's* comment suggests that, aside from their humanity, the magistrates may also have been offering expiation for the earlier bloodshed in hopes of restoring peace. That was, at any rate, the immediate result. The rioters celebrated the surrender of the prisoners with a triumphal procession, but peace returned. Two weeks later, however, the dockyard workers had the audacity to smash their way into the magistrates' committee room and rescue another arrested rioter.[119]

In more general terms, the lord lieutenant hoped that the magistrates and Volunteers would be able to restore order "without the necessity of having recourse to any violent means." The magistrates refused to use lethal force because they were humane, because bloodshed would have only increased social conflict and exposed them personally to retaliation or odium, and because other means of restoring equilibrium were available.[120] That combination of mildness and conciliation was the reciprocal half of Devon's "protocol of riot."

The county of Devon was also a community in the sense that it was governed and knit together by a cohesive ruling class. Their recognition of a protocol of riot was reflected in the lord lieutenant's reaction to the mobbing of the king in London in October 1795. He condemned that riot as "far derogatory, not only to the character of Englishmen, but even of an English mob."[121]

The county's ruling class took a more principled view of riot and social order than hard-pressed local officials. The conspicuous official positions of the lord lieutenant and the district military commander gave them a compelling legal obligation to restore order. More broadly, the class interests of the peers and top gentry of the county—the leaders of the Quarter Sessions and the county lieutenancy—provided motives and means to act. On the whole, the peers saw themselves as standing far above the conflicting material interests of farmers and hungry townspeople. They did not feel immediately threatened by riot. All seemed to agree that restoring authority was far more important than asserting narrow material interests. Some believed in mediation, some believed in strict protection of the markets, but all agreed that social peace required a durable solution to popular grievances. In practice, politics took precedence over legal or economic dogma and sharply modified the application of abstract principles of authority, property, and the freedom of the markets.

Devon's ruling class was led by vigorous and intelligent officials whose social and economic power gave them the means and the understanding to effect a long-lasting reconciliation of interests. At the top of the Devon hierarchy were three peers and a general. The Earl of Fortescue, the lord lieutenant, was a vigorous and highly principled leader who personally supervised in detail the affairs of the county lieutenancy, and particularly those of the dozens of local Volunteer Corps. More than most lords lieutenant he was also a powerful force in the Quarter Sessions.[122] His unusually full and well-organized correspondence shows that he was an active and well-informed administrator. Lord Rolle was a justice of the peace and a Member of Parliament from 1789 to 1796 before he inherited his father's title. He was also an eccentric ("the strong-lunged member who coughed down Burke") who operated quasi-independently of the county hierarchy, by mutual preference. But most of all Rolle fancied himself a soldier. He was simultaneously commander of the South Devon Militia Regiment and of no fewer than five Volunteer and Yeomanry Corps. Lord Clifford was a Roman Catholic and thus ineligible for official posts, but he performed a crucial service as chairman of the Committee of Internal Defense, which supervised the county subscriptions for the Volunteers. All three peers lived on their Devon estates for much of the year, Lord Fortescue at Castle Hill near South Molton, Lord Rolle at both Stevenstone near Great Torrington and Bicton in East Devon, and Lord Clifford at Ugbrooke near Chudleigh. Fortescue and Rolle were two of the wealthiest landowners of the county. The fourth key gentleman in Devon was the commander of the western military district, Lieutenant-General J. G. Simcoe, who had settled on his estate near Honiton upon retirement as governor-general of Canada in 1796. Years and family traditions of administering their estates made these men familiar landmarks in their neighborhoods as landlords, employers, customers of tradesmen, and patrons of churches, charities, and local recreations.[123]

Their connections with local communities enabled them to measure crisis quickly and personally. In 1801 Lord Fortescue listened firsthand to the expostulations of the poor at the South Molton market. He and Lord Rolle toured the county during the unrest to watch the state of the markets. General Simcoe made local inquiries. He had initially feared that "Jacobins" instigated the riots of 1801, but he discovered "there was no disloyalty at the bottom of these insurrections, only absolute want. The illness of the peasantry in the parishes in my vicinity all proceed from this source, as I am assured by medical persons of integrity and capacity."[124] In 1795, Lord Clifford picked up local rumors of plans for a riot in the parishes around him, and he correctly foresaw that the "low and inadequate price of labour" would cause a disturbance.[125]

Their instinctive response to unrest was to use their own wealth and influence to underwrite order in their own neighborhoods. Fortescue bought "great quantities" of grain to sell to the poor of Barnstaple and South Molton at very reduced prices in the winter of 1795. In the spring of 1801, he kept close watch on the South Molton relief program, to which he was a substantial contributor. Lord Rolle bought two shiploads of wheat and rice to be sent down from London to two areas of the county. He later ordered the steward of his estate to take his remaining corn into the Torrington and Barnstaple markets and to urge the neighboring farmers to do likewise.[126] He and Lord Clifford also exerted decisive local influence over farmers in their neighborhoods. No doubt the local efforts of these peers were important in keeping their home towns free of riot. Fortescue certainly believed that his neighborhood had been quiet in the spring of 1795 because of voluntary increases in laborers' wages and relief subscriptions for the poor, both of which he led by example. Fortescue went on to draw the moral that gentlemen should lose no time in "affording immediate and effectual relief for the poor,...for unjustifiable as riots always are, yet every measure should be taken to prevent the provocation to them which the distresses of the labouring class...but too much occasion."[127]

Lord Clifford insisted in 1801 that his local connections would enable him to preserve the peace of his neighborhood: "The respect I have received from the people and support from the principal inhabitants around me leaves no doubt in my mind that the storm has passed us." Like Fortescue in 1795, Clifford believed that authority had to rest on an effective response to the distress of the people: "Nothing but the greatest energy on the part of Government and meeting grievances wherever they are to be found can restore Subordination to the [laws?] and make us a United people."[128] Hence the peers' local ties rendered riot at least politically intelligible, though not legitimate.

This pragmatic view of social order—that social equilibrium rested upon reciprocal duties, not on unconditional deference— also shaped the peers' economic ideology. Their notions of how the market should operate were intimately bound up with their prescriptions for social peace.

Some county leaders were as ready as local officials to compel the farmers to contribute to social peace. Lord Rolle condemned "the impolicy or really impropriety of the farmers asking and taking such extravagant prices for their grain." He saw the duty of the leading gentry as that of impartial arbiters of conflicting interests. He wrote to Fortescue: "Your Lordship's sentiments entirely coincide with mine respecting the opulent farmer, or farmers in general who have a quantity of corn to dispose of. The prices are very exorbitant. Compulsion you cannot use, and they are deaf many of them...to every persuasive advice—I have almost said humanity. To steer between the two and do justice to both is the arduous and difficult task."[129] In January 1801, after riots nearby, Lord Rolle persuaded his neighbors and tenants in half a dozen parishes to supply the poor with corn at low prices.[130] In response to the Exeter rioting two months later, some gentlemen there took out newspaper advertisements ordering their tenants to take their grain to market on pain of nonrenewal of their leases.[131] At the same time, the clerk of the county Quarter Sessions busied himself riding around the neighborhood of Exeter trying to persuade the farmers to supply the markets in order to restore peace. He wrote to Fortescue, hoping he and other gentlemen would also exert their influence.[132]

The chairman of the Quarter Sessions took up a position midway between "paternalism" and laissez faire. He snorted that Rolle's pressure on the farmers was a "bonus for insurrection." He came down on the side of order even while he recognized the farmers' provocative behavior, writing, "I fear the farmers have carried the price to too great a height. Wheat at 20s. or 1 Gn., Barley at 15s. and butter at 16d., is more than ought to have been exacted. They are aware of it, and many of them in private have confes'ed it to me today. However, they must be supported, or infinitely worse consequences will ensue. God send us well out of it. Next to a religious riot, I dread a riot on the score of provisions."[133]

Finally, some of the county rulers had by 1801 converted to the laissez faire doctrines preached by the Duke of Portland: that scarcity was a natural disaster, and that the security of the markets must be preserved so that free trade and "rationing" of supplies by high prices might prevent famine.[134] This doctrine confronted Lord Clifford with the most painful dilemma of his life. Threats of a riot at Chudleigh in 1801 prompted a parish meeting at which Lord

Clifford assured his neighbors and tenants that law and the rights of property guaranteed their freedom to dispose of their grain as they wished. But, he continued, "after ascertaining the matter of right they were to consider what part of their right they were inclined to abandon for the preservation of the public peace." If any of them decided to lower their prices out of prudence, he would personally repay their losses. They agreed to lower their prices, and riot was forestalled. When Lord Clifford was criticized by General Simcoe, though, he replied defensively, with great rhetorical flourish, that property was sacred. He added that reducing consumption, if possible, would be the only remedy for scarcity, and that "security of conveyance of articles of provision and a peaceful freedom of the markets would still bring forth a sufficiency of food."[135] At the crisis, though, social peace and the reestablishment of legitimate authority outweighed such economic abstractions. Historians have discussed the transition from paternalism to laissez faire at length,[136] but in practice, politics rather than ideology was still decisive in Devon.

The most ardent convert to the doctrine of the "freedom of the markets" in Devon was the lord lieutenant. In 1795 Fortescue had believed that the market people in many towns had taken advantage of the soldiers quartered among them to raise their prices, and he suggested that the town authorities exercise their right to regulate prices. In 1801, however, he agreed with the Duke of Portland that the only permanent basis for peace was "the perfect restoration of the freedom of the market and hence the return of every other article of provision to its least price." So strongly did he believe this that he dared to advise some clamoring poor people in the South Molton market simply not to buy from farmers who had not lowered their prices.[137] But even Fortescue's belief was qualified in practice, as I will show.

General Simcoe, the military commander of the western district, agreed that interference with the freedom of the markets would turn scarcity into famine. But Simcoe also made more abstract analyses of the origins and the "extensive consequences" of the riots. He believed that all social subordination had broken down. He deplored the "ruin of all hold on the people that was heretofore in the landed interest. . . those who. . . from their benevolence and understanding deserved, and had obtained an influence over" the common people. Simcoe drew alarming parallels with Continental revolution, fearing that the "infection" of "anarchy" would reach "the capital" and that it would lead to "rebellion." "Every man of property ought to be on it," he wrote

Fortescue. To act against "the Insurrection," the "system" among the rioters must be met with "equal system among the supporters of civil society...all persons, more especially, those of property & distinction, should unite as one man in that arrangement, which under the authority of the civil magistrates, may best apply the military force to the protection of the law of the land...and avoid the fatal consequences that must follow the continuation of such lawless acts."[138]

Simcoe deployed troops to cordon off Devon from the continuing unrest in Somerset. He impatiently suggested setting up summary tribunals to override the borough magistrates' jurisdiction.[139] He also insisted that the "peasantry" be politically separated from the townspeople and returned to the restraining influence of "the patronage of their landlords." Then, once he recognized that "misery" rather than Jacobinism was behind the riots, he urged that the magistrates hold local Sessions to hear the "peasantry's" complaints and to protect them from the self-interest and intimidation of the overseers.[140] To some extent Simcoe's worries were justified—the independence and militancy of the east Devon woolen workers were well known—but his vivid imagination and his foreign experience exaggerated his fears. And perhaps so did his newness to Devon and his military habit of anticipating the worst outcomes. At any rate, his lurid fears contrast with the prosaic confidence of the county's peers.

The county leaders' ultimate goal was to restore authority, property rights, and the freedom of the markets, but they had to compromise each of those principles. Fortescue returned from London to Devon at the beginning of April 1801 armed with instructions from the Home Secretary to reestablish order.[141] The three main points of his program were to make a show of force, to prosecute rioters, and to establish a comprehensive relief program. While Simcoe busied himself with the deployment of regular forces, Fortescue sought to stiffen the backbone of the Volunteers. The riotous Brixham Volunteers were formally disarmed and disbanded, and official notices of that action were sent out as lessons to other corps. Other Volunteer units were tested in various ways. Many were mustered and required to sign declarations that they would serve against rioters; recalcitrants were expelled.[142] But as rioting ended, pressure on the Volunteers eased. Simcoe declared that, "In a civil view the restoration of tranquility will much depend on not considering too harshly the faults of the Volunteers. They are misled but not Jacobins."[143] For indeed, the gentry could not dispense with the Volunteers' services. At least nine corps were called out on permanent duty in April. And the latent antagonism of town and country could be harnessed to help keep the peace. The gentry and farmers together raised several new corps of Volunteers and Yeomanry made up of countryfolk, who were presumed to be more reliable than townspeople against rioters.[144] Fortescue personally toured the country, shoring up weak magistrates and, particularly, spurring the town authorities in Dartmouth, Totnes, Bideford, and Plymouth Dock to do their duty.[145]

These reassertions of authority were mostly symbolic; order was not restored by a direct physical confrontation between mobs and official forces. Fortescue did not want a bloody clash with rioters any more than other Devon magistrates did. More important, the rioting had already ceased by the time his show of force was under way,[146] in part because the magistrates had regained control, especially in the larger towns of Exeter and Plymouth, by mobilizing large numbers of special constables and by making a few exemplary arrests.[147] But also, the rioters, by taking direct action and by triggering compromises on food supplies and relief programs, had already achieved as much as they could hope to. At the same time, even where troops were called out to guard the markets, continued pressure from the townspeople inspired farmers in Okehampton, Bideford, and Torrington to reduce prices "voluntarily." Lord Fortescue reported that farmers were now secure enough to bring their corn to market, "and though they have abated something of their prices (which were before extravagant beyond the extent of fair speculation), yet they have been induced to do so purely by fair competition and from a calculation of reasonable profit." But aside from the pressure of public opinion, he added, anticipation of the county's relief supplies had helped force prices down. It was hardly a victory for unadulterated freedom of the markets![148]

The second leg of Fortescue's program was the prosecution of the rioters, one of the most critical "costs" for rioters to calculate. Douglas Hay has shown brilliantly how class interests were served by the discretionary workings of criminal justice in the eighteenth century.[149] In no instance was the "politics of justice" more evident than in the treatment of rioters, at every step from arrest to punishment. While rioters often said "they might as well be hung as starved," the politics of justice opened up much more varied and subtle prospects. Arrests were made in fewer than half the riots, and far fewer than half the arrested rioters were convicted of any offense. That was not because justice was baffled by the rioters' anonymity but because justice was intended to be exemplary and instructive. The magistrates meant to punish enough rioters to demonstrate that riot was not *legitimate,* and that the legal authorities would reclaim their monopoly on coercion, but not so many as to outrage the public. Such arrests were believed to have quieted Exeter in 1801. But the sentences given convicted rioters were relatively light, generally ranging from one week to six months in prison. Moreover, the longer rioters put off their trial, the more the timeliness of exemplary justice cooled, and the more likely they were to be acquitted.[150]

Conversely, only rarely was it necessary to reaffirm the protocol of riot by drastic example. In 1795 the rioters at the Bellmarsh mill had far exceeded the conventional limits to violence by destroying the mill's machinery and beating the miller. One Thomas Campion had made himself conspicuous by carrying a flag, and so was a marked man from the moment of the riot; he was tried and condemned at the Summer Assizes in August.[151]

Campion was not hanged at the county's usual place of execution in Exeter but was taken seventeen miles down the road in a mourning coach to the scene of the riot. The procession was staged for maximum dramatic impact: Campion's coach was attended by an array of hundreds of militiamen, Volunteers, cavalrymen, and even an artillery detachment. The escort was ostensibly to prevent rescue, but it also impressed the gravity of the occasion upon the troops themselves, in that year of rioting militiamen. Indeed, Devon was quiet that August, while the rest of England seethed with violence. So effective was the lesson, so deep the local scar made by that single execution (among the dozens of executions of unhappy sheep stealers and pickpockets), that when I visited the area in 1970, 175 years later, both the present Lord Clifford and the last miller's widow spontaneously told me of that hanging!

In 1801, Lord Fortescue at first asked for a Special Commission to make some drastic examples of the rioters, but instead, the exemplary sacrifice was provided by neighboring Somerset. Two rioters who had broken into a Taunton breadshop during the Assizes were condemned and quickly hanged. General Simcoe and the Duke of Portland regretted the lesson but hoped it would prove salutary.[152]

Fortescue's determination to provide examples in 1801 was thwarted in some instances by local complications. Sometimes witnesses were clearly intimidated, as they were at Modbury. Nor were officials immune from threats. An anonymous letter to the

magistrates of Modbury promised bloody retaliation if they continued their prosecutions. That threat had the reverse effect,
however, for it made the magistrates even more determined to
prosecute the rioters.[153] At both Brixham and Totnes, Fortescue
was frustrated by more subtle processes. He had especially hoped
to make an example of the officers of the Brixham Volunteers, to
indict them "on such charges as will I believe prove capital," but he
had to report later, "I am sorry to find that [the evidences] against
them have fallen short of the expectations I had reasonably
conceived." The magistrate Fortescue had sent to investigate
found not only that the officers had been compelled to lead the
mob and had actually helped prevent violence, but also that
community leaders and victims were unwilling to prosecute.[154]

At Totnes, too, the rioters could not be disentangled from the
rest of the community. Only one victim protested strongly enough
to bring the Totnes events to the notice of the county authorities,
and he could find no sympathy among his neighbors. Evidence
melted away as witnesses modified their stories and as implausible
alibis were accepted. The investigating magistrate ultimately let the
rioters off with apologies, "concluding that [prosecutions] would
rekindle the flames which had been extinguished and not answer
the design your Lordship [Fortescue] had in view." The crown's
law officers concurred.[155]

The third leg of Fortescue's peace program was relief. At the
same time, relief was the ultimate achievement of riotous politics.
In both 1795 and 1801 riots elicited large voluntary subscriptions,
especially in Exeter but also in the other towns, that dwarfed the
"pure" charity extended before the riots.[156] In both periods,
magistrates also called upon the central government for special
relief supplies. Finally, rioting in 1801 called forth an unusually
thorough and sophisticated county relief program. Before the
rioting, the Quarter Sessions had ignored the relief legislation
passed in December 1800 (41 Geo. III, c. 12). But the social crisis
prompted Fortescue to convene the county magistrates to imple-
ment that legislation through resolutions requiring every parish to
stock imported substitute foods, such as rice and fish, to sell at
low, subsidized prices. The Quarter Sessions were then adjourned
through biweekly petty sessions to hear parish officials certify that
they had fulfilled the provisions of the legislation to the letter.
Explicit instructions were drawn up to prevent offense to the poor
by overseers; and they were to be paid for their extra duties, so as
to reduce profiteering. Two provisions are particularly noteworthy
because politically they aimed directly at the presumed rioters:

first, the subsidized supplies were to be sold, not only to regular paupers, "those Descriptions of Persons...who actually receive Parochial Assistance, but likewise any other Persons, who, though their Situation places them above such Predicament, yet, from the present pressure of the times, find themselves unable to meet the prices of the necessaries of life.—[the latter] will...be assisted...without being thereby brought into the Description of Persons receiving Parochial Relief." It was just this class of people, the semi-independent artisans and laborers, who had been the chief rioters; this relief program was designed not only to alleviate their hardship but to do so without stigmatizing them as paupers. Second, the magistrates altered the original text of a resolution in an important way, to declare that, after the public relief effort had been mounted, everyone should avoid further riots, for "they would then proceed only from the Wicked Views of bad and designing people."[157] By adding the subjunctive phrase *would then,* the magistrates changed an impolitic condemnation of rioters to a harmless platitude.

The resolution of the crisis of 1801 did not simply return Devon to the status quo ante. Worries of men like General Simcoe about the dangers of popular triumphs helped to sustain a campaign to raise more Yeomanry corps in Devon following the rioting of 1801.[158] Obviously, reliable armed force would be only one factor among others in maintaining Devon's social equipoise. But when the dust had settled, Fortescue was able to reply flatly, to a gentleman who feared popular sovereignty and revolution, that the magistrates' relief measures would prevent "apprehension of further distress," that the relief importations would lower prices, and that two more important points had been gained: the public, the middle-class sympathizers with the mobs ("well-meaning and not uninformed people who agreed with the...vulgar"), had been convinced that interference with the farmers would turn scarcity into famine. Second, "the enforcement of the civil power has likewise been another end gained," and would, he hoped, "not cease with the exigency that gave rise to it."[159] Whether or not Fortescue was right, the key point is that he regarded the crisis as a political battle won, not as an insurrection crushed.

At the end of the eighteenth century, social relations in Devon had produced riot as a frequent, conventional, and successful form of political action by the common people. Far more decisive than the ideological contest between paternalistic and laissez faire doctrines were local social structures that gave the common people real if limited power over their supplies of food.[160] No doubt future commercial developments would remove the grain trade from such direct community controls, but in 1801, the people of Devon did not yet need to accept the harsh teaching of political economy— that high prices and acute hunger were *necessary* to "ration" food supplies over a bad season. Against such scientistic logic, riots forced community and county leaders to mobilize their wealth and administrative resources to provide food for the working classes at reasonable prices. Devon's towns provided rioters with rich traditions of collective action and a stock of experienced leaders. Their stable and intimate community life provided memberships that enabled them to act coherently and purposively to carry out shared moral and political objectives. The durable bonds between rioters and authorities allowed each to calculate and to influence the actions of the other. Balanced between traditional patronage ties and plebeian autonomy, Devon's communities provided optimal conditions for classical political "bargaining by riot"—for frequent, disciplined, and successful riots. Devon's community politics and its riots probably represent the mainstream tradition of English food rioting, for similar patterns of behavior have been discovered in riots elsewhere.[161] Those patterns and that type of community politics were neither unchanging nor universal, however. Devon's community politics were "optimum" both as a phase of social evolution and as the midpoint of a spectrum of contemporary communities.[162] Manchester furnishes a revealing contrast.

3

Manchester,
a Town of Strangers

The trade of this Country...produces...a very
numerous and *foreign* population,...estranged,
unconnected, and in general composed of
persons who are in a species of exile.

—Thomas Butterworth Bayley,
Justice of the Peace, 19 July 1791

In 1795 and 1800 Manchester's markets resounded with riots that
were most unlike the communal "rituals" of Devon's riots. Crowds
of women and children seized and scattered food and smashed
shop windows. The magistrates called out the cavalry and forcibly
drove the crowds away. Food riots in Manchester were feeble, or
disorderly, or both. As a form of community politics, riot had
become obsolescent, primarily because rapid urban growth had
swamped the kinds of vertical ties and horizontal memberships
that had supported it in places like Devon. "Vertically," Manchester's governing elite confronted a broad spectrum of urban
disorders with impersonal remedies designed to eliminate "nuisances." Crowds, too, came to be seen as "nuisances," rather than
as constituents of community politics. "Horizontally," the common people could not rely upon communal forms of action, and
the continual influx of newcomers to the city made construction of
new bases for collective action a long and arduous task.

New, impersonal social relations began to emerge. The history
of social crisis and conflict between 1790 and 1812 suggests that
class polarization in Manchester in large part grew out of the
structured alienation of urban politics and out of particular violent
moments. I follow E. P. Thompson's conception of *class* (not *a*
"class" or classes) as a historical process and *relationship*.[1] Class
happens when as a result of experience a group of people come to
feel and to articulate their common interests as opposed to those of
other groups of people. It is this double relationship of solidarity
and antagonism that I mean by the word *class* in this book. It also

seems to me that some degree of generalization is part of class consciousness as people come to perceive their position and that of their antagonists as part of a *system* of social relations. Hence I take as a sign of emerging class the capacity of working people to conceive of their plight, and of possible remedies to it, in terms that go beyond the concrete, the local, and the personal objects of "classical" riots. In Manchester, hardship, industrial proletarianization, and political radicalization all contributed to the process of class, but they hardly ensured working-class solidarity or determined the form it would take. Direct political and physical confrontation in riots also contributed to class. The riots of the Luddite year of 1812 revealed both the degree of class polarization that had developed and the partial replacement of riot by wider political movements and aspirations.

The experience of Manchester illustrates the disintegration of social networks under the impact of urban explosion. Manchester, with its sister town Salford, was already a rapidly growing town of 20,000 by the late 1750s. By 1774 population had increased to 27,246. By 1790 that figure had doubled, and by the census of 1801, it had tripled to 84,025, with another 4,000 in the suburbs of Ardwick, Chorlton Row, and Hulme. The next decade added nearly 20,000 more inhabitants to Manchester and its suburbs. Manchester was already the boom town of the Industrial Revolution when in 1784 a French visitor wrote that it was "large and superb...built almost entirely in the past 20 to 25 years."[2] After the American War of Independence, industrial expansion created new jobs that attracted many demobilized soldiers. By the 1790s "the town extended on every side and such was the influx of inhabitants, that though a great number of houses were built, they were occupied even before they were finished."[3] Industrial employment also allowed people to marry earlier and to have larger families, for even young children could be sent out to work. "We are well off for hands in Manchester," Robert Southey was told. "Manufactures are favourable to population, the poor are not afraid of having a family here."[4]

Growth in Manchester was triggered by the boom in the cotton industry following the mechanization of spinning in the 1770s and 1780s. Nationally, cotton manufacturing consumed 5.1 million pounds of raw cotton in 1781, 28.7 million pounds in 1791, and 56 million in 1801, leveling off for seven years before soaring to 91.5 million pounds in 1811. Manchester's growth before 1790 probably depended more on its status as a commercial and marketing center for the growing industry in the satellite towns and in the hinterland, but beginning in the early 1780s, steam came to Manchester. It was used to lift the water needed to power spinning machinery, first Richard Arkwright's waterframe, then, in 1790, the spinning mule.[5] That brought spinning factories from the rural streams to the towns: "In consequence of this, waterfalls became of less value; and instead of carrying the people to the power, it was found preferable to place the power amongst the people, wherever it was most wanted."[6]

Spinning mills sprang up rapidly in Manchester after 1790. Previously, steam engines in combination with waterwheels may have been used in Manchester to power machines used for cotton preparation and finishing processes—carding, dyeing, printing, and so on. By 1790 the town apparently had two spinning factories that used steam, though a few others may have existed, judging from the number of steam engines. By 1795, there may have been seventeen or more cotton mills; by 1800, "dozens"; by 1802, fifty-two spinning mills; by 1803, sixty-five cotton and woolen mills; by 1809, sixty-four cotton-spinning factories; by 1811, seventy "concerns;" and by 1816, between forty and seventy mills. These figures reflect the rapid expansion of the cotton industry that took place primarily between 1790 and 1802, despite the economic crises of 1793, 1797–1798, and 1799–1800. The trade leveled off when war resumed in 1803 and remained uncertain until 1809, when it boomed for a year, before entering the slump in 1811–1812 that helped bring on Luddism.[7]

The spinning mills by no means dominated employment, for the capital of the cotton district was not a one-industry town. Joseph Hanson, a former manufacturer, estimated in 1811 that there were 9,000 spinners in Manchester and its vicinity; the urban population was 107,000.[8] Other estimates from this same time suggest that there were about 13,000 spinners.[9] Hanson estimated that the weaving branch of the trade employed 12,000 weavers in Manchester.[10] The expansion of the cotton trade led to corresponding growth in firms making machinery, some of which pirated Matthew Boulton and James Watt's patented steam engine, and in a host of other auxiliary trades. Paper mills turned out wrapping paper and fine writing paper for letters and bills. Tin-plate workers, braziers, clockmakers, harness makers, and of course curriers all contributed the rollers, wheels, and belts for the spinning machines. Many artisans and foundry and construction workers began to advertise as shuttle makers, loom makers, and millwrights. Finally, because Manchester remained a regional headquarters for the marketing of such provisions as oatmeal, fruits, and vegetables, as well as for luxury goods—silver, jewelry, coaches, wines, barometers, and mirrors—it employed hundreds of artisans, shopkeepers, carters, and porters.[11]

This diversity of trades, together with the size and rapid growth of the town, made collective action more difficult in Manchester than in smaller, more stable, one-industry towns. The newness, numbers, and economic and cultural heterogeneity of the common people meant that they did not share long-experienced member-ships and traditions of collective action that might support com-mon perceptions and coherent and spontaneous crowd behavior. While cotton spinners and weavers were undoubtedly the most visible groups of organized workers, they were still only a large minority of Manchester's workers. Their interests and activities were bound to be sectional—pertaining to only a section of the town's people—rather than communal—representative of the common interests of all.

Indeed, Manchester's magistrates were troubled by the town's apparent "disintegration." It seemed to Thomas Butterworth Bayley, the rock on whom the Manchester Bench was founded, that rapid growth had produced a city of strangers: "...the trade of this County is wonderfully prosperous. [But] it produces its attendant evils; amongst those I include a very numerous and *foreign* population (especially from Ireland), estranged, uncon-nected, and in general composed of persons who are in a species of exile...We have also now a very general spirit of combination amongst all sorts of labourers and artisans, who are in a state of disaffection to all legal control."[12]

This tension between estrangement and *legal* control epitomizes Manchester's community politics, for the spontaneous political reciprocity of riot could no longer work, and solutions to crises would either be institutionalized or would not exist. In August 1786, for instance, the magistrates for Salford Hundred (the Manchester district of the Lancashire Quarter Sessions) passed a long resolution deploring an apparent crime wave. They lamented that "idle, disorderly and dangerous persons of all descriptions" were "wandering about," and that the "commission of offenses hath increased to an alarming degree." They hoped that Sunday schools would restore the moral integration so obviously lacking and would "produce an happy change in the general Morals of the People, and thereby render the Severities of Justice less frequently necessary."[13] Indeed, the Sunday school movement had been launched two years earlier with another jeremiad on urban decay: "The hardest Heart must melt at the melancholy Sight of such a

Multitude of Children, both Male and Female, in this Town, who live in gross Ignorance, Infidelity, and habitual Profanation of the Lord's Day. What Crowds fill the Streets! tempting each other to Idleness, Play, Lewdness, and every other Species of Wickedness."[14]

"What Crowds fill the Streets!" That exclamation, with its sense of foreboding, was in part a reaction to the leviathan pressure of anonymous urban masses; it was also a reaction by an Enlightened, moralistic temperament against the old, plebeian culture that the immigrants had brought to town with them. In 1792 the authorities had tried to prohibit throwing at cocks on Shrove Tuesday, for example.[15] Even the luxuries of peace and prosperity in 1802 brought evils in train—particularly, the profanation of the Sabbath. That year the boroughreeve and constables warned townsmen that "a much greater degree of irregularity and dissipation prevails at present than at any former period. —It is most particularly to be noticed on the Sabbath day, when many very improper practices are witnessed—Numbers of boys and even men frequently meet in the outskirts of the town, and amuse themselves with battles of dogs, and of cocks, with gaming, running races, and other similar diversions." The officials did not want to brandish their authority unduly, but they hoped that the "well-disposed" inhabitants, and "all who possess any influence over those around them" would by setting an example help to restore order.[16]

Contemporaries sometimes explained such debauchery as a result of prosperity. The leading spinner, John Kennedy, remembered that the early boom in factory construction had corrupted workers and cut them loose from older customs: "With the advance of wages their dissipation increased...Having lost their attachment to rural employment and the avocations they had left, and being united by slender ties to their new employers, they became unsettled, and more indifferent than formerly to the good opinion of their neighbors; and consequently became less respected by them." But urban life and the regularity of factory work also had "good effects on the habits of the people...they became more orderly in their conduct, spent less time in the ale-house, and lived better at home."[17] These glimpses of tension between polite piety and rough culture—made menacing when transported to the anomie of the boom town—and between factory discipline and dissipation suggest the kind of cultural confrontation that was all the more evident in riots.

But Manchester was also infamous for its squalor and poverty, to which its anomie was sometimes attributed. John Ferriar's description of the cellar dwellings of the poor anticipates Engels's more famous exposé of Manchester's slums in *The Condition of the Working Class in England* in 1844. Ferriar reported, "The number of damp, and very ill-ventilated cellars inhabited in many parts of the town, is a most extensive and permanent evil...[a] deplorable state of misery." Ferriar also condemned some cotton mills for damaging the workers' health through uncleanliness, lack of ventilation, and nighttime working.[18] Dr. Thomas Percival added that while night work and long hours destroyed the health and "vital stamina of the rising generation," they encouraged "idleness, extravagance, and profligacy in the parents; who, contrary to the order of nature, subsist by the oppression of their offspring." He added that factory work deprived children of education and moral and religious instruction. In 1795 Dr. John Aikin had written in a similar vein that, as Manchester rivaled London in its booming growth, "so it unfortunately vies with, or exceeds, the metropolis, in the closeness with which the poor are crowded in offensive, dark, damp, and incommodious habitations, a too fertile source of disease!" Twenty years later Robert Southey damned Manchester and all her works, echoing the Board of Health's indictment of child labor, night work, and crowding in the factories. Factory children grew up "without decency... hope...morals...religion...and shame, and bring forth slaves like themselves to tread in the same path of misery." He, too, commented on the horrible cellar dwellings of the poor and added that, despite workhouses, charities, and prisons, the poor had become "more numerous, more miserable, and more depraved; and this is the inevitable tendency of the manufacturing system." The poor, thought Southey, had become brutes incapable of seeking more than the gratification of immediate wants.[19]

Finally, the war against France may have destabilized Manchester society even further. By 1796–1797 the town was less crowded than it had been in 1793. "The Recruiting service, as was natural, flourished in proportion to the depression of trade."[20] And the stagnation of business since the war began, wrote Sir Frederic Morton Eden in 1795, had caused thousands of workers to enter the armed forces. Their wives were thereby thrown onto the poor rates, and the "excessive number of necessitous females" may have swelled the food riot mobs of those years.[21]

What institutions shaped social relations between the powerful and the numerous in Manchester? What agencies tried to pacify the poor by welfare and police? Manchester entered its industrial adolescence governed by parish and manorial institutions. It did not have a municipal corporation, which many agreed might have restricted economic growth or promoted disruptive political factionalism.[22] Authority was exercised by an energetic establishment of wealthy merchants, enlightened physicians, and Tory Churchmen. They governed through a set of interlocking institutions, the Court Leet of the Manor, the parish vestry, a new police commission, and the bench of county magistrates. It is easy to criticize these bodies for their inefficiency, lack of vision, frequent apathy, and occasional corruption. But the town fathers were hardly complacent about urban growth. There was no "abdication of the governors."[23] Signs of vigor and reform could be found in each of the governing institutions. The town fathers also created a complementary network of voluntary organizations to defend mercantile interests, provide welfare services, promote political mobilization, and maintain social control. If Manchester was poorly administered by modern standards, it was governed better than most contemporary towns.

Yet these reforms gave Manchester's social politics an artificial cast. Because the reforms were a class response to the threat of sudden urban disintegration rather than the products of slower, organic evolution, they tended to substitute the one-sided interest and direction of the propertied classes for the rough political reciprocity that characterized patronage—and riot—in older towns. The laboring poor were *objects* of social policy, not political participants having a power to be reckoned with. Moreover, the magistrates could not easily communicate with crowds in a Babylon of newcomers lacking a common language or culture; clearly riots would be perceived as nuisances, not as occasions for political bargaining.

Manchester's oldest organ of government was the ancient Court Leet of the Lord of the Manor, descended of course from the manor of medieval days when Manchester was a mere village.[24] The town's chief public representative, the boroughreeve, was elected annually by the court's jury of leading citizens. He was usually an Anglican Tory merchant or textile manufacturer. The boroughreeve did not have the legal powers of a magistrate; his primary function was to call and preside over the ad hoc town meetings that voiced public opinion and launched municipal improvements. The boroughreeve also disbursed the town charities, known as the boroughreeve's charities. Almost all the boroughreeves came from the same compact social circle, but their annual rotation in office probably prevented them from using the charities as an enduring form of partronage network, as could be done in towns governed by old borough corporations, which tended to be fixed oligarchies. For instance, when the radical Thomas Walker became boroughreeve in 1790, he took steps to break the custom of treating "individuals only" (that is, political friends rather than the general public) at the annual town celebration of the king's birthday.[25]

The Court Leet also annually elected two gentlemen to serve as unpaid constables to maintain peace and order and to disburse town funds. A salaried deputy constable, paid £150 per year, actually managed the town's beadles and night watchmen, and he also swore in the town's two hundred special constables annually. They were organized by districts, each led by two members of the middle class. The police of Manchester in the 1790s thus seemed to depend in large part upon voluntary but organized middle-class support rather than upon traditions, institutions, or patronage.[26]

The deputy constables of this period engaged in old-fashioned corruption, but it was not sufficient to form a political machine. Richard Unite, the deputy constable from 1792 to 1796, was also a salaried Overseer of the Poor, charged with administering poor relief. His career combined political Loyalism with extensive racketeering. Unite condoned and apparently even encouraged the "Church and King" mob of December 1792.[27] He squeezed his offices for all they were worth. He solicited presents from innkeepers in return for favoritism in the billeting of soldiers. He milked both thieves and their victims. He paid the poor in counterfeit coin. He even offered to oblige friends or, for a fee, acquaintances by arresting their enemies as vagrants or "by locking up a troublesome wife as a lunatic."[28] But Unite's corruption seems to have been merely individual graft undertaken in a spirit of free enterprise. It could not have been extensive enough or sustained long enough to knit together the kind of patronage networks found in the parliamentary boroughs, where patrons treated voters at election time, supported public causes, and distributed personal favors over a period of years.

In any case, Unite's tenure was short. After a tireless campaign led by one reforming zealot, Thomas Battye, Unite was deprived of his offices. A few years later Joseph Nadin became deputy constable. Nadin was hardly impartial, but he was efficient. He became notorious for his avid pursuit of radicals, especially in 1812 and at the Peterloo massacre of 1819. He too was said to operate through a ring of spies and paid informers, but although he became a wealthy man in office, he was never charged with fraud or corruption.[29] He not only kept the confidence of his employers but was given increasing responsibilities for supervising the different sets of watchmen and firemen provided by the town. Nadin's kind of brute efficiency, while hardly modern or bureaucratic, does represent a step away from the more informal kinds of corruption and mob rule practiced by Unite and a step toward more professional peace keeping, which was all the more galling to some plebeians just because it was politically biased.

Besides peace keeping, the Court Leet also played a narrow but important role in supervising markets and curtailing nuisances. The court appointed leading citizens to more than one hundred unpaid offices, such as "Scavenger," "Market-looker," and "Muzzler of Mastiff Dogs." Everything depended upon the voluntary exertions of these officers. In 1788, the steward of the manor deplored the "sluggish and inactive" exercise of the court's powers and called upon the gentlemen of the jury to revive the court's prescriptive powers.[30] The officials did prosecute public nuisances. Scores of individuals were fined during the wars for encroaching on the public footpaths with dangerous cellar entrances or dung heaps, for allowing their pigs to run loose, or for permitting their factories to pour out noxious smoke.[31]

Most important, the town's officials still regularly supervised the food trade at the beginning of the 1790s. In 1788, the steward of the manor had emphatically warned against "corrupt or unwholesome victuals" and false weights and measures. Indeed, dozens of vendors and shopkeepers were fined all through the period of 1790 to 1810, most of them for false weights and measures, a few for bad veal, or even "stinking beef."[32] Such enforcement was not merely perfunctory. The fines ranged from 1 gn. to £10 and occasionally up to £20. In 1793, the market-lookers seized 120 underweight sacks of potatoes, and in 1795, a woman was jailed for eighteen days for assaulting a market-looker while he was performing his office.[33] During the food shortage in the summer of 1795, the boroughreeve and other gentlemen personally went to the market, checked weights, and seized food being measured fraudulently. So while the Court Leet can hardly be accused of "zeal" and "courage," its measures against market frauds and nuisances demonstrate that such ancient machinery was "lamentably inefficient but not...entirely inoperable."[34] By contrast, the Court's prosecution of the old "moral" offenses of forestalling, regrating, and engrossing ceased in this period.

Stronger signs of civic vitality surfaced elsewhere. In 1792 a special statutory authority, the police commission, had been created to clean, light, and watch the streets. The commissioners were drawn from the ranks of manorial and church officials and any other important property owners they might co-opt. Not until 1799 did they begin to use their broad powers. In that year Charles Frederick Brandt, an energetic merchant, became boroughreeve and revived several municipal projects. The police commissioners reformed their shaky finances, and over the next several years began to fulfill their mandate to police the streets.

These were also years of reform and conflict in Manchester's administration of poor relief. In late 1789 a town meeting resolved to build a new poorhouse, and it appointed a committee of leading citizens to supervise construction. The building was designed to be spacious, even elegant, and to provide superior care for the growing numbers of paupers. Its construction did not, however, symbolize thorough reform of the administration of the poor laws in Manchester, for even the blue-ribbon building committee sometimes failed to muster a quorum. As early as 1794 the new building itself seemed to have become "a receptacle of vice, filth, and disease."[35] The parish officials in charge of poor relief in this period have been condemned by modern historians as "a slack and incompetent set of High Church Tories."[36]

Scandal and the heavy burden of poor rates provoked an investigation in 1794 by the recently organized Committee of Associated Ley-payers (a ley was simply a local tax or "rate"). The ley-payers' report depicted a ring of corruption. They likened the parish accounts to a "whirlpool." Fraud and misappropriation of funds were rife. Churchwardens co-opted their successors, and so abuses were covered up. Overseers of the Poor gave generous relief payments to their employees; some overseers who were shopkeepers manipulated relief so as to encourage their own trade. At least one churchwarden employed paupers for his own gain at the town's expense. The struggle for reform was long and dogged, since the impetus came from outside the entrenched establishment. Reforms of the workhouse rules and closer supervision of the collection and disbursement of funds began in 1794. By 1802 some of the abuses had been corrected, and by 1808 the churchwardens had begun to undertake more regular and efficient supervision of the accounts.[37]

While it would be most interesting to reconstruct in greater detail the networks of patronage emanating from the parish vestry and from the police organization run by Unite, it is doubtful that the web of political influence would have been extensive enough to link the Anglican-Tory wing of the town's establishment with great numbers of lower-class Mancunians. It is quite possible that such networks may have helped to mobilize a few Loyalists in the early 1790s. But the growth of the town to nearly ninety thousand by 1801 would have defeated even a much more determined effort to build a political machine. As it was, such small-scale corruption probably benefited only a few minor officials and their "dependents," paupers who ordinarily were not assertive enough to become rioters. The reform measures themselves slowly eroded such networks. In short, parochial institutions did not provide sufficient opportunities for patronage to sustain a political matrix in which bargaining by riot could be practiced.

Furthermore, even the patronage that did exist was largely separated from the real locus of police authority in Manchester. The ultimate responsibility for public order rested on the shoulders of a half-dozen county justices of the peace, who lived in and near Manchester. They met quarterly with justices from Bolton, Rochdale, and the neighborhood as the Quarter Sessions for Salford Hundred. From 1795 the magistrates took turns holding Petty Sessions twice a week in Manchester to consider industrial disputes and appeals against the actions of poor-law officials.[38]

Before 1790, the bench was dominated by gentlemen and clergymen like John Gore Booth, Esquire, of Salford, or the Reverend Maurice Griffiths, Fellow of the Collegiate Church. But at least by 1795, a majority of the Manchester magistrates were retired merchants or manufacturers from mercantile families. These included: Thomas Butterworth Bayley (1766—the year of his earliest known service); Peter Drinkwater (1792), cotton spinner; Henry Norris (1794), Esquire, cotton merchant; John Leaf (1795), check and fustian cloth manufacturer; John Simpson (1795), cotton spinner; Thomas Richardson (boroughreeve 1795; justice of the peace 1797), timber merchant; Captain Richard Atherton Farington (1800), merchant; Matthew Fletcher (1804), linen draper; and John Silvester (1808), merchant.[39] Most of these men were self-made— their stars rise through the successive editions of the Manchester business directories. John Leaf, for instance, first appeared on the horizon in 1772 as "check manufacturer, Salford Cross," then "check and fustian manufacturer," then "check manufacturer" with a house *and* a warehouse (at separate addresses), and finally as "Esq., Belle Vue, Pendleton."

The Manchester magistrates had none of the family tradition, the patronage, or the experience that helped equip magistrates of the landed classes for governing—and for bargaining with rioters. Moreover, having lived by the market, they governed by the market, protecting food markets from mobs and labor markets from combinations of workmen. Finally, the magistrates shared some of the activism that promoted business growth and stimulated civic improvement, activism that erected a new prison and a new poorhouse when the older institutions became overcrowded, created a recovery house for fever victims, and devised "efficient" ways of dealing with food crises that did not include accommodating rioters.

The chairman of the Manchester bench, the enlightened despot of the town, was Thomas Butterworth Bayley (1744–1802).[40] Bayley was the son of a wealthy merchant, a Dissenter, and his two sons were merchants too. So were many of his relatives. He had been educated at that seed-bed of Enlightenment, the University of Edinburgh, "to qualify him for the rank and duties of a country gentleman." Bayley was a "Whig of the old school," a supporter of Christopher Wyvill's campaigns to reform Parliament, and a promoter of the campaign to abolish the slave trade. He was a man of broad religious principles, a trustee of the Cross Street Unitarian Chapel, but he was "cordially attached" in his mature years to the Church of England, though without "enthusiasm or bigotry."

Bayley was a relentless improver. He helped found the Manchester Literary and Philosophical Society, which gathered the illuminati among Manchester's doctors, industrialists, and gentlemen, to discuss mental disorders, demography, physics, rational principles of taxation, scientific principles of dyes and mordants, and much more. Among the many objects of his practical energy were agricultural experiment, poorhouse administration, public health, child labor legislation, Sunday schools, and Volunteer corps. Bayley also organized the weekly rotation of county magistrates staffing Manchester's Petty Sessions. His most enduring monument was the new prison for Salford Hundred, constructed according to the most modern principles of John Howard, the prison reformer, and emphasizing solitude and work discipline. Opened in 1790, it inevitably became known as the New Bayley Prison.

His seemingly boundless energies did not escape criticism, of course. One enemy referred to his political ambitions as "Quixotism," and his closest friend, Thomas Percival, conceded that Bayley verged on dilettantism. It was also charged that Bayley was sometimes a busybody "as a private Gentleman...so indefatigable...that...he investigates the cupboard of every cottager in his neighborhood—with a manifest intention to suppress Luxury in its infancy." He was hot-tempered, though never, said Percival, on the bench. But he was known to be a stern, unbending judge, deaf to pleas for mercy or favor: "As a magistrate, —his Worship is so strenuous a defender of the Laws, that even those which are generally esteemed lenient, —when dealt out with his spirited exertion, —have in their consequences, —by moderate Men, —unwittingly been called severe."[41]

Bayley was equally rigorous on the streets. He was said to prefer to quell riots with "temperate firmness, and authority mixed with conciliation," rather than military force and bloodshed. "He has been known to ride into the midst of an enraged multitude, armed with stones and bludgeons; and when exhortations and threats availed not, has assisted personally in the seizure of their ringleaders."[42] But even this accolade suggests that Bayley's style did not enhance his ability to communicate with the townspeople.

Above all, Bayley joined with other Manchester leaders— doctors, lawyers, and businessmen—to set up a plexus of philanthropic ventures that complemented the work of the established institutions. The infirmary, established in 1755, had in 1765 added on one of the nation's first municipal asylums for the insane. In the 1790s sermons given in all the churches and chapels helped establish a dispensary and a lying-in hospital for poor women.[43] Bayley was elected president of the newly formed Board of Health in 1796. It soon established a House of Recovery for patients with contagious fevers. The Stranger's Friend Society, run by Methodists, visited and relieved newcomers to Manchester, especially the Irish, who did not meet the local residence requirements that would have entitled them to ordinary poor relief.[44] The gentlemen of Manchester also sponsored a series of subscriptions to relieve the poor in hard times. The Soup Charity was the most impressive of these, but committees "for Distributing Provisions and Coals to the Poor," "for the General Relief of the Poor," "for the Health of the Poor," and so on were also formed. Partly because of Bayley's death in 1802 and partly because food riots ceased between 1800 and 1812, such efforts lapsed almost entirely for ten years.[45]

The town fathers created two other agencies in answer to the problem of urban degeneration. Sunday schools were begun in 1781. They were energetically promoted by a town meeting and by the magistrates as an explicit measure to overcome social disorder and moral disintegration, and "to call in a sense of religious obligation to the aid of industry." By 1795 the Manchester Sunday schools had enrolled five thousand pupils. In 1801 the Anglicans began the annual Whitmonday processions of Sunday school children that soon became a mainstay of local social life.[46]

The town fathers also created a Volunteer movement that was very different from Devon's. In Devon, where real strategic necessities were pressing, the Volunteers enlisted a cross-section of the common people who were not necessarily Loyalists and who also became leading food rioters. In Manchester the Volunteer movement was permeated with political Loyalism from the beginning. Certainly the leadership remained in "reliable" hands. By the peace of 1801, three regiments of Volunteer infantry of up to one thousand men each had been formed. Their commanders were T. B. Bayley, the Tory James Ackers, and another "Church and King" supporter, John Silvester. These men were prominent merchants, gentlemen, or both; there is no sign that the officers were popularly elected, as were the butcher, tavern keeper, and postmaster who became Volunteer officers in Devon. When war resumed against Napoleon in 1803, the Tory establishment still dominated the leadership of the revived Volunteer Corps, which by 1804 had grown to six thousand. The exceptions were George Philips, a former radical who made a fiery statement against the usurper Napoleon, and Joseph Hanson, a gentleman maverick of whom more later.[47]

The Volunteers probably helped to integrate Manchester socially. Their routine activities as well as their participation in patriotic holidays gave the thousands of working men who joined the Volunteers a sense of camaraderie, an *esprit de corps* that differed from that of Devon's Volunteers in two ways. First, the Manchester Volunteers were probably more an associational than a communal organization, choosing their men from all parts of the large town, not simply institutionalizing the existing bonds of a small town's working classes. Second, camaraderie certainly had a different meaning and function for Manchester's Volunteers, led by members of the bourgeois oligarchy, from that in Devon, where many Volunteer corps embodied plebeian independence. Manchester's Volunteer Corps might have helped to deter riots, and they plainly withdrew several thousand men from the pool of people available for food rioting.

The Volunteers do not seem to have had much of a role in riots at all until 1808. They were not organized in time for the food riot of 1795, and the riots of 1800 were too small to require their being called out. In 1808 the Volunteers finally had a chance to act, and they proved their social loyalties by patrolling against the weavers in the strike of that year.[48] They were not apparently active in the riots of 1812.

The development of the Volunteers was consistent with the

larger pattern of Manchester society. The town's old parish and manorial institutions were too slender to supply significant networks of patronage. Still, the town fathers were not complacent about the challenges presented by Manchester's growth. They launched a voluntary bureaucracy to attack specific nuisances, poverty, and disease. But they found it much more difficult to promote social cohesion in the industrial Babylon—to capture the loyalties or refashion the culture of the industrial immigrants. The Sunday schools and the Volunteer movement were a beginning, but most of the common people seem to have remained estranged from the elite, and at the same time atomized among themselves.

4

Cavalry and Soup Kitchens

Food riots in Manchester in 1795 and 1800 clearly reflect the breakdown of social networks, the erosion of the discipline and ideology that shaped classic riots, and the modernization of the market that placed it beyond the control of direct action. When dearth appeared in 1795, Manchester had not had a major food riot for a generation. Perhaps that is why the authorities responded with mostly symbolic gestures. In 1795 the wheat harvest was deficient throughout the country, and the Lancashire potato crop was ruined by frost.[1] Prices rose to a peak in August, and the Manchester magistrates reported in late July that "disturbance...looks at present with a threatening aspect."[2]

At the Saturday market on July 25, some Manchester gentlemen, presumably acting as market officers, seized defective weights and underweight measures of butter and distributed the butter to the poor at the workhouse. The *Manchester Mercury* warned consumers to be vigilant against the "great evil" of market fraud and commended the intervention.[3] The following Monday the Manchester justices met to try to find ways to supply "this populous Town and Neighborhood with Bread." They ordered that beginning August 10 only "standard wheaten bread" (made with the whole grain rather than only fine white flour) be sold in Salford Hundred to economize on the use of wheat. They also recommended that everyone reduce consumption of flour and, in particular, that "wealthy Individuals" not purchase more wheat or flour than they needed for immediate consumption. The coarser wheaten bread was probably not welcomed by Manchester workers, who had already developed a taste for white bread.[4] These efforts were too little and too leisurely to alleviate dearth, and they may have actually aggravated social tension by spotlighting inequalities of wealth and cheating in the markets.

In any event, disorderly rioting occurred the next time the magistrates intervened in the market. Thomas Butterworth Bayley, together with the boroughreeve and other gentlemen, returned to the potato market on Thursday, July 30, to examine the weights and scales of the vendors.[5] A crowd of women and boys gathered to watch. They began to quarrel with the market people, and the crowd became a violent mob. Ignoring the boroughreeve's attempts to appease them, they threw potatoes into the street and smashed the front windows of the flour dealers' warehouses and homes. The growing crowd then trooped over to the house and warehouse of Martin Marshall, one of the prominent corn dealers in Deansgate. They "deliberately" destroyed Marshall's windows, doors, shutters, and, according to one account, a great part of his furniture. Marshall was one of the Court Leet's "Officers [to inspect] Corn Weights and Measures."[6] The blatant conflict of interest between the roles of merchant and market official must certainly have undermined the public's trust in the effectiveness of the Court Leet's supervision of the markets. Marshall eventually collected £121 from Salford Hundred for the damages to his property.

The next morning, crowds of women gathered again, this time at the New Cross Market, just east of the central market district, on the edge of the workers' suburb of Ancoats. They seized a cart bringing meal into the town, opened the sacks, divided up the meal, and scattered it. They broke more windows at flour shops in the neighborhood before order could be restored.[7] The destruction and seizure of food reflects the demoralization of riot, by which I mean the disintegration of restraints sanctioned by either customary morality or tactical prudence. Though it was hardly random, the Manchester rioting took the form of a unilateral crowd action to punish dealers, rather than disciplined bargaining within a social and moral framework that included both magistrates and dealers.

The traditional tactic of popular price-fixing was not quite extinct in Manchester, but it appeared only vestigially in the food riots of 1800, when hunger and unrest again swept over England. In that year more than two hundred food riots occurred from Berwick to Pevensey. Towns like Birmingham, Oxford, Nottingham, and London each witnessed days of furious attacks on mills, shops, and warehouses. At least fourteen riots occurred in the cotton district.[8] In that context, Manchester's food riots were surprisingly feeble. In late January 1800 "a large body of women" seized potatoes in the potato market and forced the owners to sell them at half price. The markets may have been disturbed for several more days.[9]

In June, rioting once again followed the official enforcement of accurate market measures, as it had in July 1795.[10] On a Saturday market day, some women tried to seize potatoes from the vendors in the markets to sell them at "their own price." Justice John Leaf lectured the women, warning them that forcible interference would dry up the markets by discouraging farmers from bringing potatoes to town. Leaf organized a cadre of special constables to sell potatoes at reduced prices, perhaps subsidized by charity funds as they had been in 1795. Many of the women were grateful, but others were so fiercely determined "to create a riot, that they abused the more orderly who had purchased potatoes, seized and threw them about." Disorder continued for several hours. Finally two or three women were arrested and sent to jail, and two of them were later sentenced to six months in jail for stealing and forcibly selling potatoes.[11]

The disorderly food riots of 1795 and the weak attempts at riot in 1800 suggest that the "moral economy" was decaying in Manchester. Germs of that ideology were probably still in the blood of Manchester's immigrants from the surrounding towns and villages where traditions of the forced sale were still strong.[12] But the norms and conventional tactics of the moral economy would have only a brief half-life in Manchester, where social structures no longer supported them.

In part, the weakness and disorder of Manchester's food riots arose from traditions of popular action very different from those of the corporate towns of Devon. The classic conventions of "taxation populaire" (the ironic French term for popular price-fixing) and effective bargaining had not become established earlier in Manchester. In the food crises of 1757 and 1762, Manchester had witnessed three violent, disordered food riots.[13] Rioters "plundered" the markets and the Mealhouse, carried away bread, cheese, meal, and flour, and even rendered food "unserviceable...in a most odious manner." They attacked and heavily damaged mills, warehouses, homes, and furniture, though not indiscriminately. In particular, they accused one George Bramall, the town's leading corn chandler, of adulterating his grain with "Acorns, Beans, Bones, Whiting, Chopt Straw, and even dried Horse Dung." Samples of the exotic additives attributed to his mill were handed around the town as black relics. The very scale of his dealings was interpreted as evidence of his design to corner the market.

The peak of the violence was the famous Shude Hill fight in November 1757. When the sheriff refused to set prices, as a crowd from Saddleworth had demanded, brickbats and musket balls flew, and four civilians and one Invalid were killed. Bitterness over "The Blood of Shulde Hill" and "those Canables" (the merchants) lasted for years.

The bitterness, destruction, and bloodshed were all quite different from the mainstream tradition of eighteenth-century food riots like those in Devon. In large part, the heavy damage in Manchester was the work of outsiders from the collieries and the country weaving-towns who probably assumed they could not be identified by the Manchester magistrates. Elements of paternalistic market regulation still survived in midcentury Manchester, but it is likely that food riots in the north of England became neither so conventional nor so frequent as in the south because the greater distances between suppliers and consumers made it nearly impossible for crowds to physically confront the producers of their food.[14]

Certainly that relationship was a compelling reason why food riots in Manchester were weak and disorderly in the 1790s. The external and internal economic networks that supported popular control of the markets by riot in Devon had long since been dissolved in Manchester. Manchester's supply lines stretched far beyond the reach of regulation by magistrates or mobs. Oatmeal and wheat for the textile workers' bread were already brought in from Wales, the Isle of Wight, and the London area by the middle of the century.[15] By the 1790s the county of Lancashire was believed to produce only one-fourth of its annual consumption of cereal. The rest was imported through Liverpool or drawn from Lincolnshire and the south by canal. The land around Manchester was being converted from arable to industrial or residential use, or else to dairy pasture or hay meadows for the town's horse power. Hence, the immediate neighborhood furnished Manchester only with vegetables and a fraction of its potato stocks.[16] It was impossible for either crowds or gentlemen to go out into the countryside to put pressure on the town's suppliers.

As Manchester's external market network receded, so the internal social ritual of marketing had long since disintegrated. It was not focused in a central marketplace by a weekly or semiweekly market day. Markets and marketplaces proliferated as the town grew. By the end of the century there were nearly a dozen separate manorial (that is, licensed by the manor) markets, including the "apple" market, the oat market, the potato market, the cheese market, the corn market, and the fish market. Most of these were still clustered around the dense tangle of streets near the Collegiate Church. But new marketplaces had begun to appear. In 1781 a second shambles market was built just outside the old area, off Market Street Lane. Between 1795 and 1804 the new shambles at New Cross became a firmly established market for Ancoats, while around 1804 additional new shambles were established at Bank-top, near Ardwick to the southwest, and at the top of Bridge Street, south of the old market center.

To be sure, custom and habit slowed the "migration" of the markets. Farmers bringing in potatoes paid their tolls at the new potato market at outlying Camp-field, then hurried on to central Shude Hill "to meet their old customers upon the accustomed place of sale."[17] But numerous presentments at the Court Leet suggest that Manchester's consumers were increasingly dependent on shops rather than on an open marketplace for staples like flour and potatoes. Flour shops were spreading out from the old market district, and a few were already serving the working-class suburbs of Ancoats and Alport. Moreover, though there were still three primary market days, provisions were sold every day of the week. Indeed, the markets were so well developed both inside and outside the town that they supplied much of the country to the north and east. The hordes of outsiders helped dilute the cohesion of the markets' crowds even further.

These developments reduced the likelihood of food riots in Manchester. In traditional towns, weekly market days and the central marketplace promoted camaraderie among consumers, while the personal exchange between producers and consumers symbolized their complementary contributions to the community and also created the possibility of disagreement and tension over the relative values of those contributions. Both sets of personal and physical relationships—among consumers and between consumers and producers—undergirded the *norms* of the "moral economy" and the *actions* of food rioters in traditional towns. Both relationships were dissolved by the dispersion of food sellers and markets in Manchester. Regulating the prices charged by dozens of shopkeepers was impossible and morally pointless, when the "real" profiteers were several steps removed from them. The potato markets at Shude Hill were the one arena where consumers still met producers. It is no accident that Manchester's food riots began at Shude Hill, but otherwise, centrifugal forces triumphed.

That dispersion plus the lengthening of the town's external supply lines dissolved the social framework necessary to support the ideology of the "moral economy." Without its guiding norms and without the traditional social relationships, Manchester's food riots lacked both discipline and effectiveness.

On the other side of the "protocol of riot," the best test of the officials' attitudes toward markets is their treatment of the nebulous practices of forestalling, regrating, and engrossing—the operations of wholesaling middlemen who bought and resold grain. According to late medieval traditions of market regulation, forestalling occurred when a dealer bought foodstuffs from a farmer before it could come to market. Regrating was buying in order to sell again. Engrossing was attempting to monopolize supplies or to corner the market. All were transgressions against the approved model of marketing whereby farmers sold directly to consumers in an open public market. Middlemen were traditionally condemned because they made money without seeming to produce anything; they were believed to be manipulating food supplies to make a profit, in other words, to be exploiting the needs of the community for their own selfish ends. No doubt speculators tried from time to time to corner the market. But merchants normally engaged in buying and selling for a profit, and so the distinction between ordinary wholesale transactions and profiteering was a matter of degree.

Hence it is less the practices themselves than their interpretation by the elite that is significant. Manchester's newspapers still condemned forestalling, regrating, and engrossing at the end of the eighteenth century.[18] But it was the opinions and actions of the officials that would enter into the calculus of riot.

By the end of the century official policies toward such middlemen were increasingly tentative. In 1788 the steward of the Court Leet included forestallers, engrossers, and regraters in a long list of public nuisances, with dunghills, houses of ill fame, and scolds, brawlers, and eavesdroppers, but he concluded that the gentlemen of the court should consult among themselves "how far all or any of these offenses. . .deserve to be punished." To be sure, the Court Leet continued to appoint "Officers to prevent Ingrossing, regrating and forestalling" throughout this period, and they and the magistrates vigorously enforced the more *objective* regulations prescribing the accuracy of weights and measures and the purity of meat and fish.[19] Those regulations might have contributed to public peace or raised moral issues, but they did not touch the delicate issue of the "just price"—the core of the "moral economy." In the summer of 1799 the Manchester boroughreeve and constables charged that forestalling, regrating, and engrossing had greatly raised prices and injured the poor, and vowed to punish the offenders with fines and imprisonment, but when the last few cases against regrating were presented before the Court Leet in the autumn, the fines of two to five pounds were reduced to a nominal fine of one shilling.[20] No longer would magistrates exorcise the old specters by selecting a few merchants for exemplary prosecution.

It is particularly striking that Manchester's authorities, unlike authorities in other towns, did not use or threaten to employ the ancient machinery of paternalistic market regulation during the scarcities of 1795 and 1800. In part this was because their reaction to popular tensions was apprehension rather than sympathy, and in part the town was too dependent on an elaborate food trade to risk interference with the markets. The chief magistrate, Thomas Butterworth Bayley, expressed these attitudes in a revealing letter that he published after the food riot of July 1795. Bayley flatly condemned the riots in a way that would have been impolitic and abrasive in a smaller community. He charged that the riots had been "excited and carried on by ill-disposed Persons . . . for very wicked Purposes."

He did not completely renounce the "moral economy," for he conceded that "Men of much Information and Reflection differ in their sentiments about the Nature and Extent of Forestalling and Engrossing." He balanced Adam Smith's arguments for the freedom of the markets against the wisdom of the ancient statutory regulations against profiteering. He warned that forestallers who manipulated local supplies of food courted legal punishment. And he hoped that the corn traders' "sense of Christian Duty" and social responsibility, as well as competition, would prevent monopoly. But he insisted that, "This very populous, manufacturing Country cannot be supplied with Corn but by Merchants and Factors, whose Capitals enable them to purchase it from all Parts of Great Britain . . . Europe, and . . . America. *Such* Forestalling or Engrossing can alone supply our Wants."[21] Thus although moral imperatives were not altogether absent from Bayley's ideology, practical considerations determined his conclusions to his own internal debate between moral criteria and laissez faire. Rioters could not count upon sympathy or neutrality from the magistrates, for the magistrates had reduced the moral economy to platitudes utterly lacking in any commitment to social control of the flow and price of food by official regulation or by the gentry's informal influence over farmers and dealers.

What is even more striking, however, was the withdrawal of the more articulate and organized groups of workers in Manchester from the politics of food riot. Ideologically, they agreed with Bayley's diagnosis. A committee of workers organized in 1799 to protest the recent Combination Act (which prohibited workers' organizations to raise wages), warned their brother workmen against riot: "...riot and disorder cannot afford even a temporary relief, and would greatly aggravate the evil, by deterring the merchant from importing corn, which in that case he could not carry to the places it is most wanted in safety."[22] Food rioters would have to face not only the opposition of the magistrates but also the misgivings of the "better sort" of workmen who might elsewhere have led the crowds.

Furthermore, popular remedies for hardship had begun to transcend the politics of direct action. Self-help was organized on an astonishing scale. A Union of Friendly Societies was formed in 1800 to counter "the avarice of speculative and interested persons" in the food trade. They collected donations of more than £5,000 and bought food, which they sold at prices "considerably lower than the shops." At one point, they had accumulated a stock of £20,000 worth of grain from the Continent. Even if sold at maximum prices, that would have fed the entire town for a week! The executive committee of the Union warned the "labouring poor" "that some evil-minded persons are endeavoring to excite the people to Riot and public Commotion," and advised the poor to "be on...guard against the artful insinuations of such Incendiaries; carefully abstain from all acts of violence and outrage; use your endeavors to prevent public tumult, knowing that it is always productive of public calamity and has a direct tendency to increase the evil it is intended to cure."[23] Although the Union of Friendly Societies failed before very long, owing to market fluctuations induced by the war, it was justified in claiming that its operations had helped to preserve the peace and tranquillity of Manchester, when towns without such organizations "were distracted with riot and confusion."[24]

The common people of Manchester had also begun to connect high food prices with wider, more abstract political issues. Their political vocabulary ranged from earthy, seditious social blasphemy to more complex analyses derived from Thomas Paine and the English Jacobins. Both were alien to the pragmatic spirit of bargaining by riot. For instance, the magistrates received old-fashioned anonymous threats of murder and ruin if they did not take steps to lower prices. In June 1800 an anonymous letter warned Bayley, "You Magistrates and Gentlemen of old England by God's laws and the church we mean to stand, and men's laws to destroy. Unless the price of provisions comes to a fair price, a famine appears in the midst of plenty. Betwixt the Badger and the huxter the poor do starve. As a caution take this writ. For a fare living on our bended knees to God we will call." Unless that came about, the writer threatened "a civil war" and the destruction of "your fine halls and your pleasure ground...either by fire or sword."[25] In November, grafitti chalked on the walls of the town "daily saluted" the public. One handbill on the New Bridge tollgate trumpeted:

> No peace, No King
>   to kill Billy Pitt it is no sin...
> We will have a big loaf for a shilling
>   or else the Justices we will be killing.[26]

In March 1801 Bayley was warned that if prices were not reduced, "measures" would be taken by "28,348" who would rise with "unnumbered" friends across England.[27] Perhaps these threats were so bitter just because the tradition of food riot was no longer a viable means of exerting popular power in Manchester in 1800; certainly the anonymity of the threats contrasts with the publicity and forthright pragmatism of Devon's rioters.

Disaffection also began to take on more sophisticated, more organized, and more radical forms in Manchester. Hardship was not the only cause of the growth of popular radicalism. But high food prices began to be blamed upon national policies rather than upon the local and individual malefactors emphasized by the "moral economy." In November 1800, Bayley reported "throughout this Country...a general Rumour of rising, *If* Parliament does *not* reduce the Price of Grain etc." He was convinced it was fomented by "the Democrats, who wish to create a general Outcry against the War, & the Ministry;—as the Causes of the Dearness of Provisions."[28] Indeed, in the following spring, a series of outdoor meetings on the moors near Manchester voiced a coherent analysis of high prices,[29] and resolutions passed by one meeting of thousands of workers at Tandle Hill, about ten miles from Manchester, blamed them on the war and charged that the war had been undertaken only to enrich contractors. The commercial and landed classes prospered, while workers suffered from taxes, unemployment, wage reductions, and high prices. Only "an immediate peace, a thorough reform in the representative system, and a reduction of the national debt" would remedy those grievances. Most significantly, the meeting concluded, "...we cordially unite in the propriety of conducting ourselves with every degree of firmness, decorum and peace; convinced that all tendency to disorder or riot must be more and more destructive of the great and valuable constitutional rights we are in pursuit of."[30] That March a clandestine meeting of Reformers at the Britannia Inn in Manchester discussed the war, high prices, and wage levels. As Alan Booth has pointed out, hunger was beginning to be combined with other political and industrial grievances.[31] Political radicalism and food riot were not necessarily mutually exclusive, but the Tandle Hill resolutions against riot suggest that as working people raised their ethical critique from the marketplace to the political system, violence began to seem a liability.

Finally, organized groups of workers rejected food rioting as a solution to hardship, in part because they were preoccupied with their own labor campaigns. Both 1795–1796 and 1800–1801 were periods of relative commercial prosperity for the cotton industry, and in both periods the weavers' wages had temporarily stabilized. In 1795 Manchester's mule spinners met the hard times with a labor combination that won higher wages.[32] In 1800 the weavers were occupied with their campaign for regulatory legislation, while a committee of tradesmen organized to protest the Combination Acts.[33] That committee's warning against food riots, the relative prosperity of the cotton trade, and the spinners' and weavers' campaigns suggest that important segments of the working classes were not available to lead food riots in 1795 and 1800. The communal solidarity that undergirded food riots in other towns had nearly broken down in Manchester.

Since some organized groups of workingmen in Manchester were preoccupied with labor organizations, one might expect that food rioting would be left to women, and indeed, both eyewitness reports and records of arrests indicate that the rioters were overwhelmingly female. That is unusual and may be significant. The prominent role of women in eighteenth-century food riots has recently been remarked upon,[34] but it is an exaggeration to suggest that most food rioters or their leaders were women. Women were specifically reported as participants in only 73 of 242 food riots between 1790 and 1810, and in 35 of these, groups that included men—colliers, tin workers, and so forth—also participated.[35] Indeed in the classical English food riots, such as those in Devon, crowds included both men and women, for they enlisted a cross-section of the communities' working classes. The fact that Manchester's food rioters were mostly women may help to explain the riots' disorderliness, for Manchester's women were less organized in trade groups and friendly societies than were the men, and, at the same time, they were less likely than their Devon counterparts to be bound into community social networks.[36] In both ways they lacked the social ties that otherwise gave both strength and coherence to collective action.

The disintegration of the old communal bases for political bargaining is especially reflected in the magistrates' actions. What is most striking is the magistrates' lack of authority over the crowds. In 1795 the rioters ignored the boroughreeve's promises of "every exertion for their interest." They continued to attack dealers' shops and houses, and they ignored the warning that the light cavalry had been summoned from the barracks, the exhortations of the boroughreeve and military officers, and the reading of the Riot Act. Likewise, in 1800 the magistrate's lecture on the need for order, and even the sale of potatoes organized by the officials, failed to calm the most determined rioters.[37] The magistrates could not speak the language of the crowd because they were not bound together by ties of social patronage and because the gentry had no means or desire to control the food sellers directly.

Impersonal police measures to restore order thus took the place of communal bargaining. Force replaced conciliation. The first day's rioting in 1795 was finally broken up only when the cavalry charged through the crowd with their swords drawn and wounded several rioters. Tumult continued in the streets well into the evening, despite military patrols. The next day the rioters were again dispersed by soldiers, and several of them were arrested. The magistrates oranized very thorough measures to secure the market on the following Saturday. They circulated handbills assuring the farmers of protection if they would bring their provisions to market. At dawn, the magistrates, constables, special constables, gentlemen, and soldiers formed patrols to guard the roads into town. The magistrates also appealed to householders and employers to keep their children and servants off the streets, and warned "good Townsmen and peaceable Subjects" not to assemble, or they would be subject to "public Notice" and "serious Consequences." Finally, they imposed an evening curfew on the streets and public houses. These measures met with mixed success. The *Manchester Mercury* conceded that some farmers had not sent their meal to market that Saturday, but the following week supplies were abundant.

In November 1799, when shortages had reappeared, but before

any violence occurred, the magistrates once again advertised their determination to protect farmers and merchants, this time because of high prices and labor unrest.[38] In May, 1800, Bayley assured the Home Office that the presence of the Fourth Dragoons was "an ample security for our tranquility."[39] What is crucial is that the magistrates had to guarantee order by force, for they could not apply moral and social pressure to farmers to lower their prices and reduce tensions. Rioters had to be suppressed as nuisances rather than treated as parties to a compromise.

Riot stimulated magistrates to begin relief measures that had, like peace keeping, also become impersonal rather than politic. The day after rioting began in 1795, Bayley and the other magistrates declared "the Necessity of a liberal Subscription to lessen the present *High Prices* of Provisions sold to the Poor." Saturday evening, after order had been preserved at that day's market, a committee of gentlemen sold a stock of potatoes in small quantities at reduced prices that apparently had been subsidized by the subscription. Three days later, officials at a public meeting thanked the dragoons for their help in quelling the riots and established a subscription fund for weekly premiums to be given to the vendors who brought the largest quantities of fish, potatoes, and vegetables to market. The gentlemen of Manchester thus tried to make up in cash incentives what they lacked in personal influence. The funds were soon used to subsidize the sale of potatoes at low prices three times a week.[40]

In November 1799, the magistrates tried to quiet hunger and labor unrest by warning against disturbance and by reviving the Soup Charity originally tried out in January 1799. The Soup Charity was the Industrial Revolution's answer to urban hunger. From Birmingham came the latest technology—great, gleaming steel "Soup Digesters" that could reduce an entire cow to enough stock for hundreds of quarts of soup and only a few pounds of waste.[41] Recipes and models for organizing the distribution of soup came from the Society for Bettering the Condition of the Poor. Three soup shops were established, one on Toll Lane, Deansgate, near the central market area, a second on Copperas Street between the Shude Hill market and working-class Ancoats, the third on Chorlton Street in the dense warrens behind the Infirmary. These shops poured out 12,000 quarts of soup a week in 1800 and 17,500 quarts a year later.[42] A separate Committee for the Relief of the Poor raised funds to resume the payment of premiums for food brought in to market, and to sell enormous quantities of potatoes (four hundred loads, or fifty tons a week), bacon (twenty-four

hundred pounds), and rice (two tons) at low prices. That committee continued its work into April, and a similar committee resumed
the work in November 1800, this time providing clothes and
bedding to the poor after visits by gentlemen, as well as subsidizing sales of rice and coal. No doubt these charitable efforts in
1799–1800 helped to reduce the people's impulse to riot in 1800.
In fact, the food riot of June 1800 occurred while soup distribution
had been halted. It was quickly resumed.

Manchester's relief subscriptions were not all immediate responses to riot. They were parts of an enlightened concept of
"police" that included social welfare and moral discipline as well as
coercion in a broad strategy of civil governance. *Police* meant the
civil health of a community—its social order and its physical well-
being were closely connected. Emergency relief subscriptions in
1784, 1789, 1791, 1793–1794, January to March 1795, and January
1799 had no apparent direct connection with riot, but in the
summer of 1795 and the winter of 1799–1800 the threat of
disturbance clearly quickened and intensified the compassionate
efforts of the wealthy—and the close connection between relief
and social stability was frequently drawn.[43]

In 1795 the Tory *Mercury* commented on the magistrates'
protection of the markets and the subsidized sale of potatoes:
"Whilst such pains are taking, the poor have nothing to fear, IF
THEY WILL ONLY BE PEACEABLE."[44] In March 1800, the Committee for
the Relief of the Poor trusted "that the gratitude of the poor will
manifest itself by assiduous industry and becoming behaviour."[45]
In November 1800, the revived Relief Committee pointed out that
the previous winter's charity had indeed restored proper subordination: "The Poor received the donations with gratitude; and by
their quiet and orderly behaviour have evinced their sense of the
favours then bestowed upon them; and also their dependence
upon the wisdom of the Legislature, joined with the beneficence of
their richer neighbors, for the alleviation of their PRESENT severe
calamities." The committee also called for a renewed devotion of
the generous impulses of the wealthy "to their own gratification—
to the rescue of the poor from want and disease, and to the SUPPORT
OF CIVIL SOCIETY, which is always exposed to violent shocks, from
the pressure of temporary scarcity."[46]

It is not historically useful to separate the undoubted
humanitarianism of these charities from their function in preserving class rule. Plebeian misery assaulted the conscience of the
wealthy and challenged their capacity for remedy, just as it
threatened to assault their property and challenge the legitimacy of

their political monopoly. But disorder had also loosened the purse strings of the gentry in Devon. It was not the connection between riot and relief that was distinctive in Manchester, but rather the mechanical nature of that relationship. Manchester's rioters themselves seemed merely to express their anger and frustrations rather than to articulate their rights in a political context, while relief was distributed in a strikingly impersonal way.

In Manchester, administrative efficiency in providing relief to the poor matched technological prowess. The Manchester Soup Charity tended to draw on great numbers of small donations garnered from subscribers who were mobilized by extensive organization, rather than to rely upon the magnetic example of a few wealthy patrons as Devon's towns did. As in previous emergency relief subscriptions, collection of the money was accomplished by thoroughly organizing the neighborhoods for house-to-house solicitations. The names of thousands of donors were published in the newspapers, including even contributors of the smallest amounts of a shilling or two, so that advertising rewarded the generous and shamed the miserly. In a way, the Manchester Soup Charity was to old paternalistic charity what the joint-stock company was to the family firm.

More important, these charities had perforce to treat the poor as a faceless mass instead of dependents with assigned places in a network of patronage. When the Soup Charity was originally established in January 1799 and revived in November, it tried to make use of personal relationships between donors and recipients. Subscribers to the fund received tickets that they could distribute to their poor neighbors to exchange for soup.[47] But soon after its revival in the winter of 1799–1800, the soup shops were forced by the sheer numbers of the needy to revert to straightforward cash sales at one penny per quart.[48] If relief was to be effective in alleviating hunger and preventing unrest, it had to be applied massively and impersonally, as a kind of social inoculation program, without regard for social and political distinctions among the lower orders.

We do not know the reaction of the "respectable" workers to charity that implicitly treated them as paupers, except that the weavers' address to the public in May 1800 argued that low wages forced weavers onto parish poor relief and extinguished their "state of independence."[49] A decade later, as both hardship and political consciousness grew, relief through charity would be positively denounced and ridiculed. Even in 1811 an address by the cotton weavers of Bolton declared that the "temporary relief" by charity was wholly inadequate for "many thousands mechan-ics . . . who of course disdain to become paupers, until forced by the arrogant lash of necessity." By 1816 both Bolton and Wigan had experienced bitter demonstrations against charity.[50]

The impersonal mass charities for the poor of Manchester demonstrate the difference between class-directed "police" and the reciprocities of the politics of riot in Devon. In Devon, relief was aimed specifically at artisans and laborers above the rank of pauper, and pains were taken to keep from stigmatizing them as paupers. Prices for subsidized food were even adjusted according to the applicant's income, and some tradesmen were turned away if they were too well off. Relief in Devon was a concession to the legitimate demands of people whose political standing was suffi-cient to win compromise and to move gentlemen to exert pressure on farmers and tenants to reduce prices.

In Manchester, by contrast, the relief charities were emblematic of social reforms on a broad front that tried to bring order out of urban chaos. The New Bayley Prison, the new poorhouse, the Board of Health, the activities of the Infirmary Committee and the police commissioners, and the reorganization of the justices of the peace were other such efforts. But this broad assault on urban problems did not, and could not, concede any political standing to the masses of strangers. Cavalry and soup kitchens stood in for compromise and patronage. The elite of Manchester had begun to treat the common people in action as a "dangerous class" even before the workers of Manchester had achieved class con-sciousness. The politics of class confrontation were a consequence of urbanization as much as of industrialization.

That conclusion is demonstrated by the contrasts not only between Manchester and Devon, but also between Manchester and smaller Lancashire towns, which were also undergoing indus-trial development. In many of these towns the "moral economy" and the ties of patronage that supported it were still viable. At Lancaster in 1800, the magistrates not only threatened to prosecute monopolizers, forestallers, regraters, and engrossers, but also promised to send their own grain to the markets to be sold in small quantities, and to "use our utmost influence with our tenants and neighbors to adopt the like salutory measures."[51] At Wigan, the lord lieutenant and eighty other gentlemen warned their tenants against speculative practices and added "that they will recommend themselves very much to our future Favor by bringing and selling at their neighboring markets Bread Corn and Meal, the Produces of their Respective Farms."[52] The lord lieutenant and the high sheriff of Cheshire led a similar meeting at Northwich to warn against both riots and "illegal practices in the buying and selling of Corn." They believed that such practices, not "an actual scarcity" had kept prices high after the favorable harvest of 1795, and they recommended to farmers "as they value their own Credit, the ease of the Country, *and the goodwill of their Landlords,* to thrash out their Corn, and bring it gradually to Market, on such moderate terms, as may with sufficient profit to themselves, enable the industrous of every description to support their Families with comfort."[53]

And at some of the country cotton towns, food riot still took traditional forms. At Oldham in 1795, 1799, and 1800 food rioters forced reductions in prices and returned the proceeds of forced sales to owners. Furthermore, in contrast with the impotence of the Manchester magistrates, Sir Watts Horton, a county magistrate of Chadderton, was able on several occasions in 1795 to persuade crowds at Oldham to disperse in a relatively good humor. That diplomacy was made possible by his efforts at a meeting of the "principal inhabitants" held the same week as one of the riots, at which he persuaded provision dealers to lower their prices to demonstrate "that they were not actuated by motives of extreme selfishness."[54] Not all food riots in the cotton district were so decorous, nor all magistrates so influential.[55] But in the smaller towns, more components of the moral economy and a more orderly tradition of food riot survived to 1800, and the magistrates correspondingly could still use their influence on their neighbors, both farmers and rioters, to bring about community compromise.[56] This contrast suggests that it was the scale of urbanization more than the qualitative changes in capital-labor relations brought on by industrialization that disrupted traditional social relations and promoted class polarization.

5

Entrepreneurial Politics

Everything now seemed to wear the appearance
of a preconcerted scheme. The same contrivances were used
as at a contested election.

—Thomas Walker, 1794

Manchester's town fathers used cavalry and soup kitchens to combat food riots and aggressive and efficient philanthropy to fend off urban degeneration. Those tactics were complemented in the 1790s by intense political mobilization of Loyalism and Reform sentiment that promoted the development of affiliations between Manchester's elite and its working classes where traditional ties fostered by patronage and social bargaining were missing. Those rival campaigns created bitter antagonisms, and those animosities led to "Church and King" riots against Reformers partly because both sides were so well organized and partly because in a "town of strangers," "sedition," in the sense of criticism of the existing constitution, was particularly intolerable to those in power.

Between 1790 and 1810 political riots were relatively more frequent in Manchester than in English society in general. Of the 617 riots in my national sample, only 63, or 10 percent, were political riots. (I use the word *political* here in its more conventional sense, to denote matters of ideology and national and local government, rather than in the broader sense of the attitudes and opinions involved in "community politics.") That is, English crowds were typically motivated by tangible objectives rather than abstract political issues. As the record of food riots shows, Manchester's society was not especially conducive to "spontaneous" collective action. However, a string of seven riots over political issues in the 1790s makes up half of the total number of riots in Manchester in this period. First, in June 1792, a crowd of Loyalists attacked Dissenters' chapels, then in December of that year, one of the most famous "Church and King" riots of the period took place. In July 1794, a working-class Reform leader was mobbed in the streets. Less than a year later at Easter in 1795, a challenge by Reformers to the oligarchy of the parish vestry created pandemonium at Collegiate Church. That winter, a final "Church and King" riot brought partisan conflict to its peak of intensity. Two less significant but bloody political riots took place in the theater the following year. With some exceptions Manchester's political riots were more focused and more orderly than its food riots. Their targets were more clearly marked and limited. The paradox is that political conflict provided a more frequent and more definite stimulus to collective violence in Manchester than did hunger—a situation exactly opposite that of the rest of England.

Manchester's political riots were rooted in and shaped by the bitter partisan conflict that developed between segments of the town's social elite. That elite included the justices of the peace, present and past boroughreeves and constables, individuals prominent in town committees and philanthropies, and the most prominent Reformers—members of the Constitutional Society, leading signers of "opposition" petitions, and the Committee of the Associated Ley-Payers. I have traced their political attachments in the rival petitions—declarations on the issues of the day—that were published in the newspapers. Those petitions, signed by hundreds of men, are the functional equivalent of borough poll-books as historical sources. Most of the several dozen leading town officials in this period were "Tories," by which I mean they supported national Tory governments and consistently took the "Church and King" side in controversies. Their local opposition was led by the thirty-four men listed in January 1793 by the Loyal Association as "suspects" whose loyalty ought to be investigated.[1]

Manchester's political elite were predominantly entrepreneurs. A few, especially among the radicals, were professional men, physicians or attorneys or, among the Tories, clergymen. But "gentlemen" were few. The great majority of both the Tory oligarchy and their opponents were merchants and manufacturers, the vigorous men who led Manchester's economic growth and established volunteer organizations to supplement the town's formal institutions.

Their partisan rivalry was so virulent because of the informality of Manchester's politics and the activism of its entrepreneur-leaders. What Manchester did not have was a municipal corporation like those of cities such as Liverpool, Nottingham, Norwich, or Leicester. I have already shown that Manchester's political system rested more on voluntary initiatives than on corporate institutions, and that the town's "chief executive," the boroughreeve, annually elected by the jury of the Court Leet, itself a panel of town fathers, executed very little—his main function seems to have been to summon town meetings when appropriately requested by "respectable inhabitants."[2] The public town meetings debated national and local issues—taxes, war, or emergency relief—and then voted resolutions expressing the town's opinion. It was at those meetings that Manchester's body politic most nearly took visible form. Such informality increased the Manichaean intensity of political rivalry, because factional politics remained almost purely ideological—"unpolluted," and hence unrestrained, by the need to compromise and coalesce over tangible interests. The people of Manchester had no Members of Parliament to elect as spokesmen for their interests—and to importune for favors to individuals or to the whole community.[3] Local Manchester politics was not anchored in such concrete staples of borough politics as town property, or enclosure and construction, and the distribution of patronage.[4] There were no traditional parties based on local interests to bind humbler freeman to the political elite. The limited amount of patronage available to the Tory oligarchy through the vestry seems to have been large enough to support only individual "rackets," not a full-fledged political machine. In short, politics in Manchester was a matter of ideological competition in a "free market" almost wholly unstructured by bureaucracy or organized patronage.

Lacking such traditional stabilizing mechanisms, and facing a growing population of working poor, the Manchester establishment was especially worried by the Jacobins' challenge to the established political order. They were not as complacent about either food riot or sedition as the more confident and experienced gentlemen of Devon. They were more willing to try to arouse the common people and to enlist them in active Loyalism.

From the 1780s onward, Manchester's elite began to form political movements, first for common commercial interests, then for more ideological purposes. To be sure, partisan divisions had occasionally appeared earlier. In 1763 the town's Tory oligarchy defeated a movement that sought to have Manchester incorporated as a municipal borough and to share power among the High Churchmen, Low Churchmen, and Dissenters.[5] But commercial unity outweighed political differences. By the 1770s and early 1780s, Manchester merchants and manufacturers had formed committees to suppress embezzlement and workers' combinations, to oppose Arkwright's patents, and to promote the cotton trade.[6] In 1784–1785, William Pitt's proposals for a tax on fustian (a cloth made from cotton and flax, at that time the chief textile manufactured in the "cotton district") and for a liberalization of the restrictions on Irish trade provoked a storm of opposition from Lancashire industrialists in the form of mass petitioning, the formation of the General Chamber of Manufacturers (with manufacturers from the Midlands), and lobbying at Westminster. Thomas Walker, the key Manchester Reformer of the 1790s and a leading fustian merchant-manufacturer, was also a leader of that lobbying campaign. When Pitt was forced to give up his measures, Walker returned home from London in May 1785 as the toast of the town. He was met by a grand procession of javelin throwers, trumpeters, the lord of the manor and the deputy constable in their chariots, mounted dragoons and gentlemen, and groups of fustian cutters, master fustian shearers, packers, dyers, velvet dressers, and calenderers (who pressed cloth), whitsters (who bleached it), and pattern-card makers carrying the flags and emblems of their trades. Many of the marchers sported the Whig colors of blue and buff. The celebration reached its climax at an elegant dinner where silver plate was presented to Walker.[7]

That episode was the high point of the commercial elite's unity, and doubtless also of Walker's personal popularity, because the following year the manufacturers split over the Eden Treaty with France of 1786, which lowered tariff barriers between England and France, including those on cloth and wines. Northern large-scale manufacturers, including the cotton spinners of Manchester, were generally in favor of the treaty and freer trade. Thomas Walker, however, led a committee of fustian manufacturers against the treaty; he was consistently protectionist—his political liberalism did not necessarily imply economic liberalism. However, other Manchester fustian manufacturers repudiated Walker's leadership, and a tumultuous town meeting approved the treaty.[8] In 1788 the fustian manufacturers crossed swords with a coalition of calico and muslin manufacturers and printers. Robert Peel, one of Manchester's arch-Tories, led the printers at a meeting of the opposing groups. Thomas Walker "speeched away for the fustian makers... at last they were so warm that Mr. Lawrence Peel [Robert Peel's son] and Mr. Walker collared each other, and all was violence."[9] It was not the last of Walker's skirmishes with Tory leaders.

The polarization of Manchester's politics was heralded by the local reaction to the regency crisis of 1788–1789. In November of

1788, the centenary of the Glorious Revolution was celebrated in Manchester with little hint of partisan discord. The following month, however, the King went "mad," and Pitt resisted the Whigs' demands for a regency that would probably put them in power. In Manchester, a public meeting on the issue resulted in such turmoil that the chairman was forced to terminate the proceedings. Petition and counter-petition were launched. Pitt's followers signed up more than 250 people. They insisted that they had sought "to procure respectability rather than numbers," for the opposition's petition was nearly twice as large. Pitt's partisans included the dyed-in-the-wool Churchmen and Tories who would virtually monopolize the town government in the 1790s: the lord of the manor, at least two merchants who became magistrates, Anglican clergymen, and many other leading merchants and manufacturers who served as boroughreeves; they also included the moderate Reformer Dr. Thomas Percival and the radical William Rigby, Jr. At the top of the opposition's petition were the radicals who were to form a well-defined party in the 1790s: Thomas Walker, Samuel Birch, Thomas Cooper, George Duckworth, George Philips, Samuel Jackson, Thomas Kershaw, Richard Roberts, and George Wakefield. In addition, a few members of the establishment who served as boroughreeves and magistrates in the 1790s also signed the opposition's petition: James Ackers, Thomas Richardson, Thomas Butterworth Bayley, William Myers, and John Leaf—all but Bayley later joined in the strident antiradical campaigns of 1790–1795.[10]

But it was the fierce controversy over the repeal of the Test and Corporation Acts in 1789–1790 that really crystallized the contending factions into opposing regiments. The Test and Corporation Acts, passed in 1673 and 1661, prohibited Dissenters from holding crown and municipal offices. Although that prohibition was frequently evaded, repeal would mean elimination of the standing insult and also of the possibility of capricious enforcement. The contest over repeal was especially heated in south Lancashire because both sides were so strong. The Dissenters' vitality was manifested in their many chapels, in their operation of the Warrington Academy, which provided higher education for Dissenters, who were excluded from Oxford and Cambridge, in their dominance (with the Whigs) of the Manchester Literary and Philosophical Society, and in their prominence in civic ventures such as the Infirmary committees. On the other hand, Manchester's establishment of merchants and manufacturers, predominantly Tory in weight and numbers, opposed repeal. The contest was not one between an entrenched Tory squirearchy and a rising liberal bourgeoisie, for both sides were almost equally bourgeois.[11]

Perhaps because repeal of the acts would make little practical difference in Manchester's informal politics, the issue took off into boundless realms of ideological abstraction as Tories and Dissenters competed to win over public opinion. The Dissenters and their sympathizers held public meetings at Manchester, Warrington, and Bolton. The more radical proponents of repeal claimed it as a natural right and bruited the possibility of abolishing tithes and the Anglican liturgy, which alarmed even their own moderate supporters like Thomas Percival. The Tories declared that repeal would be "subversive of our Constitution in Church and State."[12] Anglican "sermons were everywhere preached" against the repealers, according to Thomas Walker, himself an Anglican, and the rector of Warrington accused the Dissenters of using "cool determined violence" to realize sinister ulterior objectives.[13] The Anglicans played on outdated fears in published advertisements and circulars that warned churchgoers to "remember who trampled upon and made shipwreck of both Church and State in the last Century, and guard against the Repetition of the like Dreaded Scene." Thomas Walker and the Dissenters answered with a broadside insisting that repeal "cannot in any wise endanger the Church of England."[14]

That exchange set the stage for a climactic public meeting on February 3, 1790. Churchmen (here meaning political supporters of the Church of England) had persuaded the boroughreeve to call and to chair the meeting, despite Dissenters' protests that partisan town meetings were not legitimate. The Dissenters attended in force, and an uproar ensued. Walker charged that the meeting room had been packed by the Anglicans and that the resolutions against repeal had been steamrollered through by the Anglican clergy, arrayed in their gowns and cassocks.[15] The contest was resumed by abusive broadsides in the streets. The Anglicans', entitled "Constitution against Innovation," congratulated "their Fellow Citizens...on the complete overthrow of the PROTESTANT DISSENTERS." The repealers replied with "A Priest's Confession,"a song with an ironic refrain that alluded to the use of mobs:

And this is Church I will maintain until my dying day, Sir,
Whatever arguments are used, *my* argument's, Huzza, Sir.[16]

The acrimonious contest over the repeal helped to create and to harden political divisions in Manchester even before the more famous controversies over the French Revolution and English Jacobinism had inflamed British politics.[17] The attempts by both sides to rally public support on the repeal issue began to prepare the ideological climate and the organizational framework for the "Church and King" riots of 1792.

In the short run, the third Repeal Bill was defeated in Parliament, and that inspired the founding of the Manchester Church and King Club on March 13, 1790. The club ordered commemorative medals struck and sported uniforms with buttons depicting Manchester's old Collegiate Church. They appointed a committee to admit members of "suitable lives and conversations." The standing toast of their club and private societies was "Church and King, and down with the Rump." They later declared that "the Corporation and Test Acts are the great bulwarks of our constitution in church and state."[18]

The Reformers countered by organizing the Manchester Constitutional Society in October 1790, composed of several merchants, manufacturers, and professional men. The Constitutional Society was committed to government by "the consent of the governed" and a "speedy and effective reform" of parliamentary representation. The Reformers apparently were still a relatively small group, while Walker tells us the main Church and King Club was but one of several.[19] Both the Church and King Club and the Constitutional Society met regularly, but bitter conflict died down for eighteen months.

Partisan rivalry did not prevent cooperation on common interests. Thomas Walker chaired or served on town committees on the manorial market tolls in 1789, and on the Excise Laws in 1790.[20] That October, Walker was elected boroughreeve of the town; his brother Richard served as foreman of the Court Leet jury the following spring.

A series of minor incidents did, however, aggravate political and personal animosities. Conflict between "liberal" Whigs and economy-minded Tories on the Hospital Board erupted at its Michaelmas meeting in 1790 into a bitter debate between Walker and barrister William Roberts, one-time steward of the manor. In November 1790, Boroughreeve Walker presided at the annual "Revolution Dinner," commemorating the events of 1688. It was a relatively nonpartisan occasion, but Roberts bitterly protested the singing of "Billy Pitt the Tory" as a partisan song. He traded angry words and even veiled threats with Walker and later blanketed the town with a crude handbill calling Walker a "BULLY, FOOL, SCOUNDREL, COWARD, and BLACKGUARD." Walker sued Roberts for libel and won £100 in damages. Walker's clashes with Roberts, as well as those with Lawrence Peel earlier and several subsequent incidents, suggest that Walker's temper and self-righteousness may have aggravated political differences and marked him out as a lightning rod for the Tories' animosity. Certainly Walker was a target of abuse in the streets. Before long his boys were to be taunted by their schoolmates, "There go Jacobin Walker's sons!" Another minor controversy arose in the spring of 1791 when Walker chaired a town meeting opposed to war with Russia and the Tory *Manchester Mercury* refused to publish the meeting's resolutions.[21]

On July 14, 1791, the Constitutional Society held a dinner celebrating the anniversary of the fall of the Bastille. Walker and his friends tried to take precautions against the appearance of any provocative political symbols or slogans, but a handbill inviting riot was distributed through the town. It sneered that, "If Englishmen had the spirit they used to have, they would, on the 14th of July, pull the house the reformers assembled at over their heads; and the brains of every man who dined there would be much improved by being mingled with brick and mortar."[22] Since Walker was still the boroughreeve, his control of the police, including the two hundred special constables, helped prevent any such outbreak of violence. That very day at Birmingham, in parallel circumstances except that the magistrates were hostile to the Reformers, "Church and King" rioters viciously attacked Joseph Priestley and others.

Political conflict in Manchester finally became openly violent in 1792, as political ferment increased. When the second part of Thomas Paine's *The Rights of Man* appeared in 1792, Thomas Walker signed a letter on behalf of the Manchester Constitutional Society congratulating Paine, and Paine replied with gratitude, "Your sincere and much obliged friend." The Manchester Society began to correspond with the "Reforming Societies in Sheffield" and the London Corresponding Society. Moreover, the Manchester radicals decided to found their own newspaper, the *Manchester Herald*. The new paper appeared on March 31, 1792, and it dedicated itself to the political awakening of "tailors, farmers, butchers, and blacksmiths," for it proclaimed its determination to be "the PAPER OF THE PEOPLE." The *Herald* printed the exchange of letters between Paine and Walker. Soon after, it reported on the celebrated visit of the Manchester delegates, Thomas Cooper and James Watt, Jr., to the Society of Jacobins in Paris. Their actions were hysterically denounced in Parliament by Edmund Burke, and the Manchester Society was made even more famous. Two new workingmen's Reform societies, the Patriotic Society and the Reformation Society, appeared in Manchester in late May and early June under the patronage of the Constitutional Society. These societies probably had only a few dozen members, so that to Manchester's Tory establishment they must have appeared not only irritating but also vulnerable.[23]

All these signs that the radicals were mobilizing provoked the Tories' retaliation in a "Church and King" riot on June 4, 1792. The immediate catalyst was the publication on May 21 of the royal proclamation against "seditious meetings and publications." That proclamation inaugurated a governmental campaign throughout the country to mobilize public opinion against Jacobinism.[24] In Manchester, the Tories, who once more held the town's major offices, decided to celebrate the proclamation with a carnival of Loyalism. They called a meeting for June 4, the king's birthday, to thank His Majesty for the proclamation. Walker and Samuel Jackson protested on behalf of the Constitutional Society that the proclamation and the Tory meeting would promote rather than prevent riot: "the obvious tendency, of a multitude of people...assembled to discuss a public measure of a most violent nature...is too glaring to be mistaken...The cause of the people would inevitably be injured by violence and tumult."[25]

They protested in vain. In the morning, the boroughreeve and constables convened a public meeting at the Exchange. A day of festivities ended, at least for the notables, with a public dinner and a ball. But that evening a crowd was drawn to St. Ann's Square by some tradesmen's fireworks. The crowd suddenly grew violent and "assaulted several peaceable spectators." Next they tore up several trees in the square and carried them to the Old Dissenters' Chapel and the Unitarian Chapel on Mosley Street. They tried to beat down the gates and doors of the chapels, yelling "Church and King!" and "Down with the Rump—Down with it!"[26] The crowd finally dispersed after midnight.

The crowd's actions were specific and symbolic. Although the mob did little real damage, the riot was a warning aimed at the social headquarters of the opposition. The century-old Old Dissenters' Chapel, or Cross Street Chapel, was "the original, and first place of worship" for Manchester's Dissenters; its congregation was "composed of persons of the first respectability." The Unitarian Chapel was one of the newest Dissenters' chapels, but "the congregation, though far from numerous...can boast as much respectability in the characters which compose it, as any in the united towns" of Manchester and Salford.[27] Moreover, this otherwise minor episode served as a rehearsal for the more serious riot of December 1792. Loyalists could see that no serious reprisals would be taken. Most strikingly, the otherwise energetic Thomas Butterworth Bayley was silent. He took virtually no part in the political conflict of these years.[28] No doubt Bayley wanted to remain above party, and his loyalties were divided. As I have pointed out, he distrusted sedition and led a Volunteer corps in 1798, but he was also a trustee of the Cross Street Chapel and a friend of some of the leading Reformers.

Political alarm and polarization grew in England that autumn with the radicalization of the French Revolution. When the Manchester Reformers called for relief donations to the beleaguered French revolutionary forces, they provoked an enraged response. On September 13, 1792, 186 innkeepers declared their "detestation of such wicked and abominable practices" that aided "the French Savages," and that they would no longer allow "infernal" clubs and societies to meet in their houses. Walker charged that the innkeepers had been instigated to such action by Tory tax collectors and others. Given the billeting and protection rackets run by the deputy constable, that may have been true. The Reform societies were thus forced to meet in private houses, including Thomas Walker's and apparently William Gorse's. As local reaction deepened, the two rival newspaper shops in the marketplace became headquarters for political news and gossip, and of course at the Tory *Mercury*, the Reformers were constantly abused as Jacobins and Levellers, while at the *Herald* "more liberal sentiments prevailed."[29]

Once again, national events touched off violence in Manchester. On December 1, a second royal proclamation ordered measures to avert the danger to the Constitution from "evil-disposed persons...acting in concert with persons in foreign parts." In Parliament most of the Whigs combined with the Tories to form a solid party of order. The government encouraged voluntary mobilization of the propertied classes against sedition. In London on November 20 John Reeves had formed his famous "Association for Preserving Liberty and Property against Republicans and Levellers."[30] On December 7, Joseph Harrop, editor of the Tory *Mercury* and boroughreeve of Salford, chaired a meeting there to form such an association and to profess "the utmost horror and Detestation" of Jacobinism.[31] The Manchester Loyalists called a meeting on December 11 for the same purpose. The meeting assembled at noon, the room "crowded in a manner never before known."[32] Robert Peel was reported to have declared, "That it was time for the people to rouse from their lethargy, for there were incendiaries in the country." (Peel later denied having said anything more inflammatory than "God save the king."[33]) The meeting resolved to form an "Association for Preserving Constitutional Order and Liberty, as well as Property, against the Various Efforts of Levellers and Republicans" (hereafter, the Loyal Association). They vowed to bring to justice the distributors of seditious doctrines and members of seditious societies. All but two of the nineteen men who served as boroughreeve between 1785 and 1804 signed the declaration.[34]

The formation of the Loyal Association set the stage once more for riot. The violence that occurred that night was neither an expression of spontaneous and general popular loyalism nor the work of a "hired band operating on behalf of external interests."[35] Rather, it was the direct outgrowth of the structured political mobilization that resulted from the polarization of Manchester's politics. The friends of order and property had clearly issued a license to riot.[36] The rehearsal had been held in June, so premeditation, or at least premonition, there certainly was. Soon after the Tory meeting broke up, Walker heard a report that "a riot...was intended to take place in the evening." The senior constable of the town directed the deputy constable to collect "as many persons as he could to oppose any riot, should there be one." Soon after dark, a few men "of the lowest order" gathered in the marketplace, crying out, "Church and King,—Damn Tom Paine," "Huzza! Huzza!" The noise and the number of people in the crowd increased, and for two hours they were inflamed by liquor and by agitators who urged them to cry out against "Jacobins and Presbyterians." The last slogan, of course, was a direct reference to the previous years' conflict.

Indeed, Walker compared the deliberate and festive mustering of the crowd to the familiar election rituals of a parliamentary borough. "Everything now seemed to wear the appearance of a preconcerted scheme. The same contrivances were used as at a contested election. Parties were collected in different public houses, and from thence paraded the streets with a fidler before them, and carrying a board, on which was painted CHURCH and KING, in large letters."[37]

Moreover, the crowd did not "run wild and riot."[38] It is their deliberateness rather than their abandon that is striking. The riot was indeed a skirmish in a limited political "civil war" rather than a "blind *pogrom* of prejudice."[39] As part of the contest for ideological supremacy, the rioters intended to silence the Reformers' *Manches-*

ter Herald and the Reform societies. They smashed the windows at Matthew Falkner and Samuel Birch's shop and house where the *Herald* was printed. And parties of rioters went repeatedly to smash windows at Thomas Walker's house. Ever since the publicans had banned radical societies' meetings, two of the three societies had met there. Walker managed to keep the rioters at bay by firing a gun over their heads. The next morning a crowd of hundreds gathered before his house where they were harangued by a man reading from a printed paper, another hint that the "disorder" was premeditated. They shouted at Walker, "Jacobin, damn the Jacobins, damn Tom Paine, down with the Rump!" Only on the second night of rioting did civil officials restrain the crowds who had again gathered at Walker's house to shout "Church and King!" Some of the rioters, however, went on to William Gorse's house on Great Newton Street, where the workers' Reformation Society met, and destroyed his windows and furniture. The crowd also apparently attacked the house of the surgeon Joseph Collier, who was also a radical.[40]

Not only were there signs that the riot had been planned, but it was clear that town officials condoned and even encouraged it. The corrupt deputy constable, Richard Unite, took up his station at Harrop's Tory newspaper office. But when a *Loyalist* gentleman asked him to stop the crowd at the *Herald* office, Unite replied, "They are loyal subjects, let them alone, it is good to frighten these people." Afterward he went to some men pounding on Falkner's door, clapped them on the shoulder, and said, "Good lads, good lads!" and boasted, "I can keep them quiet by giving them good words!" Other people of *"respectable appearance"* were seen stirring up the crowd with applause and cheers of "Church and King for ever, lads, down with the Rump!"[41]

Other officials were negligent in their duties, especially on the first night of the riot. When Reformers applied to the town's constable and a magistrate for help, they were turned away complacently and insultingly. Then Nathaniel Milne, a magistrates' clerk and an ardent "Church and King" man, told them it was a "scandalous, shameful, abominable business to call out a magistrate on such a trifling piece of business as the breaking a few windows." The town officials neglected to call out the standing corps of special constables or the regiment of dragoons quartered in the town that was mustered and ready to march. Only after Walker had fired over the heads of the crowd did the officials appear on the scene to ask *him* to desist, and to be scolded by him in turn. Walker's account of official complicity was not challenged, nor were any rioters apprehended or prosecuted, although town officials did deny that there had been a plot.[42]

There is no evidence to support the contention that the crowds were a lumpenproletariat made up of the least skilled, least educated, least organized, and poorest workers in town, along with "hooligan and even criminal elements." We simply do not know precisely who the rioters were. One witness observed that they were *not*, to his surprise, "unlettered and destitute of property," though he may have meant the "managers" of the mob.[43] But subsequent developments suggest that Manchester's Church and King clubs could successfully compete with the democrats in recruiting fustian cutters, shearers, shoemakers, and other tradesmen in Manchester.[44] There is no concrete evidence that the crowds were really mercenaries, and the conspiracy interpretation also fails to explain the relative discipline of the crowd: did not "Church and King" rioters need some prior ideological commitment to be effective wreckers—to limit themselves to meaningful targets and to pass up targets of opportunity (for loot)? On the other hand, one cannot infer that the "Church and King" rioters represented unanimous popular Loyalism. In a town of 80,000, a small but militant crowd of a few hundred could be noisy and aggressive enough to silence others.[45] Both "parties" had appealed to the common people, and both had won supporters. But the Reformers generally left rioting to their opponents, because they themselves tried to appeal to reason, because they were physically outmatched, and because violence was not a useful tactic for bringing about constitutional change.

Partisan conflict was the one sector of Manchester's community politics in which "vertical" networks of ideology and affiliation connecting the authorities and the plebs made collective violence both frequent and coherent. That conflict, originally between segments of the town's social and economic elite, was fought with a distinctive combination of old and new weapons. "Old-fashioned" riot was an important weapon in the Tory arsenal— old-fashioned in the sense that it was limited and conventional, and in the sense that "Church and King" riots played the same role in battles over political "turf" that election riots did in parliamentary boroughs, as Thomas Walker himself remarked. The initial advantage in those contests naturally rested with the Tory wing of the establishment, for it had the most members and the greatest wealth among the elite, and it controlled the major newspapers and the only patronage that was available through the town government. At the same time, both sides used new political techniques by seeking to mobilize supporters through appeals to ideology instead of through old-fashioned patronage,[46] and by promoting associations that for the first time drew the artisans of the town into politics.

The Tories moved to shift the conflict onto safer ground while consolidating their victory in the political marketplace. First, they emphasized that the license to riot was not a blank check, by their restraint of the crowd at Walker's house, and the next day, by the Loyal Association's pious declaration of "concern" over the violence and by the more sincere reminder to their fellow townsmen that Salford Hundred would have to reimburse the victims for damages. They promised to help the boroughreeve and constables prevent further violence, and, somewhat ambiguously, they called upon townsmen to prevent "every Meeting of others, that is likely to produce Riot and Disorder."[47]

Second, the Loyalists took up the weapon of legal harassment. The riot of December 1792 had not silenced the *Manchester Herald*, so the Loyalist Association sent an issue of the *Herald* to the Treasury Solicitors. Charges were brought against the editors; they fled to America, and the paper folded. The committee of the Loyal Association also called for an inquiry into the loyalty of thirty-four leading radicals. They did not immediately pursue their prey, but in 1793 a member of one of the Reform societies, Benjamin Booth, was convicted of sedition. Finally, the Loyalists brought ten of the radicals to trial at the Lancaster Assizes in April 1794 on a charge of conspiracy to overthrow the government. Although Walker and the others were easily acquitted when the state's key witness was revealed to be a perjuring drunkard, Walker was financially crippled by the legal expenses.[48]

Third, the Loyal Association welcomed the crystallization of popular loyalism into more orderly forms. Already in 1790 several other Church and King clubs besides the elite parent organization had been formed.[49] At the time of the riot, at least one other club existed. The Loyal Association thanked the Hibernian Church and King Club for its loyalism and its condemnation of "wild Theories and seditious Doctrines respecting the Rights of Man." Within two weeks, the Loyal Association greeted another Church and King club that met at the Weavers Arms public house.[50] The Association's members had originally been, and probably remained, drawn from the manufacturing and mercantile elite of the town: almost all the boroughreeves and constables of the 1790s and all the leading members of the Manchester Commercial Society were members.[51] But soon after the riots, associations of Loyalists began to proliferate, perhaps as the result of a propaganda campaign by the parent group. Two clubs in Manchester and Salford thanked the town officials for their defense of Loyalist honor against Walker's charges of conspiracy. By February 1793, the parent association had exchanged correspondence with seven other clubs around the town, at least five of which survived for years after 1792. New ones were continually being formed. The clubs marked the formal enlistment of the lower orders into the ranks of the Loyalists, for fustian cutters and shearers, glaziers, shoemakers, and other artisans and tradesmen were members.[52]

This emergent Loyalist popular culture was steadily regularized by its relations with the parent Loyal Association. In November 1794, the plebeian Loyal Associations formed a committee of delegates and offered to sponsor an armed Volunteer Corps. They very deferentially sought the approval of "the original Mother Association at the Bull's Head," "that Association of Gentlemen," "our leading Townsmen, who, in a pecuniary Point of View, have the utmost to be directly solicitous for. . ." Their offer was rejected, for reasons we can only speculate about,[53] but in April 1795, the fraternal bonds of loyalism were drawn tighter. The parent Loyal Association resolved that twelve other "loyal associations co-operating with this society be entered upon the books . . .1, [the club meeting at] The Crown and Cushion [a public house]; 2, Black Moor's Head. . ." and so on. The parent association also appointed gentlemen representatives to attend the monthly meeting of the united delegates' committee.[54] In December 1795 the Loyalist apparatus was wheeled into combat against the Reformers once more, when a Loyalist mob attacked a radical protest meeting.

In February 1797 the military aspirations of the popular Loyalists were finally requited, partly because of the threat of invasion by the French. The Manchester Volunteer Corps was founded at a meeting of the town oligarchy at the Tory Bull's Head Inn that included political "neutrals" like the Old Whig Thomas Butterworth Bayley but was dominated by arch-Tories like John Kearsley, John Ackers, and James Ackers, an ardent "Church and King" man who was made the first colonel. At that meeting, the Loyal Associations once again offered to form Volunteer corps and "disclaimed all party considerations." No doubt the first Manchester and Salford Volunteers were essentially the Loyal Associations in uniform. Some of the working-class support for the Volunteers was doubtless motivated by patriotism rather than out-and-out Loyalism. Among the friendly societies that subscribed to the

Volunteer fund, the Loyal and True Friendly Society of Middleton may be suspected of political as well as comradely loyalty, but not necessarily the Amicable Female Society or the Union Society.[55]

In February 1798, the consecration of the unit's colors—a sort of baptism for new Volunteer Corps—was the occasion for yet another festival of loyalty, this time without window-breaking. The town officers and the Volunteers paraded solemnly around the town to Piccadilly, where they were greeted by a "large number of Loyal Associations" assembled with "their respective flags." The Volunteers were congratulated for offering "to preserve and secure internal tranquility and social order." The procession ended at the Collegiate Church with a sermon that lamented the necessity for war against enemies of Britain's religion and laws and the danger posed by societies in Britain that abetted them. The day concluded with more secular forms of communion: a dinner, toasts, and a social "assembly" for the gentry, and convivial "meetings" at many different houses for the lesser sorts.[56]

The *Manchester Mercury* warned the sponsors of new Volunteer corps to investigate their enlistees carefully to prevent the Jacobins from infiltrating the ranks.[57] In the dark days of November 1800, when Thomas Bayley feared an uprising fomented by "the Democrats," he took some comfort in reporting that Manchester's (by then three) corps of Volunteer Infantry were recruited "from the common Mass of Artists (sic) & Labourers, but selected with care. They mix with the whole Body, and are useful to spread Loyalty & *detect* & suppress Sedition & Mischief, & *thus* are *very* well employed."[58]

The Volunteer movement in Manchester thus seemed to be a more decidedly partisan institution than it was in Devon, where Volunteers seemed to "represent" smaller, homogeneous communities not so politically aroused, and where the threat of invasion was more immediate.[59] To be sure, given the invasion threat of 1798, there was just enough real justification for preparing for home defense to attract even those not affiliated with the political factions.[60] But the Loyalist origins of the Volunteers gave them a partisan aura that shone, though not provocatively, on the days of the annual field reviews, the king's birthdays, and so on, with only a slight interruption during the period of the truce with France from 1801 to 1802. The number of Volunteers was not large: by 1801 perhaps three thousand men were enrolled; in 1804, after war resumed, some six thousand. But as I have said, these organized legions withdrew one of the few networks of comrades in Manchester's amorphous society from the pool of men available for riot. And however primitive their training, here were several thousand men, armed and drilled weekly and avid in their political attachments. No doubt they would have made quite a respectable showing as street fighters—even if soldierly discipline broke down—had they ever confronted an "insurrectionary" uprising of working-class radicals, who after all could only meet secretly in tiny cell groups and who had little opportunity for practice in collective action. No doubt when the dark days of 1800–1801 saw sedition on the walls, United Englishmen in the chimney snug, and radicals meeting on the moors, the gentlemen of Manchester were comforted by the knowledge that the traditions of their Volunteers had included a period of seasoning as "Church and King" rioters.

While the Tories were consolidating their political phalanx and druming up prosecutions, their opponents had not been idle. The year after the Walker riots, an organized challenge to the "slack and incompetent set of High Church Tories" who controlled the administration of the parish emerged. It originated when the poor rates, or "leys," were sharply raised by parish officials in 1793, a year of commercial distress.[61] Some of the ley-payers formed a society of Associated Ley-payers (ALP) whose committee investigated the parochial administration and ultimately published *A Report of the Committee of the Associated Ley-payers in the Township of Manchester* on April 9, 1794.

The conflict over parish affairs was rooted in "objective" issues, but partisan antagonisms repeatedly surfaced. The impetus for reform came in large part from the upper ranks of the politically active opposition, not from "nonpartisan" small rate payers. Of the eight identifiable leaders of the ALP, one was a doctor, and five others are identified as gentlemen or merchants in John Scholes's directories for 1794 and 1797.[62] Four members of the ALP committee, together with eight other men, were appointed to a town committee of inquiry in November 1794 to follow up the ALP report.[63] That committee included two attorneys, two gentlemen, six merchants or manufacturers, a tallow chandler, and one whose occupation cannot be identified because he was one of the town's many James Smiths. The political attachments of these sixteen men were quite clearly marked: three were on the Loyal Association's "suspects" list, two others were veteran Reformers, and twelve signed at least one of the opposition peace and protest petitions of 1795.[64] Two members of the ALP and two members of the committee of inquiry were politically neutral.

The committee of the ALP first asked the magistrates for

information but received a high-handed retort from Thomas B. Bayley, who declared that "the mode of their application was wrong, their interference improper, and that in his opinion the accounts were very right and proper."[65] (He was later forced to eat his words and express his "good wishes" to the committee.) So the committee of the ALP set about to reconstitute as best they could one year of the town's accounts, which they described as a "whirlpool." In their report, they concluded that the poor rates had been unequally, illegally, and arbitrarily assessed. In particular, "stock in trade" and spinning machinery, as well as canal tolls and a great deal of newly built housing had not been rated. Hence unfair burdens were thrown on small rate-payers while merchants and manufacturers paid far less than their share.[66] These "pocketbook" grievances probably increased the support of the opposition Reformers from tradesmen. The ALP also condemned patronage, charging that the parish officials were appointed from motives of "private friendship" and "personal attachment" while other "fitter" candidates were passed over, and they attacked a wide variety of other negligent and corrupt practices.[67]

The *Report* insisted that "the society [of Ley-payers] has no political relation," and that propriety rather than partisanship had motivated their criticisms,[68] but partisan ramifications were unavoidable. Among Constable John Leaf's accounts the committee found three juicy items: a charge of 19s. 6d. "To at Jockey Club and T. Paine's works by order of Mr. Leaf," on December 11, 1792, the date on which the Loyal Association was founded and the rioters had attacked Thomas Walker (*The Jockey Club* was a radical publication, which the magistrates bought to get evidence against radicals); £106 19s. 6d. in June 1792 for the expenses of Nathan Crompton, Samuel Clowes, Jr., Joseph Thackeray, and John Ford—the first three, at least, staunch "Church and King" men—on their trip to London to present the town's address on the first proclamation against sedition; and £31 6s. 6d. for celebrating the king's birthday, the day of the June riot in 1792. If the constables wished to treat their friends on such occasions, the committee urged, they ought to pay for it themselves, as Thomas Walker had done as boroughreeve in 1791, rather than take it out of the poor rates.[69]

The 1794 *Report* of the Ley-payers stimulated some immediate reforms in the assessment and administration of the poor rates.[70] But it had hardly touched Richard Unite, the deputy constable who had encouraged the "Church and King" rioters in December 1792. Soon after that demonstration of his political reliability, Deputy

Constable Unite had also become a salaried Overseer of the Poor, and "during the next few years he feathered his nest very energetically" by extortion and corruption.[71] Among other things, he had converted the system of bastardy payments made by putative fathers into a lucrative scheme of blackmail.[72]

The Associated Ley-payers' revelations touched off a long one-man crusade by Thomas Battye, a law stationer, accountant, and estate auctioneer, to expose Unite's monstrous enterprises. Battye was apparently a nonpartisan muckraker.[73] In October 1794 he challenged Unite to produce the missing bastardy accounts that were supposed to be kept in a "red basil book" among the parish records. He sent his challenge to the *Chester Courant*, which he chose as the only available "independent" medium free from "m[inisteria]l influence," unlike the *Manchester Mercury* and the *Manchester Chronicle*.[74] Battye insisted strenuously that his motives had nothing to do with partisan conflict, despite rumors to the contrary: "...an impression...has been industriously attempted to be made on the public mind—that this subject has been taken up from party or political motives...Politics have nothing to do with *local* regulations; and it is absurd to suppose that the CHURCH or the STATE can be endangered by an enquiry into the conduct of a *deputy* constable, or a *deputy* overseer."[75]

By early 1796, however, even Battye had to recognize that his campaign had rekindled party animosities. He remarked that when the justices had approved the overseers' accounts despite public clamor, "the common topic of discourse was of the cat's paw of party," and he twice lamented that the "inveteracy of party spirit existing in Manchester opposes an almost insurmountable barrier" to reform, and that the criticism of the deputy constable "has been considered as an attack on the whole body in office." Writing in December 1795, Sir Frederick Eden found that "Manchester is much divided into parties" over the administration of the parish.[76]

The parochial controversy and the conflict over national politics both reached violent climaxes in Manchester in 1795. Battye's challenge forced the town officials to call a public meeting on November 26, 1794, so that Unite might either be dismissed or cleared of "so foul an accusation."[77] The meeting was long, crowded, and heated. It appointed a committee of twelve to investigate Unite. As I have explained above, the membership of that committee reflected at least a temporary victory of the town's opposition over the Tory oligarchy. But the immediate outcome of the Unite case was decided by partisan power. When the committee was ready to report in March 1795, the Tory borough-reeve and constables refused to reconvene the adjourned meeting on the grounds that Unite's conduct should be judged in the courts, not in a public meeting that could neither acquit him nor fire him.[78] The ALP was thereby forced to stop the proceedings against Unite, at least temporarily.

But that same year, they next sought to challenge directly the Tory monopoly of parochial office. Their *Report* had complained that the churchwardens were in effect simply co-opted by their predecessors rather than freely elected at a public meeting, hence abuses were easily kept secret. The Associated Ley-payers hoped that the inhabitants would exercise their rights at the annual Easter parish meeting. At the meeting at the old Collegiate Church, the challengers did indeed make "a very strong attempt... to over-rule the usual mode of election." They proposed and vigorously insisted upon a reform list of officials, and when James Smith, an Associated Ley-payer, spoke for the reform list, the Tory James Edge, a member of the Loyal Association Committee of 1793, seized him and tried to throw him out of the church. That created "a great tumult," and "the parish officers embraced the opportunity of declaring their own friends to be duly elected, without ever taking the sense of the meeting by a division, which was repeatedly desired."[79] The Tory *Mercury* naturally saw public consensus rather than brute force at work: "On the names being distinctly put in the accustomed way, an approbation so decided was given to the measure, as to prevent, we hope, a contest of the like nature from happening again." The *Mercury* immediately added, "The doctrine of *Church and King* must still be supported," almost involuntarily revealing that parochial conflict had hardened partisan divisions. In October 1796, after two more of Battye's exposés had been published and another heated parish meeting had been held, the Court Leet Jury finally dismissed Unite.[80]

The final contest over national politics also took place in 1795. In January the parties skirmished by petition and counter-petition to Parliament. The opposition petitioned for peace with France, and the food shortages of that year probably widened the base of their support. However, the furious food riot of July together with the Easter battle over the parish administration, probably redoubled the Tories' determination to beat down the opposition. And their success in reimposing order by using cavalry and soup kitchens to pacify the townspeople may have emboldened them to unsheath the weapon of riot once more.

Among the hundred-odd proponents of peace were prominent

veterans of the Constitutional Society, six of the Loyal Association's "suspects" of 1793, and twelve members of the Manchester Literary and Philosophical Society, including Thomas Percival and Robert Owen. The Tory counter-petitioners included most of the magistrates and boroughreeves of the period, except Charles Frederick Brandt, a future boroughreeve (1799–1800), who stood above partisan politics for most of the period.[81] The Manchester and Salford Loyal Association charged their opponents with "lusting for power and popularity."[82] That April they cemented their fraternal ties with other associations, and December thus found the Loyalists ready to march into battle for "Church and King" in Manchester. The catalyst for the riot came once again from London. In late October the London Corresponding Society had staged a huge demonstration against hunger and Parliamentary corruption. Three days later, the king had been mobbed on his way to open Parliament by crowds crying, "Down with Pitt!" "No war!" "No King!" Pitt seized the opportunity to introduce on November 10 two bills against sedition: the first made it treason to speak or write against the constitution; the second prohibited meetings of more than fifty people without the prior permission of a magistrate, who might also stop the meeting and arrest the speaker. The threat to civil liberties from these measures touched off a storm of protest by Reformers across the country before and after they were passed into law.[83]

In Manchester the two bills rekindled the partisan struggle. The boroughreeve chaired a town meeting to congratulate the king on his escape. But the Reformers soon emerged again in force. Both Walker brothers and eleven of the thirty-four "suspects" of 1793 took part in the December contest. Led by George Lloyd, Samuel Greg, and Thomas Percival, they circulated handbills advertising a petition against the two bills. In reply, the several Loyal Associations of the town launched a counter-petition in favor of the two bills. It was passed by the "Loyal and well-affected Inhabitants" of the town and neighborhood at a meeting on November 20 chaired by James Ackers, leader of the original Loyal Association. The following week Colonel Stanley, Member of Parliament for Lancashire, presented the Loyalists' petition, signed by 7,351, to Parliament, while the Whig leader Charles James Fox presented the Manchester opposition's petition, signed by 4,303.[84] First round to "Church and King!"

The conflict that followed gave rise to a revealing controversy over what constituted a legitimate expression of the town's opinion. The Reformers requested that the boroughreeve and constables call a town meeting to petition the House of Lords against the threat to the freedoms of press, speech, and meeting embodied in the bills against sedition. But a Loyalist counter-requisition attempted to stand pat on the result of the previous petitions, arguing that the rival petitions to the House of Commons had already fully expressed the town's opinion. Significantly, they disdained to point out that they had "outscored" the Reformers, but they did complain that every effort was being made "to inflame, and even call into act, the public mind." The staunch Tory boroughreeve and constables rejected the Reformers' request on account of "the Impropriety of holding a Town's Meeting at this Time." Not to be stopped, the Reformers then published a direct appeal "To the Inhabitants of the Town" for a public town meeting on Monday morning, December 7, even though only the borough-reeve and constables could legitimately call a town meeting. When the lord of the manor denied the Reformers the use of his New Market Hall, they hurriedly issued several thousand handbills informing the public that the "Town's Meeting" would take place at eleven o'clock in a field near St. John's Church.[85]

The Loyal Association at the Bull's Head Inn replied with 4,000 more handbills inviting "all true Friends to their King and Country" to meet at the same time at the New Market Hall, but they hardly intended to rely on the spontaneous stirrings of loyal breasts.[86] Earlier that week, several of the affiliated loyal associations had declared their detestation of "wicked incendiaries" and "pernicious Doctrines," their determination to bring their authors to "Justice," and their intention "at all Times to co-operate with the Mother Association at the Bull's Head" and with other loyal associations "in any measures they may from Time to Time find necessary to adopt for the. . . Security to the Peace of the Town and Society in general."[87] The day before the scheduled meetings, the Bull's Head Loyal Association put the finishing touches on their order of battle. They resolved "that every support possible shall be given by this meeting to the other loyal associations on Monday, the 7th instant," and "that this and the other loyal associations be requested to meet at the New Market Hall, to-morrow morning (the 7th inst.) at ten o'clock."[88] The time chosen clearly suggests their plan to muster and then march to disrupt the opposition's meeting.

The next day the scheme was almost flawlessly executed. According to the Tory *Mercury*, twenty-five hundred Loyalists met at the New Market Hall and listened to "very animated and argumentative" speeches from several Churchmen. The meeting unanimously approved the two bills against sedition as necessary "to guard us from the horrors of anarchy and devastation." Meanwhile, a half-mile away, the rival meeting passed a petition to the House of Lords expressing their alarm at the two bills and one to the House of Commons calling for "Peace and Plenty" and lamenting the war and its burdens: deaths, debt, taxes, scarcity, and high prices. They had just passed the resolutions when a crowd from the Loyalist meeting rushed onto the field, routing the peacemongers with mud and stones. The parchment petition, according to a Loyalist account, "was carried, indeed, most unanimously, by the indignant Populace to the Market-Cross, and there burnt, amidst the Acclamations of their *immense Majority*."[89] The next day protest petitions were torn from the hands of people who had collected hundreds of signatures in nearby Stockport and Royton.[90]

The authorities were little more effective than they had been at the "Church and King" riot of 1792, and much more lax in restoring order than at the food riot in July 1795. The *Mercury* praised the magistrates and town officials for their "vigilant and active exertions," but they had failed to prevent window breaking at a bookseller's shop and harassment from mobs around the houses where the opposition's petitions were left for signing. The magistrates bound over a cotton spinner, a nailer, and a hat finisher to keep the peace for their participation in those incidents, and a joiner who was a special constable was bound over for rescuing one of the rioters who had been taken into custody. A Salford dyer was forced to apologize publicly to avoid prosecution for throwing a stone at Thomas Walker in Manchester. He declared he had been given the stone "for that express Purpose, by a Person whom I do not know, genteelly dressed in a green coat." The magistrates also bound over an Anglican curate, the Reverend Thomas Chambers Wilkinson, to appear at the Quarter Sessions on a charge of inciting the Loyalist invaders at the peace meeting. At the January Sessions, the bill of indictment was ignored by the reliably Tory grand jury, but in case they were needed, "a considerable number of totally respectable inhabitants" were standing by to testify to his proper conduct.[91]

The contest over the petitions of 1795 marked a climax in the crystallization of partisan politics in Manchester. Each side referred to the other as a "party," apparently for the first time.[92] Such mutual recognition implied that instead of shifting factions competing for an undifferentiated public, Manchester had developed enduring organizations based upon divergent political ideologies.

Their definitions of "public opinion" epitomized those ideologies. The Tories clung to the time-honored legitimacy of the indivisible town meeting. Their meeting on the sedition bills had ascertained, "decidedly and unequivocally," "the sense of the Public." Not only did the *Mercury* estimate their attendance at five times that of the Reformers' meeting, but more important, the Tories tried to insinuate that their meeting at the New Market Hall was the *only* town meeting, because it had been properly, or at least publicly, advertised. (Ironically, they had to argue that the public had been responding to the original invitation, however illegitimate, of the peace party.) They declared that the Loyal Association was only a "very small Part of that immense multitude" that assembled, and concluded, "the Fact is, the Public assembled at the New Market Hall, and their Opinion was 'fairly taken.'"

The Loyalist petitions themselves were couched in the language of consensus. They began, "We, your Majesty's most loyal and dutiful Subjects, *the* inhabitants of the towns of Manchester and Salford..."[93] This plebiscitarian rhetoric helps to explain the Tories' claim that "the Populace" had destroyed the opposition's petition. The Tories hardly even bothered to condemn the violence, and their accounts of it positively crowed: the riot had "clearly shown the unshaken Loyalty of the People." The Tories thus interpreted the riot itself as the final work of the public.[94]

If the Tories looked back to some symbolic consensus, the Reformers' rhetoric looked forward to pluralism and the counting of individual votes. Their petitions began more pointedly, "the *undersigned* Inhabitants of the Town and Neighborhood of Manchester..." (my italics). Their resolutions were carried by "an immense Majority," not unanimously, as the Tories had boasted of theirs. And while the Tories had the old-fashioned power of office and muscle on their side, the Reformers claimed the more modern superiority of numbers. Their claim, unchallenged by the Tories, was that 17,826 people had signed the petition to the Lords against the two bills while 12,185 had signed the Loyalists' petition.[95] Raw numbers, not formal procedures that were stacked against them, expressed the sense of the public for the Reformers.

By December 1795, even more than in 1792, the partisan rivalry of Manchester had become precisely like that of "a contested election" in a traditional borough, even down to the tallying of "votes" and well-orchestrated Loyalist riots. The orderliness imposed by that rivalry is underscored by the contrasting wildness in a few political riots motivated by spontaneous hatreds rather than structured rivalry. In July 1794, John Cheetham, sometime secretary of the workingman's Reformation Society, was mobbed by a group of people near the New Bayley Courthouse, apparently following a sedition trial at the Quarter Sessions. One voice called out, "Now, wenches, at him!" and the crowd jostled him, stoned him, broke into the house where he sought refuge, and dragged him several hundred yards by the hair before the constables could rescue him. He was seriously injured. The *Manchester Mercury* half condoned his punishment as deserved by anyone who would criticize the government at that time.[96] The Tories had used the hangers-on around the New Bayley Courthouse as that kind of informal pillory before. When Benjamin Booth had been arrested for sedition in 1793, he was twice deliberately "expose[d]... to the fury of the populace."[97]

Two minor riots in 1796 echoed the partisan battles of the previous year. In February and again in May, violence erupted in the Manchester Theater. In both instances the singing of "God Save the King" was called for and some members of the audience resisted. Officers of the Eighth Dragoons attacked the dissidents with drawn swords. In the February riot at least, the "obstructionists" had brought along bludgeons, and in the turmoil several people were cut and wounded. (The most seriously hurt was the merchant William Johnson Edensor, a member of the peace party of January 1795 and a future boroughreeve, who received a cut in the arm.)[98] Those three riots in 1794 and 1796 led to more serious personal injury than any of the "Church and King" riots had. The contrast suggests that more injurious rioting could result when the rioters were free-lance enthusiasts, acting out of pure ideological commitment, whereas the well-organized partisan conflicts provided motives but also constraints for collective action.

After 1796, no more partisan violence occurred in Manchester. The parties apparently continued to exist—certainly the Loyalist cause endured in the Volunteer movement. The struggle over the parish's administration continued at a lower level until Unite was relieved of his offices, but Battye continued his exposés of abuses of power through 1801 and beyond. Perhaps the reforms he eventually induced cut into the parochial patronage available to the Tory ring, just as the "economical reform" campaigns since 1784 had reduced Parliamentary patronage at the national level. At the same time, the town government was being put on a sounder footing, particularly with the activation of the police commission in 1799–1800, under the impetus of the Tory establishment, particularly of the boroughreeve, Charles Frederick Brandt.[99] Brandt was also a key figure in the soup kitchens of 1799–1800 and in the merchants' organizations that reawakened in 1800–1804. Besides being active in the leadership of the Volunteers, the Tories also dominated other major civic institutions, such as the Infirmary and the Lying-In Hospital. But leading Reformers were also active on the boards of such institutions as well as taking a minority role in the police commission.[100]

Nevertheless, the mass petition campaign of December 1795 was a harbinger of a development that would go far beyond the constraints of partisan conflict among Manchester's elite, for the efforts of both sides, marked by the incidents in Stockport and Royton in 1795 and the "votes" of thousands of common people, represent the emergence of a *regional* popular political movement.[101] In the remaining years of the Napoleonic Wars that mobilization would be spread and reinforced by the immediate pressures of hardship arising from food shortages and industrial change and by a series of workers' campaigns. By 1808 and 1812, that mobilization bore fruit in substantial strikes and demonstrations. At the core of that process was the organization of the weavers.

6

The Mobilization
of the Weavers

The history of food riots in Manchester reveals how the traditional frameworks of community political bargaining dissolved and were replaced with impersonal means of managing crises. The development of partisan conflict in the 1790s involved consolidating a phalanx of Loyalist Associations from the riots of 1792 into more permanent Volunteer organizations in 1797–1798, while at the same time hardship, the impact of the war, and political appeals increased the numbers of those willing to challenge Manchester's Tory establishment. Conflict between workers and employers and magistrates was a third dimension of the social alienation and polarization of Manchester's community politics. The broad outlines of the cotton workers' collective actions have been described by several historians.[1] However, conventional explanations of working-class solidarity in this period—hardship, proletarianization, ideological radicalization—are not sufficient to explain the workers' *capacities* for collective action nor in what way that action was new. To understand that history one must recast it in the light of Manchester's community politics. The crucial fact is that the textile workers—especially the mule spinners (operators of the spinning mules) and hand-loom weavers—were new groups of workers in 1790, "created" and assembled by the appearance of new technology and by Manchester's rapid industrial growth. Both geographically and culturally, they were recent immigrants into a new urban industrial world. They lacked the long traditions of collective action of London's artisans or Devon's woolen workers or food rioters. They had to organize themselves on the basis of regional and industrial, rather than local and communal, solidarity (see Figure 9). Weavers especially had to overcome the obstacles to

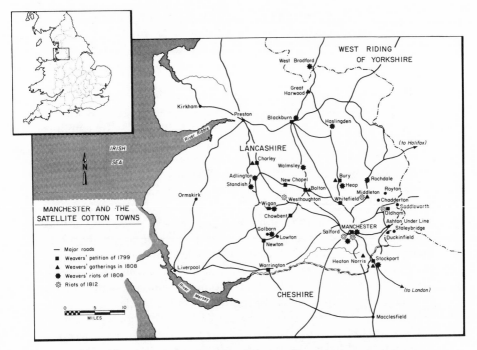

Figure 9. Manchester and the satellite cotton towns.

such unity posed by rapid industrialization and the handicaps to collective bargaining created by their alienation from the town's authorities. As their organization and their perceptions grew beyond their local and concrete work experience, they became aware of the industry as a whole, of its political context, and of their roles in both. That mobilization was an important part of the emergence of class.

A few signs of solidarity among Manchester's workers appeared before 1790. Elementary signs of trade consciousness appeared in civic processions at the time of George III's coronation and Thomas Walker's triumphant return to Manchester in 1785, when the town's various trades paraded in costume, with "colours."[2] Significantly, no cotton weavers and of course no mule spinners appeared as a group. Probably the best-organized workers in Manchester in this period were the journeymen calico printers. (Calico was a relatively coarse all-cotton cloth originally imported from India but now manufactured and printed in England.) In 1786 the calico printers locked horns with their employers over the introduction of machinery.[3] By 1803 they had formed an extensive combination to petition Parliament to extend the Elizabethan apprenticeship law in a way that would restrict the employment of apprentices. Their petition failed, but they won partial concessions. No doubt their skill, high wages, and physical concentration in towns and in factories made their strong combinations possible.[4]

The most successful trade unionists in Manchester were the mule spinners. The mule spinners were a new breed of workers, the spinning mule having been invented only in 1779 by combining the rollers of the water frame and the drawing-out bobbin carriage of the spinning jenny into one machine. For more than a decade mules were employed in small shops and factories, but in the 1790s, first waterpower, then steam was used to drive the mules, and mule spinning factories began to multiply in Manchester.[5] The mule operator required skill to tune the machine, a fine touch, and physical strength,[6] so mule spinners tended to be adult males. Strength and skill were not an absolute obstacle to the employment of women, however, and the early spinners' combinations in Manchester envisaged women members,[7] and female spinners certainly existed in both the mule and the throstle branches of spinning in the 1830s.[8] But social attitudes seem to have restricted the numbers of women employed, both because women tended to leave work after they married in order to care for children, thus interrupting their development of particular skills, and because the adult mule spinner supervised a team of assistants, which seemed to require the "patriarchal" authority of a man.[9] In any case, the adult mule spinners were already becoming an "aristocratic" elite among members of the cotton trades. Their skill and authority enabled them to control recruitment to their jobs and to command high wages. Their high concentration in the factories and in towns facilitated their organization and picketing. Their key role in the production process meant that the strike of a few spinners could bring entire factories and hundreds of other workers to a stop. Their masters (employers) were vulnerable to work stoppages because their heavy investment in fixed capital required them to keep the machinery running if possible even during slumps in the market. And the high profits of the early days of factory spinning meant that employers were more ready to concede to workers' demands than to risk losses.[10]

For all these reasons durable combinations of workers appeared early among the Manchester spinners. As early as 1792, the Manchester spinners formed a friendly society that set forth rules providing for "union shops." All spinners were to have membership tickets and no spinner was to work in a shop where there had been a "lawful turnout," that is, a strike properly declared by the union.[11] In 1795 the mule spinners met "the present excessive Price of Provision" with two strikes. In February and March, they "turned out" to resist a reduction in their wages. They denied the masters' allegations that nonstrikers had been "dragged from their places, menaced by members of their club, and compelled...to loiter about the streets in idleness." The spinners apparently were promised a raise, but the masters later denied it. In August and September, however, the spinners made "an almost general turn out for an extravagant advance of wages," and after holding out for a month, they won nearly their whole demand.[12]

Since employers were more willing to advertise for replacements than to bargain with "wicked Combinations,"[13] picketing was necessary to make a strike effective and it was probably used in 1795 despite the spinners' denials. Of course when they had registered their friendly society's rules with the magistrates in April 1795, the spinners dutifully passed resolutions to expel any member guilty of assaulting an employer, damaging property, indulging in riotous conduct, or combining to raise wages.[14] Nevertheless violent direct action was used again in 1798. In early February, striking spinners assembled "in considerable numbers in [the center of] Manchester, [and in suburban] Ardwick, Chorlton Row, and other places" to enforce strike demands, assaulting and abusing would-be strikebreakers. They were apparently successful despite the proclamation by magistrates Bayley, Leaf, and Simpson that those who disturbed the peace would be "punished with that severity which is due to such violent and unwarrantable proceedings." In March, striking spinners assembled at a factory to harrass strikebreakers who had been hired for reduced wages. They broke the windows of the factory but were eventually dispersed by the magistrates and cavalry. One of the rioters was sentenced to three months in prison.[15]

The spinners encountered the magistrates' hostility not merely because their strikes were violent but also because Manchester's elite was so alienated from its common people, as the food riots of 1795 had shown and as the weavers strike of 1808 would reemphasize.[16] The spinners' sustained leverage is suggested by their recurring strikes and combinations: at Stockport in 1796, and at Manchester and Salford in 1797, 1801 (twice), 1803, 1804, 1805, and 1807.[17] Although these episodes were nonviolent, in three instances leaders of the combinations were sentenced to three months in prison. On two of those occasions the chairman of the Quarter Sessions issued "a most impressive warning" to the prisoners and their colleagues. And in October 1803 the master spinners (employers) formed an association against the mule spinners' "dangerous and wicked combination to compel the master spinners to raise their wages." They raised a "fighting fund" of £20,000 to finance prosecutions of striking mule spinners, to support individual firms in their resistance to the combinations, and to encourage masters to train substitutes.[18]

Such nearly continuous and often successful collective action by the mule spinners set the stage for the first appearance of a general union of Lancashire spinners in 1810. The spinners were trying to capitalize on a wave of prosperity by raising the piece rates paid in the country towns to the rates paid in Manchester. That would stop the country manufacturers from undercutting (or perhaps even competing efficiently with) Manchester's spinning firms, which had better access to raw cotton. Hence the general union of 1810 demonstrated the spinners' perception of the necessity to cooperate throughout the entire labor market in their trade. Their union extended from Manchester north to Preston, east to Staleybridge, and south to Stockport and Macclesfield. The General Union was conducted by a "general congress" at Manchester composed of forty or fifty delegates elected by clubs of spinners in Manchester's factories and in the country. The union had planned to conduct a rolling strike, calling out a few mills at a time and supporting them from the contributions of employed spinners. But the masters out-maneuvered them by locking out whole districts, so as to break the unions' funds. The strike lasted three or four months, chiefly in the neighborhoods of Staleybridge and Preston. Eight to ten thousand workers struck or were turned out. The spinners, who may have been only 10 percent of the total number, received strike pay of 12s. a week. In all, some £17,000 was disbursed, and Manchester alone contributed as much as £600 per week to the strike fund. According to a later account, many of those thrown out of work paraded the streets of the smaller cotton towns shouting and hooting at their enemies' houses. Some factories were attacked and "blacklegs" (strikebreakers) were confined to the mills in a virtual state of siege. The strikers held out until their funds, savings, and disposable furniture had run out, and then the strike collapsed. There was little or no crowd action in Manchester itself. Several spinners convicted of riot and assault at Staleybridge were sentenced to twelve months' imprisonment. But many convictions under the Combination Acts of 1799–1800 were quashed owing to legal technicalities. The collapse of the strike caused great hardship, and according to John Doherty, the abandonment of the union, but by 1811 mill strikes were again taking place in Manchester. E. C. Tufnell, a Benthamite poor law inspector in the 1830s, even claimed that Lancashire Luddism had its roots in the strike of 1810.[19]

In any case, the strike of 1810 was important for three reasons. First, it climaxed more than a decade of organized action by textile workers. Second, it demonstrated the enlargement of the mule spinners' horizons of perception and organization to include the entire labor market. Third, the well-organized but nonviolent actions of Manchester's strikers contrasted with the more demonstrative crowd actions of the workers in the satellite towns. Physical coercion was not often used by the well-organized spinners, but neither was it alien to them. Furthermore, the organization and actions of both the mule spinners and their masters reflect the degree of polarization of social relations in Manchester. The sectional organization of the spinners and their frequent success in raising their wages probably diverted them from taking part in the communal collective action of food riot, although their widened horizons and their experience of the masters' and magistrates' hostility made them potential recruits for the even broader campaigns for political reform.

Hand-loom weavers, as a group, had overwhelming handicaps that contrasted at every point with the strengths of the mule spinners and that made collective action very difficult. To begin with, the weavers had no skill that could provide bargaining leverage or give them control over entry into their occupation. It took only three weeks to teach a prisoner in the New Bayley Prison to weave calico, while muslin weaving could be learned in six weeks by "a lad of fourteen."[20] Accordingly, tens of thousands of newcomers flooded the weaving trade during its rapid expansion in the period of the Napoleonic Wars. Irish peasants, many of them experienced cottage-weavers, poured into Manchester in the 1790s.[21] Women and children flocked to the looms in cottages, cellars, and small shops as spinning machines displaced them from their traditional by-employment or as their weaver husbands and fathers went off to war. By 1808 it was thought that half the weavers in the district were women and children, though that was probably an overestimate.[22] They were joined by agricultural workers induced "to forsake the spade for the shuttle"; workers from declining trades, including other textile industries and lead mining; and even "the dregs, the runaways, and the outcasts of eighteenth century society."[23] Indeed, by 1800 it was no doubt already true that hand-loom "weaving, next to general labouring, was the grand resource of the northern unemployed."[24]

The number of hand-loom weavers exploded from 75,000 to 225,000 between 1795 and 1811, by one estimate.[25] They crowded into the "offensive, dark, damp, and incommodious habitations," and particularly into the disease-ridden cellars of Manchester and other towns, and they "thickened" the villages and the country districts around Manchester and the satellite cotton towns.[26]

The cotton hand-loom weavers were offspring of the Industrial Revolution as surely as the new factory workers, for the Industrial Revolution included not only technological change that created factories but also economic growth through the extension and intensification of capitalist forms of production still carried out in workshops and cottages. The cotton hand-loom weavers were the classic exemplars of "proto-industrialization," a process whereby economic growth took place by exploiting abundant supplies of cheap labor using hand techniques of production, not new power-driven machinery.[27]

Indeed, proto-industrialization itself increased the supply of labor in the long run by providing opportunities for employment that stimulated population growth, in the short run by providing an easily learned form of work that might enlist the unemployed and underemployed members of families. The hand-loom weavers illustrate a monstrous supply curve of labor, the other end of what is known in economics as the "backward-bending supply curve of labor," in which workers aiming for a customary standard of living reduce their work hours and increase their leisure time as wages rise, instead of trying to maximize their income by working the same number of hours. The converse side of that curve is that, as wages decline, workers supply more, not less, labor to the market in order to achieve a subsistence income. They might do this by working eighteen hours a day rather than twelve, or by sending more members of the family into the labor market.[28] This is what the hand-loom weavers did. Proto-industrialization, the interaction between surplus labor, profit inflation, and industrial growth, was not merely a *preliminary* phase of the Industrial Revolution, but was a crucial and central mechanism of economic growth for at least the first two generations of the revolution in cotton manufacturing, and even longer in the "sweated trades," such as garment making.[29] The almost infinitely elastic supply of weaving labor was the chief obstacle to the task of organizing the hand-loom weavers.

Since the cotton hand-loom weavers were largely a new and

uprooted group of workers, they had almost no stock of traditional defenses. The only germs of previous collective action were few and far between. The check weavers and small-ware worsted weavers had created strong combinations in 1758 and 1759, but they were completely suppressed. In 1781 another contest between the small-ware weavers and their masters had been settled after a stern warning from the Manchester magistrates against "dangerous" and "unlawful combinations."[30] The only successful instance of collective bargaining by the cotton hand-loom weavers is that of the Bolton and Bury weavers, who apparently had an agreement on wages with their masters that lasted from 1792 to 1798.[31] It was an arsonist acting covertly, not a crowd acting publicly, who burned down Messrs. Grimshaw's power-loom factory in Manchester in 1792.[32] The thin tradition of collective action in the cotton industry and in the trades from which it drew its recruits was simply swamped by the rapid influx of newcomers after 1790.

The weavers also lacked traditional institutional defenses. Apprenticeship, for instance, could hardly be maintained when expansion of the industry was so rapid and the "mysteries" of the trade so flimsy. In 1782 the weavers' last attempt to assert the rights prescribed by the sixteenth-century statutes on apprenticeship had been roundly rebuffed by the organized masters of Manchester and therefter, apprenticeship survived primarily as a means of binding pauper children as cheap labor.[33] Nor could the weavers rely on the magistrates' setting of wage rates. The last mention of such a practice came in 1779 when several weavers' societies had addressed the Home Office to request legal enforcement of set wages.[34] Furthermore, the mode of appeal to the magistrates to intervene in disputes with employers was extremely cumbersome.

The weavers did have one important base for organization, the friendly society. In 1802–1803, there were more than 1,000 friendly societies in Lancashire, with a total membership of over 100,000, far more than in any other county.[35] Some of the friendly societies in Lancashire went back at least to the 1750s. In 1792 the United Benefit Societies of Manchester held meetings to concert proposals on a forthcoming parliamentary bill on friendly societies. In 1800 a Union of Friendly Societies in Manchester acted as a consumers' cooperative, selling food cheaply in a time of high prices. Friendly societies also took part intermittently in festive processions and in making group donations for the support of the Volunteers.[36]

It is difficult to say what impact these friendly societies had on the mobilization of the weavers. F. M. Eden, author of the weighty compendium *The State of the Poor,* distrusted the societies' alehouse meetings because they faciliated "combinations for improper purposes in trade, religion, and politics."[37] In 1808 the friendly societies of the region did help finance the weavers' delegation to Parliament, and they lent money to weavers who were out of work because of the strike that year.[38] The members of the Bolton area societies that participated were said to have been principally cotton weavers.[39] There is no doubt that the spinners' societies were at the core of their successful militancy, but otherwise, friendly societies may have been relatively weaker in Manchester than in most other cotton towns. Eden, for example, did not discuss Manchester's friendly societies in his report *The State of the Poor,* though he gave detailed coverage to the societies in other towns.[40] And because Manchester was such a large town, its friendly societies enrolled a much smaller proportion of the population than friendly societies in other cotton towns.[41] The greater density of such workers' social organizations in the satellite towns may have been responsible for the stronger roles those towns played in the weavers' campaigns of 1799–1808.

The structure of the "putting-out" system of production was a final obstacle to collective organization of the weaving trade. The weavers employed by any one merchant-manufacturer worked either in their own cottages or in small workshops scattered throughout the town and countryside. Weavers made individual bargains with their master at the master's warehouse, when they picked up the yarn to be woven and the specifications of the kind and pattern of cloth to be produced. "Prices" (wages) varied not only with the state of the market but also with the quality and pattern of the work given out. When weavers returned the finished cloth to the warehouse and claimed their wages, there were frequent disputes over the quality of the work done, over whether the assigned pattern had been carried out, and over defects, stains, and "damps"(since both raw material and finished cloth were measured by weight to prevent embezzlement, the weavers could be accused of wetting the cloth to make up the weight of any missing yarn). At worst, masters might even reduce the price paid for weaving from the agreed contract just because the markets had fallen, and the weavers would be forced to accept these reductions for several reasons. They might be unable or unwilling to change employers because they were in debt to them, or because a change would require an expensive and time-consuming change of the pattern set on the loom, or simply because trade was bad and alternative employment was unavailable. In theory, a weaver might apeal to the magistrates to have the contract upheld, but that might cost more time or money than the weaver could afford and was no help if the weaver needed money immediately. In at least one instance, a manufacturer called on a magistrate to threaten a reluctant weaver with jail.[42] The dispersion of the weavers' contracts over space and time and the variety of cloth woven meant that it was nearly impossible for weavers to bargain collectively. Moreover, the flexibility of the system put all the bargaining power in the hands of the employer. Since the looms were in the weavers' homes, the employer had little fixed capital to keep in operation at fixed costs, and he could lay off and take on weavers as the market fluctuated.[43] This putting-out system of employment and the relatively unskilled nature of the work meant that a simple mass withdrawal of labor was not likely to be an effective bargaining tactic. The manufacturer would either draw upon his accumulated stocks of cloth or else hire new weavers who would be scattered and thus difficult for the strikers to prevent from working.

The hand-loom weaver was essentially a "free" wage laborer, a proletarian in the sense that he or she was absolutely dependent on the sale of his or her capacity for labor to a capitalist employer.[44] Cotton hand-loom weavers were not, for the most part, artisans displaced from an old craft tradition or possessed of some degree of control over the process of production. Although weavers often owned their looms and the "implements" required to work different patterns, owning such equipment was a liability when patterns changed. The weaver had very little real freedom, faced with a glutted labor market, falling wages, rising food prices, and a twelve- to eighteen-hour workday. Cotton weavers had been predominantly wage earners and not weaver-farmers even before 1780.[45] Even those who had gardens that could supply part of their food depended on their wages to pay the rent of their cottages and gardens. In other words, they did not possess access to enough productive resources to render them independent of the labor market and of their wages for their livelihood. Moreover, it is misleading to describe weaving as "a kind of by-occupation for the aged, the unmarried sisters and daughters, and the growing children in a family."[46] That may have been the case after 1820 when the power looms began to depress the weavers into unfathomable misery, but before that date, the impression given by the sources is that weaving was typically a full-time occupation.[47] Women and children contributed not a "supplement" to family income but a crucial portion of the minimum necessary for the family's survival.

To sum up, the great mass of hand-loom weavers entered the Industrial Revolution as one of its newest, largest, and most characteristic contingents. They were not artisans displaced by machines who could draw both strength and resentment from lost craft traditions.[48] Rather, they were newborn proletarians, virtually naked of any collective armor. Their proletarian status was in itself no guarantee of a capacity for collective action. Yet by 1808 they were able to orchestrate an effective strike across the whole weaving district of south Lancashire. They transcended both their weaknesses and the parochial limits of traditional collective action. How was this accomplished?

The most direct stimulus to mobilize came from a disastrous decline in wages. By the late 1790s there was a glut of weavers in the labor force. Despite some evidence of local demand for weavers as late as 1800, wage rates had already begun to fall.[49] In the bad year of 1799, weavers claimed that rates for piecework had been cut by more than 50 percent since 1792, and in addition, the length of the pieces woven for the standard rates had been increased.[50] The most optimistic figures for the period indicate a drop in the piecework rates of more than 25 percent between 1796 and 1799, and the true picture for many weavers was probably worse.[51] The impact on their family budgets was aggravated by an inflation of food prices of some 30 percent during the 1790s, even before the great food scarcity of 1800.[52] But economic misery probably undercut as much as it promoted collective action, for weavers were prone to work longer as wages dropped, and to accept more and more unfavorable terms out of desperation. The physical weakness that no doubt accompanied food shortages was not an asset in collective action.

The process of constructing a workers' movement required the weavers to perceive their common interests, and to organize across the entire cotton region. The weavers' direct experience had made them aware of their position in the wider labor market. The geographical mobility of the trade was their first teacher, for weavers changed masters or even towns when higher wages were offered.[53] The ease with which they could be replaced if they refused a master's terms brought home the knowledge that any solution must embrace the whole labor market. The weekly "bearing home" of work to the warehouses fostered regular contact between weavers from different communities. Samuel

Bamford, the radical weaver, told how he and his uncle would load up the "bearing home wallet" with finished cloth and tramp the seven miles over the fields and lanes from Middleton to Manchester, where he met other weavers at the master's warehouse. On the way home, they might travel in groups for protection, and they would stop at the public houses frequented by weavers. "There the wallets or 'pokes'...were piled in a heap, ale was ordered, seats drawn round the fire, pipes were soon lighted, news interchanged with the host or some of his company..." Such contacts, together with weekly meetings of the local friendly society, provided occasions for keeping abreast of trade conditions in different firms and communities.[54]

Second, the war with France widened the economic and political perspectives of the weavers, probably more directly than did arguments about natural rights. In 1793 and 1796, and especially after the intensification of economic warfare in 1806–1807, war and peace had immediate repercussions on weavers' earnings, because employers passed the effect of trade reductions on to the workers in the form of lower wages.[55] When the weavers brought in their finished work, they might hear their masters blame wage reductions on the war. The employers might complain of "Hamburgh being taken, or that such a Person had failed...or that the markets are so low." One weaver testified, "Sometimes they laid it to the war, sometimes to the badness of the market."[56] No wonder the *Manchester Mercury* cautioned the weavers in 1798 against supporting the possibility of an ignominious peace. No wonder Manchester greeted the peace preliminaries in 1801 with guns and bells, and no wonder that peace petitions signed by eighty thousand people were sent to Parliament from Bolton and Manchester in 1808.[57]

Third, foreign conditions made markets unstable, and that forced the weavers to think in *industrial* rather than in individual or local terms. William Radcliffe, a cotton manufacturer from Stockport, liked to titillate his weavers by telling them their pay came from London, Amsterdam, Moscow, or even "Bucharia, a rich trading country, lying north of Persia and Hindostan." Wage reductions might be attributed to falling markets, to "others ...working for less money."[58] Especially after 1801, the instability of the trade—and earnings—was increased by the cutthroat competition of "men of little capital" who would go down in flames, dumping their goods on the market below cost as they sold out.[59] Weavers argued that the evil of "masters striving with each other to lengthen pieces and reduce wages" called for regulation of the trade.[60] The force of this direct education in economics drove weavers to seek a solution in collective action that would encompass the whole industrial district. The leaders of the Bolton weavers rejected the offer of a possible local compromise by saying, "other places were similarly aggrieved, and a general Remedy was necessary."[61]

And so in the spring of 1799 the weavers began to organize regionally. They formed an association to petition Parliament for the regulation of the cotton industry. Their campaign initially sought a more efficient means of settling disputes than the cumbersome appeal to the magistrates.[62] It did not seem to be spurred on by immediate hardship, for the cotton industry in the first half of 1799 was generally prosperous.[63] Their strategy of acting "not from any power of their own but by appealing to Government"[64] recognized their weaknesses in trying to bargain collectively. Their original declaration was signed by thirty delegates from thirteen towns, at least some of whom represented large and active branches of a federation of weavers with headquarters at Bolton. They tried to appeal to many sectors of public opinion. They asked their masters to consider the rising prices of the necessities of life. They reiterated their common interest with the employers in ending price cutting and exportation of cotton yarn. They appealed to the nobility and gentry by demonstrating how much rates for piecework had fallen. They proclaimed their steadfast loyalty to king and country and disavowed any inclination toward riot or sedition, and they declared that the charge against them of Jacobinism was only a "mean artifice" of their enemies: the "late laws on meetings" (meaning the acts against sedition of 1795–1796) were directed against "that wild democratical fury that leads nations into the vortex of anarchy, confusion, and bloodshed." They sought to impress upon both "ignorant" magistrates and reluctant colleagues their legal right to meet to petition Parliament.[65] The weavers' tone was assertive, but they were careful to avoid "political" aims and to appeal to common interests.

However, although they appeared to conduct their business with "great openness and apparent loyalty,"[66] the Weavers' Association aroused the suspicion and hostility of the magistrates from the beginning, partly because the kind of organization was so new. The Weavers' Association was a network spread across the cotton district, organized by committees and delegates; it was not the more familiar local trade club. Justice Bancroft of Bolton found it ominous that the weavers documented their case by citing wage reductions for velverets, when that sort of cloth was not even made in Bolton, where the complaint and the association originated. The magistrates feared "that Associations of such a magnitude and professing to move the County, might be ultimately dangerous."[67] Moreover, the Society of United Englishmen had already been founded in Lancashire in 1797. The magistrates there were keenly watching and prosecuting all persons suspected of sedition.[68]

Hence the magistrates of Wigan and Bolton reported that the new association "seems to threaten harm." Despite the weavers' clearly stated objectives, the magistrates worried that "their publications and the arrangement of the Plan are able and great." Bancroft wondered "how far Politics might be blended with it" and remarked that "the Arrangement of their Plan had something of a Jacobinical aspect." "Nineteen out of twenty" of the member weavers were "loyal sober and industrious," "but their leaders are the reverse." The weavers' declaration was "calculated greatly to inflame and mislead the laboring class" who were "happy and contented" "before these arts were used to disturb their peace." Accordingly, the magistrates of Bolton prohibited the weavers from meeting in public houses, despite "the odium of the prohibition."[69]

The Home Office concurred with the magistrates' suspicions. The Weavers' Association was not illegal, and possibly not even seditious, but it could be "converted at any time into a most dangerous instrument to disturb the public tranquility." The Home Office therefore recommended that the magistrates employ spies to watch the Weavers' Association to detect any wider ambitions they might have.[70]

Meanwhile, in June 1799 Pitt introduced the first Combination Bill prohibiting labor combinations, making reference to combinations in the north, probably meaning the Weavers' Association.[71] The bill speedily became law, and it heightened social tensions in Lancashire. By the autumn of 1799, high bread prices, unemployment, and wage reductions had deepened the dissatisfaction of the cotton workers. In late October, delegates from the Manchester trade societies of fustian cutters, shoemakers, machine makers, cotton spinners, and calico printers published a handbill protesting the injustices of the Combination Act. The chief Manchester magistrate, Thomas B. Bayley, confused that protest with the weavers' campaign. He believed that the weavers and spinners were being invited to petition Parliament against the Combination Act, and that the handbills had an "obvious tendency to produce Insurrection." He claimed that workers threatened "desperate things against some of the Masters."[72] The Home Office replied that of course the Combination Act could have no connection with wage reductions, and it recommended that the magistrates use conciliation, relief, and firm warning "to restore the influence of the magistrates over [the weavers]."[73]

The Manchester magistrates' public reactions once more expressed the anxiety they felt toward the alien masses of the town they governed, all the more so since the Weavers' Association had seemed to spring out of thin air among workers who were previously unorganized.[74] Bayley agreed that the magistrates should combine "great Tenderness towards our distressed Poor" with "Firmness to execute the laws," including the Combination Act.[75] In late November, the Manchester magistrates issued a handbill warning against attempts to "excite a spirit of dissatisfaction amongst the weavers and others employed in the manufactures of this County." They promised severe punishment to offenders and attributed the hard times to Divine Providence, which was chastising the people for their failings. They flatly rejected any notion of regulating wages: "The Price of Labour ought and must be free and unshackled, it is governed by a greater or less Demand." They repeated their warning against seditious societies. The magistrates also published a handbill promising to protect farmers frequenting the Manchester market, thus implying that riot threatened, and they reestablished the soup kitchens.[76]

By the spring of 1800 the weavers' petition had collected twenty-three thousand signatures.[77] Their petition complained that wage reductions, were "oppressions...effectuated by a powerful combination of the master weavers or manufacturers...of so much Secrecy, Wealth and Power" that the weavers were powerless to combat it.[78] And when the weavers' delegates testified before a parliamentary committee in May, Thomas B. Bayley wrote to oppose their bill. Although Bayley had earlier supported some regulation of wages to conciliate the poor,[79] he now declared that "much of sedition had mixed itself with the weavers' petitions and bill...the measure they solicit is altogether so obscured and impracticable" that he hoped its defeat would be *"very speedy and by a great majority* in a full house." He added that "the 4th Dragoons now at Manchester are an ample security for our tranquility."[80] Like the food rioters, organized weavers were a "nuisance," to be met with cavalry and soup kitchens.

The magistrates' November warning drew two separate replies from the workers. The trades protesting the Combination Act denied that they had any seditious intentions. Almost condescendingly, they warned distressed workmen, apparently the weavers, to avoid riot. They declared that the wise dissatisfaction among the workers came not from clandestine sources but from their reading the Act itself or its abstracts, great numbers of which had been sold by the booksellers. Dissatisfaction would have to be very great indeed, they argued, "before a number of men, who had neither time nor money to spare, could be called on by their brother workmen to bring forward such a petition." Finally, they flatly rejected the magistrates' economic theory: "We believe the price of labour to be now shackled, so as to be highly injurious to the community...The price of labour neither is, nor ought to be, governed by the demand...yet we believe the legislature might adopt regulations which would make the demand both regular and increasing."[81] The last presumably referred to the war or to the weavers' proposals for industrial regulation.

The weavers also answered the magistrates, in a public statement in the *Manchester Gazette*. (It was refused by the *Mercury* and *Chronicle*.) They flatly denied any connection "with political societies of any description." They declared that the masters' "impositions" upon the workers made the proposition that "wages [were] free and unshackled" merely a common fallacy. They also issued a barrage of statistics and calculations to indicate how their earnings had fallen since 1792.[82] While it would be unrealistic to suppose that there was neither sympathy nor cooperation between the two groups, the campaigns were publicly separate. They had different objectives, and they arose from different kinds of organizations—established local trade societies with treasuries on the one hand, and a new and narrowly focused regional association to finance the weavers' appeal to Parliament on the other.[83]

Despite Bayley's opposition, Parliament passed the Arbitration Act, which provided procedures for arbitrating disputes between weavers and masters.[84] Hundreds of weavers took advantage of its provisions to settle individual disputes, but the masters soon found ways to evade them. While the Act was in effect, the magistrates settled most of the appealed cases in favor of the weavers. But an incident in December 1800 both revealed Bayley's hostility to the weavers and made his anxieties about their insubordination something of a self-fulfilling prophecy. Several hundred weavers at Whitefield had tried to use the arbitration procedures for collective bargaining by presenting their claims simultaneously. The case was referred to Bayley. He delivered a forceful sermon to the hundred or hundred and fifty weavers who crowded the courtroom. He had been on the bench for thirty years, he said, and he was ready to hear any complaint a weaver might make. The present laws were sufficient to protect them against their masters. Bayley "tossed the Act of Parliament by" and said, "You are many of you Weavers, I would have you not to mind Mr. Holcroft, or this new Law"; further, he advised them "to go home and mind their Business and not be persuaded by cunning, artful, and designing men against their own interest." James Holcroft, secretary of the Weavers' Association and the organizer-arbitrator in this case, could only reply "that he was not to be intimidated by anything which was said from the Bench."[85] Such a stinging demonstration of class antagonism in the context of war, rising food prices, and falling wages went far to reinforce the connections between hardship and politics that had begun to be widely appreciated during the petitioning for peace in 1795.[86]

While social alienation prevented the magistrates from taking any conciliatory actions toward the weavers, their reactions to the weavers' campaign were also strongly influenced by the tide of sedition in south Lancashire that rose with the price of bread in 1800–1801, for the weavers' frustrations were flowing into wider currents of political disaffection. By the middle of 1800, Justice Bayley was reporting great suffering among the poor of Manchester who were "supposing they starve amidst plenty." As I have said, Bayley himself had received a violent threatening letter.[87] As the crisis deepened, bitter threats against the magistrates and government mingled with cries for bread. "The public eye is daily saluted with sedition in chalk characters on our walls," wrote Bayley, "and whether the subject regards Bread or Peace, NO KING introduces it. This is a shocking idea to be thus familiarized."[88] The "coalition between Jacobinism and distress" alarmed the Reverend Bancroft of Bolton, and Bayley wrote that the Jacobins blamed the scarcity on the war and not on the seasons. "This scarcity is the great mountain from which they build, and this calamity they boldly attribute to our government," wrote Justice Singleton of Wigan.[89] By the spring of 1801, the king and the Constitution were cursed in the public houses and on the streets. In Manchester, "the subversion of government by a complete revolution [was] the general subject of conversation among the lower orders," and Bayley hoped that the government would promptly take measures to relieve the poor.[90]

But besides such general ferment, more alarming forms of organized discontent began to sprout from the fertile soil of dearth. The magistrates confronted a spectrum of evidence ranging from florid spies' reports of revolutionary conspiracies to public demonstrations of popular support for political reforms, which seemed quite radical in that climate of alarm and repression. The question of the extent of the Jacobin underground in Lancashire cannot be fully examined here, but at least its relationship to the weavers' campaign can be indicated.[91]

At one extreme, the more lurid spies' reports tended to be vague in details and to speak of plans for a general rising, of pikes secreted in Birmingham and Sheffield, and of great numbers under oath, ready to seize the arms of the Volunteers and to attack the banks.[92] Somewhat more plausible accounts of radical activity around Ashton and Oldham came from an informer "A," through an intermediary to Justice W. R. Hay of Dukinfield. "A" was a long-standing acquaintance of both his supervisor and of some of the radicals, and his reports contain the prosaic detail that one would expect of earnest working-class insurrectionaries. "A"'s friends had their French correspondents, their comrades in Southwark, and their vague plans to seize the arms of the Manchester Volunteers, but they were reticent rather than grandiose about their political goals and principles, beyond their aim to "overturn the Tyranny." Their society claimed 1,531 members in branches in Manchester, Bury, Bolton, Oldham, Rochdale, and Glodwick Hamlet. "A" attended a meeting of delegates who came from seven towns to the Seven Stars public house in working-class Manchester to discuss the strength of the society and to sing political parodies of the Psalms.[93]

How far we should accept "A"'s description of these rather conventional insurrectionaries is hard to say, but more concrete evidence of radical activity exists. One William Gallant of Bolton, twenty-three years old, was arrested in March 1801 and convicted and hanged in September for attempting to seduce two dragoons from their sworn allegiance. Drunk, young, and naive he may have been, but in his final confession he did not deny his offense. He only regretted that he had fallen in with the "wicked, ill-designing" men who pushed him forward.[94]

Furthermore, a radical Reform society or societies was connected with seven men who were convicted of administering unlawful oaths in separate episodes in Bolton and Chadderton. The oaths were probably those of the United Englishmen. The seven were transported. One of the Bolton men, William Moor, wrote thirty years later (when he had nothing to gain or lose) that his society had been "the Political Union for a Reform in Parliament," and that the oath committed members to seek "an equal representation of all the people of England." When the Bolton men were hauled off to Lancaster Castle, a crowd gathered and began to stone their military escort, an earnest of growing popular sympathy for the secret societies.[95]

Such societies may have been the instigators of several large meetings in the spring of 1801 at which both politics and the weavers' plight were discussed. At the Britannia Inn in Manchester on March 16, the constables broke up a meeting of 150 men "of the lowest order," 50 of whom were arrested. This meeting apparently discussed a petition for redress of grievances: the war, high food prices, and wage regulation. The magistrates could not obtain evidence of anything more offensive, and they were ultimately forced to release the prisoners.[96]

Three larger meetings took place on the moors, near Manchester's satellite cotton towns. On the first Sunday morning in April, several thousand "sons of labor" with "meagre countenances and tattered clothes" gathered at Tandle Hill near Royton, between Oldham and Rochdale. This meeting passed nine resolutions that were printed in the *Manchester Gazette*. They protested that the war had caused high food prices; that it had enriched contractors at the expense of the laboring poor; that the heavy national debt and taxes were borne by the poor while the landed and commercial interests flourished as rents and prices rose; and that the fall in wages meant starvation for "nineteen out of twenty of the community." Only "complete" remedies would suffice: "an immediate peace, a thorough reform in the representative system, and a reduction of the national debt."[97]

A month later the magistrates expected another meeting at Tandle Hill, but it was held instead at Bucton Castle, four miles east of Ashton, on May 3. This meeting drew more than five thousand people, some coming from Manchester, twelve miles away, with hopes ranging from peace to revolution. A man read a paper attacking the national debt and declaring taxation for the war an unjust burden on working people. He promised "if they were all of his mind and stick to him, he would lower things very soon." The magistrates and cavalry dispersed the crowd before the meeting could really get under way.[98]

A third meeting at Rivington Pike near Bolton drew only about two hundred people, apparently because of growing repression: the arrests of those suspected of sedition the previous two months, the reported activities of spies, and the discharge of "Jacobin" workers by several employers.[99] The Royal Horse Artillery and Justice Fletcher broke up the meeting before dawn and arrested twenty-two people, including sixteen weavers, together with two spinners, two coal miners, a mason, and a brazier. The cavalry, returning with their prisoners, found that the "rioters" had blocked the road with boulders.[100]

The social crisis of 1799–1801 in south Lancashire promoted a rapid and crucial transition in the weavers' perceptions and capacity for collective action. Their inability to bargain collectively in Manchester either as food rioters or as workers had forced them to look beyond the framework of community politics and prompted them to form the Weavers' Association for the limited objective of industrial legislation. The shortages of 1800 certainly aggravated their suffering, for workers were forced to sell their belongings to buy food,[101] but their frustration also increased with the inadequacy of the Arbitration Act and the hostility of the magistrates, which propelled them to make contact with more radical politicians and with their more far-reaching analyses. By 1801 the weavers' grievances had taken their place beside the war, parliamentary Reform, and bread prices on the agenda of popular public meetings, and the weavers themselves attended these political discussions. Indeed, the weavers' campaign for an amendment of the Arbitration Act had been "a means of combining and stimulating the people" to attend the mass meetings on the moors.[102] In sum, the weavers' growing unity was a product of hardship, of the experience of class antagonism in industrial relations, of the ideological context provided by popular radicalism, and of the character of community politics in Manchester.

The alarmist Colonel Fletcher of Bolton believed that "the cotton weavers' [second] petition to Parliament [was] of Jacobin origin," and that its proponents actually hoped for its defeat so that more weavers would convert to radicalism.[103] If Fletcher oversimplified by conflating the agitations, it would be equally unrealistic to draw too sharp a dividing line between the clandestine networks and insurrectionary plots described by the spies and the open protests of those attending the large meetings, with their petitions and program for industrial and political reform. The aims of the Reformists and of the underground wings of the popular movements were similar enough and the demonstrations of popular support for the radicals broad enough that groups like those described by "A" might well have existed on the fringes of the larger Reformist movement.[104] Revolution, parliamentary Reform, effective legislation, or simple collective bargaining were all equally hopeless and "radical" in Manchester and the cotton district in 1801. The significance of the Jacobin underground does not lie in its real potential for insurrection, for the difficulty of even traditional forms of collective action and the physicial strength of the authorities were only too obvious.[105] Rather, the boasts about revolution were, like threatening letters, "reveries of rebellion":[106] "revolutionaries" might win plebeian sympathy and shelter (even if not commitment to insurrection) because their plots served a vital psychological function, leavening the more sober (but futile) movements with wishful fantasies and establishing a kind of emotional counter-theater to the authority of the rulers. Radical— which is to say seditious—ferment was, like an inkblot, hard and tangible at the center and fuzzy at the edges. And both plebs and magistrates might project their antagonistic fantasies upon it.

Finally, it is worth remarking that the stronger and more overt organized support for weavers and radicals came from the cotton towns that were satellites of Manchester, not from Manchester itself. All of the weavers' public addresses, the chief officers and most of the delegates of the Weavers' Association, and the majority of the weavers' witnesses before parliamentary committees be- tween 1800 and 1808 came from Bolton and the smaller towns.[107] Moreover, the three mass outdoor meetings in the spring of 1801 had taken place on the moors near Bolton, Rochdale and Oldham, and Ashton, eight miles and more from Manchester, though to be sure it was safer to meet in the countryside, away from the magistrates and their troops.

Although the cotton industry produced similar class relation- ships in Manchester and in the smaller towns, the greater intimacy of the satellite towns made it easier for people to act together. Bolton, the next largest town, was growing more rapidly than Manchester, but it was less than one-fourth as large. Bolton had long been a semi-autonomous weaving center, so most of its industry, unlike Manchester's, was concentrated in one or two trades.[108] Partly for this reason the Bolton and Bury weavers boasted the only collective agreement between masters and weav- ers in Lancashire in the 1790s, and the organizing involved in that arrangement may have produced experienced leaders for the larger Weavers' Association.[109] The friendly societies also enrolled a much higher proportion of the population in Bolton and the other satellite towns than in Manchester.[110] As a further suggestion of plebeian autonomy, the only worries about the reliability of local Volunteer corps as riot police were voiced by gentlemen of the satellite towns, not Manchester.[111]

Perhaps the weavers in Bolton were more active because closer relations between weavers, manufacturers, and magistrates both aggravated the weavers' grievances and helped sustain their campaign. The last weavers' address from Bolton in 1800 had complained bitterly of the "sudden transition" of upstart masters from "penury to opulence," thanks to the unreasonable level of the employers' profits,[112] yet established manufacturers like Thomas Ainsworth of Bolton also came around by 1808 to support a minimum wage so that the instability caused by the speculations of "men of little capital" would be eliminated.[113] It was at Bolton that the Reverend Bancroft, suspicious as he was of the Weavers' Association, met with the weavers' officers at the very beginning of their campaign and offered to convene a meeting of the "eminent Manufacturers" to seek a compromise.[114] It was in the satellite towns where more orderly, though often bitter, food riots took place in 1795 and 1800–1801.[115] Thus, although the weavers had the difficult task of looking beyond parochial issues to encompass the entire regional labor market in their organization, the local bases of collective action already existing in the smaller cotton towns eased the way.

Between 1801 and 1808 the weavers were almost continuously active in petitioning Parliament for labor legislation. Agitation for an amendment to the Arbitration Act had already figured in the public meetings on the moors in the spring of 1801. By Feburary 1802 the weavers of Lancashire, Cheshire, Yorkshire, and Derbyshire had submitted their petition.[116] They immediately found the mercantile might of Manchester arrayed against them. The same merchants' elite that had dominated the political affairs of Manchester held a series of public meetings beginning in February 1802 and organized a special committee led by C. F. Brandt to oppose the amendment and, if possible, to repeal the act. The committee was instructed to communicate with other cotton towns, and it spent £2,000 to vigorously oppose the weavers.[117] In the following year, several petitions came from manufacturers for and against the legislation. A Select Committee took evidence from both masters and men, and in 1804 an amending Arbitration Act was passed. It proved to be useless to the weavers, as masters evaded its provisions and magistrates failed to enforce it. In 1805 the manufacturers of Bolton met with the weavers' leaders to petition Parliament jointly for legislation to regulate wages. Once more the magistrate Fletcher of Bolton worried that "the disaffected" were busily and ominously organizing the weavers. He also believed the weavers' campaign and disaffection were connected with agitation against the Corn Law of 1804. The weavers' application to Parliament in 1806 got nowhere because of a change of the ministry. Early in 1807 a petition signed by 130,000 weavers of Lancashire, Cheshire, Yorkshire, and Derbyshire again asked for legislation to regulate wages.[118]

Trade depression stimulated renewed debate on war and peace in 1807, especially after August, when Napoleon began to enforce his blockade of the Continent, and in December when the United States closed its ports to foreign commerce. By 1808 weavers were earning an appalling average of only six shillings a week, about half of what they had earned in 1799. Partisan politics revived in Manchester and south Lancashire. In Manchester a group of younger Reformers failed to get the boroughreeve to call a public meeting, but they circulated a peace petition that gathered forty to fifty thousand signatures. Joseph Hanson, one of those Reformers, published a long statement that blamed the misery of the workers on the war.[119]

In December 1807, the idea that hardship might be eased by political change was revived near Bolton. A group of men known to be connected with the Jacobin agitation of 1801 promoted a meeting near Oldham on Christmas Day that passed resolutions for peace by acclamation. The audience of "the industrial class of manufacturers" was estimated to be ten thousand strong by sympathizers, but only five hundred by spies. That meeting also condemned withholding information about popular distress from the king. At about the same time, a "treasonable paper" was picked up on the road near Bolton that explicitly connected the war with hardship. It began, "No King No War The Downfall of the Trade will be the Downfall of the Nation," and it added, "if there was no King & a new set of Ministers... the working People might Earn a Living."[120]

Early in 1808, Bolton manufacturers were blaming the war for low wages, in an effort to enlist the weavers' support for a peace petition. The weavers, however, were suspicious. The Bolton Weavers' Committee publicly warned weavers that the people petitioning for peace were the same employers responsible for wage reductions. They feared that the peace petition might be a trap and that any such evidence of "a disloyal or riotous spirit would blast every prospect of relief from Government." Justice Fletcher was pleased that the Weavers' Committee had detached themselves from the peace petitioners, but he warned the government to reinforce that development by receiving the weavers' latest proposal sympathetically: "To secure these Men by Attention to their Application... will tend much to give a right Biass to the

Weavers' Affections both on this and future Occasions."[121] Nevertheless, the Bolton peace petition contained thirty thousand signatures, no doubt many of them from weavers who had drawn their own conclusions about the war and wages.[122]

Hence the weavers petitioned Parliament for minimum-wage legislation in February 1808 in an atmosphere of taut political expectancy as well as acute hardship. The weavers sent witnesses to Parliament financed by loans from the friendly societies. Many Lancashire manufacturers and some London merchants also supported the application. For indeed a minimum wage might have checked cut-throat competition at the weavers' expense and thereby stabilized the industry's and weavers' hours.[123] The climax came when the government half-heartedly introduced a minimum wage bill on May 19 and then withdrew it.[124] But now nearly a decade of organization enabled the weavers to go beyond petitioning to collective action.

The failure of the minimum wage bill touched off the great weavers' strike of 1808. The news of the bill's defeat reached Manchester on Sunday, May 22. On Tuesday morning two thousand weavers gathered at St. George's Fields on the outskirts of the town. They waited outside a public house where their "delegates" were meeting. They ignored the admonition of the magistrates and the deputy constable to disperse, replying "they would rather die on the field, than go home and see their families starved; they could not live on the wages they had."[125] Despite their peaceful though stubborn demeanor, the boroughreeve, constable, and magistrates perceived them as a "mob" and as "an alarming and tumultuous assemblage of misguided and disappointed Weavers." Accordingly, the magistrates called out the cavalry, read the Riot Act proclamation, and after waiting an hour, ordered the dragoons and constables to disperse the weavers. The senior magistrate even warned the Home Office not to believe any exaggerated accounts it might receive.[126]

The next morning the strike began in earnest. Small parties of strikers collected shuttles (the key part of the loom, for it carried the bobbins of weft thread) to force weavers to leave work and close their shops. More than five thousand weavers assembled peacefully, again at St. George's Fields, their number perhaps now swollen by recruits from the country. They told the boroughreeve "they could not live on their wages; and it was time to endeavor to get them mended." He replied that they had chosen a wrong method and that if they did not disperse quietly, he "should consider them a mob, and treat them as such." He did consent to set up a meeting of their delegates with the magistrates, at which the weavers appealed for help in starting negotiations with the masters. The boroughreeve had at least negotiated courteously with the crowd, whom he called "my lads." But the magistrates refused even to parley with the weavers' delegates. They declared: "It is the opinion of the magistrates that under the existing circumstances they cannot treat with men deputed from a large body of men, assembled in a tumultuous and unlawful manner. If they disperse, and go peaceably and quietly to their homes, the magistrates will take their situation into consideration [and] be ready to attend to any representation which may be made in a proper and peaceable manner." When their delegates read that reply, a murmur ran through the crowd. They said "they might as well remain there and be killed, as go home and see their families starved."[127]

The boroughreeve then summoned the magistrates and the cavalry, but the crowd held its ground, encouraged by the appearance of their most prominent sympathizer, the radical manufacturer Joseph Hanson. When Hanson rode onto the field, the crowd huzzaed so loudly that Hanson fell off his startled horse and soon left the field. Near nightfall the magistrates read the Riot Act proclamation without effect. They then ordered the dragoons to "scour" the ground. The cavalry made several furious charges across the field. One man who threw a brickbat at a dragoon's horse was instantly shot and killed, and a few others were injured, one critically. One Manchester historian compared that event to Peterloo: "It was the 16th of August 1819 on a smaller scale."[128]

The killing, and even more generally their recourse to force, threw into sharp relief the magistrates' complete estrangement from the weavers. Not a trace of sympathy for the weavers can be found in the reports of the three Manchester magistrates active during the strike.[129] In part their hostility to the collective organization of the weavers was rooted in a pattern of class response. As I have shown in Chapter 3, merchants and manufacturers had long been prominent members of the Manchester bench.[130] The senior magistrate, R. A. Farington, was probably a gentleman, but he seems to have been a merchant at one time.[131] Farington and J. Silvester, another magistrate, had also been staunch members of the "Church and King" establishment that included most of Manchester's manufacturers and most of the other active justices in the 1790s. Indeed their hostility was increased because of suspicions, which they had also expressed in 1799–1801, that the strike might have political undertones. The Tory Silvester suspected "an organized system of keeping the Weavers afloat to obtain Petitions for Peace." Farington feared that "the dissatisfied part of the weavers, or perhaps their leaders, had an object in view beyond an advance in wages, something of a political nature."[132]

Finally, the magistrates acted out of fearful incomprehension, which reflected the anonymity and alienation of Manchester's community politics. The senior magistrate, R. A. Farington, confessed his "want of knowledge of the manufactory." He dismissed the weavers as "misguided," "ill-judging," and he declared that collective bargaining was impossible. He worried about "the vast populousness of [the town and neighborhood and] the very unprotected state in which a vast property is necessarily placed."[133]

Accordingly, he and his colleagues treated the strike as a problem of public order, rather than as an occasion for mediation. "Peaceable," that is, individual and deferential, appeals for relief would be heard, but any attempt to act collectively was tantamount to riot and would be sternly suppressed.[134] Farington repeatedly emphasized that the peace of the town depended on the presence of the cavalry, and the magistrates used patrols made up of cavalrymen, and constables to protect nonstriking weavers bringing in cloth.[135] They also offered a reward of fifty guineas for evidence against any who might interfere with "industrious weavers," and they threatened to prosecute such interference as felony.[136] Significantly, neither before nor during the strike were public relief subscriptions mounted as they so often had been in the past. The weavers' suffering before the strike seems to have been ignored, while charity during the strike would only prolong the weavers' resistance. Instead, the authorities rewarded the "well-disposed" weavers who returned to work with "a very liberal distribution of money issued from the parish table." Such relief payments to strikebreakers were a perversion of patronage and, with the cavalry to "maintain the proper ascendancy,"[137] served only to deepen the lines of class conflict.

The punishment of the Manchester rioters was not severe, but it was certainly ample demonstration of the authority of the law. Many strikers were taken into custody, and more than thirty were bound over on recognizances to appear at the July Quarter Sessions. Most were discharged on bonds to keep the peace, but nine were found guilty of riot and picketing and were sentenced to between one week and one month in prison.[138]

The Manchester magistrates did, however, display their vindictiveness by their showcase prosecution of Joseph Hanson. The punishment of Hanson also allowed them to settle old personal and political scores. Hanson had been a member of the Reformer's opposition party in 1795 and 1798; he was a commander of a Volunteers corps, and in 1804 he had become embroiled in a bitter personal conflict over military seniority with J. L. Phillips, a pillar of the establishment. That same year, Hanson stood as a radical candidate for Parliament against the landed and industrial interests of the borough of Preston and committed himself to promote the weavers' minimum wage bill if elected. He was defeated. Later that year he was a leader of the peace movement, and he resigned his commission in the Volunteers to protest the continuation of the war.[139]

At the weavers' second public meeting in Manchester, on May 25, Hanson rode dramatically onto the field. He told the weavers that he was sorry they had lost their bill, that his father had made his fortune from the weavers' labors, and that they should stick to their cause and he would continue to support them provided they dispersed peacefully. His accusers charged that Hanson had also said that "neither Nadin nor none of his faction should put them off the ground that day."[140] Joseph Nadin, the deputy constable, was a vigorous enemy of radicals.[141] The reference to "Nadin and his faction," whether or not Hanson actually said it, shows that the animus against Hanson went beyond personal hostility and "treason" to his class, and also that the partisan conflict of 1807–1808 colored the magistrates' handling of the weavers' agitation.

Hanson was tried in May 1809, fined £100, and imprisoned for six months.[142] But his popularity had been confirmed. When he visited Preston a month after the strike, he was greeted with wild acclamation. After his trial, nearly forty thousand weavers donated a penny each to present him with a gold cup. The liberal Manchester historian of the next generation, Archibald Prentice, declared, "The effects of this ill-advised prosecution were long and injuriously felt. It introduced that bitter feeling of employed against employers which was manifested in 1812, 1817, 1826."[143]

Even more striking than the magistrates' repression, the clandestine and impersonal conduct of the strikers in Manchester contrasted sharply with overt actions by crowds to enforce the strike in the country. Despite, or perhaps because of, the severe police measures in Manchester, the strike was effective for about three weeks. But after the killing at St. George's Fields, there were no more mass meetings in Manchester. The town remained quiet on the surface, and great numbers of weavers strolled peacefully around the streets in small groups. Nevertheless, thousands of looms were silenced in the town and its neighborhoods. "Negotiations" between weavers and masters took place not over a bargaining table but by an exchange of offers and demands contained in handbills posted on the walls or printed in the newspapers.[144] The strike was apparently directed by a committee that met secretly. The magistrates' discovery and arrest of the committee members helped bring the strike to an end.[145] Most significant, the strike was enforced covertly—by threats and handbills posted on walls, and by small flying squads of strikers who rushed into shops to take the shuttles from those they found at work before the patrols could catch them. In many cases, the work of nonstriking weavers was destroyed by "utter strangers."[146]

The strike was surprisingly successful. A week after it began, the manufacturers met and offered a 20 percent wage increase. At first the more militant weavers rejected the offer, and held out for the full 33⅓ percent they had initially demanded.[147] They continued to enforce the work stoppage for several weeks. But after a month, the majority of weavers had returned to work, apparently satisfied with the moderate increase in wages.[148]

Crowd action was not a part of the Manchester strike until the bitter end. However, near the end of June, large groups of the last holdouts gathered in the neighborhood of St. George's Fields and stopped all the looms in the area. They burned several "respectable" manufacturers in effigy and prevented weavers from leaving or entering the town with work. Vitriol was squirted on the looms through broken windows or dropped into workers' cloth-bags, and some pieces of cloth were cut in the looms. Women were reported to be particularly "turbulent and mischievous" and intolerably insolent to the soldiers and constables, "confident of deriving impunity from their sex." Patrols of dragoons were able to suppress the disturbances after three days. That desperate attempt to revive the strike, the only episode of crowd violence in Manchester, was said to be the work of the Irish.[149] The neighborhood had some years earlier been an Irish ghetto.[150]

Indeed Irish clannishness and militancy may have been one of the strands that helped to knit together the weavers' organization. Certainly the magistrates repeatedly singled out the Irish as the most militant supporters of the strike. Another strand may have been personal contacts in neighborhoods, for many of the arrested weavers lived near each other. And of course the friendly societies, though few were made up entirely of weavers, gave the strikers financial support and probably some solidarity that facilitated the collective action.[151]

Perhaps these specific bonds, together with nearly a decade of campaigns for various petitions, helped establish some footings for collective action in the great chaotic town. Certainly the Manchester weavers' combination had performed an impressive feat in sustaining the strike as long and as solidly as they did. The secretive, almost anonymous, conduct of the strike in Manchester was not simply the result of intimidation by the cavalry patrols, as witness the crowds' defiance at the beginning and end of the strike. Rather, it reflects the newer, more impersonal form of association that was to grow up in new industrial cities where the social framework for disciplined direct action by crowds could not exist, and where the ripening of a supportive, working-class culture and community was still years in the future.

Throughout the rest of the cotton district, the actions of the strikers reflected a spectrum of types of communities in which they worked.[152] In the larger towns like Stockport and Bolton, the weavers assembled in nonviolent mass meetings like the early ones in Manchester.[153] But in the middle-sized towns and in the villages, the strike was enforced by overt, disciplined crowd action. Groups of one hundred or two hundred weavers marched through town and country collecting shuttles to stop work. Many of the weavers seemed to be as eager to surrender the shuttles as the strikers were to collect them. For the most part, these were transactions between neighbors. The crowds allowed their victims to mark their shuttles for identification and told them they might have them back "next Wednesday." They stored the shuttles nearby so they could be reclaimed without difficulty. At least one magistrate found that the victims later refused to identify those who had taken their shuttles.[154]

Unlike the Manchester strikers, the country weavers also confronted particular employers personally. At Oldham and Heap, crowds forced leading manufacturers to sign wage agreements.[155] The crowds were not altogether good-natured. Several minor assaults occurred, and at Oldham and Blackburn the weavers broke the manufacturers' windows. At Oldham, however, the strikers' leaders publicly apologized for the broken windows of manufacturers who had sympathized with the weavers.[156] Only one riot ended in more serious damage. At Rochdale, the crowd progressed from gathering shuttles to stoning the magistrates' office, then to rescuing the bags of shuttles and the prisoners taken by the special constables to the jail, and finally to burning the jail itself.[157] Rochdale was one of the most populous weaving parishes. In 1795 the magistrates had suppressed a food riot with needless bloodshed, so social relations there were peculiarly embittered. For the most part, though, the country riots were spontaneous and focused, based upon personal contacts and antagonisms, and reminiscent of communal food riots or machine breaking rather than of the more systematic and impersonal strike in Manchester.

The country magistrates were not generally any more sympathetic to the weavers than their Manchester counterparts. Social relations between workmen and masters in the smaller towns in the cotton industry did not differ that much from those in Manchester, though the smaller towns had fewer dragoons with which to break up the crowds. One magistrate in the country near Manchester did speak with a crowd of strikers and promised to report their suffering to the government. The Mayor of Wigan also recognized the extreme suffering of the weavers, but he attributed it to bad trade. He sought to make a legal example of one of his prisoners by prosecuting him for felony, which "would have great effect on the minds of the people [so] as to bring them to immediate subjection."[158]

At least one country squire, however, resorted to a display of old-fashioned personal influence. Sir Richard Clayton was a crusty old justice of the peace in the village of Adlington near Chorley. When the strike began, he decided to exert his "impressive and extensive" personal influence to keep the "entire peace of ye neighborhood," a populous and extensive district. Sir Richard's policy was "firmness and resolution in conjunction with some civility." He thrived on personal confrontation. He visited and admonished those of his neighbors he thought most likely to become unruly. He twice persuaded crowds of weavers to disperse, and from one weaver he even elicited the wonderful promise to notify him immediately "if any rioters should come from a distance." When a crowd from another neighborhood collected shuttles at the nearby village of Standish, he went the next morning "without a single attendant" to the house where the shuttles had been stored, made a "peremptory demand" for them, and restored them to their owners. Sir Richard's confidence in his authority over his neighbors remained unshaken.[159] There is little sign in his reports that this amiable dinosaur had any notion of what his neighbors were up to and why, but his robust reliance on old-fashioned personal interest and influence makes a refreshing contrast to the anxious and impersonal police measures of the Manchester magistrates.

More generally, the weavers' strike of 1808 was the culmination of nearly a decade of impressive organizational effort by the weavers' committee. To bargain effectively, the weavers had to conceive and concert their action across the whole regional labor market. Their perceptions widened from an individual to a collective level, and from particular to systemic issues through their own work experience, through the ideology that the radicals provided to connect hardship with politics, and through their collective experience of class alienation in the apathy and hostility of magistrates, manufacturers, and Parliament. But beyond perception, the strike of 1808 required the cooperation of both the "older," more organic solidarities of the country towns and the newer, more impersonal networks of that vast Babylon, Manchester. The strike of 1808 was a transitional movement that reveals how class evolved out of both old and new forms of community politics.

7

Reprise: 1812

The events of 1812 in Manchester were a reprise that finally wove together the motifs of popular mobilization during the wars: political alienation, hunger, and the weavers' frustration. The year 1812 was a nightmare year for the rulers of England and for the magistrates of Lancashire. Harvest failures in 1810 and especially in 1811 sent food prices rocketing upward. Economic warfare with France and America brought acute depression to the cotton trade from 1810 to 1812. Luddite machine-breaking riots began in Nottingham in 1811, and in 1812 the West Riding croppers' resistance to labor-saving machinery climaxed in April with a bloody battle at Cartwright's Rawfolds mill. The merchants and magistrates of Manchester were in one month confronted with a riot at the Exchange Hall, a week of violent food rioting in Manchester and the satellite towns, and armed assaults on factories in nearby Middleton and at the Westhoughton mill near Bolton. The horror deepened at the end of April with the assassination of the manufacturer William Horsfall near Huddersfield, and in May with the assassination of the prime minister in the lobby of the House of Commons, an event that was greeted with popular rejoicing in Bolton and in several other English towns.[1]

Since 1808, the weavers' thwarted pursuit of industrial remedies for their low wages had become channeled much more directly into support for radical political reform. That process has recently been reconstructed in detail, and only the milestones need be remarked here.[2] After the great strike of 1808, prosperity returned to the weaving trade in 1809–1810, but only temporarily.

From 1809 onward, a Lancashire-Cheshire weavers' association was revived, especially in Bolton and Manchester, and became linked with Carlisle and the Scottish textile centers. In 1810, nearly eighteen thousand people signed a congratulatory address from Manchester to Sir Francis Burdett, Radical Member of Parliament for Westminster, who was imprisoned by order of the Speaker of the House of Commons for challenging the right of the House to jail a radical for contempt. In May 1811, a public meeting in Manchester launched a petition for relief from unemployment and dearth that was signed by forty thousand people. Parliament's utter failure to respond stimulated a campaign for peace and parliamentary Reform by weavers and by a committee of the Manchester trades, who approached several gentlemen of the opposition party for support. The most important fruit of that activity was a pointed address in November 1811 on parliamentary Reform. In the words of John Knight's famous paragraph to the weavers, "Had you possessed 70,000 votes for the election of members...would your application have been treated with such indifference, not to say inattention?"

The social ferment of 1812 extended beyond the campaign for Reform. But strikingly, the impulse toward collective violence seemed to be stronger in the satellite towns and villages than in Manchester. By the winter of 1811–1812, magistrates in the Manchester area were receiving reports of insurrectionary plans and, particularly, of popular intentions to attack factories, especially at Stockport. On Sunday, April 5, 1812, delegates from the weaving towns met in Salford and agreed on a plan to attack factories in Manchester, Bolton, and Stockport on the following Thursday, April 9. But on Monday, April 6, a larger committee of representatives of the Manchester districts rejected the plan.[3] Two weeks later, rioters attacked the Middleton factory and the Westhoughton mill near Bolton. However, no industrial rioting took place in Manchester in 1812. In rejecting the plan to attack the factories, the Manchester delegates doubtless considered the troops quartered in the town and the difficulty of launching crowd action in "disorganized" Manchester. It was also easier for spies to infiltrate a large committee representing the many trades of the town than a more compact and intimate committee in a one-industry satellite town.[4]

The Manchester trades' meeting did help set the stage for the Exchange Hall riot of April 8. The Tory party in Manchester had foolishly requested the boroughreeve to convene a public meeting on April 8 to express support for the Tory government retained by the Prince Regent, the future George IV, on his assumption of full royal powers.[5] The retention of the unpopular Tory government had dashed popular hopes that a Regent might install the Whigs and a new policy. The Manchester Tories had counted blindly on the neutrality, if not the support, of the workers.[6] The well-to-do Reformers in Manchester, however, resolved to turn out enough of their sympathizers to defeat the Tories' resolutions. They diligently circulated handbills in the town and countryside decrying the "distress and wretchedness unexampled." They called upon "those inhabitants who do not wish for an increase of taxes and poor rates—an advance in the price of provisions—a scarcity of work, and a reduction of wages... to go to the meeting... at the Exchange and oppose the 154 persons who have called you together." At the same time the Reformers asked the secret Manchester workers' committee to help them mobilize opposition to the Tories.[7] This may have been a defensive measure to co-opt Manchester's plebeian radicals so that they would not join forces with those who were promoting the alarming increase of sedition in the countryside. By the end of the month in which the Exchange riot and several "Luddite" incidents elsewhere had occurred, the Reformers' *Manchester Gazette* was urging the laboring classes to shun "this bloody league" and to remember that "the interests of the rich and the poor are not in opposition to each other."[8] Class anxieties had emerged even within the ranks of the Reform party.

The Tories' promotion of their meeting was even more inflammatory. Once again, they raised their eternal cry of "No Popery!": "Should you not this day give your support to the PRINCE REGENT, you may in a very short time, expect a revival of the days of Bloody Queen Mary, where your ancestors were tied to a stake and burnt alive. The active opposers of the present Government have pledged themselves to sanction the Popish Religion, and, as BUONAPARTE is the head of that religion, your universal cry should be "No Pope Buonaparte."[9]

But it soon became clear that they had badly misjudged popular opinion. The Tories tried to recall the storm that now threatened to overwhelm them. The boroughreeve and constables declared that the meeting could not take place since an architect had ruled that the staircase of the Exchange Hall could not bear the weight of the expected crowd. The announcement was both too late and insulting. By noon, thousands of people, including some working-men and boys from the country had gathered in the marketplace around the Exchange. Some entered the building, and finding the main hall locked, gathered in the newsroom to wait. The men and boys in the stately newsroom began mockingly to read the papers to each other, and then to push each other around. That skylarking turned into a sack of the Exchange's newsroom and dining room. First the windows, then the chairs, tables, chandeliers, and maps were smashed. "A valuable portrait" of Colonel Stanley, Member of Parliament for Lancashire, did not escape. At the same time the much larger crowd outside the Exchange passed by acclamation the radical resolutions of the London Common Hall that called for the correction of abuses and the reform of Parliament. The committee of gentlemen Reformers meeting nearby had meanwhile adjourned, not wishing to be implicated in the riot. By one o'clock the magistrates and the cavalry had driven away the crowd by force.[10]

The Tories tried to dismiss the riot as the work of mischievous boys and ignorant men.[11] Even the liberals tried to separate the riot from the more "sober" resolutions of the crowd, and to interpret it as the result of an explosion of frustration over the cancellation of the meeting.[12] But other observers drew a more interesting connection between the riot and the partisan controversy of the past. One "Pacificus" noted that party violence and the cry of "No Popery" had also figured in the riot of December 1795.[13] J. E. Taylor, who was prosecuted for libel in connection with the opposition handbills, later traced a path from the "Church and King" riots of the 1790s through the killing of 1808 and the riot of 1812 to the Peterloo meeting. One old Radical veteran of the witch-hunts of the 1790s chuckled to Archibald Prentice, "But we had no Church-and-King mobs after that!"[14] In a sense, the sentiment was anachronistic: no "Church and King" mobs had been possible in Manchester since the hardship of 1800–1801.

Yet in another sense, the riot was more significant than is often realized. It was a neat counterpoint to the Reform resolutions passed by the crowd outside. That acclamation marked the coming of age, and literally the coming out, of popular Reform sentiment in Manchester. It was the most public mass endorsement yet of Reform in Manchester, a far cry from the nocturnal meetings on the moors in 1801, or even from the smaller meetings of Reformers that gradually emerged from secrecy into the light of day in the summer of 1812.[15] Those meetings in 1812 mark the merging of political radicalism and industrial grievances,[16] and point ahead to the popular Reform campaigns that were to reach their climax at Peterloo.

But the riotous part of April 8 also had its role in that process. The sack of the Exchange resembled nothing so much as a theatrical desecration of the very shrine of Manchester's ruling class. The Exchange had only been opened on the king's birthday in 1809, amid great civic celebration. It had been paid for by years of donations from Manchester's commercial elite. More than any other building, it was the capitol of cotton capitalism, "appropriated to the use of merchants meeting on business," "intended to unite as much convenience and elegance as possible."[17] The blasphemy of that commercial tabernacle by the rough and mocking hands of the country bumpkins was the first collective violence against the Tory oligarchy. For the first time, the Reformers rather than the magistrates appeared to "license" public political violence. The sack of the Exchange Hall added expressive overtones of defiant political emancipation to the sober Reform movement, just as "reveries of revolution," though also a fringe, had "psychodramatic" functions for plotters, magistrates, and their audience, the common people.

Perhaps the Exchange Riot loosened some inhibitions against violence in the Manchester area.[18] In the following weeks of economic hardship and growing anger in the countryside, crowds rioted for food in Macclesfield, attacked factories in Stockport, and roamed the countryside at night, extorting money from householders in the week of April 14 and 15.[19] The "Luddite" phase of the Lancashire riots reached its climax the following week in two peculiar episodes. The armed assaults on the Middleton power-loom factory, only seven miles from Manchester, originated in a food riot at Oldham, and they were carried out by colliers and weavers from the Oldham, Saddleworth, and Ashton area.[20] The leaders of the secret Manchester workers' committee barely prevented a contingent from leaving Manchester to join the attack at Middleton on April 21.[21] By contrast, the destruction of the Westhoughton mill near Bolton was unusuallly well disciplined and was probably instigated by *agents provocateurs*, spies paid by the magistrates.[22]

In the meantime, disorderly food rioting broke out in Manchester itself. That rioting manifested the underside of class in Manchester, the less "politicized" alienation that fed the more organized, "progressive" Reform currents. The rioting was more furious though no more coherent than the riots of 1795 and 1800. And the magistrates' response was even more harshly coercive. In the week before the rioting social order was already beginning to break down. The cavalry patrolled the streets at night, but street lamps were broken on the outskirts of the town, and on the night of April 15, a group of people forcibly seized some bread from a shop in a working-class district of Newton Lane. In the fracas, one poor woman was badly hurt, and eight or nine assailants were arrested.[23] The following Saturday, April 18, a great increase in potato prices provoked "great disorder and confusion" at the Shude Hill potato market, where the riots of 1795 and 1800 had begun. A crowd made up mostly of women demanded that prices be lowered. When the sellers refused, the crowd seized most of the produce in the market and began carrying it home. The civil and military authorities soon intervened, however; they subdued the rioters and arrested several women. Some sort of mutual agreement was struck between buyers and sellers, and potatoes were sold in small quantities at little more than half the original price.[24]

Forced sales and outright seizures of food continued to be intermingled when rioting spread outward on Monday, April 20. In the morning, a crowd of men, women, and children appeared at a shop at Bank Top, on the southeast side of Manchester. They overturned a cart loaded with half a ton of potatoes on its way to the shop and cried out, "We will have them at 8^d a score," but one violent woman, Hannah Smith, swore and exclaimed, "Damn them we will have them for nothing!" She threw down a basket of potatoes, then filled up her apron from the potatoes in the street and ran away. The crowd carried off most of the remaining potatoes. That afternoon Hannah Smith and a crowd of two hundred people appeared at a second shop. They forced the shopkeeper to sell his potatoes at a loss. But Smith, the leader of the crowd, said, "We will not be satisfied with Potatoes," and she threatened to stop butter carts and horses bringing milk to town and reduce the prices of those goods. If the owners would not take that price, she declared she would have butter and milk for nothing, and exulted that she could raise a crowd in a minute. When someone mentioned the name of a constable, she cried out, "I would have him to mind or he will be hanged up I know he will."[25] Violent rioting also took place in working-class Ancoats around the New Cross market. A cartload of meal going out of town was seized and overturned, and the rioters carried the meal away. The tumult caused all the shops in that quarter to close. The cavalry was called out to disperse the crowd after the reading of the Riot Act, and several more women were arrested.

Finally, in still another location that day, rioters broke the doors and windows of a shop in upper Deansgate and stole large quantities of bread, cheese, and potatoes.[26] Once again the military and civil authorities stopped the rioting, and six were arrested. That ended the violence, but rioters were reported to be meeting in the fields, devising fresh plans.[27] In the next few days, "parties of the disaffected and disorderly" called on gentlemen's houses in the neighborhood of Manchester and demanded money and provisions.[28] On April 26 and 27 the town was alarmed by the sudden appearance of thousands of strangers in the town.[29] Two weeks later a gang of "desperate villains" broke into a farmer's house in Newton Lane, beat him and wounded him, and ransacked the house.[30] Such signs of social dissolution continued to appear in Manchester and its hinterland even while radical reformers and insurrectionaries tried to harness popular discontents to their program.[31]

Certainly the magistrates and gentlemen of Manchester perceived the food rioting as part of the much more threatening wave of machine breaking and preparation for insurrection. There is no note of sympathy for the sufferings of the poor in the public pronouncements of the magistrates, nor any invocation of the social responsibility of food sellers. Rather, their reactions took the form of increased cavalry patrols and proclamations promising protection to the farmers and vendors and warning the peaceable inhabitants not to be led astray by the "wicked and evil-minded" instigators of riot.[32] Most significantly, the town fathers had not revived the soup kitchen during the hard winter of 1811–1812. It was only in late April, after the riots, that the soup kitchens were once again called into service, even more obviously than before as an instrument of order rather than humanity.[33]

The arrested food rioters of Manchester were ultimately called upon to expiate Luddism, sedition, and social blasphemy. Although they might have been tried at the ordinary Summer Assizes, they were instead thrown together with the machine breakers and the seditious conspirators of Bolton to be tried in May by the Special Commission that had been created by the government to strike terror into the districts disturbed by Luddism. The presiding judge delivered a portentous charge to the grand jury that "shop breakers" and "food stealers" were guilty of felony without benefit of clergy. Four of the seven Manchester food rioters charged were convicted and hanged. Those food rioters accounted for half the death sentences passed by the Special Commission in Lancashire, even though much more physically violent unrest had occurred at Middleton and Westhoughton. The hapless food rioters were required to serve as a drastic example to the more serious rebels beyond the gentry's reach.[34]

In that year of Luddite rioting in the north, that springtime of both disciplined industrial action and insurrectionary plotting, violence in Manchester was very strikingly neither. The "classic" politics of bargaining by riot had long been obsolete in Manchester. The poor prospects for direct action were manifest in the hesitations of the Manchester workers' committees. Instead, class alienation emerged full-blown in both "rational" Reformist and elemental "expressive" demonstrations. Taken together, the systemic project of Reform, toughened by concrete, immediate experience, and the bitter fury of the riots of 1812 marked out a trajectory for the development of class in Manchester that it would follow for the next three decades.

8

The Agrarian Equipoise

The Duke of Devonshire decided that he must take the view
of his broad and prosperous acres. He did not want his view
spoiled by the sight of any ragged, dirty laborers, and so he
gave orders that his people should all keep themselves indoors
on the day. However, one of the rude hinds crouched under a
hedge with his pig next to the road on which the duke's carriage
must pass. As the duke drove by, this man thrust his pig up,
so that his pig might see His Grace.

—Told by J. H. Plumb, Oxford University, 1965

If one measured the social climate of the eighteenth-century
countryside not in the comfortable mahogany parlors of the gentry
but in village beer-shops and at earthy fairs, if one consulted not
the landowners' diaries and letters to their estate stewards but the
local columns of country newspapers, the anxious reports of
magistrates, and the crowded Quarter Sessions dockets, one
would be most skeptical about the mythology that reciprocal
paternalism and deference held country folk in thrall to the gentry.
When hard times rubbed harmony thin, one might hear or read
alarming "threats dropped by individuals," such as, "To men and
the gentlemen of Culliton [Colyton]: if we have not got things more
reasonable than what we have now you must expect. . .the town
shall be burned level to the ground and the lake shall run with
blood as it doth now with water and we have all drink our
damnation to it 452 of us. . ."[1] Nor was the pastoral care of men of
the cloth always cherished by their flocks. The rector of Whitburn,
for example, was rudely warned, after a row of his young trees had
been cut down one night: "Mr. Simins, take notish of this you have
taken every opportunity to robin the Pour of Whitburn But you
may look for your House Ben seat on fir the first opportunity."[2]

Such threats were chilling not only because they profaned the
paternalism of the gentry, but also because the blazing barn or hay
rick only too often followed them.[3] On occasion, gangs such as the
Comet, or "Cow-meat," Society of Leicestershire or the self-styled
"white boys" of south Yorkshire terrorized the countryside by

maiming cattle or sheep at night.[4] Even in daylight the poor were not always dutifully humble. At Barton, near Lancaster, for example, a justice of the peace tried to reason with a crowd of country folk who had attackeed some carters and farmers with bludgeons, but "they defied all laws, damned the Justices," and threw stones at the magistrate and constables.[5]

Yet despite verbal and physical turbulence, agrarian society was nearly untouched by riot. By *agrarian society*, I mean parishes with populations of no more than fifteen hundred inhabitants, in which a "majority" of the families were employed in agriculture, as reported in the census of 1811.[6] Riot remained a tradition of the towns. Three-fourths of the riots in this period took place in towns of two thousand or more inhabitants (see Table 2); man for man and woman for woman, townspeople were six times more likely to riot than people in parishes having fewer than two thousand people. London, "the infernal wen," had one-fifth of all the riots in this period, and the thirteen largest towns of England together fostered nearly as many, about one in six. Those towns ranged from the new industrial boom towns like Manchester, Birmingham, Sheffield, and Leeds to old regional centers with strong corporate traditions like Norwich, Nottingham, and Bath.[7]

But riots were not at all the product of large-scale urbanization. If one person in six in England and Wales lived in London and the great towns, a similar number dwelt in middling and small towns of from two to twenty thousand inhabitants—the ancient county towns like Carlisle, Chester, Exeter, and Oxford; the old industrial centers like Derby and Leicester and new ones like Walsall and Wigan; and the small weaving or mining towns—which, as a group, were every bit as riotous as the large towns. It is only when we leave the towns behind, including a considerable number of small market towns of between one and two thousand people, that "quiet" returns.

Country people who were chiefly farm laborers very rarely rioted. Only 40 riots, less than 7 percent, of the national sample of 617, can be considered "agrarian riots."[8] Yet well over half the English and Welsh people lived in small villages, and more than one-third of all British families were employed in agriculture.[9] The countryside—excluding rural industrial and mining districts—resembled a great agrarian sea, turbulent below but calm on the surface by contrast with the tumultuous islands of the towns.

The seeming paradox of agrarian folk who were quite demonstratively disrespectful to the gentry yet nonriotous confirms the strong relationship between rioting and community politics. The

Table 2. Riots and towns in England and Wales, 1790–1810.

Towns and places		Riots		Population		Riots per 10,000 people
Population	Number	Number	Percent of total	Total in 1801	Percent of national	
Over 100,000[a]	1	123	19.9	900,000	9.8	1.36
20,000–99,999	13	102	16.5	636,000	6.9	1.60
10,000–19,999	37	66	10.7	478,000	5.2	1.38
5,000–9,999	about 230	69	11.2	1,251,000[b]	13.6	1.50
3,000–4,999		63	10.2			
2,000–2,999		56	9.1			
1,000–1,999	—	46	7.5			
Under 1,000	—	52	8.4	5,903,000	64.4	0.23
Unknown[c]	—	40	6.5			
Total	—	617	100.0	9,168,000	99.9	0.67

Sources: National sample of 617 riots reported in the *London Observer*, the *Morning Chronicle*, the *Annual Register*, or H.O. 42, for 1790–1810. Population figures for London, M. Dorothy George, *London Life in the Eighteenth Century* (London: Penguin Books, 1966), p. 619; for towns over 10,000, B. R. Mitchell and Phyllis Deane, *Abstract of British Historical Statistics* (Cambridge: Cambridge University Press, 1971), pp. 24–27, adjusted for town areas by reference to the census of 1801 (*P. P.*, 1801–1802 [112], VII).

a. London, including Southwark.
b. Derived from figures given in Thomas A. Welton, "On the Distribution of Population in England and Wales . . . ," *Journal of the Royal Statistical Society*, 63 (1900), 560.
c. Includes places for which the census of 1801 gives no population figure, and riots attributed only generally to a county or district like the Forest of Dean.

experiences of Devon and Manchester show that individuals' anger and frustration—that brought on by economic hardship, for instance—are necessary but not sufficient to explain *collective* violence. Once again, the shape and frequency of riots were the product of a community's "political" networks that encouraged or prevented bargaining by direct action. Did villages lack such networks? How did the specific structures of agrarian society foster or, more typically, prevent collective "bargaining" on such issues as food prices, recruiting, wages, and enclosure?

Food riots in the countryside were not only rare but also undisciplined. Of course, rural villages could not so easily muster a crowd of fifty (one of my criteria for riot) but smaller mobs could be just as bitter. When a dozen rioters threw down a load of flour at the Yarpole turnpike gates, for example, their female captain told the carter, "We will not hurt you because you are a servant but if your master was here we would kill him."[10] The few instances when country rioters did invade a town showed that they were not regular participants in either market or political transactions, for neither they nor the magistrates observed the classic "protocol" that food rioters in Devon followed. In December 1795 a crowd of villagers from Little Barton drained a sluice in Mildenhall to stop a boatload of grain bound for Cambridge. After dark, a crowd of 150 people returned to take out all the wheat and left the barley untouched. Their anonymity was not secure, however, since they had been observed, and they were intimidated by the arrests made the next day into returning their booty.[11] That autumn, a similar crowd of three or four hundred people from Diss and the neighboring villages had intercepted a train of wagons carrying grain bound for Ipswich. The crowd agreed to let the barley go, but they insisted that the wheat, the more palatable grain, should remain, and they ripped open one of the sacks to make sure the bargain was being kept. The next day the villagers tried to plead with the magistrate for better wages and lower food prices. He replied vaguely that their complaints would be addressed, especially since Parliament was to meet soon (one can almost hear the laborers snort!), and he urged them to go home. Instead, they moved on to a merchant's granary, which they threatened to break open. They were finally dispersed, not after gaining concessions from the merchant, but after sixty armed gentlemen, constables, and the Suffolk Yeomanry Cavalry had arrived and begun to make arrests.[12]

Apparently, country rioters could not rely on community networks of mutual obligation to support any realistic bargaining. None of the agrarian riots took the classic form in which crowds in the marketplace forced food dealers to lower their prices. In a few instances, villagers seized food and sold it outside the markets, but more often they either took grain without payment or attacked mills, as they did, for instance, at Dereham and Kinginhall in Norfolk, and Sandford in Oxfordshire in 1800.[13]

To some extent, farm laborers were insulated from the markets, because they handled the grain themselves, and in hard times, they could either pilfer it or purchase it directly from their employers.[14] But direct sales were no guarantee against hunger and unrest, for prices that were bargains in times of dearth—7s. or 8s. a bushel—were nevertheless higher than in normal years, and that could still spell disaster for the precarious family economies of the laborers.[15] For example, one Oxfordshire gentleman farmer reported that he and some of his neighbors would sell wheat at 7s. a bushel to their laborers, "but this will not do as a general relief throughout the county." He doubted that supplies would last until the harvest, and he later added, "I have succeeded by the bribe," but "no substitute for wheaten bread can be found. . . our labourers will not be satisfied without it." Moreover, Nathaniel Kent, an authority on Norfolk's agriculture, noted that an increasing number of farmers disdained to sell grain in small quantities to the poor. They preferred to "carry [it] all to the towns. A farmer is even unwilling to sell the labourer who works for him a bushel of wheat. . . the very persons who have the advantage of their labour. . . are often their greatest oppressors; and as the principal farmers of every parish are generally the overseers of the poor, their complaints are frequently made to a deaf ear."[16] Indeed, most of the evidence for direct sales to laborers comes from outside the regions of the most intense capitalist farming of East Anglia and the Home Counties.

Field laborers were also shielded from market fluctuations by receiving parish relief. Under the arrangement known as the Speenhamland plan, relief was given as a supplement to low wages, and the amount of relief was determined by the prevailing price of wheat and the number of children in the laborer's family.[17] Town workers, more directly exposed to the market than poor farm workers, were also more prone to take direct action when food prices became unbearably high. For example, at Winkleigh, Devonshire, six "tradesmen" (artisans, not merchants) forced their way into a sale of cheap grain subsidized by the parish for which they had not been poor enough to qualify. And after a riot at Branscombe in Devon, Lord Rolle explained the "turbulent... spirit" of "the mechanics and manufacturers": they "undoubtedly have more reason to complain than the labourers in husbandry, who...have wheat at 8s. bu. and Barley at 4s." A Surrey magistrate concurred: "the little tradesmen and householders of a country town...certainly feel the pressure of the times more severely than labourers and actual paupers."[18] Nevertheless, being shielded from the market by relief was not an unmixed blessing, for it meant that the farm laborer's income was in part a low wage and in part a payment set by political and administrative means which increased his social subservience.

On one hand, relief and the direct sales of food by employers shielded farm workers from having to deal with the marketplace. On the other hand, they prevented the villagers from mingling in the market-town's society. If the village laborer did go to a market town, he was not likely to find himself among a familiar crowd of neighbors, fellow Volunteers, labor militants, or political allies. Indeed, the weekly round of market days provided townspeople with important social rituals that knit them together, but those rituals were missing from village life.[19]

Furthermore, when food shortages precipitated town-country tensions, farm workers found themselves on the "wrong" side. Unlike workers in town, a farm laborer could rarely afford to challenge the farmer—his employer and probably also the overseer of his parish relief—in the marketplace. The other side of cheaper food—wages subsidized by the poor rates and the opportunity to receive charity—was a stifling dependence, a vulnerability to what E. P. Thompson has called "the revenges of village paternalism." The day laborers of Heacham, Norfolk, resented the practice of "selling [the laborer] flour under the market price, and thereby rendering him an object of a parish rate." It was "an indecent insult on his lowly and humble situation (in itself sufficiently mortifying from his degrading dependence on the caprice of his employer)."[20] And so, when they did rise, villagers preferred to tackle town merchants, millers, or carters, rather than farmers in the marketplace, or to come *into* a town (away from the village) to appeal to a magistrate over the heads of their farmers.[21] Indeed, the threat of being victimized could release powerful emotions in the field hands. At Abergele, Denbighshire, a crowd of a hundred, armed with weapons that were probably reaping hooks, beat an employee of one Mr. Hughes almost to death. A month before, the employee had warned Mr. Hughes's workmen that if any joined a mob "they should be discharged from Mr. Hughes' service."[22]

Such threats, implicit or explicit, were probably the most important factor in denying village laborers the psychological and political leverage necessary for effective rioting. Their vulnerability insured that they did not riot frequently, and that when they did they would act anonymously, in a quick raid into a town, perhaps under cover of night, or by resort to such clandestine forms of protest as threatening letters or arson. Conversely, that anonymity, together with the "desperation of impotence" and the absence of a bargaining framework, helps to account for the laborers' violence of language and action—their lack of restraint in destroying millworks or in seizing grain outright, for instance—once beyond the tight constraints of their own village world.[23]

One cluster of riots may be an exception that proves the rule that farm workers were generally too constrained by village society to riot. In general, agrarian food riots were either isolated incidents or else occurred in the wake of risings by townspeople or industrial workers. The only county to have a significant number of agrarian food riots was Norfolk, with six. Of course, Norfolk was a major grain exporting region, and four of those riots took the form of intercepting shipments of grain, but the rest of East Anglia was also a breadbasket, yet country people rioted only in Yeaxley, St. Ives, and Mildenhall, and the last two were good-sized market towns.[24] Most of Norfolk's country riots clustered in the triangle stretching south from Norwich to Thetford and Diss in part because of the precocious political development of this region. In 1792 it was reported that radical Reform clubs had been established "almost in every village" of Norfolk. At Saxlingham, a town in the disturbed triangle, a radical in a cockade hat drew the direct connection between politics and hardship one October Sunday in 1795. He explained to his "Fellow Citizens" that "the present and unnecessary war" and the "defective representation" were the causes of "poverty and famine." Although he warned them not to riot, the radicals may have furnished the networks and the critical perspective conducive to riot. It was at Larlingford near Thetford in that triangle that rioters were to resist the Militia Bill in 1796.[25]

Perhaps Norfolk's farm workers were already involved in an agricultural system more oriented toward capitalist practices than most of rural England, and therefore providing greater freedom from village "paternalism" and its controls. Although expert writers on agriculture like William Marshall, Arthur Young, and

Nathaniel Kent all commented on the special alertness and industry of Norfolk field hands, wages in Norfolk were lower than those in agricultural counties closer to London. Perhaps the lack of alternative industrial employment helped keep wages down, for domestic spinning around Norwich had declined, and in Norwich, weaving had stagnated. Furthermore investors were buying up small farms in Norfolk to create larger, more profitable ones. Finally, the system of "open" and "closed" parishes was well established in Norfolk by the late eighteenth century.[26] A "closed" parish was one in which local authorities—the squire and the farmers—kept new cottages from being built in order to keep poor laborers from gaining residence (or settlement) and thereby becoming candidates for relief from the local poor-rates. "Closed" villages got their labor from neighboring "open" parishes—rural slums that allowed anyone to settle, and so harbored large working "gangs" of farm servants, but that were too poor to pay much relief. That system of settlement implied a proletarianized work force whose relationships with farmers had been reduced solely to wage payments, and probably also a casualized labor force that provided a pool of "surplus" labor to be on call for intermittent work. In short, the Norfolk workers were "free laborers"—free to take their chances on the market, unencumbered by customary obligations and relations, with farmers and squires, and so, like the proletariat of rural industries, "freer" to riot than the vast majority of their rural counterparts.

Villagers did not often clash with military forces in riots. Soldiers in transit were most frequently quartered in the towns, and the inevitable friction with civilians erupted in a great many public-house affrays as well as some large brawls. But a few rural melees showed what fierceness villagers could display when provoked.

Villagers despised soldiers for the same reasons townspeople did: they perceived them as the dregs of the cities, they dreaded the "repeated assaults and irregularities" perpetrated by the troops, and they hated the Irish, which was the nationality of many of the recruits.[27] Not surprisingly, most of the rural battles with soldiers took place at fairs, where country folk congregated and where tensions were heightened by the carnival spirit and abundant drink, and by sexual rivalry.[28] Before a bitter battle at Wadley Fair, for instance, magistrates had asked the government to move a detachment of "ferocious" "villains," raw Irish recruits whose "savage behavior" had disrupted "the normal intercourse of husbandmen at fairs and markets."[29]

Indeed, the soldiers were usually the aggressors in such fracases, but the country folk were usually the victors, owing to their numbers and a home-ground advantage. At the Farnham, Surrey, Fair in 1800, Irish soldiers tried to form a ring around two sparring civilians. When resisted by the crowd, they began to beat and drive the country people with their bludgeons. But the laborers counterattacked with hop-poles, killed two privates, and seriously wounded twenty others. A coroner's jury ruled the deaths justifiable homicide. At Claxton Fair in 1807, soldiers and their women companions tried to take over a room at the Blacksmith's Arms where country people were dancing. But the mob overwhelmed them, despite their drawn bayonets, and chased them back to their barracks. One private was killed. At the subsequent trial the accused killers were acquitted.[30] The outcomes of such contests only made soldiers more contemptible in civilian eyes, and they may help to suggest why the cavalry, not the infantry, was necessary for controlling crowds.

Villagers had little occasion to riot against recruitment. If they were little involved in the towns' food markets, as consumers or as rioters, so they were also not part of the great urban man markets, where recruits were a commodity like beef, and where press gangs and crimps culled their prey from the teeming waterfronts and slums. The only significant rural resistance to recruitment occurred in 1796–1797 when the government sought to raise a supplementary militia of some sixty-four thousand men. That project provoked a series of riots, beginning with four in Lincolnshire, that spread across Northamptonshire (four riots), Norfolk (two), and Cumberland (three) and reverberated in Barmouth (Merionethshire), Wing (Buckinghamshire), Oswestry (Shropshire), Stowe on the Wold (Gloucestershire), and Bakewell (Derbyshire). A similar riot had taken place at Denbigh in 1795 against the act for manning the navy through parish quotas for recruits. The story of the riots against the Supplementary Militia Act has recently been told, but their exceptional features may be better appreciated if they are compared to other riots and disturbances.[31]

Three features of the Militia Act riots are noteworthy. First, the rioters were almost entirely country people, despite the fact that the Act applied to *all* parishes and despite the rarity of agrarian riots on other issues. Second, unlike almost all other rioters, these rioters challenged the legal authority of the magistrates directly. Their objective was simply to stop the execution of a parliamentary statute, even though the Act's lack of ambiguity might seem to offer little hope of success. Third, although their challenge came from an unexpected quarter—rural England was assumed to be the secure "rear area" of social conflict—and although it elicited stern measures of repression, nevertheless, in many places the rioters achieved their key objective.

All the riots followed a similar pattern that was dictated by the administration of the Act. Each county was required to send a certain number of recruits to man the expanded militia, so first, each county lieutenancy was to hold a general meeting to divide the county's quota among its various subdivisions. Next, parish constables were to take lists of all the eligible men in each parish to a meeting of the deputy lieutenants of that subdivision. At that meeting, the deputy lieutenants would draw by lot the names of the men who would be liable to serve for each parish. Rioters aimed to break this process locally, at its most vulnerable point. They intercepted the constables on the road to the meeting and destroyed the lists, or else they burst into the subdivision meeting and chased the gentlemen from the room. At Cockbridge (Cumberland), for instance, they cast the deputies' papers into the fire, not sparing even the New Testament.

The first remarkable feature of the Militia Act riots is that almost all were carried out by country folk—chiefly the servants of the prominent farmers and the sons of the smaller farmers in Lincolnshire, the villagers from the neighboring parishes at Larlingford, Norwich, Kettering, Clipstone, Denbigh, Cockbridge, Penrith, and Bakewell, and the "mountaineers" from Grizedale Forest at Ulverston, including laborers and husbandmen, a village butcher, and a carpenter.[32] In most riots men of different villages acted together (it is striking that no women were reported among the crowds). In large part, this unaccustomed capacity for collective action was artificial, imposed upon country people by the balloting process itself, which touched every village and every cottage. To a far greater degree than either market or work conditions, it provided both a common grievance and a concrete threat, a target on which the young men of a neighborhood could focus.

Resistance centered in the rural areas because country men seemed to have less change of escaping service in the militia than did men in the towns. The elaborate balloting procedures for the old militia, established forty years before, had long since lapsed, most completely in the largest, most rapidly growing urban and industrial districts. There it was much easier for the draftees to abscond. By the 1790s most members of the old militia were substitutes who had enlisted for bounties, rather than ordinary citizens selected by lot. Indeed, militia regiments had begun to use recruiting parties to secure such substitutes, usually finding them in the towns and industrial areas. Moreover, by 1796, because of the population growth in those areas, the counties were bearing an unfair burden in meeting the old quotas. For all these reasons, purely rural counties like Lincolnshire almost certainly had to obtain more militiamen from the villages. Hence, although the Supplementary Militia Act of 1796 allowed for substitutes, that provision was understood locally in the light of previous experience. In the industrialized neighborhoods of Halifax, most parishes seemed to have little difficulty in finding "volunteers" (at a high price).[33] But in rural Lincolnshire, misunderstanding over substitutes aggravated other existing tensions.

The riots began in north Lincolnshire (in the district known as Lindsey) because of its peculiarly chaotic administration, not because of any unusual economic hardship, for wheat prices there in 1795–1796 had been close to or below the national average price, and by late 1796 they had receded to their normal levels. Moreover, at 10s. 6d. a week, the field laborers of Lincolnshire were among the highest paid in the land.[34] But the old system of lists and ballots had not been implemented for years.[35] Lincolnshire was hardly unique in that respect, but the execution of the Act of 1796 did appear to be a threatening innovation. More seriously, the colonel of the north Lincolnshire battalion, the lord lieutenant's own son-in-law, had failed to keep the parishes informed of attrition in the ranks, through death, desertion, or discharge, of the men serving for them, in contrast with the colonel of the south Lincolnshire militia. Ordinarily when such vacancies appeared, the parish for whom the dead or discharged man had served would be obligated to replace him. Hence if balloting were required, only scattered individual parishes should have been affected. But in both 1795 and 1796 the precepts from the north Lincolnshire lieutenancy's general meeting required *all* parishes to supply lists. That may have been necessary because of the colonel's derelict record-keeping, but the effect of such a requirement was to make all parishes liable for filling the quotas of a few, and that would outrage villagers who thought their obligations had already been met. That seems to be why Sir Joseph Banks, the county's leading gentleman, blamed "the whole origins of these Riots [on] the execrable carelessness of the Duke of Ancaster's drunken son-in-law and his Battalion clerks."[36]

The compiling of lists for all parishes may also have been an attempt to fulfill (for the first time) the requirements of an act of 1786 calling for up-to-date accounts to the Privy Council of available manpower—Banks did not know—but whatever the reason, that irksome innovation soon became hopelessly entangled with the requirements of the new Supplementary Militia Act. The general lieutenancy meeting for 1796 was held on September 30 rather than in October as required by law. That special meeting was technically to proceed under the legislation for the old militia, for the Supplementary Militia Bill was introduced in the Commons only on October 18, and it received the royal assent on November 11. The purpose of the special meeting was to fill up vacancies in the old militia. But also, in August 1796 the Home Office had requested in a letter that the lord lieutenant, the Duke of Ancaster, report the number of men in the county available for militia service, presumably in order to calculate the quotas for the new militia. The duke turned the letter over to the clerk of the general meeting, and it seems to have been the clerk's idea to call an early special meeting that would order all parishes to compile lists of eligible men and so kill two birds with one stone.[37] Not only did that set in motion a collection of lists earlier than that required under the new act—which explains why the riots began in Lincolnshire between October 29 and November 9, before the new act was passed—but also, the haste and irregularity of the proceedings undermined the magistrates' credibility in their dealings with the villagers.

Reports of the new bill has appeared in the local press from October 14 onward. Hence, the magistrates' assurances that the subdivision meetings were not being held to provide men for the new militia rang hollow. At an earlier meeting in 1795, the magistrates "were unable to explain to the people whence this unusual mode of summoning [all the parishes] arose." In 1796, Thomas Coltman, the chairman of the Quarter Sessions, could not discover the number of replacements needed until after the riot at Horncastle had started. Sir Joseph Banks deplored the lack of "...information which might enable us to quiet the minds of the people by telling them exactly what is required of them."[38]

Lincolnshire was also the first to witness resistance to the militia balloting in 1796 because of local precedents. In 1757 when the balloting process was instituted for the old militia by the Militia Act of that year, the areas around the Humber, particularly Lincolnshire, were the scene of the earliest and most serious rioting. Those riots forced the lord lieutenant to call off the selection meetings. At the national level, the militia legislation was amended, explained to the public more clearly, and used only intermittently until the threat of a French invasion in 1759.[39] From the grass-roots perspective, resistance by riot had succeeded.

Forty years later, the Lincolnshire rioters' initial success was even more dramatic. In the autumn of 1795, a large group of people assembled at Spilsby with a flag and paraded around the town. The magistrates and deputy lieutenants called off the meeting they had scheduled for that town to avoid a riot. In May, 1796, a second meeting was cancelled owing to the absence of Thomas Coltman, the chairman of the Quarter Sessions, but "the Country people who conceived they had gained a victory at Spilsby before were now convinced in their minds that if sufficient opposition was given to the magistrates, meetings would not be held and they would be forever free from serving in the Militia."[40]

Besides their rural character, another striking feature of the Militia Act riots was their violent boldness. While most other rioters preferred to enlist the magistrates' sympathy, the Militia Act crowds challenged the legal and social authority of the magistrates directly and without truckling to them. If any forelocks were tugged, they were those of gentlemen and constables. The crowds were unusually large, ranging from two or three thousand in Lincolnshire to over a thousand in Kettering. Unlike most other rioters, almost all the mobs against the militia were armed, typically with "large sticks and bludgeons." In Denbigh in 1795, a mob threatened to assault the magistrate and to pull down his house, and forced him to sign a promise not to enforce the militia or navy acts. The magistrate regretted "having lost so much of the confidence of the lower class of people...who hitherto have always treated me with the highest respect." He blamed "the Methodists."[41]

The roughest and least deferential rioters were the backwoodsmen from the hill and forest parishes of northern Lancashire and Cumberland. At Penrith a "set of desperate fellows" armed with clubs broke into the room where the officials were sitting, seized their papers "by violence," burned them, and subsequently threatened to burn down the George Inn if they proceeded. At Cockbridge, a crowd struck their bludgeons through the window and wainscoting of the meeting room. They forced their way into the meeting with "vollies of Oaths," bludgeons poised. Those at the back called out, "Cowards! Push Forward! Strike!" One magistrate was struck "a violent blow on his head with a Bludgeon," another averted attack, he believed, only by advancing to the middle of the crowd with his head bared. Then the magistrates left town. At Ulverston, the magistrates and Deputy Lieutenants were held "in *Durance Vile*" for three hours by the crowd, but the rioters "durst not strike." The officials won their freedom by ordering a barrel of ale sent to the Town Cross, but not before they had promised not to proceed with the balloting.[42]

Such violence was not simply a flash of spontaneous fury, for at Denbigh and Cockbridge, as at Kettering and in Lincolnshire, men from the country parishes had assembled in advance to march on the meetings. Nor was their militancy simply fueled by alcohol: at Cockbridge "they kept nearly all sober to the last." Only after their objectives were achieved did they get down to serious, or rather uproarious, drinking. Rather, these backwoodsmen were probably emboldened to attack the magistrates because they expected the justices not to recognize them, or at any rate, not to possess any means of social or economic retaliation.[43]

The Lincolnshire mobs generally preferred carnival to mayhem, although at Caistor they were reported to have beaten the constables "cruelly" with their own staves, and at Horncastle they had held up the constables by the ears when they would not surrender their lists. But generally they blocked the meetings successfully without physical assault. Their triumph was heady. At Horncastle, for example, the rioters procured blue ribbons for cockades, some of which they wore triumphantly to church the following Sunday. At Spilsby, one party led by flag and fifes marched through the town, after they had stopped the meeting, and rapped at the Reverend Edward Walls's door (Walls was a magistrate and deputy lieutenant) saying, "Sir, you'll observe we don't demand anything, but hope you will give us something to drink." At Alford the following week, the crowd levied graduated contributions on the inhabitants: "gentlemen, 5s, Parsons, 3s, and the rest in proportion." They were scrupulous enough to give change of 5s. 6d. when one gentleman had to give them half a guinea. The rioters' extortions, there and elsewhere, however, were by no means always so polite. Indeed, such rude solicitations were partly an extension of the "sturdy begging" that customarily followed village games and fetes, an expression of the carnival atmosphere of a world turned upside down, a reminder of the contingency of wealth and authority, a sense of euphoria when authority had been so forcefully defied. After a week of turbulence, the villagers of south Lindsey were reported to have been "confident in their strength and certain that the civil authority will be unable to resist them!"[44]

The consequences of the Militia Act riots must be weighed at two levels. Immediately, of course, the rioters had succeeded in stopping the execution of the Act. Accordingly, the magistrates sought to restore order, make shattered authority whole, and enforce the law. They had lost face by the rioters' outrageous behavior, for, as Sir Joseph Banks wrote, "the whole power of executive Justice has been seized out of the hands of our magistrates by these young men and no one can tell in what manner young men will use power while in their hands."[45]

And so force, not persuasion nor merely "theater," was necessary. In Shropshire, Lord Clive declared that military force "alone will be sufficient to produce due obedience to the Laws and and Respect to the Magistrates." The Lincolnshire magistrates asked the Home Office to send cavalry under the command of an "experienced temperate officer...These rash mistaken people wd. quickly feel their own inferiority and return to their duty."[46] Once the cavalry began to arrive on November 11, they were stationed in seven towns across Lindsey (north Lincolnshire), and no further sign of riot appeared.

The Lindsey magistrates used the backing of the military to reassert the authority of the law. Banks insisted "that some examples should be made before conciliation is resorted to. A Low person who has successfully insulted a magistrate or beaten a constable is apt to be proud of the deed & to set up for a hero if he or persons who have committed similar enormities are not punished."[47] Examples were made. Thomas Coltman led a party of cavalrymen on a fifty-mile night raid to seize prisoners in the villages and "to strike terror into the mob..." For the maximum dramatic effect, the prisoners were sent off to Lincoln Castle escorted by cavalry with drawn swords.[48] The politics of justice determined their fate at the March Assizes. Four were sentenced to six months' imprisonment on a lesser charge of obstructing a constable, and they were bound by recognizance to keep the peace for five years. A fifth, William Catliff, "a hardened and irreclaimable thief," was tried on a capital charge of robbery and sentenced to hang. But, not wishing to create any martyrs, the gentlemen and magistrates successfully petitioned for his reprieve and for his transportation (to Australia) so that he would no longer be able to corrupt "inexperienced young lads."[49] They had deliberately kept back additional capital charges at the trial "in order that he might be saved."[50] Banks had believed that six to ten prisoners would be "a sufficient example to others," and Coltman assured him later that only "very few were selected for prosecution to save both blood and money."[51]

Finally, to round out repression the gentlemen undertook to raise troops of Yeomanry Cavalry, especially at Horncastle. That went smoothly enough, although the farmers, who were afraid of their servants, were reluctant to join. But Banks was glad to have subdued the county "without bloodshed."[52]

Yet at another level coercion and terror were not sufficient to restore order and authority. No one wanted to contemplate an indefinite military occupation of Lindsey. Viable class rule required some attention to the grievances of the rioters. One wealthy and perspicacious widow who had parleyed with a mob suggested that public explanations of the legislation might dispel the "misunderstandings" of "those poor misguided People... for they seem only to want conviction of the truth."[53] However, too much emphasis should not be placed on simple "clarification," for the rioters had real grievances that required concessions, not merely "enlightenment."

First of all, service in the militia could seriously disrupt the family economy of a workingman, especially because embodied militia units served far from home. In theory, his family was to be supported by a parish allowance, but those allowances were all too frequently disputed, bungled, late, or insufficient. Hence the resisters' opposition was not entirely a matter of abstract principle. At a shilling a day for the period of training, the young laborers would lose one-third of their average wages. At Caistor they had avowed "if the gentlemen would stand forward and pay them for their loss of time in having their exercise they would to a man stand true to their King and Country."[54] The procurement of substitutes was another sore point. The rioters at Horncastle said "they had offered the Evening before to subscribe a Guinea each; [subscriptions and even insurance clubs for hiring substitutes for those actually drafted were common practices] but were told every seventh man would be wanted and that 5 Guineas would not excuse them."[55] Other rumors had it that subtitutes would cost "two or three guineas apiece," and at Horncastle rioters told one magistrate, "We will neither go nor pay." When told a substitute was likely to cost them less than a guinea, they "appeared satisfied." Nevertheless, at least one sign that resistance derived not just from economics but also from class hostility appeared in Lincolnshire, as it had in 1757: near Boston, one group of rioters told a magistrate, "No poor man should be compelled to fight for lords and rich men."[56] In effect the exemptions and the costs of substitutes made the militia ballot a regressive tax on the poor.

Such sentiments were rarely rooted in politically sophisticated radicalism.[57] The "miscreant mountaineers" in Ulverston voiced the more typical "pre-political" levelling attitudes. They "amused themselves by treating [the magistrates], the Government and Church with every degree of contempt and insult they could devise...their whole Demeanor, Gestures, and Language were Revolutionary. Their general Exclamations were, 'Down with the Rich! No Militia! Why should we fight for them—If the French come they will not hurt us—They will only plunder those who have already too much. We can be no worse, but may be gainers.'"[58] For one awful moment it must have seemed to the magistrates that the infernal spirit of the threatening letters had taken flesh!

But in Lincolnshire, magistrates were confident of the loyalism of their countrymen. Time and again the rioters cried out, "God save the king!" even when they coupled it with "No New Militia!" or "Damn Pitt and the Justices!"[59] No doubt shouting "God save the king!" was partly a prudent talisman against a charge of sedition, for the rioters were fully aware of their legal liabilities, particularly in the open-field (as opposed to forest) society of Lincolnshire, where there could be little hope of maintaining anonymity. One rioter there surrendered his cudgel immediately on the request of Justice Coltman. Another deliberately broke his iron-tipped plank hook when he was warned "that it was particularly punishable...in a Riot."[60] Banks concluded, "the mob itself indeed was loyal for tho their cry was, no requisition, they repeatedly said, we will Fight the French whenever they come. Why do not the gentlemen come out, we will go with them anywhere."[61]

The last phrase reveals one of the most significant and complex facets of the riots. One of the chief fears of the rioters was that once in the militia, they would be drafted into regular regiments and sent abroad, a lethal sentence, given the high risk of contracting deadly fever in the West Indies, for instance. "They swear they will die in the streets before they will go."[62] The fears may have been based on a cause célèbre of 1756, when men who had enlisted in the army had been sent abroad contrary to their expectations. In fact, the Supplementary Militia Act specified that the militia was to be returned home after three weeks' training and to be embodied (called out and placed on a formal military status) only in the case of an actual invasion. That much was public knowledge. But the government might depart from its promise—such fears were hardly groundless.[63]

In any case, the question of foreign service immediately raised the issue of the local gentlemen's service as officers. In the past, gentlemen, especially those of leading families, had been unwilling to serve as militia officers.[64] The common people seem to have felt that the best insurance that the new militia would remain at home was for the political heavyweights of the county to "stand forward" as officers to share the social burden of service. The best evidence for this is the modification of the new militia's organization that was demanded by the gentry after their repeated discussions with some of their young neighbors who had been among the mobs.[65]

Richard Ellison, chairman of the Lincoln subdivision Quarter Sessions and Member of Parliament for Lincoln, sharply criticized the government's new Militia Act: it had driven a fatal wedge into the natural social networks of the country, "at the moment when almost everything depends upon conciliating the general Body of the people...Instead of calling upon Men of property to stand forward & by their example & participation...please & encourage the lower Classes—a Requisition is made upon Persons [while] Property [is] nearly excluded." Although Ellison counted himself a strong supporter of the ministry, he deeply lamented the slovenliness of the militia legislation: "I fear that in the insolence of large majorities *within* [Parliament] Ministers are induced to pay little attention to the more important majorities *without* & that they calculate nothing beyond getting the undigested Bills into Acts, & they leave the consequences to the Shoulders of Magistrates and Country Gentlemen."[66]

The promise that local gentlemen would head the new militia was the keystone in the campaign to restore peace in Lincolnshire. The Home Office recommended a large meeting of county leaders to impress the people.[67] The government also sent down a printed copy of a handbill that gave a brief explanation of the Act.[68] Joseph Banks agreed on the wisdom of publishing "resolutions...to conciliate the minds of our mistaken countrymen," after an example had been made of the rioters.[69]

The government's explanatory handbill was printed in the *Lincoln, Rutland, and Stamford Mercury* on November 18 and over the next three weeks. It was designed to meet the rioters' objections head on. The men enrolled would be called out only *"within their own counties, for the space of Twenty Days."* During that time they would receive a shilling a day, plus provisions for "SUPPORTING THEIR FAMILIES." *"No further service"* would be required except "in the event of an *actual Invasion*." Most important, the notice emphasized that the new force would be "conducted by proper officers, selected from their own Neighborhood."[70] The deputy lieutenants and the magistrates circulated the printed notices widely "for the information and satisfaction of the County." They publicly emphasized that the supplementary militia would be officered by "Persons selected from their own Neighborhood."[71]

Nor were these promises hollow. As early as November 15 Banks suggested "we incline here to enroll ourselves in the New Militia & to Find substitutes among our Farmers' sons," so as to have "a Militia we can depend upon." On November 21, Banks and Lord Gwyddir formally offered their services to the government as colonel and lieutenant colonel of the new Lincolnshire Battalion, as an example to "their Tenants and neighbors."[72]

The government did not reply to this offer until late December, and then they reaffirmed the original disruptive policy. If embodied the supplementary militia was to be incorporated into the battalions of the old militia, and all offers of service from local gentlemen would be refused. The gentlemen of Lincolnshire protested loudly, for they were certain the apparent breach of faith would renew the rioting. Ellison and his colleagues even threatened to resign their posts as magistrates and deputy lieutenants.[73] The West Riding magistrates were pressing s similar case. One of them urged the Lincolnshire gentry to persevere, and declared, "I should prefer a cell in Newgate, with any consequences that might ensue, to the knocking out the brains of my Neighbors in order to conquer prejudices so wantonly and wilfully raised."[74]

The government gave way. They agreed to the Yorkshire demand for new battalions under local officers. Joseph Banks and the Duke of Ancaster made the case for Lincolnshire. Finally, in late March the government granted Lindsey similar terms, though both agreements were kept "unofficial." At Bawtry (Nottinghamshire) public quiet was restored by similar concessions. In Buckinghamshire, after the magistrates and Yeomanry had vigorously hunted down and prosecuted the ringleaders of the riots there, the Marquis of Buckingham was able to secure terms for having local officers similar to Lindsey's.[75]

The Militia Act riots were altogether remarkable. They demonstrated that country folk were not incurably passive or deferential. Conversely, the social emergency brought on by the balloting revealed that agrarian authority rested upon coercion, not "theater." The Militia Act had created an unusual, even "artificial," basis for collective action, one that was normally missing in disputes over food prices and wages. It was that provocation to unwonted plebeian assertion that the gentry hated. At first glance they seemed to have no room for conciliatory manuevers, for they were bound to execute the law. Eventually, however, they managed to sidestep the thrust of the crowds' animus and to assume their preferred role as broker between plebs and government. For the law, not the magistrates, was the primary target. Before compromise was achieved, however, the eruption of social blasphemy and fierce repression revealed that beneath the quiet surface of rural society, considerable antagonisms simmered.

A surprising number of farm laborers' wage movements—nearly two dozen—occurred in the 1790s. Like threatening letters, arson, food riots, and resistance to the Militia Act, such movements demonstrate that not all farm laborers fitted historians' and contemporaries' conventional stereotype of apathy and ignorance. It is true that farm workers formed labor combinations much less frequently than did industrial wage earners. Indeed their tactics for obtaining higher wages are revealing. In my national sample, only two of the forty-odd labor riots involved farm laborers using physical coercion. Like other workers, farm laborers usually acted to gain higher wages rather than to defend themselves against wage cuts. But the relative rarity of such wage movements (and their use of indirect means to exert pressure on employers) are clues to the insurmountable obstacles they faced in trying to bargain collectively in the framework of agrarian society, even when the war period improved their economic prospects.[76]

Agricultural wage rates in the eighteenth century were low and stagnant until 1790, except where alternative urban and industrial employment was available, in Lancashire and around London.[77] In the 1790s, however, there were many complaints of "a scarcity of laborers" in East Anglia, Hampshire, Cambridgeshire, and Cumberland. That scarcity was blamed on "the rage for building... the flourishing state of commerce" and manufacturing, and the canal mania.[78] Moreover, enclosures and the expansion of cultivation to meet the demands of war required hedges, ditches, drains, buildings, roads, land clearings, and the more-intensive cultivation of such crops as turnips—all of which required more labor. Finally, the army, navy, and militia absorbed half a million of the underemployed.[79]

The result of such pressures on the labor market was a steady and considerable rise in money wages that kept pace with the cost of living up to 1810, except during the dearths of 1795 and 1800 (see Table 3).[80] Arthur Young believed that the Board of Agriculture's surveys showed a general increase in farm wages of some 40 percent between the early 1790s and 1803–1804, especially in such agricultural counties as Lincolnshire, Norfolk, and Huntingdon-shire.[81] Such evidence is far from establishing what the standard of

Table 3. Agricultural wage rates and the cost of living, 1790–1810.

Year	A. Gilboy-Boody cost of living index 1700 = 100	B. Column A when 1790 = 100	C. Bowley index of agricultural money wages	D. Column E when 1790 = 100	E. Phelps Brown and Hopkins cost of living index
1790	133	100	100	100	871
1791	131	98	104	100	870
1792	140	105	108	101	883
1793	148	111	111	104	908
1794	168	126	115	112	978
1795	179	135	126	125	1091
1796	153	115	138	133	1161
1797	152	114	143	120	1045
1798	165	124	149	117	1022
1799	229	172	153	132	1148
1800	252	189	157	180	1567
1801	190	143	160	201	1751
1802	—	—	162	155	1348
1803	—	—	164	146	1268
1804	—	—	177	150	1309
1805	—	—	189	175	1521
1806	—	—	198	167	1454
1807	—	—	198	164	1427
1808	—	—	198	169	1476
1809	—	—	198	186	1619
1810	—	—	198	192	1670

Sources: Column A, Elizabeth W. Gilboy, "The Cost of Living and Real Wages in Eighteenth Century England," *Review of Economic Statistics* (August 1936), 134–143, reprinted in B. R. Mitchell and Phyllis Deane, *Abstract of British Historical Statistics* (Cambridge: Cambridge University Press, 1962), pp. 346–347. Column C, A. L. Bowley, "The Statistics of Wages in the United Kingdom during the Last Hundred Years," *Journal of the Royal Statistical Society*, 62 (1899), reprinted in Mitchell and Deane, *Abstract*, pp. 348–349. Column E, Price of composite unit of consumables (1451–1475 = 100). E. H. Phelps Brown and Sheila V. Hopkins, "Seven Centuries of the Price of Consumables, Compared with Builders' Wage-Rates," *Economica* (1956), reprinted in *Essays in Economic History*, vol. 2, ed. E. M. Carus-Wilson (London: Edward Arnold, 1962), p. 196.

living was in this period. Unemployment and underemployment are impossible to calculate, but probably declined in this period. Nonmonetary payments rising in value could add nearly 20 percent to wages paid in cash.[82] They could be calculated precisely. For instance, in 1793 the "hinds and bound men" (servants hired on annual contracts?) from around Alnwick met to demand specific increases in the amounts of feed, pasturage, coals, and potatoes that they were paid. In market values, their demands represented an annual increase of more than 25 percent.[83] On the other hand, as the real value of such payments soared, farmers were almost certainly eliminating them, and the working poor were losing both rights of access to the commons and the privilege of buying small quantities of grain directly from the farmers.[84]

What was clear and disturbing to the gentlemen and the farmers was that money wages rose substantially during the wars. Ordinarily, wage rates were far more firmly rooted in custom than were prices; they fluctuated far less, and they had long been stable in most places. In addition, they were even more deeply embedded in a moral economy than food prices—human labor was the commodity; "the labourer is worthy of his hire," began the farm workers at Heacham in Norfolk in 1795. Hence, to landowners, the rise in wage rates represented a shocking increase in the farm laborer's dignity, and so evoked deep feelings from both employer and employee. Thus, though the Alnwick laborers' meetings had not been "riotous," "yet the circulation of their resolutions at this time may have serious consequences."[85] How far were such wage increases the direct result of collective pressure?

The geography of the two dozen farm "wage movements" in this period is revealing. With a few exceptions—isolated episodes in Wiltshire, Somerset, Northumberland, Devon, and Berkshire— the farm workers' protests clustered in East Anglia and in the Home Counties, particularly in Hertfordshire, Kent, Surrey, and Sussex. These were among the areas where the commercial development of agriculture was most advanced, whether by enclosure and the "Norfolk system" of crop rotation, or by intensive market gardening for the metropolis. There, wage relationships were probably increasingly reduced to a cash nexus, ruled by impersonal changes in the market than being determined by custom. The Home Counties were also the places where employment opportunities of the metropolis beckoned—building and commerce or enlistment in the army or the navy—and therefore could pull farm wages up. However, only the Alnwick farm servants made explicit references to other workers' wage increases as part of their own argument. At the same time, the capital's demands for food were felt most keenly in the southeast. And wage claims clustered in the dearth years 1795 and 1800, when they were typically joined to complaints over high food prices. At Thatcham, Berkshire, for instance, three or four hundred laborers gathered in 1800 to ask that wages be made higher or food cheaper. At Monkton, Kent, in 1795, farm workers demanded and won concessions on both food prices and a wage increase.[86]

The southeast was also the area where the farm laborers' friendly societies were thickest on the ground. Even sympathetic contemporaries feared the "independence" that the friendly societies seemed to foster. Their chief drawback was their tendency to engage in "mutinous" disputes with employers. Their monthly meetings and rituals helped sustain a submerged rural "working-class culture," the "dark side" of the village.[87] Moreover, a friendly society could offer workers partial independence from parish relief. Hence the density of friendly societies in agrarian counties provides a rough index of villagers' capacity to organize and act collectively. Six of the agricultural counties that had the greatest number of friendly societies were also the areas where the farm wage protests took place. Likewise, the heartland of capitalistic agricultural progress, Norfolk, Suffolk, Essex, and Surrey, had the greatest proportion of friendly society members in their population in 1801, except for the industrial counties (see Table 4).[88]

The labor market and friendly societies were only the beginning of a capacity for collective action. In the face of formidable social obstacles, they were not enough to permit the success that might have encouraged more frequent collective action. In only a handful of cases did anything like collective protest bring positive results in the form of increased wages. In 1792 the justices of the peace in counties around London "forestalled unrest" by raising the wages of day laborers. The success of "negotiations" at Monkton has already been mentioned.[89]

But the only known success of collective direct action by farm laborers came at Crediton, Devon, in 1795. For several years, the lord lieutenant, Lord Fortescue, had blocked proposals at the Quarter Sessions to raise farm workers' wages, arguing that farmers would "take umbrage at the Gentlemen being generous at their expense." Wages remained "low and inadequate" according to Lord Clifford.[90] However, as food rioting reached its climax in April 1795, a handbill was circulated that invited laborers and gentlemen in half a dozen parishes to a general meeting in Crediton. Threats of apocalyptic justice were combined with

Table 4. Counties and friendly societies, 1796 and 1801.

Counties	Number of friendly societies		Society members per 100 people (1801)
	1796	1801	
Agricultural			
Suffolk	219	235	10.0
Essex	182	205	8.1
Surrey	130	188	6.3
Norfolk	145	185[a]	6.7
Kent	13	158[b]	4.7
Buckinghamshire	30	44	3.7
Hertfordshire	31	33	3.0
Herefordshire	32	32	3.2
Sussex	29	31	1.8
Wiltshire	19	30	1.5
Cambridgeshire	17	20	2.0
Lincolnshire	53	15[c]	2.3
Oxfordshire	26	15	1.2
Rutland	11	14	7.7
Berkshire	12	14	1.2
Huntingdonshire	11	—	2.6
Bedfordshire	5	9	1.3
Mixed, and Industrial and Commercial			
Lancashire	452	820	11.0
Devonshire	—	156	4.1
Nottinghamshire	92	141	9.1
Somerset	114	132	4.0

Sources: The categories of counties are those listed in Phyllis Deane and W. A. Cole, *British Economic Growth, 1688–1959*, 2nd ed. (Cambridge: Cambridge University Press, 1967), pp. 108–109. The number of friendly societies for 1796 is from Witt Bowden, *Industrial Society in England towards the End of the Eighteenth Century*, 2nd ed. (London: Frank Cass, 1965), pp. 296–297, and for 1801, from Frederic M. Eden, *Observations on Friendly Societies* (London, 1801), p. 7. Friendly society members per 100 people are based on a ratio of Eden's estimates of members in 1801 to county populations from the census of 1801. Calculated in Christopher A. Kojm, "The English Friendly Societies, 1760–1830" (B.A. thesis, Harvard University, 1977), p. 72.
  a. Outside Norwich.
  b. Outside Canterbury.
  c. Lindsey, excluding Lincoln.

reason in the laborers' appeal for higher wages. If the gentlemen wished to receive "mercy and forgiveness...at that Great trybunal Day" (when even the justices would be judged), "should ye not likewise therefore have Mercy Upon your poor Destressed Brethren." "Extreme want" and natural justice called for an increase in wages from 1s. to 1s. 6d per day, "or to be settled according to the price of wheat," with "hours to Labour and Lyqour as usual," for the cost of living had recently doubled. But if the gentlemen refused to treat in "amity Peace an Concord," then "this Great assembly will Open the Period of Death Gain or perish at the attempt to the End that our Little ones for want perish not." A poetic conclusion tried to wash away any hint of sedition:

God Bless our Gracious King and send
Health and Prosperity may his Days attend
May his Ruleing Subjects Humanity then show
Any Pay unto the Poor what they to them do owe.[91]

Compassion, reason, and prudence should do what simple justice required; the laborers did not beg for charity.

In the event, some two hundred farm laborers and laboring poor assembled at the appointed time and began to make threats against the local flour mills. The magistrates and gentlemen managed to disperse most of the crowd, but a knot of militant women stood defiant. The Royal Cornwall Militia helped arrest three "most refractory" women, one of whom was convicted of assault, the only reported physical violence.

The next day the Quarter Sessions raised the daily wage from 12d. to 14d., in view of the high price of food and the distress of the poor, despite Clifford's reiteration of Fortescue's opposition. Clifford himself drew the moral: "Everything is now perfectly quiet; the large subscriptions for procuring corn & the good sense of the Grand Jury at the Quarter Sessions in recommending the increase of wages for the Labourers has produced the best effect."[92] It was the lone achievement by direct action taken by farm laborers in this period.

The Crediton meeting was also the nearest farm laborers came to confronting their employers directly. Since individual farms typically employed small numbers of field hands, it was nearly impossible for workers to bargain collectively with their employer. In the context of relatively low-skilled work and a relative labor surplus in most areas, militants risked being easily replaced. Further, regulation by the magistrates of the laborers' wages was not quite defunct, and of course, the Speenhamland policy of supplementing inadequate wages with poor relief reinforced the implicit assumption that remuneration was more a question of social policy than of what the market would bear. In short, farm wages were considered to be more a public and social matter than a private contractual one. That may explain why farm laborers, especially, often tried to organize a local "general strike," that is, to enlist the workers of a whole neighborhood and to appeal to the gentlemen and magistrates rather than to confront their own employers directly. In a dispute over gleaning in Exning, for instance, the laborers assembled and paraded to Newmarket and back with "a flag of defiance and music."[93] The gentlemen perceived such movements as a kind of "insurrection" and combated them with repression and relief, as questions of public order, instead of treating them as conflicts requiring private economic bargaining.

All these tendencies appeared in the only other coercive farm laborers' movement of this period, a strike-demonstration in the Essex marshes in 1800. On June 11, "Captain" John Little of Steeple led a large body of men around to various farms. They were joined by many "infatuated" men, and they were said to have enlisted others by force. They said they would stop any work being done until wages were raised or the prices of provisions lowered. "They were to have a flag, and when they became 200 strong, they were to take the horses from the ploughs, and have everything their own way, but. . .they agreed they would neither *kill* nor *slay*."[94] All the marshmen in the district were reported to be privy to the rising. By dusk they had mustered nearly one hundred men at the town of Southminster. But the Reverend H. Bate Dudley, the local magistrate, raised the hue and cry against them and stopped them in their tracks. The ringleaders were tried at the August Assizes for conspiracy, combination, riot, and assault (for forcing laborers to join them). Lord Kenyon, who had become famous for his Assize sermons against forestalling and regrating, now redeemed himself socially with a grave homily on the enormity of such a "conspiracy," "little short of raising troops and levying war against the King and government of the country. . . many thousand lives have been sacrificed in riots and insurrections which had beginnings as small and leaders as insignificant as the present."[95] He handed down a crushing sentence: John Little and two others were imprisoned for twelve months and bound over to keep the peace for seven years by recognizances of £100! Two months later the gentry were still glowing: the chairman of the Quarter Sessions, at Kenyon's suggestion, thanked the Reverend Dudley for his "spirited exertions" to defeat a "desperate conspiracy and insurrection" and bring the ringleaders "to an exemplary punishment."[96]

In what seems like a similar episode, some laborers had gathered at Warehorne, Kent, in January 1794 and tried to persuade laborers from Kennardington and Shadoxhurst to join them. Their leader was charged at the Assizes with conspiring "to raise and levy an insurrection and Rebellion within the Kingdom" to force the king to introduce reforms such as raising the wages of day laborers. He had aggravated his offense by boasting that he would join the French if they invaded. For, he told one witness, "It can be no harm to you or any of the middling sort of people. We are as much imposed upon as they are in France." He was punished heavily for his indiscretion, with consecutive jail terms of one year each on charges of sedition and conspiracy.[97]

When the avenue to open collective bargaining was blocked by repression, popular discontent was diverted to sabotage. The Hertfordshire-Bedfordshire border witnessed one such progression. In March 1793, soon after the war began, people gathered at Baldock, Hertfordshire, then fanned out through several nearby Bedfordshire villages, calling on the laborers to join them to lower bread prices and raise wages. The local gentlemen were afraid the Bedfordshire Militia would be unreliable in the event of a riot. "Where it would end if it once broke out, God only knows...as I do assure you from all I hear, the people's minds are all so poisoned with pernicious doctrines that the outrage would be very violent and serious. I dare say that when once the common people are let loose, no property is safe, they think then of nothing but plunder." Laborers also gathered at Potton, ten miles north of Baldock, to clamor for an increase of wages. They were persuaded to disperse, but one gentleman conceded that their complaint was "not without reason" and hoped that the Quarter Sessions would consider it.[98]

Two years later, as food prices rose, unrest moved in the opposite direction across Hertfordshire. The people around Buntingford, Hertfordshire, about eight miles east of Baldock, met in great numbers in March 1795 and seemed ready to try to force an increase in wages. The magistrates nipped that agitation in the bud by arresting one of the ringleaders. That July an anonymous, threatening handbill was picked up in the yard of the Angel Inn at Buntingford. It claimed to speak for a league of nine parishes around Buntingford: "...we will do some Mischief if you don't lower the Brade [bread] for we cannot live...we have give you a fair offer to do it before you too have your Town & Towns set on fire."[99] The threats seemed to reflect the laborers' growing rage at their lack of any real power.

At the same time, the farmers' servants from around Hoddesdon, fourteen miles south of Buntingford, had begun to collect in small parties, "with the Intention of exacting by Menaces & Force, an Increase of Wages." They recruited support and threatened to strike. Most disturbing to the magistrates, many of the laborers were members of "certain Friendly Societies" in Hoddesdon, and they had withdrawn their funds from these societies, "for the express purpose of standing out against their employers." Rumors flew that several "considerable farmers" were hoarding grain and that government imports had not been used to reduce the London food prices as much as possible. Justice William Baker hoped that the government would keep the London food prices down to soothe the countryside.[100]

The gentry braced itself to meet the storm. Baker tried to pinch off nodes of unrest by warning the publicans not to allow "people to remain in their Houses tippling &c, especially tomorrow." Most important, the gentry renewed the collection and distribution of relief subscriptions that had carried the poor of Hertford and the smaller towns and villages through the winter but that had been exhausted on June 10. They mustered special constables and the Yeomanry in case of "disagreeable circumstances."[101] Baker was greatly relieved to report finally that the "disturbances...we were taught to expect at Hoddesdon...have blown over." He feared that someone might propose raising wages at the next Quarter Sessions, which might cause some "public mischief," but he also felt that no one else would support it, "considering...the relief" that had been provided.[102]

That is not quite the end of the story. In the spring of 1795, in March 1796, and in the summer of 1800, five suspicious fires destroyed the property of farmers popularly rumored to be hoarders.[103] In the hard winter of early 1800, a notice posted in the marketplace at Hitchin called "all poor treadsmen and Laborers [to] lay all work aside and meet togeather in a bodey...for your work all you can do will not support you & your family." Charity was now treated with contempt: "our Soupmaker may come with doctrine of fine speech as keeping a clean house and the wife to give a smile." At harvest time, popular tensions increased as prices rose sharply again. Baker blamed the high prices on speculation, but he could not say so publicly, "for fear of worse mischief...[of] Riot and Destruction of the most horrid kind."[104] And so, just as the laborers, blocked from open bargaining, turned to arson and violent threats, the country magistrates, unfamiliar with the "protocol" of riot, were prey to exaggerated fears of popular uprising.

If repression diverted pressures for higher wages to sabotage, so the complementary policy of giving relief in lieu of wages also destroyed the laborers' bargaining position. What became the "Speenhamland" policy kept remuneration securely within the discretion of the gentry and rate payers. One of Arthur Young's correspondents stated this policy quite baldly: "It is here judged more prudent to indulge the poor with bread corn at a reduced price than to raise the price of wages."[105] Moreover, the lord lieutenant of Norfolk sneered that relief was preferable to "high wages which [the laborer] would insist upon being continued or probably spend at the Alehouse instead of supplying his family."[106] But the Marquis of Buckingham had misgivings about the Speenhamland strategy. His investigation of an arson epidemic in Essex prompted him to condemn "that combination *amongst Farmers* on the subject of labourers wages, that throws them all upon the parish rates. A system that...is destructive of every vital principle of Government."[107]

Just as the "public" character of farm wages forced the laborers to appeal to the magistrates rather than to their employers, the gentlemen usually responded to such appeals with words of "charity." At Lewes in February 1801, for example, villagers armed with large sticks told a magistrate they would "throw off labour" unless they "lived better." The magistrate then ordered their parish officers to increase the amount of relief they received. In April 1795, a body of laborers at Ardingly warned the parish officers that unless their wages were "augmented," they would become "burdensome" to the parish. At Eatonbridge, Kent, laborers besieged the house of the overseer of the poor for hours with the demand that he call a vestry meeting to raise their wages. When Lord Townshend heard threats of a strike and of an attack on the millers at Fakenham (Norfolk), he ordered the rangers (Yeomanry) to protect the millers, and he increased relief. He could not understand why relief had not previously prevented unrest.[108]

For indeed, laborers did not accept relief in lieu of wages with humble gratitude. At East and West Rudham, near Fakenham, for example, laborers assembled to demand of a parson-magistrate that wages be increased and food prices lowered. He admonished them to complain only in a "respectable," not an illegal fashion, and he reminded them of the existing provisions for relief. But the crowd only grew larger, so he arrested their ringleader with the help of "several respectable Farmers" (of the Yeomanry). That autumn, an assembly of day laborers at nearby Heacham condemned subsidized grain sales as "not only an indecent insult... but a fallacious mode of relief, and every way inadequate." They planned a campaign to petition Parliament for a sliding scale of wages pegged to the price of wheat prices. The justices at the Bury (Suffolk) Quarter Sessions asked their county Members of Parliament to introduce a similar measure. They were moved to act by a gathering of the poor of seventeen parishes on Hadleigh Common. That assembly protested to the directors of the House of Industry (the parish workhouse) that a bushel of wheat cost more than a man earned in a week. The magistrates of Berkshire and Hampshire also supported the concept of raising wages to meet the cost of living. But Samuel Whitbread's Minimum Wage Bill was defeated in Parliament both in 1796 and 1800.[109]

The laborer's distaste for charity was as much a question of digestion as of dignity. From Maldon, Essex, came a bitter, anonymous protest against the repulsive soup and the coarse bread the poor were given in lieu of reasonably priced flour:

> The hogs Rise up in Jugment for eating of their food...
> I mean your Brothscribers for you'l surley go to hell...
>   Charity Broth one penny a Quart [contains]
>   Migges Maggots and Quids of Tabbacco
>   & All for one penny per Qt.[110]

And so, ultimately relief itself became the subject of dispute. The laboring poor felt they deserved good bread. At Chidingfold, near Midhurst, the poor intimidated the parish officers into giving them relief in money instead of the rice provided by the Relief Act of December 1800. At Sharborough Castle, Surrey, the poor signed an agreement to refuse relief offered in the form of either coarse flour or substitute foods such as rice and fish. They carried banners from house to house in protest. At the poorhouse at Lingfield, the magistrate heard sixty people complain of the rice and of the very bad flour required by the recent Act. He had to concede that the samples of bread they showed him were "extremely indifferent." They complained it was "disagreeable to the taste (as indeed it was) as utterly incompetent to support them under their daily labour and productive of bowelly complaints to them and to their children in particular." They blamed the millers for adulteration of the flour. At nearby Gosden near Horsham, however, the poor took direct action: they seized and destroyed the new coarse cloth the miller used to sift flour in complying with the new Act.[111]

Historians once thought that Speenhamland relief demoralized field laborers, but Mark Blaug argues that it was poverty owing to overpopulation that pauperized the farm workers.[112] The evidence concerning the laborers' futile wage movements suggests, however, that a surplus of laborers in the context of constrictive social mechanisms accounted for the laborers' weak bargaining position. For even when wartime economic pressures gave the farm workers an advantage, though only temporarily, the farmers' "combination on the subject of labourers wages,"[113] repressive prison sentences and the magistrates' use of the cavalry, and class interest in Parliament closed off appeals for either a "moral economy" of labor or direct collective bargaining by riot or strike. The field hand was left instead with discretionary "relief," in the form of vile soup and coarse bread. Yet, farm wages rose during the wars, even if the farm workers did not share fully in the farmers' prosperity. If they were harshly prevented from open collective bargaining, who can say how much arson and threatening letters compelled such concessions?

One outstanding popular grievance of this period was conspicuous by its absence from violent conflicts. Despite the "availability" of riot as a form of popular politics, there were almost no riots against enclosures. Enclosure meant the extinction of common rights on lands shared or jointly operated by all or many members of a community. Such lands might include open fields, commons used chiefly for pasture, and waste land, which was often a source of brush firewood for the poor. Once enclosure was agreed upon by the landowners of a community and sanctioned by a court decree or a private act of Parliament, an impartial committee (or "commission") divided up the land in the community so that all landowners received compact blocs equivalent to their original scattered strips and rights. They then enclosed their property with hedges or fences and farmed it individually. Landless members of the community usually did not receive compensation for their loss of access to the commons and waste land.

The period 1790–1810 witnessed the culmination of parliamentary enclosure (enclosure sanctioned by private act of Parliament), as the wartime boom in the demand for farm products provided strong incentive to extend and intensify cultivation. The number of enclosure bills submitted to Parliament each year rose to unprecedented peaks in the 1790s and 1800s.[114] Yet only 6, or 1 percent, of the 617 riots in the national sample were enclosure riots. Even if incidents recorded in the records of the Quarter Sessions and the Assizes are added to the sample, only a dozen enclosure riots come to light.[115] The reasons for their rarity confirm the relationships between riots and community politics.

The character and impact of most enclosures did not provoke immediate popular outrage. First, it is now generally agreed that late eighteenth-century enclosures did not reduce yeomen farmers to wage laborers, and that enclosure commissioners were scrupulously fair in compensating small property owners. Second, enclosure by act of Parliament was typically only the last stage of a long process of enclosure by private agreement. For England as a whole, the previous century of private enclosure probably wrought more economic and social transformation than did the parliamentary enclosures of the late eighteenth century that were more "visible" to contemporaries and to historians. Both reasons probably account for "the small volume of organized protest"—and riotous opposition—from *propertied* villagers.[116]

But was the loss of access to the commons a serious grievance for cottagers and laborers? The most balanced review of the evidence concludes that, by the enclosure of common wasteland, the "thin and squalid curtain... which separated the growing army of labourers from utter proletarianization was torn down."[117] The extent to which compensatory allotments were made for laborers' gardens is still uncertain. It may be that village laborers were willing to exchange their "birth right" on the commons for the pottage of increased employment brought by enclosure. The point is that such an exchange would leave laborers more completely at the mercy of farmer-employers by depriving them of alternative sources of support—pasture, firewood, and so forth. That is "proletarianization." In view of laborers' protests against receiving relief in lieu of higher wages, it seems fair to say that "more and more regular employment—at least for a time—did not compensate for the poor man's loss in independence."[118]

In a few instances, precisely those issues provoked the laborers to violent resistance. At Streatham Common, the Duke of Bedford had formerly given the furze (brushwood) to the poor, but in 1794 he sold it. A crowd of the poor then gathered to set the furze on fire. "The conflagration was tremendous, but the neighbors rather prevented than lent any assistance for extinguishing it," said one account. The duke had also enclosed some land formerly used for the poor peoples' cattle, but the fences around it were destroyed, allegedly by six masked men in a hackney coach! At Maulden, crowds of two hundred people obstructed the work of the enclosure commissioners. The common had provided the poor the "privileges" of digging turf and pasturing cattle. The enclosure act for this piece of land required part of the common "to be given up to the poor in [place] of those privileges...but they are not contented with part of the common and claim a right to the whole." Moreover, the compensation made to the poor for the loss of their turf-digging rights was fuel allotment: "The trustees (the rector, the churchwarden, and the overseers) were to distribute the turf to poor families and were to pay any surplus from the rent of the herbage to the poor rates." Once again, as in the payment of relief in lieu of wage increases, a right claimed by the poor was converted into an additional discretionary lever for the authorities. The enclosure was ultimately carried out under cavalry guard, though not without resistance.[119]

The riotous resistance at Maulden might have been repeated scores of times, but it was not. There were probably many instances of small-scale or clandestine resistance to enclosures that simply went unreported. At Mere, Wiltshire, and Gillingham, Dorset, which were three miles apart, two groups of ten men were charged with demolishing fences "lately erected" for enclosures by act of Parliament.[120] Countless episodes of small groups' pulling down or invading "enclosures" are recorded in Quarter Sessions and Assize indictments. However, they are reduced to the opaque legal charge of "forcible entry."[121] The formalized language of the indictments makes it impossible to know whether these incidents represented social resistance to enclosures or private, perhaps family or clan, disputes over title to property. Further detailed local research may clarify this problem.

In any case, the rarity of full-scale riots against enclosures bears out in a negative way the relationship between riots and community politics. A parliamentary enclosure provided precious little ambiguity and little division within a community that poorer villagers might use to gain public support for collective resistance. In order for enclosure to be undertaken at all, agreement had first to be reached among the owners of the majority of the community's land, and that left the people without property politically isolated. Then, too, resistance to enclosure would mean a direct challenge to the local squire's or parson's interests, for enclosures were usually promoted by the larger proprietors, while those with the right to collect tithes (including parsons) were generously compensated for any losses caused by the rearrangement of land.[122] That made conflict over enclosures very different from food riots or labor disputes in which the targets were socially "middling" third parties upon whom crowds and magistrates might bring pressure, and whose interests might be compromised by the authorities out of sympathy, "justice," or prudence. Moreover, magistrates were bound by social and legal duty to enforce the law, including an act of enclosure, by military force if necessary. At Maulden, Justice Webster called for the cavalry, "for if ye poor people are suffered to make laws for themselves, we shall very shortly have no Government in this County." At Wilbarston, rioters were forced to act out their submission to such authority by taking part in the physical work of enclosing the land.[123]

To put the point slightly differently, most riots were generally effective bargaining tactics for "volatile" issues, such as food prices, where immediate material concessions were after all only temporary, even though the successful use of political leverage by a crowd would have a lasting impact on community politics. The ruling class was more uneasy about popular protests over low wages and the use of machinery, not only because wage rates were "stickier" than food prices (and so increases would tend to be permanent), but also because collective bargaining infringed upon an employer's assumed freedom to dispose of his property and upon his social authority over his workers. Finally, riots against enclosures were completely inadmissible, for enclosures were a real and permanent change in the organization of capital, and riots were not allowed to interfere with the political or economic constitution.[124] So the structure of politics surrounding the process of enclosure provided the people with little hope or opportunity to resist.

The status of the victims of enclosure also disabled potential rioters. The great majority of all rioters were one rank above the poor, possessing just enough independence, physical stamina, and networks of social communication to support riot. Enclosures, however, bore hardest upon the lowest members of village society—the cottagers, laborers, and paupers who depended on the commons. Indeed, "the poor" were more prominent in the few recorded enclosure riots than they typically were in food riots. At Maulden, Streatham, and Bintry, for instance, the rioters were all described as "the poor."[125] At Bintry and Headington, the rioters were common laborers and women. Only at Wilbarston and Sheffield did more clearly mixed crowds seem to have rioted.[126]

The poor were apparently too vulnerable to victimization, and too little bound together by social networks, perhaps even too geographically mobile,[127] to concert collective violence. In short, enclosures made their greatest impact on precisely that part of the population least capable of resistance by riot.

Two final examples are exceptions that prove the rule that the village poor could not resist enclosures successfully by rioting and hence riot did not become established as a means of resistance to enclosure. At Otmoor in 1801 an enclosure was successfully resisted by both legal action and riot, but the decisive opponents were gentlemen, not crowds of poor people.[128] The most violent enclosure riot of the period occurred at Sheffield in July 1791. Trouble began when enclosure commissioners at nearby Hallam and Stannington were violently prevented from marking boundaries. "No King, No Church" was chalked on doors and walls all over Sheffield. "Considerable bodies of disorderly people" threatened freeholders who supported the enclosures, burned their "farming property" (implements), and broke their windows. The magistrates anxiously summoned dragoons from York and Nottingham. The troops' sudden arrival at Sheffield on Wednesday morning, July 27, excited great alarm and curiosity. People poured out into the streets. That night the crowds attacked the jail and released all the prisoners being held for debt, then marched to Broomhall, the seat of the Reverend John Wilkinson, a justice of the peace, who had been one of the prime movers of the enclosures. There they broke windows, burned library books and tables, and set eight large haystacks on fire. Driven away by the dragoons, the rioters moved on to the residence of V. M. Eyre, steward of the Duke of Norfolk, where they broke the windows of the house and the Roman Catholic chapel. The duke was one of the principal promoters of the enclosure act. The next two days, special constables and troops patrolled the town, but crowds gathered, a barn was burned, and "No King!" "No Corn Bill!" and "No Taxes!" were chalked on the walls. The enclosures in Sheffield were blocked for at least a week, and damages of nearly £1000 were eventually paid to the victims.[129]

That riot illustrates several important points. First, Sheffield was not a sleepy country village but a booming "new" industrial town, with a population of independent artisans who lacked "all decent subordination" to their masters, and who were soon to found and maintain one of the strongest radical movements in the country.[130] The enclosures were so unpopular that the magistrates were afraid to communicate openly with the government.[131] At the same time, the slogans on the walls, including "Liberty or Death," reflected antagonisms that ran deeper than anger over the enclosures. The frantic magistrates believed that instigators from Birmingham's Priestley riots had tried to incite the Sheffield crowds "to bring about a Redress of Grievances as they had done."[132] Second, the violence really intensified after the troops arrived. In 1795 Sheffield was to have one of the most serious town-military riots of the period.[133] Third, when opposition to the enclosures led to the attack on a magistrate's house, the establishment reacted with chilling severity. The judge at the York Assizes promised the Sheffield prisoners that their punishment would be an example to others. One of them, John Bennet, was singled out by the government "as a fit object of punishment, a person who had actually set fire to the house of a magistrate, and though his youth on any occasion might entitle him to some hopes of mercy; yet the enormity of the present offense was such that to save him would be to encourage crime; and...if the prisoner was found guilty...his punishment would serve as a solemn lesson to those unthinking men who had been concerned in the riots at Sheffield."

Bennet was convicted and hanged. But in deference to community feeling, four other rioters were acquitted or released.[134] Sheffield's riot helps to illustrate why enclosure riots were so few. Bennet's execution underlined to all the danger of attacking a magistrate, and even violent hostility in a militant industrial town would only stall enclosure; it could not reach the vital processes whereby enclosures were awarded and troops were sent out to enforce them. How much more futile then would enclosure riots have been for the village poor.

On the whole, agrarian society did not provide a conducive environment for collective bargaining by riot. By contrast with Devon's horizontal and vertical social networks, in the countryside one set of such networks was too sparse, the other, too tight. On the one hand, except for members of some of the friendly societies in the south, villagers lacked the public organizational networks that townspeople were able to use for effective collective action. Only the recruitment for the militia seemed capable of temporarily creating a strong base for collective action in the agricultural regions. The farm servants' youthfulness, as well as their practice of annually changing masters (and often villages), prevented them from establishing the solid social networks that supported riot elsewhere.[135] At the same time, farm laborers were *too* dependent:

at every turn their grievances ran directly up against the interests of those whom they depended upon for employment, relief, and justice. Relief certainly served as a social anodyne, but instead of being wrung from the rich as a result of the collective pressure of the common people, relief was deliberately substituted for the increases in wages that were justified by market pressures, just to inhibit the assertion of rights and to enhance the means of social control.

Finally, since agrarian society had not hammered out a tradition of collective bargaining by riot, when country folk did riot, they were likely to go beyond the protocol normally observed by town rioters and to give vent to their pent-up resentments that were aggravated by their galling powerlessness. They seemed to hope to deflect the consequences of that violence with the cloak of anonymity—often in riot, always in sabotage. Conversely, magistrates were likely to perceive such uprisings in the countryside as petty treason, as insurrectionary, or socially blasphemous, in large part because their own personal interests, authority, and myth of paternalism were directly challenged. Hence, they reacted sternly with the full force of the law to confirm the futility and prohibitive costs of riot in the countryside.

9

Riots and Community Politics in Historical Perspective

At the end of the eighteenth century, riots were the most common and effective form of popular politics. They were not simply "spontaneous" eruptions motivated by hardship or other grievances. Rather, the frequency and tenor of riot depended on a community's social networks and political processes. In the classical, mainstream tradition of riot, dense, stable, and partly autonomous networks among the common people enabled crowds to act coherently. Vertical, reciprocal relationships between the plebs and the powerful ensured that a "protocol" of riot would be observed by both sides. That mutual familiarity enabled rioters to calculate the possible gains and costs of riot, and it enabled magistrates to understand riot and to carefully adjust their responses.

Small-town Devon had the optimum balance between plebeian autonomy and the close-knit horizontal and vertical social ties that formed the framework for classical community bargaining by riot. Riot called into action and tested those sociopolitical relationships. In Devon's towns, the prescriptions of the "moral economy" could be enforced. Riot was not merely "theater," but neither was it unambiguously crime. Moreover, the success, frequency, and discipline of riots were closely bound together. Riots were frequent in towns like Devon's because they were successful local politics, in part because their discipline enabled the common people to exert maximum pressure on particular targets while the "protocol" of riot precluded direct challenges to the authority of the gentry that would raise the costs and lower the prospects of success. And they were disciplined in large part because of solid conventions born of frequent practice, and because the rioters' heritage of success gave them confidence that local politics might once more satisfy their claims and reaffirm their role in the community.

If Devon stood at the center of a spectrum of community politics, Manchester and agrarian society marked out the opposite ends of that spectrum. In Manchester rapid urbanization overloaded the local social and economic networks; magistrates confronted a "city of strangers." Those social circumstances, together with the far-flung system for supplying the town with food, made the "moral economy" impracticable. For a time, fierce partisan antagonisms created "artificial" frameworks for political mobilization and collective action. But hardship and alienation forced the textile workers to forge new, sectional, independent vehicles for collective action that received their baptism of fire in the weavers' strike of 1808. Their continuing frustration ultimately provoked class defiance in 1812. At the other end of the spectrum, farm workers' bonds of solidarity were too sparse, while social controls over work, relief, and justice were too formidable and constrictive for them to practice the assertive direct action of "classical" rioters.

That spectrum of riots and community politics seems to illuminate the "politics of riot" in other communities as well. Disciplined food riots and "paternalistic" responses like those in Devon predominated in many of the older, more stable, county towns, in medium-sized market towns, and in small manufacturing centers, from the West Country through the Midlands to East Anglia, and even in Yorkshire and Lancashire—towns like Oxford, Cambridge, Canterbury, Aylesbury, Chichester, Sudbury (Suffolk), Wells, Banbury, and Nuneaton.[1] In such towns the common people still carried political clout, and the magistrates were still willing to act as mediators, not only in food riots but also in labor disputes and conflicts over impressment.[2] In Mansfield (Nottinghamshire), for instance, "proto-industrialization" had loosened but not destroyed the traditional social frameworks when food rioting occurred in September 1800. The local magistrate deployed the Oxford Blues (a unit of regular cavalry) and vetoed a relief subscription for fear it would "seem...we had allowed them to make terms with us." But he also persuaded the millers, "Flour men," and the farmers, whom he blamed for the crisis, to supply the town with flour and grain at reduced prices, for "...when good is my aim, I scruple not to exceed the bounds of my authority."[3] Significantly, price controls soon had to be abandoned, and that may well mark the end of a practicable "moral economy" in Mansfield.

Likewise, each of the dozen or so great provincial towns might be ranked along that spectrum of more or less stable, dense, and cohesive social frameworks. Each town was a unique compound of old and new. Norwich, for instance, was a stable, even stagnating manufacturing and market town with one of the broadest parliamentary franchises in England. According to the Webbs, the municipal corporation of Norwich disposed of "extensive patronage," so that "the whole internal life of the Corporation took the form of a struggle for its patronage—for the admission of Freemen, the appointments to the numerous petty offices, the filling of vacancies at the Hospitals, the grant of Outdoor Relief,...even the privilege of admission to the workhouse,...appointments to the salaried force of Watchmen...[and] all contracts for the hospitals or the workhouse." One of the most visible forms of patronage at Norwich was the charity—bread, coals, and cash—the aldermen lavished on their poor neighbors (and doubtless constituents) in hard times—so lavish that food riot seems almost to have been eliminated from town politics. In the only significant food riot of the period, women marched a malfeasant miller to the Guild Hall to demand that the town authorities deal with him.[4] The desire not to offend working-class electors motivated the elite to avert industrial conflict, and even to prevent the use of labor-saving machinery in Norwich's worsted industry.[5] Parliamentary elections themselves were frequently riotous contests and served as popular referenda on the war and its impact on the town's welfare. The "precocious" political arousal of the workingmen of Norwich by their active involvement in electoral politics; the impact of hardship aggravated by industrial stagnation; and the even division of the town's establishment between the Whigs and radicals and the Tories—all promoted the growth of an unusually vigorous Jacobin movement, one whose coalition partners were strong enough to prevent its being silenced by "Church and King" riots, for they could obtain no "license" in Norwich. It was no accident that the plebeian electors who had experienced locally the tangible benefits of the franchise—and had fought over the tangible injuries of national policies, especially the war—should be among England's most ardent supporters of wider suffrage.[6]

Another of the great towns, Birmingham, was "new" and growing rapidly like Manchester. And yet Birmingham had an older and more coherent tradition of popular political articulacy and action, owing to the town's close connections with neighboring parliamentary constituencies. A dense matrix of popular clubs and "opportunities for social meeting" mitigated the centrifugal effects of rapid growth. To a large degree, relatively conservative traditions among Birmingham's artisans allowed a "local pre-industrial sense of community" to survive despite the town's expansion.[7]

Against that background, Birmingham's riots were transitional mixtures of order and disorder, bargaining and violence. The Priestley riots of 1791 in Birmingham were the most violent riots of these two decades. They grew directly out of the hardening polarization within Birmingham's bourgeois elite. The riots were "licensed" by the local magistrate, in the sense that he condoned them, but the crowd exceeded their "license" and made riot too dangerous a weapon to be used again in partisan conflict. In the food shortages of 1795 and 1800, "Job Nott's" obsequious warnings against riot competed with seditious handbills and slogans chalked on the town's walls. At the same time, some of Birmingham's artisans were prosperous and self-reliant enough to have become the main stockholders in one of the town's two flour mills. In sum, signs of both cohesion and breakdown appeared in Birmingham's social relations, and so also in the town's riots. On the one hand, traditional forced sales of bread, potatoes, and butter by crowds in the marketplace were central features of several food riots in Birmingham in 1800. But on the other hand, both in 1795 and 1800, crowds furiously attacked James Pickard's steam-powered flour mill.[8]

The magistrates' reactions combined force and conciliation. When direct exhortations to the rioters failed, they called in the cavalry. Two rioters were shot in 1795, and two in 1800, though as a result of skirmishes between the crowds and the troops, not by order of the magistrates. In both 1795 and 1810 some of Birmingham's food rioters were sentenced to death, but in 1800 some of the most respectable inhabitants of the town successfully petitioned for leniency for rioters of otherwise good character.[9]

Paternalistic charity and influence mingled with laissez faire economic doctrines in the relief programs set on foot by Birmingham's magistrates and gentlemen. In 1795 subscriptions were collected to purchase relief supplies at Liverpool, but the supplies were sold in Birmingham at the going market rate rather than at a reduced price. However, in 1800, gentlemen actually created a fund to take over Pickard's mill and run it as a public service. They sank thousands of pounds into the effort. Even more remarkable, the magistrates of Birmingham and nearby Bilston still called upon landed gentlemen to induce their neighbors and tenants to supply the town with food at reasonable prices.[10] Despite Birmingham's size and growth, therefore, a thicker tissue of social relations seemed to have modified the kind of class alienation so evident in Manchester.

The most riotous town in the kingdom was Nottingham. Its riots resembled both Manchester's and Norwich's. Nottingham's old municipal corporation and broad electorate for both local and parliamentary elections provided ample opportunity for the distribution of patronage and for partisan conflict—in other words, for intense political participation by the workingmen. Nottingham also had an old stocking-knitting industry that had a tradition of bargaining between the stocking-knitters and their employers; occasionally the magistrates mediated between them. But Nottingham was too large, too polarized between capitalists and wage earners, and too rapidly growing to contain social relations within traditional bounds. The riots there combined violence and bargaining: twice in the early 1790s rioters were killed in Nottingham, and the bitter "Church and King" riot of 1794 was more destructive than any but the Priestley riots.[11]

The food riot of September 1800 epitomized the workings of social politics at Nottingham. Crowds made up mostly of women broke shop windows, stole bread, scattered "adulterated" flour and plundered barges and warehouses. But they also observed traditional rituals, forcing food dealers to reduce their prices in some instances. The local authorities did not react with simple, impersonal police measures. They certainly tried to protect the markets with all the civil and military force at their disposal, but they also applied their corporate and personal influence directly to the markets. The mayor and magistrates quickly procured grain to be ground and sold to the poor at prices and in quantities they could afford. The Yeomanry were asked to send in their own corn to be sold at low prices. The high sheriff and "County Gentlemen" met at the Shire Hall and agreed to compel their tenant farmers to bring their grain to market at low prices. Several gentlemen subsequently promised to compensate their tenants for any losses.[12]

The texture of riot politics in Nottingham was thus more bitter than in Norwich and more impersonal than in Devon. But the magistrates' actions were more "politic" than in Manchester, no doubt because of the political standing of Nottingham's thousands of plebeian voters, who had to be placated and not flatly repressed. At the same time, the cohesive but violent crowds seemed to be shifting away from communal bargaining toward class conflict. A letter from a Nottingham rioter or sympathizer crowed:

Thus has the price been lowered almost four pounds a quarter by nothing but the courage of the people in declaring against oppression but what scarred the Gentlemen the worse was to see the Union of parties their being no Scrats [aristocrats] nor painites nor no such Song as God Save the King to be heard and the conduct of the people on tuesday who stood the fire from the Yeomanry with such an undaunted courage that astonished the Gentlemen . . . Thus has two species of Vilians [farmers and flour sellers] been brought to reason by the courage of the Tradesmen and Inhabitants of Nottingham, and convinced I am that the people United may and can shake of any species of oppression at any time they think proper.[13]

"The people" exulted: they had once more enforced their claims in community politics.

These vignettes suggest that the interaction of a town's growth rate, industrial structure, and political "density" set up important tendencies and limits for the incidence and character of riot. Relative stability and density of social relationships permitted riotous "bargaining"; instability promoted the cruder use of force by both rioters and authorities. At the same time, many of these episodes suggest that this was an important period of transition in community politics, and hence in the character and incidence of riot. But before that suggestion is elaborated, London's experience must be considered.

The metropolis was a social universe *sui generis*. Some features of its social conflicts are familiar enough—resistance to recruiting, the political turbulence of Wilkesite, Radical, and Loyalist crowds, the strikes and riots of well-organized craftsmen.[14] But in addition, fully half of London's riots in this period sprang from other than "mainstream" political and economic sources. For example, crowds attacked unpopular individuals—an elderly pickpocket in 1790, an accused wife-murderer in 1808, a group of homosexuals in 1810, and many more.[15] Theater audiences exercised their venerable prerogative of helping to determine the cost and content of their entertainment. The uproarious "Old Price" rioters at the Drury Lane Theater in 1809 used "Old Price" songs, dances, hats, and placards to force the management to rescind new price increases—an urbane enforcement of the "moral economy." Brawls pitted Irish men and women against police officials who intruded into their neighborhoods and disrupted their "cock-and-hen" social clubs. More than once the men of Munster joined battle with the men of Connaught in Sunday donnybrooks that appeared to be more sport than politics.[16]

Perhaps the most peculiar feature of conflict in London was the extreme rarity of food riots, but some of the explanations offered for their infrequency do not seem to hold.[17] It has been suggested, for instance, that London, as both the hub of the corn trade and the object of governmental concern for the peace of the capital, had access to more supplies of food. Now, if the capital was better supplied than the provinces, it should have had lower prices, but London's prices were close to the national average for this period (see Figures 2 and 3; Middlesex prices substitute for London's). Moreover, although the Assize of Bread (which limited bakers' profit margins) was probably more regularly promulgated in London than in other towns, it too fluctuated, almost as sharply as the wheat prices. In 1795 it increased by nearly 70 percent over the previous five-year average, while in 1800 it doubled the average of the more normal years of 1796–1798.[18] Hence London's unique geographical and political advantages were of little comfort to consumers in the market and at the shops, for they did not seem to have reduced hardship. Another explanation for the infrequency of food riot in London is that the suburbs shielded the capital from invasions by hungry rioters from the countryside. But most English food riots were the work of hometown consumers, not "invaders." London's food rioters, too, were city people. Finally, as I have shown, country people did not usually enter into food riots.

It has also been suggested that intensive relief efforts forestalled riot in London—a much more likely explanation, though it remains undocumented.[19] This explanation also directs our attention away from simple price analysis. For if relief efforts did prevent riots in London, they apparently did so without raising or lowering market prices. In order to feed perhaps hundreds of thousands of London consumers without increasing the demand for grain so as to raise prices above the national average, London relief committees would have had to operate outside domestic market channels, by direct purchase of grain on the Continent.[20] Conversely, in order to be effective without lowering prices, relief would have to have reached consumers who were otherwise too poor to generate effective demand, who would otherwise simply have starved. All this is highly speculative, though plausible. The point is that the supplies of food available for London's consumers were probably affected as much by sociopolitical motivations as by purely economic pressures.

A further likely explanation for the rarity of food riots in London is that neither the social structure nor the ideological climate of London was conducive to the politics of riot and the ideology of the moral economy.

However, although the political and economic contexts of London's riots have been explored, a full appreciation of the grass-roots social foundations for collective action must await further research at the parish and neighborhood level. It is striking that many of London's crowds arose from recognizably coherent groups and traditions: artisans' and coal-heavers' combinations, Westminster electoral committees, Irish neighborhoods and factions, activist theater audiences. Nicholas Rogers's study of Westminster election riots in the 1740s has disclosed a running contest between a powerful "machine" based on patronage distributed by courtiers and aristocrats and an opposition of "independent" tradesmen resting on a number of taverns and coffee houses and on the efforts of an Independent Electors' Society.[21] George Rudé has suggested that the major disturbances in late eighteenth-century London "were almost exclusively centered in the older areas of declining or stagnant population: the cities of London and Westminster, the Strand, Spitalfields, Finsbury, Whitechapel, and the Minories," together with several expanding districts, notably Southwark. Rudé believes that such old and settled areas provided a firmer basis for a *"camaraderie* of rebellion," born of long association, than either newly settled quarters or the warrens in slums like St. Giles-in-the-Fields.[22] Perhaps further study of riots and local social relations in London will illuminate the balance between patronage and autonomy, and between "camaraderie," organization, and disintegration in the experience and politics of London's common people.

But finally there is the question of how changes in riots and community politics shed light upon the evolution of English society. Both the number and character of riots in this period suggest that the older tradition of bargaining through riot reached its climax in these two decades. At the same time, even in the "classical" social environment of Devon, as well as in the quieter countryside, signs of social transition appeared. Those signs multiply and intensify as we move across the spectrum, through the older great towns to Manchester. Does that spectrum of communities have an analog in change over time? Does the history of riots provide insights into such developments as the rise of class politics? Conversely, how did social changes affect the frequency of riots, the occasions of riot, and the usefulness of riot as a form of social politics?

Changes in social protest during the Industrial Revolution have most often been explained by a "sea-change" in popular mentalities, or else by the transition from "pre-industrial" to industrial society. The "sea-change" in mentalities has been described in several ways. It is sometimes argued that as "the governors" abdicated their social responsibilities for the welfare of the laboring poor, as paternalism yielded to laissez faire, so the common people renounced deference for defiance.[23] The evolution of popular political attitudes in the eighteenth century is usually described as one from "instinctive" popular loyalism to radicalism, owing to the combined impact of Jacobin ideology and economic hardship.[24] Alternatively, less empathetic historians treated riot as inherently primitive behavior, and assumed that popular salvation began with "enlightenment," when the common people forsook riot and embraced their proper destiny in the shape of parliamentary Reform.[25] More generally, many historians have regarded traditional rioters as backward-looking, striving to recover "lost rights," by contrast with modern, forward-looking movements that strive to claim new rights by progressive change.[26]

Historians who have emphasized the shift from "pre-industrial" to industrial society have often been engaged in the search for the origins of the modern labor movement. According to the prevailing consensus, in eighteenth-century "pre-industrial" society, trade unions were impossible to sustain. At the same time, family economies were acutely vulnerable to harvest failures. Hence food riots rather than labor combinations were the typical way of defending the common people's standards of living. As industrialization promoted labor organization, strikes replaced food riots as the most common way of defending living standards.[27]

But the relationships between riots and community politics suggest a new perspective on the history of popular movements. Riots *appear* to have ceased to be the predominant form of popular politics in the nineteenth century, but not merely because of political "enlightenment" and industrial change. Rather, the provocations to riot that had been most important before 1815 either ceased in the nineteenth century or receded beyond the reach of direct physical action and community bargaining. At the same time, the optimum community frameworks for bargaining by riot, exemplified in Devon's market towns, became less common because of rapid urbanization. These trends are particularly clear in the history of four of the most common provocations to riot: friction with the military, food prices, labor disputes, and political conflicts.

Clashes with the military accounted for nearly one-fifth of the riots in this period. They owed little to ideological or social change and were not especially backward-looking. Only the rural riots against the Supplementary Militia Act in 1796–1797 fit Charles Tilly's model of "reactive" resistance to the new demands for manpower by a more ambitious state, and even that resistance could be overcome by compromise.[28] Otherwise, neither crimping of recruits for the army nor impressment of sailors were innovations, given the frequent wars of the eighteenth century. At Newcastle in 1793 and in the early stages of the great Spithead Mutiny in 1797, sailors rioted not against a new loss of liberty but against low naval pay and poor working conditions.[29] Likewise, soldiers' mutinies in England were almost never rebellions against military authority as such; instead, they were a form of collective bargaining over pay arrears or resistance to harsh discipline or to service in Ireland or the West Indies.[30] All such clashes disappeared after the Napoleonic Wars, when recruiting parties and marauding Irish recruits no longer disturbed the lives of English men and women. In other words, a significant number of traditional riots ceased to occur for reasons unrelated to social change. Their absence contributed to an optical illusion by leaving the remaining industrial and political disputes more prominent among the causes of collective violence than they had been in the eighteenth century.

Food riots certainly seemed to have reached their peak in the late eighteenth century. It is often said that food rioters looked backward and sought to restore the "just price"; that they were trying to enforce ancient forms of market regulation while the magistrates were increasingly becoming converted to laissez faire doctrines; and that rioters were resisting the new strains placed on local supplies by urban areas and a growing national system of food marketing. First of all, rioters did not base their claims to legitimacy on ancient paternalistic practices. Nor did they seek to restore the "just prices" of some prior golden age. In Devon, for instance, the rioters of 1795 merely sought the prices of the previous year, while in 1801 the prices they set in their contracts were compromises between "normal" and crisis levels.[31] If food rioters were not particularly backward-looking, the decline in food riots does not represent a shift from traditionalist to progressive ideology.

Nor can food riots be explained as local reactions against the growth of a national market system.[32] The chronologies of food rioting and of capitalist market development do not match. Most riots were not reactions to *new* market pressures. For instance, only a minority of the food riots of the 1790s can be shown to be responses to new urban demands transmitted by canals.[33] Both the establishment of many town food markets and conflicts between local needs and middlemen's trade go back to at least the seventeenth century. It is not surprising to discover that food riots occurred at least as early as the sixteenth century, though it is difficult to know if these were the first, or how widespread they were. Moreover, the outlines of a national market existed at least by 1750, if not before—and yet by 1800 its complete triumph was still in the future.[34] For food riot seemed to be most viable precisely in places like Devon, where mobs and magistrates could still control those who supplied local food markets. Elsewhere, the development of a national market meant both that towns like Manchester were tapping food supplies beyond their physical control, and that local farmers could escape local controls by sending their grain to alternative markets—as happened at Nottingham and Mansfield.[35] So, far from promoting food riots, the growth of the national market was beginning to make them obsolete by 1800.

Hence the second half of the eighteenth century, particularly the crises of 1766, 1795 and 1800, was the golden age of food rioting. On the one hand, food marketing was completing its transition from late medieval regulations and conceptions into fully capitalistic practices, although residues of paternalism and social patronage allowed rioters some hope of appealing successfully to the magistrates. On the other hand, the growth of towns and of rural industry meant that working people had reached the midpoint in their emergence from rural society, with its close social and economic controls (on them and on farmers), to capitalistic market society, in which they would be "free laborers" and cash customers. In other words, probably the maximum number of semi-autonomous consumers still lived in the hundreds of local communities like those of Devon where food riot could work. In 1766 widespread food rioting was still apparently new enough to alarm the gentry as a symptom of unprecedented plebeian autonomy.[36] The food riots of the 1790s were not nearly so alarming, because they were familiar as well as disciplined. Food prices were still the most manageable issue within the framework of community politics.

Classic food riots virtually ceased after 1820. In part, this may be a sign that, as industry grew, more people thought and acted as *workers* in labor movements than as members of communities united by more general interests as *consumers*.[37] Indeed, both at Manchester and Norwich in the 1790s some well-organized workers had already deliberately eschewed food riot as being politically and economically counterproductive.[38] But a much more obvious reason for the decline of food rioting after 1820 is simply that food crises ceased to be as acute and as general as they had been before. Food prices dropped steadily over the next generation, although they still fluctuated. And the system of marketing food evened out its distribution and removed its supplies and suppliers beyond the reach of localized riots. At the same time, industrial growth, increasing mobility, and urbanization almost certainly made dense and stable communities like Devon's exceptional rather than common. In sum, popular price fixing was no longer practical economics or practical politics. Moreover, when food riots did occur in nineteenth-century industrial towns, they tended to take the form of unilateral punishment and plunder of food dealers.[39] That reflected the polarization of community politics in those towns. No doubt the demise of the classical traditions of food rioting deprived the English common people of important practical experience in the use of collective action.

Besides military and food riots, labor conflicts were a third important category of riots in this period. Labor riots in the eighteenth century have generally been regarded as a sturdy but primitive "pre-industrial" ancestor of modern industrial trade unionism. According to this view, the dispersion of small-scale production in cottages and workshops prevented the formation of durable trade unions. Like other "pre-industrial" protest, labor riots looked backward. They sought to recover lost rights, such as a "just wage," rather than to look forward and claim new benefits. Such riots were typically defensive: collective action could only fitfully be galvanized by new machinery that threatened jobs or by wage cuts in a time of depression. Only when industrialization clarified capital-labor antagonisms and when the proletariat was concentrated in factories and cities (and mining villages) could workers learn the "rules of the game" of collective bargaining, develop "habits of solidarity," and build durable trade unions. Then they were able to take the offensive, to strike for wage increases when the economy was improving.[40] However, this model (here greatly simplified) seems to exaggerate the significance of technological change in determining labor relations and, implicitly, to overemphasize the textile workers' reactions to the Industrial Revolution.

A more comprehensive view of the evolution of labor relations would emphasize the earlier formation of trade unions, their predominantly "offensive," forward-looking tactics, and the greater influence of nontechnological social factors on collective action. First, in the eighteenth century, riot was by no means the sole recourse of workers unable to sustain durable combinations. C. R. Dobson's study of nearly four hundred eighteenth-century labor disputes has recently confirmed that actions taken by trade unions spread across the century and across many geographical areas and trades and were not merely confined to London artisans and West Country textile workers.[41] Violence was not simply the consequence of a primitive stage of labor organization, for industrial riots often originated with better-paid and organized workers. In addition, riot was only one tactic for pressuring employers collectively. Well-organized workers shifted readily between strikes, riots, appeals to magistrates, litigation, and petitions to Parliament, from the early eighteenth century right through to the Nottinghamshire Luddite movement of 1811–1814.[42]

Second, collective action was predominantly offensive rather than defensive. It was also focused much more on wages than on technical change. The impression that eighteenth-century protests were defensive may be rooted in an over-emphasis by historians on the fortunes and actions of the textile workers, for they did promote one-third of the labor disputes of the eighteenth century, many of which were to resist wage cuts or the use of new machinery.[43] But even their resistance to new machinery may have been exaggerated. As Hobsbawm pointed out long ago, the key issues in many episodes of machine breaking were employment and the standard of living. At Shepton Mallet in the West Country, woolen workers' initial hostility to new machines in the 1790s was overcome after they agreed to permit a test of their impact on emnployment.[44] On the other hand, cottage-based textile workers were not always able to resist mechanization, for the machines that replaced them might be in factories hundreds of miles away.[45]

For all eighteenth-century labor disputes, Dobson concludes that "technical change as such was not a major source of conflict." Rather than structural changes such as technological innovation, apprenticeships, or work discipline, "the most important single source of industrial conflict was the money wage."[46]

Workers' combinations for higher wages were typically offensive rather than defensive. Outside of the textile industry, declining wages were not a major issue. On the contrary, "claims for wage *increases* to offset rising prices were almost universal from the 1760s onwards." Demands for wage *increases* constituted an increasingly large majority of all disputes over wages and hours from 1741 onward, and indeed a majority of all labor disputes from 1761 onward.[47]

The national sample of labor *riots* in 1790–1810—a narrower category than Dobson's labor disputes—reinforces these findings. Of nearly forty-five labor conflicts involving violence in this period, thirty-six, or four-fifths, were occasioned by wage disputes. Only seven involved resistance to new machines—all but one in the hard-pressed woolen industry of the West Country. Only one riot occurred over apprenticeship. Of thirty-six riots in which wages were at issue, thirty-four involved workers' demands for wage increases. To be sure, the Lancashire weavers in 1808 struck for wage increases to stem a long-term decline, but the Tyneside sailors and farm laborers sought to catch a rising tide.[48]

Third, workers' capacities for collective action were determined by other social factors than the divorce between capital and labor that the Webbs' classic *History* emphasized.[49] Dobson points out that "the most consistently successful bargainers were those with a permanent base for continuous association...not necessarily the workplace." He accepts Clark Kerr and A. Siegel's hypothesis that "isolated masses" of workers in homogeneous "separate communities" had important bases for collective action. The "house of call," a public house where workers in a particular trade like portering waited to be called to a job, was another very important base for collective solidarity. Community politics certainly affected workers' bargaining strength, positively in the case of midcentury woolen workers in Devon and the Tyneside sailors in the 1790s, negatively for Manchester's weavers and farm laborers. Magistrates often mediated between workers and employers. And sometimes workers would appeal to wider community sympathy in their struggles against the "selfish" and injurious introduction of labor-saving machinery.[50]

All of these factors underscore the continuity of labor traditions and their essential pragmatism. They suggest that the Industrial Revolution, classically associated with cotton-manufacturing technology, did not produce a sharp break in the tactics or bases of workers' collective action.

More broadly, the history of industrialization had been revised. Alongside the dramatic innovations in machinery, much greater emphasis must now be given to proto-industrialization—that is, to the increase in production not by technical change but by the great multiplication of outwork in cottages and small shops by wage earners under the direction of merchant capitalists.[51] That process took advantage of great supplies of unskilled labor, and even added to them. For employment stimulated population growth and also brought into the labor market new workers, particularly women and children, who had previously not been earning wages for their family. Part of that process entailed the division of labor to use cheap, unskilled labor to perform work formerly done in craft shops. An urban analog of proto-industrialization, the use of sweatshops rather than cottage industry, had by the mid-eighteenth century already begun to divide some London trades into "honorable" (craft) and "dishonorable" (mass production) sectors. These crucial dimensions of the Industrial Revolution, the growth of capitalism, and the proletarianization of industry probably affected more workers, at least up to 1830, than the more dramatic and familiar technological innovations symbolized in the steam-powered cotton factory.[52] The important point is that proto-industrialization and its urban analog widened the labor market beyond the reach of local and corporate bargaining and direct action. Like the nationalization of the food market, proto-industrialization knocked the props from under a locally enforceable "moral economy." At the same time, the centers of industrial growth were shifting away from the experienced and incorporated (organized) textile workers of the West Country and East Anglia to the mushrooming towns and country districts of Lancashire and Yorkshire. While older bases of collective action were being left high and dry, newer ones were forming with great difficulty, which depended on the cooperation of town and country workers.

One example of that kind of cooperation was the Lancashire hand-loom weavers' strike of 1808. Another was the first phase of Nottinghamshire Luddism in 1811–1812. For at least two generations before 1810 the Midlands stocking-knitting industry had expanded rapidly in country districts and villages outside the older centers of Nottingham and Leicester.[53] Much of that expansion was made possible by resorting to cheap methods, such as the manufacture of "cut-ups" and the use of "colts." "Cut-ups" were articles such as gloves or stockings made by cutting pieces out of a large piece of knitted material and sewing the edges together, rather than knitting one continuous garment. "Cut-ups" required less skill and so could employ cheaper labor, but they were also likely to fall apart when used. "Colts" were young workers who had not served an apprenticeship. "Colts" and "cut-ups" made possible cheap mass production that undercut the craft traditions and the wage scales of experienced stocking knitters. The Luddites protested the making of "cut-ups" and the use of "colts."[54] Thus, they were resisting the "soft" side of the Industrial Revolution—rather than its "hard" side, new labor-saving machines, for new machines were not an issue in the Luddite riots in Nottinghamshire.

A wage agreement between Nottingham master hosiers and their employees—stockingers, or framework knitters—had helped to maintain peace in the industry between 1787 and 1807, even while such "abuses" were gathering.[55] Negotiations between sympathetic larger hosiers and framework knitters continued up to and through the first year of the Luddites' direct action. But all attempts to fashion a new agreement broke down because it was impossible to get the lesser hosiers to cooperate. One breakdown of those negotiations in early 1811 triggered Luddism directly.[56] The Luddite rioters first began to break the knitting frames in country villages, rather than in the towns of Nottingham or Leicester, not simply because enforcing order was a simpler task in the towns, nor yet because the town stockingers were well-paid sophisticates and the country workers were roughnecks.[57] For, ample evidence suggests that the town and the country stockingers united as one body to support both organized frame breaking and peaceful efforts at petitioning Parliament.[58] Rather, the outbreak and location of Luddism seem to have been determined by the necessities of bargaining.

The first objective of Luddite direct action was apparently to compel the country hosiers operating beyond the reach of the town-based negotiations to participate in a new wage agreement. Initially, the Luddite rioters were very selective, concentrating their attacks on the machines of country masters who employed "colts" and manufactured "cut-ups."[59] In sum, Luddism in Nottinghamshire was decisively shaped not by the recent imposition of laissez faire capitalism upon old craft traditions[60]—for those traditions had been breached much earlier—but by the failure of the organized negotiations to govern the entire geographically expanding industry. That failure required, but ultimately frustrated, cooperation between town workers and their country cousins. Nevertheless, the Luddite rioting in Nottinghamshire illustrates how industrial and social geography required workers to transcend their traditional milieus of local bargaining.

After this period, it seems fruitful to ask how far nineteenth-century trade unions and wider collective action by workers were undergirded by local communal ties. Such ties could be survivals from the past, as was the leadership of the artisans who led some of the "Captain Swing" riots of farm laborers against threshing machines in 1830.[61] Otherwise, local working-class networks had to be reestablished after the most disruptive phase of rapid industrialization and urbanization had passed. The best example is the interweaving of workplace, trade union, chapel, parliamentary constituency, and community in the common lives of the coal miners,[62] interweaving that certainly promoted collective political strength as well as solidarity in strikes and riots. How far such networks underlay collective action in other trades remains a question that would repay further investigation.

Finally, besides recruiting, food, and labor conflicts, riots over national political issues and ideologies raise questions about the political evolution of the English common people. The prevailing assumption has been that during the wars with France, dominant popular ideological commitments shifted from dyed-in-the-wool Loyalism to radicalism. In the first place, recent research has shown that Loyalism was hardly instinctive. The interest, participation, and partial independence of the common people in political conflicts was fostered as early as the 1760s by the growth of literacy and the popular press and by tavern discussion groups and debating societies. That popular political articulacy was stimulated in places like Birmingham and Norwich by parliamentary contests, and it was brought into focus by the crude but charismatic John Wilkes, who combined radicalism with roguery in his challenges to Parliament in the 1760s. In Birmingham, the people's political attitudes were too complex to be assigned simply to a Loyalist or radical pole.[63]

Second, within the framework of community politics in the 1790s it is evident that rioters were neither deferential to local authorities nor ideologically traditionalist. Conflicts over national issues deeply divided the bourgeois elites of various towns according to their interests, ideological and religious commitments, and attitudes toward social change; it is hardly surprising that the more articulate members of the working classes should also have been polarized by interest and perception. Were "Church and King" mobs expressing "spontaneous" popular loyalism or were they true "'mobs' in the sense of hired bands operating on behalf of external interests?"[64] The dichotomy is too simple. If such mobs had been merely hired, it is surprising that more conclusive evidence never leaked out. Certainly local officials were more likely to "license" a mob's loyalism than its radicalism. No doubt earnest Radicals were more likely to avoid violence, both because of its political and legal liabilities, and because the logic of riot (as normal politics) was irrelevant to the logic of constitutional reform. Nevertheless "Church and King" mobs did not possess a perfect monopoly on ideologically-motivated violence. The Whig mobs of Nottingham and Westminster, the antiwar rioters of Norwich, and the insurrectionary radicals on the edges of Sheffield riots all did their share.[65] In short neither the "Church and King" mobs nor their radical opponents represented the sole "authentic" *vox populi*. The small number of "Church and King" riots scarcely warrant the inference that the common people were instinctively Loyalists.[66]

The war years did not witness a simple spiritual progess of "the people" from "natural" but "backward" loyalism to "enlightened" radicalism; what was genuinely new during that time was an unprecedented widening of the organized political public on both sides. Rather than conversion, the significant transition was mobilization, the emergence of perceptions and oranizations having regional and national, not merely local, horizons. In Manchester, the Loyalist mobilization was as innovative as the radical in its use of the press and associations. Moreover the thesis of a "sea change" in mentalities by political conversion or "enlightenment" is too rationalistic—it exaggerates the degree to which people changed their minds as a result of merely intellectual process such as new insights or arguments. The praxis of popular radicalism was rooted in tangible experience—of hardship and its connection with the war, as well as of the alienation of community politics in places like Manchester. Hence as the wars stretched on, hunger, war-induced unemployment, and the frustration of petitions for industrial regulation recruited massive support for parliamentary Reform in London, Manchester, Nottingham, and Yorkshire; practical electoral experience sustained the strong radical movement at Norwich.[67] In short, the radical critique of "Old Corruption" could gain the most converts when it could be most closely tied to the common people's direct experience of either hardship or political participation.

One might speculate that the practical results achieved by riots as a form of community politics in the eighteenth century dampened popular enthusiasm for more abstract and long-range political changes like constitutional reform. But it seems clear that the declining effectiveness of riot as community politics after 1800 helped to redirect plebeian energies and perceptions toward national political reform. The Lancashire weavers' campaign was certainly channeled toward Reform by the manifest futility not only of petitions to Parliament but also of local bargaining. Moreover, just as food and labor markets were moving out of local control, so other issues of popular welfare were being decided by Parliament rather than by local authorities. Hence the common people would gird themselves for contest in a national arena.

Nevertheless, the apparent demise of riots as local politics in the later nineteenth century was not a simple "transition to order."[68] First, the implied order-disorder dichotomy distorts the significance of earlier riots as intelligible politics. Second, the payoffs from such national political campaigns still had to be demonstrated before they could gain popular support from their promise as well as from people's frustration. The most convincing demonstration came a generation after the French wars, in the crucial contest over the New Poor Law between 1835 and 1839, because it brought the concrete significance of national policies right to the doorsteps of the working poor and because a combination of "new" political mobilization and "old" local direct action with parallel resistance by gentlemen and local officials won modifications of the New Poor Law in the north.[69] Hence the anti–Poor Law movement was one of the crucial bridges between the radical Reform agitation of 1831, the factory reform movement of the 1830s, which also mobilized northern workers, and Chartism, the climactic movement for working-class rights. All three of the precursors of Chartism, national programs that bound together local movements, involved direct action that was both instrumentally aimed at concrete objectives and expressive of pent-up anger and defiance—including, for instance, the Reform Bill riots of 1831 in Nottingham and Bristol and the anti–Poor Law riot in Todmorden.[70] The mixed "victories" of these campains gave the Chartists a sense of momentum and frustration, because their limited success pointed toward both the necessity and the promise of political mobilization on a broader front.

Furthermore, the history of British riots does not suggest a "transition to order" after 1850, despite the increasingly national scale of labor and political conflict and the advent of a "viable class society."[71] Charles Tilly has insisted that collective violence is not inherently archaic but that it has regularly flowed from the more routine social and political processes of modern Western society. Britain's experience, at least up to World War I, supports that contention, for between 1865 and 1914 Britain saw more than 450 riots.[72]

To some extent the growth of the industrial economy itself created new occasions for conflict by bringing large numbers of Irish immigrants into direct confrontation of bitterly antagonistic English workers in south Lancashire.[73] But among other sources of violent conflict was the growing distance of national political and collective bargaining agencies from grass-roots concerns.[74] At the same time, bases for collective action were proliferating as working-class associations and trade unions were established and as a mature working-class community life settled down after the period of the most rapid and disruptive urbanization.[75] When national bargaining frameworks failed to satisfy popular demands, and when the underside of a "viable class society" was persistent class inequality in wealth and power that fueled resentment, the late-Victorian working class could once again draw upon the forceful traditions of their grandparents.

Finally, one might ask what light the history of eighteenth-century riot throws on the questions of class and hegemony. Class, E. P. Thompson insists, is a relationship between groups of people that grows out of their historical experience. Between 1780 and 1830, Thompson adds, most English working people came to feel an identity of their own interests against those of their rulers and employers.[76] I would add that in Marx's discussions, the experience of class is determined by the whole system of property and power that enables some people to dominate others. Therefore, full class consciousness comes when that system of property and power as the source of class antagonisms of feeling, interest, and experience is perceived.[77]

It is just that systemic perception that seems lacking in the great majority of riots. I say "seems" because for the most part we must make inferences from the rioters' behavior, for direct evidence of their mentality is scarce. What can be inferred from the mainstream tradition of riot—from the rioters' discipline and the issues and targets they chose to act upon—is that most rioters confined their actions and objectives, their practical intentions, to the concrete, the particular, and the local. They did not challenge directly the whole system of property and power. As long as the politics of riot was reasonably effective in winning redress of their grievances, it was dangerous folly to raise the stakes by attacking those magistrates whose immediate neutrality and sympathetic action against the targets were necessary for the riot's success.

On the other hand, their actions were not passively acquiescent. Rioters modified the property rights of farmers and food dealers, for instance, and their exertion of force at the margin of legitimacy and illegality was a real if limited exercise of political power. In short, riots were not simply a functional confirmation of the status quo (or else why were rioters sent to jail?). Rather riots were a dynamic constituent moment in the system of property and power.

Rioters were pragmatic, not revolutionary. If the public actions of hundreds of crowds can be taken as more representative of the English common people than the elusive activities of revolutionary conspirators, revolution was not imminent in this period. Subjectively, while the Jacobins' or United Englishmen's cell groups and anonymous letters furnished a realm for revolutionary fantasies, in broad daylight rioters were too pragmatic to try conclusions quixotically with a government that hundreds of limited tests of strength (in riots) had shown to be strong enough, physically and politically, to defend itself easily. Objectively, Theda Skocpol has shown that social revolutions have been the product not of the intentions of a revolutionary movement or class, but rather of rare conjunctures of circumstances that created revolutionary situations.[78] England was never near such a combination in the late eighteenth and nineteenth century—hundreds of riots did not "add up" to a revolutionary sum. If the manifest futility of insurrection needed demonstration, it was provided by the Irish Rebellion of 1798, when a peasant insurrectionary movement much more numerous and better armed than the English revolutionaries was rather easily defeated by a poorly-led military force on alien ground.[79]

Yet if the English common people were not inclined toward insurrection, that is no proof of the "hegemony" of their rulers. The theory of hegemony holds that England's rulers maintained their position primarily by ideological and cultural domination rather than by superior economic and military power.[80] The concept of hegemony suggests that the common people were persuaded by theater and indoctrination to submit to their own subordination—otherwise, it is implied, they would have rebelled. However, the foremost proponents of theories of ruling-class hegemony in the eighteenth century, E. P. Thompson and his colleagues, are those who have done the most to reveal the robust autonomy of plebeian culture, to recapture the widespread social antagonism expressed in threatening letters and in the defiance of class "privileges" by poaching, for example—to which must be added the nondeferential assertiveness of rioters.[81] Hegemony could not ensure that the common people "were likely to get more from a loyal petition than from a riot."[82] For the lesson of riots was precisely the opposite. In most cases it was not until the common people undertook direct action, with its physical risks and real costs, after petitions had been ignored, that they won real concessions. The costumes of the gentry's theater of hegemony—the judges' wigs and gowns that proclaimed the majesty and impersonality of the Law—were like the emperor's new clothes. They convinced the actors but not the audience for whom the show was intended. Riots regularly demonstrated that politics rested on force—from both sides—not on ideology or mythology.

For this reason I have emphasized palpable "vertical" relationships and reciprocities under the rubric of social patronage, rather than under the insubstantial ideological tissue of "paternalism" and deference. Riots were the mode of conflict in the framework of patronage politics. In this period patronage politics was beginning to break down and class politics was forming. That shift began to take place not primarily from ideological changes (Perkin's "abdication of the governors" or Thompson's counter-revolution),[83] nor from political repression, nor from the proletarianization that was only one dimension of capitalist development. Class alienation emerged where the social frameworks that had supported a viable means of political bargaining by riot had broken down. Manchester's experience represents an extreme, "pure" form of that alienation, though other forms were possible—witness the Nottingham letter of 1800. So at one end of the social spectrum, and, to repeat, as that breakdown became more common and as issues receded beyond the reach of riot, class politics grew. The forces that shaped it were the impact of urbanization on community politics and the nationalization of political conflicts as much or more than changes in ideologies or workplace relations.

The legacy of riots to the future political evolution of the English people was not so much one of proto-class struggle and hardly one of incipient revolution. Instead, the legacy of riot was the deeply engrained experience of a quasi-independent citizenship capable of enforcing its claims and of sharing, to a real if limited extent, in the exercise of power and the definition of rights. It was that lost independence[84]—not the futile dream of revolution—that was to be the real measure and goal of popular movements as the common people became a working class.

Abbreviations

Manuscripts in the Public Record Office, London

Assize	Court of Assize Rolls, Process Books, and so forth
H.O.	Home Office files
K.B.	Court of King's Bench
M.A.F.	Ministry of Agriculture, Fisheries, and Food entry books
P.C.	Privy Council correspondence
P.L.	Palatinate of Lancaster (Court of Assize)
T.S.	Treasury Solicitor files
W.O.	War Office files

Other Manuscripts

D.R.O., 1262M	Lord lieutenant's public papers, 1781–1831, in the Devon County Record Office, Exeter
BRL	Birmingham Reference Library
B.L., Add. MSS	British Library, Additional Manuscripts
Clifford papers, GCLM	Papers of the Clifford family in the possession of the Right Honorable Lord Clifford, Ugbrooke House, Devon—General correspondence, 1800–1813, letters miscellaneous, 1800–1804
Exeter C.R.O.	Exeter City Record Office, miscellaneous boxes and Exeter Quarter Sessions records
LCL Banks	Joseph Banks Collection in Lindsey County Library, Lincoln
U.N., PwF	Portland papers, University of Nottingham
Q.S.	Quarter Sessions records

Newspapers and Journals

Ann. Ag.	*The Annals of Agriculture*
AR	*The Annual Register*
BG	*Aris's Birmingham Gazette*
CI	*The Cambridge Intelligencer*
EFP	*The Exeter Flying Post*
GM	*The Gentleman's Magazine*
LCh	*The London Chronicle*
LCo	*The London Courier*
LdsI	*The Leeds Intelligencer*
LEM	*The Evening Mail* (London)
LG	*The London Gazette*
LiRSM	*The Lincoln, Rutland, and Stamford Mercury*
LMCh	*The Morning Chronicle* (London)
LP	*The London Packet*
LObs	*The Observer* (London)
LSt	*The Star* (London)
LT	*The Times* (London)
MG	*The Manchester Gazette*
MH	*The Manchester Herald*
MM	*The Manchester Mercury*
NC	*The Newcastle Courant*
NCh	*The Norfolk Chronicle*
Reg. Times	*The Register of the Times*
RM	*The Reading Mercury*
ShI	*The Sheffield Iris*
SWJ	*The Salisbury and Winchester Journal*
SYM	*The Sherbourne and Yeovil Mercury*
YC	*The York Courant*

Other Abbreviations

H.C.J.	House of Commons Journals
P. P.	Parliamentary Papers

Manuscript Sources

Public Record Office, London

H.O. 42	Home Office: in-letters, domestic, 1790–1810
H.O. 43	Home Office: entry-books, domestic, 1793–1796, 1800–1801
H.O. 48	Law Officers reports and correspondence, 1801
H.O. 50	Home Office: in-letters, military, 1794–1801
H.O. 51	Home Office: out-letters, military, 1790–1800
M.A.F. 10	Ministry of Agriculture, Fisheries, and Food: registers of reports of corn prices to the Receiver of the Corn Returns, 1795–1796, 1800–1801
W.O. 1	Secretary at War: in-letters, 1793–1800
W.O. 13	War Office: monthly returns and annual pay lists, Devonshire Volunteers, 1794–1801
W.O. 40/17	War Office: in-letters miscellaneous, domestic disturbances
K.B. 8/83	Court of King's Bench: records of the Special Commission of 1795
T.S. 11	Treasury Solicitor: briefs and depositions
Assize 2	Assize Order Book, Worcestershire, 1797
Assize 4 and 5	Assize Rolls, Oxford Circuit (Oxfordshire, Monmouthshire, Worcestershire, Herefordshire, Gloucestershire, Berkshire), 1791–1793, 1795–1797, 1800–1801, 1803–1806
Assize 21	Assize Indictments, Western Circuit (Devonshire, Cornwall, Wiltshire, Somerset, Dorset, Hampshire), 1796–1801
Assize 23 and 24	Assize Process Books, Western Circuit, 1790–1810

Assize 25	Assize Rolls, Western Circuit, 1801
Assize 31	Assize Gaol Delivery Calendar, Home and Norfolk Circuit (Kent, Sussex, Surrey, Bedfordshire, Norfolk, Suffolk, and Essex), 1793–1797, 1800–1801
Assize 35	Assize Rolls, Home and Norfolk Circuit, 1793–1797, 1800–1801
P.L. 27	Assize Depositions, Lancashire, 1797, 1800, 1808
P.L. 28	Assize Gaol Delivery Book, Lancashire, 1797, 1801

Devon County Record Office, Exeter

1262M	Lord Lieutenant's public papers, 1781–1831, and Lord Fortescue's personal accounts
	Quarter Sessions Rolls, 1793–1802
	Quarter Sessions Order Book, 1788–1802
	Land Tax Assessments, 1799–1802, Totnes, Modbury
269A/PO2	Modbury Overseers of the Poor, Accounts, Out-Relief, 1795–1803

Exeter City Record Office, Exeter

Exeter Quarter Sessions Minute Book, 1788–1798, 1800–1801

Miscellaneous Boxes 4, 5, and 10, 1793–1801

Exeter City Library, Exeter

Ilsington Parish Register Transcripts, 1760–1801

Modbury Parish Register Transcripts, 1750–1801

Birmingham Reference Library, Birmingham

Manuscript diary of Edward Pickard

British Library, London

Add. MSS 35667	Hardwicke papers, 1796

Lindsey County Library, Lincoln

LCL Banks 3	Papers of Sir Joseph Banks, 1796–1797

Scottish Record Office, Edinburgh

The Melville papers, 1790–1795

Ugbrooke House, Devon

The Clifford papers, papers of the Clifford family in the possession of the Right Honourable Lord Clifford, 1794–1801

University of Nottingham, Nottingham

PwF   The Portland papers, 1793–1800 (the 4th Duke of Portland was the Home Secretary from 1794 to 1801)

Lancashire Record Office, Preston

Lancashire Quarter Sessions Indictments and Recognizances, 1795–1796, 1808
Lancashire Quarter Sessions Order Book, 1795–1796, 1808

Oxfordshire Record Office, Oxford

Oxfordshire Quarter Sessions Rolls and Minute Books, 1799–1801, 1804–1805

Staffordshire Record Office, Stafford

Staffordshire Quarter Sessions Rolls, 1796

Warwickshire Record Office, Warwick

Warwickshire Quarter Sessions Rolls, 1795–1810

Notes

1. The Politics of Riot

1. *LMCh*, 14 Aug. 1795 (italics in original).

2. The following is based primarily on two accounts unique among the sources for this period: "an account given by the people of Barrow and [one] by the Cavalry of the late dreadful event," in *LCo*, 15 Aug. 1795.

3. A. Temple Patterson, *Radical Leicester: A History of Leicester, 1780–1850* (Leicester: University College, 1954), p. 77.

4. One or more rioters were killed in 37 of the 617 riots in my national sample (discussed below), or about 6 percent. That is doubtless an exaggeration of the true proportion, for riots involving fatalities were more likely to be reported in my sources than were nonfatal riots. In those 37 riots, other rioters were the killers on 10 occasions, and various members of the peacekeeping forces in 19 cases.

5. The Yeomanry was typically composed of small farmers and middle-class citizens affluent enough to provide their own horses, for the Yeomanry was the cavalry branch of the Volunteers, corps organized from 1794 onward as local auxiliaries of the militia. See Leon Radzinowicz, *A History of English Criminal Law and Its Administration from 1750*, vol. 4, *Grappling for Control* (London: Stevens & Sons, 1968), pp. 112–114.

6. The figure 1,000 is a rough but reasonable estimate based on a comparison between my national sample of 617 riots (discussed later in this chapter) drawn from a limited number of sources, and several local studies, which have used many more local sources and so presumably have identified most significant riots. My own study of Devon in Chapter 2 deals with 43 riots, of which 33 are included in my national sample. Roger Wells's study of Yorkshire mentions 23 riots, of which 7 are included in the national sample (Roger A. E. Wells, *Dearth and Distress in Yorkshire, 1793–1802*, Borthwick Papers no. 52 [York: Borthwick Institute of Historical Research, University of York, 1977], pp. 24–34). Alan

Booth's "Food Riots in the North-West of England, 1790–1801," *Past and Present*, 77 (Nov. 1977), p. 90, lists 46 "disturbances," of which 12 are in my sample. The criteria used to identify riots or "disturbances" are not specified in either study, however, and almost certainly differ from mine. John Stevenson counted 144 riots in London between 1790 and 1810, whereas my sample includes 123 London riots (John Stevenson, *Popular Disturbances in England, 1700–1870* [New York: Longman's, 1979], p. 306). Stevenson's criteria for counting "disturbances" were the involvement of three or more people, mutual intent, and violence.

7. The use of wheat in hair powder and starch was also banned. See Walter M. Stern, "The Bread Crisis in Britain, 1795–96," *Economica*, 31 (May 1964), 178–184. For the production census, see W. E. Minchinton, "Agricultural Returns and the Government during the Napoleonic Wars,"*Agricultural History Review*, 1 (1953), 29–43.

8. See K.B. 8 / 83. I am grateful to E. P. Thompson for this reference.

9. Of course magistrates responded with great determination, though not panic, to violence in prolonged labor disputes, on Tyneside in 1792 (Norman McCord and David E. Brewster, "Some Labour Troubles of the 1790's in North East England," *International Review of Social History*, 13 [1968], 366–383), in Lancashire in 1808 (Chap. 6), and in the West Country in 1802 (H.O. 42 / 65 and 42 / 66, John Jones, Jr., to the Home Office, 18 July to 3 Aug. 1802).

10. For election rowdyism, see Elie Halévy, *England in 1815*, 2nd ed. (New York: Barnes and Noble, 1961), pp. 150–151. Both the hobbyhorse and "throwing the hood" included rough competition between two sides and the enforced levy of drink money from spectators. See Dorothy Gladys Spicer, *Yearbook of English Festivals* (New York: H. W. Wilson Co., 1954), pp. 17–20, 51–56. For other crowd festivals and sports see Robert W. Malcolmson, *Popular Recreations in English Society, 1700–1850* (Cambridge: Cambridge University Press, 1973), pp. 16–40. For instances of wife sales, see *LCh*, 9–11 Nov. 1790 (Ninfield Stocks, Sussex), where the meaning of the ceremony as a cheap divorce is explained and even commended to the middle classes; *MM*, 24 Aug. 1802 (Smithfield); *BG*, 3 March 1800 (Stafford); *LMCh*, 24 May 1806 (Smithfield). At Burton Fair, a young woman of Swadlincote, abandoned by her husband and hence "chargeable on the parish," was even sold in the marketplace by a parish officer, and delivered in a halter! (*LCh*, 6–9 Feb. 1790.)

11. For the ceremonies surrounding public hangings at Tyburn, see Peter Linebaugh, "The Tyburn riot against the Surgeons," in Douglas Hay et. al., *Albion's Fatal Tree: Crime and Society in Eighteenth-Century England* (New York: Pantheon Books, 1975), pp. 65–69, 111–117. On gleaning, see Spicer, *Yearbook*, p. 43. On amusements, see E. P. Thompson, *The Making of the English Working Class* (New York: Vintage Books, 1966), pp. 403–412, and Malcolmson, *Popular Recreations*, pp. 118–157.

12. This statement is based on my reading of the records of four Assize Courts and five Courts of Quarter Sessions for the period.

13. Assize 24 / 43 and 25 / 2 / 24, Wiltshire, Summer 1803.

14. For attacks on officials, see Assize 24 / 43, Somerset, Summer 1785; Assize 35 / 234, Kent, Lent 1794 (Minster); Assize 24 / 43, Wiltshire, Lent 1796 (Salisbury); Oxfordshire Q.S. Rolls, Epiphany 1798 (docs. 28–31: Wroxton), and Epiphany 1809 (docs. 11–14: Chelgrove). For instances of violent rescue, see Oxfordshire Q.S. Rolls, Easter 1799, Michaelmas 1800, and Michaelmas 1801; and Warwickshire Q.S. 32 / 3, Loose Indictments, Bundle 1, Easter 1802.

15. The three indicted rescuers had family names different from those of the girls (Oxfordshire Q.S. Rolls, Trinity 1805 [docs. 26–27], and Minute Book, I / 7, Trinity and Michaelmas 1805). Moreover, Douglas Hay's brilliant analysis of poaching has shown that a *pattern* of illegal individual "transgression" must be considered in the context of social politics, and perhaps of proto-class conflict (Douglas Hay, "Property, Authority and the Criminal Law," in Hay et. al., *Albion's Fatal Tree*, p. 253). But the "private" character of most small conflicts suggests that legal definitions of riot are of little use in selecting significant social conflicts. The common law defined riot as violent cooperation of three or more people; the Riot Act (1 Geo. I, st. 2, c. 5) specified twelve. John Stevenson provides a useful summary of the law on riot in his *Popular Disturbances*, pp. 5–7.

But the Riot Act was infrequently used. The Riot Act proclamation was rarely read to warn crowds, and few rioters were indicted in this period for felony under the Riot Act. Most rioters who were tried were charged with misdemeanors: that allowed the magistrates some flexibility in determining the seriousness of the offense (for instance, in assessing the value of damaged or stolen property) and of the punishment in a highly-charged social context.

16. "Private" is used here to distinguish riot against particular enclosures, for example, from riot against enclosure in general, which was legally treason. Richard Burn, *Justice of the Peace*, 18th ed. (London, 1797), IV, 110–113. Compare W. S. Holdsworth, *A History of the English Law*, 15 vols. (Boston: Little, Brown, 1922–1966), VIII, 324–331.

17. By contrast with early seventeenth-century riots, which functioned as "a form of petitioning in strength and in deed" (John Walter and Keith Wrightson, "Dearth and the Social Order in Early Modern England," *Past and Present*, 71 [May 1976], 32).

18. See Natalie Zemon Davis, "The Reasons of Misrule: Youth Groups and Charivaris in Sixteenth Century France," *Past and Present*, 50 (Feb. 1971), 41–75; and E. P. Thompson, "'Rough Music': Le charivari anglais," *Annales, Economies, Societies, Civilizations*, 27 (March-April 1972), 285–312.

19. J. G. Nichols's notes to *The Diary of H. Machyn, Citizen and Merchant Taylor of London, from A.D. 1550 to A.D. 1563*, ed. J. G. Nichols, Camden Society publications, vol. 42 (London: Camden Society, 1848), quoted in W. Carew Hazlitt, *Faiths and Folklore of the British Isles: A Descriptive and Historical Dictionary* (New York: Benjamin Blom, 1965), II, 551.

20. Assize 5 / 117 / I and 2 / 26, Worcestershire, Lent 1797. At Bourton, Oxfordshire, the crowd uttered "divers noises, indecent contemptuous reproachful and provoking words, speeches and expressions concerning Elizabeth Williams," the wife of John Williams, on two separate occasions (Oxfordshire Q.S. Rolls, Epiphany 1804).

21. See, for example, Assize 24 / 43 and 25 / 2 / 25, Wiltshire, Lent 1804.

22. Thompson, "'Rough Music,'" p. 306. Quotation is from H.O. 42 / 26 / 36, Robert Spillman, 25 Aug. 1793. In the well-organized sailors' strike at South Shields in 1792, reluctant and even tardy comrades were driven naked through the town (H.O. 42 / 22, Joseph Bulmer, 1 Nov. 1792, and Thomas Powditch, 3 Nov. 1792).

23. After two royal proclamations against sedition in 1792, Paine was tried in absentia on 18 Dec. 1792 and outlawed, and *The Rights of Man* was condemned as seditious libel. See Chap. 5 and Thompson, *Making of the Working Class*, pp. 105–106. For examples of Paine effigies see *EFP*, 13 Dec. 1792 to 3 Jan. 1793 (Devonshire); *LObs*, 23 Dec. 1792 (Kent); *YC*, 7, 14 Jan. 1793 (Yorkshire). For incidents at Handsworth: Staffordshire Q.S. Rolls, Epiphany 1796; Creech St. Michael: Assize 24 / 43, Somerset, Summer 1795; Dartford: *LEM*, 15–17 Sept. 1800; Rochester: *CI*, 5 Dec. 1795; West Riding: H.O. 42 / 91, "statement," January 1807, enclosed in J. W. Heaton, 3 Jan. 1807; tax officials at unspecified places: *LMCh*, 19 May 1798; at London: *LMCh*, 19 Dec. 1797; at Southampton: *LMCh*, 26 Nov. 1799; and at Tewkesbury: *LMCh*, 29 March, 3 Sept., and 14 Nov. 1805. In the 1804 Middlesex election, Sir Francis's carriage was repeatedly drawn by the "mob" (*LCh*, 7–9 Aug. 1804; *LObs*, 12 Aug. 1804; Thompson, *Working Class*, p. 458). See also Stevenson, *Popular Disturbances*, pp. 188–189.

24. John Jamieson, *Dictionary*, quoted in Hazlitt, *Faiths and Folklore*, II, 563.

25. Thompson, "'Rough Music,'" p. 290.

26. Stevenson, *Popular Disturbances*, pp. 50, 165; and Michael Ignatieff, *A Just Measure of Pain: the Penitentiary in the Industrial Revolution, 1750–1850* (New York: Pantheon Books, 1978), pp. 20–24, 42–43, and 88.

27. For Durham, see Hazlitt, *Faiths and Folklore*, II, 563. For other trials, see Assize 5 / 117 / I and Assize 2 / 26, Worcestershire, Lent 1797.

28. David Williams, *The Rebecca Riots: A Study in Agrarian Discontent* (Cardiff: University of Wales Press, 1955), p. 56.

29. Or rather, as Thompson nicely puts it, "The 'music' expressed effectively the opinion of the community, or at least of a fraction of the community sufficiently important and aggressive...to intimidate or silence those who, while perhaps disapproving of the ritual, also disapproved to some extent of the victims" ("'Rough Music,'" p. 291).

30. Thompson observes that lynching is the exact opposite of *charivari*. "Unmitigated physical violence" contrasts with violence which is "distanced, ritualized, and symbolic" ("'Rough Music,'" p. 308, n. 84).

31. The cornerstone of the modern historical study of riots has been George Rudé's *The Crowd in History: A Study in Popular Disturbances in France and England 1730–1848* (New York: John Wiley and Sons, 1964). On food riots see the pioneering work of R. B. Rose, "Eighteenth-Century Price Riots and Public Policy in England," *International Review of Social History*, 6 (1961), 277–292; R. F. Wearmouth, *Methodism and the Common People of the Eighteenth Century* (London: Epworth, 1945), pp. 20–25; E. P. Thompson, "The Moral Economy of the English Crowd in the Eighteenth Century," *Past and Present*, 50 (Feb. 1971), 76–136; John Stevenson, "Food Riots in England, 1792–1818," in *Popular Protest and Public Order: Six Studies in British History, 1790–1920*, ed. R. Quinault and J. Stevenson (London: George Allen & Unwin, 1974), pp. 33–74; Wells, *Dearth and Distress*; and Booth, "Food Riots." On urban riots, see George Rudé, *Wilkes and Liberty* (Oxford: Oxford University Press, 1962); Rudé, *Paris and London in the Eighteenth Century: Studies in Popular Protest* (London: Collins-Fontana, 1970); and R. B. Rose, "The Priestley Riots of 1791," *Past and Present*, 18 (1960), 68–88. On machine breaking and "Church and King" riots, see E. J. Hobsbawm, "The Machine Breakers," *Past and Present*, 1 (1952), 57–70; Rudé, *Crowd in History*, chaps. 4, 5, and 9; and Hobsbawm, *Primitive Rebels: Studies in Archaic Forms in Social Movement in the 19th and 20th Centuries* (New York: W. W. Norton, 1959), chap. 7. On Luddism, see Frank Ongley Darvall, *Popular Disturbances and Public Order in Regency England* (Oxford: Oxford University Press, 1934); on the Swing riots, E. J. Hobsbawm and George Rudé, *Captain Swing* (New York: Pantheon, 1968); on Rebecca, Williams, *The Rebecca Riots*. This is of course only a sampling. For a complete bibliography up to 1979, see Stevenson, *Popular Disturbances*, pp. 324–362. The word *impressionistic* is intended not to undervalue the analytical contributions these and other studies have made but only to suggest that the historians did not specify how they selected the riots they chose to study, and, in most cases, what they defined as a riot.

32. Except negatively. For instance, the usual explanation for machine-breaking riots is that eighteenth-century workers lacked the resources and habits that modern trade unionists relied upon to conduct strikes. (Hobsbawm, "Machine Breakers," pp. 57–60). Food rioters are said to have been trying to reassert the faded traditions of official market regulation (Thompson, "Moral Economy," pp. 108–109).

33. R. C. Cobb, *The Police and the People: French Popular Protest, 1789–1820* (London: Oxford University Press, 1970), p. 89.

34. Thompson, "Moral Economy," pp. 78–79, 94–107.

35. On food riots, see Stevenson, "Food Riots," pp. 33–74. On military friction, see Clive Emsley, *British Society and the French Wars, 1793–1815* (London: Macmillan, 1979); and J. Stevenson, "The London 'Crimp' Riots of 1794," *International Review of Social History*, 16 (1971), 40–58; Christopher Lloyd, "The Press Gang and the Law," *History Today*, 17 (1967), 683–690; Norman McCord, "The Impress Service in North-East England during the Napoleonic War," *The Mariner's Mirror*, 54 (1968),

163–180; and McCord and Brewster, "Labour Troubles," pp. 377–383. For civilian-military friction see Chapter 8, and John Howard Bohstedt, "Riots in England and Wales, 1790–1810, with Special Reference to Devonshire" (Ph.D. diss., Harvard University, 1972), pp. 60–62 and 66. On political conflicts, see Albert Goodwin, *The Friends of Liberty: The English Democratic Movement in the Age of the French Revolution* (London: Hutchinson & Co., 1979), pp. 180–182, 213–215, 233–237, 263–267. The classic study on labor troubles is Hobsbawm, "Machine Breakers," pp. 57–70. A recent excellent survey of eighteenth-century labor disputes is C. R. Dobson, *Masters and Journeymen: A Prehistory of Industrial Relations, 1717–1800* (London: Croom Helm, 1980).

36. George Rudé, *Ideology and Popular Protest* (London: Lawrence and Wishart, 1980), p. 136, as well as elsewhere, has suggested that two out of three eighteenth-century riots were food riots. But Rudé's sources— especially *Gentlemen's Magazine*—probably exaggerate the proportion of food riots by emphasizing the cluster of food riots in years of dearth and underreporting the steadier occurrence of various scattered riots year in and year out.

37. On the impact of enclosures, see J. D. Chambers, "Enclosure and Labour Supply in the Industrial Revolution," in E. L. Jones, ed., *Agriculture and Economic Growth in England, 1650–1815* (London: Methuen & Co., 1967), p. 117.

38. See the family budgets provided in F. M. Eden, *The State of the Poor*, 3 vols. (London, 1797), and David Davies, *The Case of Labourers in Husbandry* (London, 1795). Compare T. S. Ashton, *Economic Fluctuation in England, 1700–1800* (Oxford: Oxford University Press, 1959), Chap. 2; and C. E. Labrousse, *La Crise de l'économie Française à la fin de l'ancien régime* (Paris: Presses Universitaires de France, 1944), pp. xxxviii-xli.

39. Rudé, *Paris and London*, p. 18.

40. For instance, C. E. Labrousse, "1848–1830–1789: Comment naissent les revolutions," *Actes du Congrès historique du centenaire de la Révolution de 1848* (Paris: Presses Universitaires de France, 1948), pp. 1–20.

41. Thompson, "Moral Economy," pp. 76–78: "How is their behavior *modified* (my italics) by custom, culture, and reason?"

42. Pointed out, for instance, in Stevenson, *Popular Disturbances*, pp. 106–108; Stevenson, "Food Riots," pp. 52–53; Booth, "Food Riots," p. 88; and Rudé, *Crowd in History*, p. 39.

43. Rudé, *Crowd in History*, p. 39, and Stevenson, "Food Riots," pp. 52–53. My preliminary findings suggest that the best economic predictor of riots was not simply the difference from one year to the next but the difference between a given year and the average price for the previous *three* years. The difference involves a more complex memory and judgment than simple reaction to an immediate rise.

44. Compare, for example, U.N., PwF 233, William Baker, 11 July 1795.

45. The phrase, expressing a widespread suspicion, may be found, for instance, in H.O. 42 / 50, A. B. Haden, 10 May 1800. Compare Thompson, "Moral Economy," p. 94.

46. Annual wheat prices from B. R. Mitchell and Phyllis Deane, *Abstract of British Historical Statistics* (Cambridge: Cambridge University Press, 1971), p. 488, multiplied by .97 to convert an Imperial quarter (of a ton) into a Winchester quarter; riots from my national sample. The Pearson product-moment correlation coefficient between annual average wheat prices and annual numbers of all riots in the national sample, 1790–1810, is 0.325. That is not significant; a coefficient of ±0.360 would have to be reached to indicate significance for a one-tailed test at the .05 level of confidence.

47. See Table 1. Noneconomic issues (all but food, labor, and enclosure riots) accounted for 52.8 percent of the total national sample. This finding is confirmed by the discussion of eighteenth-century riots in John Stevenson's comprehensive survey, *Popular Disturbances*, chaps. 1–4.

48. Using annual figures for food riots and for wheat prices (for which see note 46), I find a Pearson product-moment correlation coefficient of 0.411, which is significant for a one-tailed test at the .05 level.

49. For the calendar year 1795, the Pearson product-moment correlation coefficient between weekly national average wheat prices reported in the *London Gazette* and food riots in the national sample is 0.198. For 1800 the correlation coefficient is −.166, and for the period January 1800 to June 1801 the correlation coefficient is −.015. None of these figures reaches the level of significance at the .05 level (±.230, for a one-year period).

50. Thompson, *Making of the Working Class*, pp. 454–456; Emsley, *British Society*, pp. 113–119.

51. See Chaps. 2 and 4.

52. Mark Blaug, "The Myth of the Old Poor Law and the Making of the New," *Journal of Economic History*, 23 (June 1963), 163, 166, and Appendix A. The Speenhamland system of poor relief is discussed in Chap. 8.

53. Compare Stevenson, "Food Riots," p. 67.

54. The social theorist Georg Simmel insisted that conflict and group social life were not antithetical; rather, conflict arose from, was reinforced by, and supported the group. See Lewis A. Coser, *The Functions of Social Conflict* (New York: Free Press, 1956). See also the discussion of "breakdown" theories of collective behavior versus "solidarity" theories in Charles Tilly, Louise Tilly, and Richard Tilly, *The Rebellious Century, 1830–1930* (Cambridge, Mass.: Harvard University Press, 1975), pp. 4–11, 271–274.

55. William B. Reddy, "The Textile Trade and the Language of the Crowd at Rouen, 1752–1871," *Past and Present*, 74 (Feb. 1977), 82–83.

56. See, for instance, classic sociological discussion of the panic following shouts of "Fire!" in a crowded theater, such as Ralph H. Turner and Lewis M. Killian, *Collective Behavior* (Englewood Cliffs, N.J.: Prentice-

Hall, 1957), pp. 88–97; and the discussion of the breakdown of collective ties in urban slum "cultures of poverty" in Oscar Lewis, "The Culture of Poverty," *Scientific American*, 211 (1966), 19–25.

57. Contemporary accounts mention not only the graziers who met the Leicester baker on the road but also that "Mr. Easton, Mr. Bramley, and other respectable persons who had been preserving the peace, were mixed with the crowd" (*LCo*, 15 Aug. 1795).

58. H.O. 42 / 34, G. W. Byne, 6 May, 1795. In 1795 the Duke of Richmond informed the Home Secretary that "by the word EXPORTATION is meant as I conceive, the carrying of wheat out of the country for the supply of other parts of GREAT BRITAIN" (H.O. 42 / 35, Duke of Richmond, 22 June 1795).

59. For obnoxious soldiers, see Emsley, *British Society*, p. 43; for sympathy for the shearmen in their campaign against gig mills in 1802, see J. L. Hammond and Barbara Hammond, *The Skilled Labourer, 1760–1832* (New York: Harper & Row, 1970), p. 171.

60. U.N., PwF 9847, Richard Eastcott, Jr., 28 March 1795 (Exeter), and Chap. 2, for episodes at Dartmouth and Totnes.

61. See, for instance, resistance at Chester: H.O. 42 / 74, statement of a meeting of the Magistrates of Chester, 29 Dec. 1803, enclosed in J. Bennett, 29 Dec. 1803, and H.O. 42 / 78, correspondence between the Chester magistrates and the Home Office between January and March 1804; for a defense of an employee at North Shields, see *LMCh*, 16 May 1803.

62. H.O. 42 / 65, Mr. Hughes, 23 June 1802; H.O. 42 / 66, James Read, 5 Sept. 1802; and Hobsbawm, "Machine Breakers," pp. 64–65.

63. Birmingham: R. B. Rose, "The Priestley Riots of 1791," pp. 80–84; Manchester: see Chap. 5; Nottingham: Malcolm I. Thomis, *Politics and Society in Nottingham, 1785–1835* (Oxford: Basil Blackwell, 1969), pp. 169–180.

64. H.O. 42 / 91, "statement," enclosed in J. W. Heaton, 3 Jan. 1807; T.S. 11 / 1099, brief in the case of the king against Joseph Mosey Allen; "Report from the Select Committee [on] the Petition of the . . . Electors of the Borough of Knaresborough," *P. P*, 1805, III, 131–159; H.O. 42 / 87, passim, especially R. Sinclair, 17 Nov. 1806; and *LCh*, 10–13 Aug. 1805.

65. Lewis Coser, in his discussion of the theories of Georg Simmel, quotes E. A. Ross's theory that different *sets* of oppositions in society (here arising out of the complex ties of members of opposing parties) "are like different wave series set upon opposite sides of a lake, which neutralize each other if the crest of one meets the trough of the other. . . one might say that *society is sewn together* by its inner conflicts." Edward Alsworth Ross, *The Principles of Sociology* (New York: Century Co., 1920), pp. 164–165, quoted in Coser, *Functions of Social Conflict*, pp. 76–77.

66. For "collective bargaining by riot," see Hobsbawm, "Machine Breakers," pp. 59–61.

67. As at Birmingham (Rose, "Priestley Riots," p. 84), and Manchester (Chap. 5).

68. As, for instance, the Nottingham election of 1802. See Malcolm I. Thomis, *Old Nottingham* (Newton Abbott: David & Charles, 1968), chap. 6.

69. Namely, the Excise Bill (1733), the Gin Act (which was "allowed to die a natural death"), the Jewish Naturalization Act (1753), and the Militia Act (1757). George Rudé, *Paris and London*, p. 339; J. R. Western, *The English Militia in the Eighteenth Century: The Story of a Political Issue, 1660–1802* (London: Routledge and Kegan Paul, 1965), pp. 142–143 and 297. See also Chap. 8.

70. Stevenson, *Popular Disturbances*, p. 174.

71. Thompson, "'Rough Music,'" pp. 308–309.

72. Lord Chief Justice Kenyon's famous charge to the Grand Jury of Shropshire was printed in *Ann. Ag.*, 25 (1795), 111–112, and in many provincial newspapers, for instance, *SYM*, 17 Aug. 1795, and *LdsI*, 17 Aug. 1795. His charge to the Grand Jury (and implicitly to the rioters) of Worcestershire is less frequently remembered. He warned those "who are so deluded as to riot" that they would dry up the markets (*NCh*, 8 Aug. 1795). See also Thompson, "Moral Economy," p. 96, n.64. Forestalling, regrating, and engrossing were offenses against the medieval notion that the buying and selling of foodstuffs ought to be direct transactions between producers and consumers in the public marketplace. Any other sorts of dealings were suspected of being attempts to manipulate common needs for selfish profits. Middlemen were condemned for that reason and because they did not seem to produce anything. Forestalling, regrating, and engrossing, respectively, involved the buying of food before it could come to market (for instance at the farm), buying food in order to resell it at a profit, or buying in order to accumulate large quantities. Wholesale merchants, of course, normally engaged in these practices; whether they were illegitimate attempts at speculation and profiteering was a question of both degree and perception.

73. The Act of 9 Geo. III, c. 29, made the "pulling down" of houses or mills a felony.

74. The Assize of Bread was the statutory authority given to magistrates to regulate bakers' profits by fixing the standard weight of a penny loaf by reference to the price of wheat. See Sidney Webb and Beatrice Webb, "The Assize of Bread," *The Economic Journal*, 14 (June, 1904), 196–218.

75. Michael Lewis, *A Social History of the Navy, 1793–1815* (London: Allen & Unwin, 1960), pp. 106–107.

76. J. R. Western, "The Recruitment of the Land Forces in Great Britain, 1793–99" (Ph.D. diss., Edinburgh University, 1953), pp. 96–98; H.O. 50 / 453, Edward Capel, 15 June 1793; and Stevenson, "'Crimp Riots,'" pp. 41–42.

77. See Thomis, *Politics and Society*, p. 60, and Dobson, *Masters and Journeymen*, pp. 121–150. The Hammonds observed that the enforcement of apprenticeship regulations in the woolen industry had fallen into disuse by 1802 (*Skilled Labourer*, p. 170). For parallel evidence, see Dobson, *Masters and Journeymen*, pp. 56–58, 60, 114, 130; Julia de L. Mann, *The*

Cloth Industry in the West of England from 1640 to 1880 (Oxford: Oxford University Press, 1971), pp. 100, 105–106, 143; and Chap. 9.

78. See Dobson, *Masters and Journeymen*, chap. 6; McCord and Brewster, "Some Labour Troubles," pp. 370–376, and in Devon, Chap. 2.

2. Devon's Classic Food Riots

1. Population figures for counties are taken from B. R. Mitchell and Phyllis Deane, *Abstract of British Historical Statistics* (Cambridge: Cambridge University Press, 1971), p. 20. For these statistical comparisons, riots are counted from my national sample of 617 riots for the years 1790–1810. Devon had 1.12 riots per 10,000. Other riotous counties were Cornwall (3.04), Nottinghamshire (1.14), Oxfordshire (1.07), Huntingdonshire (1.05), Surrey, excluding Southwark (1.04), and Kent (1.00). The figure for London was 1.26.

For this chapter on Devon, the "national" sources used for the national sample have been supplemented with local sources, the most important of which are the rich and well-organized county lieutenancy papers (D.R.O., 1262M).

2. U.N., PwF 9847, Richard Eastcott, Jr., 28 March 1795; *LCo*, 2 April 1795; and *LMCh*, 1 April 1795. In the second half of 1794 wheat prices in Devon had risen from just under 7s. a bushel to nearly 8s. a bushel (*LG*, 1794).

3. H.O. 42 / 34, Richard Eastcott, Jr., 30 March 1795.

4. Sources are given in full in John Bohstedt, "Riots in England and Wales, 1790–1810, with Special Reference to Devonshire" (Ph.D. diss., Harvard University, 1972), p. 342.

5. In 1799 Devon wheat prices had risen from about 7s. to just over 12s. a bushel; barley prices, from 3s. 8d. to a peak of 8s. a bushel (*LG*, 1799).

6. D.R.O., 1262M / L59, deposition of Henry Penney, 12 April 1801, included in Giles Welsford, miscellaneous documents, n.d.; and H.O. 42 / 62, Thomas Kitson, 1 May 1801.

7. Compare E. P. Thompson, "The Moral Economy of the English Crowd in the Eighteenth Century," *Past and Present*, 50 (Feb. 1971), 110–112.

8. H.O. 42 / 62 / 254, Giles Welsford, miscellaneous documents, n.d.

9. H.O. 42 / 62 / 35, Charles Farwell, 10 May 1801.

10. H.O. 42 / 62 / 254, in Giles Welsford, miscellaneous documents, n.d.

11. Ibid.

12. M.A.F. 10 / 283, and H.O. 42 / 62 / 130, William Adams [1 June 1801].

13. H.O. 42 / 61, John Pulling [4 April 1801].

14. *LG*, 1795–1796. From September to November, 1795, Devon wheat prices were as much as 15s. per quarter ton higher (15–20 percent) than the national average, but Devon was quiet.

15. H.O. 42 / 61, Giles Welsford, 4 April 1801.

16. See Thomas Tooke, *A History of Prices and of the State of Circulation from 1793–1837*, 6 vols. (London, 1838–1857), I, 181; and *GM*, 65 (1795), 162, 181. On wages, see A. L. Bowley, "The Statistics of Wages in the United Kingdom during the Last Hundred Years," *Journal of the Royal Statistical Society*, 62 (1899), 562. Bowley's index of English agricultural money wages increases from 53 in 1790 to 67 in 1795 to 85 in 1801. On burial, marriage, and conception rates, see Bohstedt, "Riots," pp. 145–152. On workers and savings, H.O. 42 / 61, James Coleridge, 29 March 1801, in J. G. Simcoe, 29 March 1801.

17. Compare Thompson, "Moral Economy," pp. 77–79.

18. "If rioters in the course of their proceedings committed a *felony* [my italics], all were equally liable for the felony." Sir William Holdsworth, *A History of English Law*, 15 vols. (Boston: Little, Brown, 1922–1966), VIII, 329–330, and X, 705. Also, 9 Geo. III, c.29.

19. D.R.O., 1262M / L53, John Underhay, 31 May 1801; Plymouth: *LEM*, 1–3 April 1801; D.R.O., 1262M / L53, notes on Modbury riots [May 1801]; H.O. 42 / 61, J. H. Rodd, 5 April 1801; H.O. 42 / 61, resolutions of the General Committee . . . [of Dartmouth], John Hine, chairman, n.d.; and H.O. 42 / 61 / 712, Thomas Kitson, 25 April 1801. The only minor exceptions to the general decorum of the Devon crowds were two cases of physical assault and one "plunder" of a farmer's cider and bacon near Exeter. One farmer, for instance, was said to be "suspended" near Modbury, but no serious injury was reported (D.R.O., 1262M / L53, notes on the Modbury riots [May 1801]). More important excesses occurred in Plymouth and in Bellamarsh.

20. Le Bon's discussion of "the collective mind," and the "savage" and "barbarian" behavior of crowds, "guided almost exclusively by unconscious motives" can be found in Gustave Le Bon, *The Crowd: A Study of the Popular Mind* (New York: Viking Press, 1960), chap. 1, and pp. 24, 26–29, 32, 36. Compare Bohstedt, "Riots," pp. 39–40.

21. E. P. Thompson, "The Crime of Anonymity," in *Albion's Fatal Tree: Crime and Society in Eighteenth-Century England*, Douglas Hay et al. (New York: Pantheon Books, 1975), pp. 304–308.

22. Thompson, "Moral Economy," pp. 95, 98, 108.

23. Exeter: U.N., PwF 9847, Richard Eastcott, Jr., 28 March 1795; for Lord Kenyon, see H.O. 42 / 61, J. G. Simcoe, 27 March 1801. For the conviction of John Rusby, a London corn jobber, for regrating, see D. G. Barnes, *History of the English Corn Laws from 1660–1846* (New York: A. M. Kelley, 1961), pp. 81–82. For forestalling, regrating, and engrossing, see *SYM*, 1795, for example, 6 April 1795, and compare Thompson, "Moral Economy," pp. 83, 88, 96, and Ray Bert Westerfield, *Middlemen in English Business, Particularly between 1660 and 1760* (New Haven: Yale University Press, 1915).

24. D.R.O., 1262M / L52, J. Willcock, 15 April 1801, and 1262M / L60, deposition of Francis G. Steer, 12 May 1801. For sickness in Devon that may have been related to hunger, see *LCh*, 9 April 1795, and H.O. 42 / 61,

J. G. Simcoe, 5 April 1801. An anonymous letter at Crediton in 1795 did complain that the cost of living had soared in the past thirty years, but this reference to the past did not come directly from rioters and the language of the letter suggests that it was not written by an ordinary laborer. The letter is reprinted in Hay et al., *Albion's Fatal Tree,* pp. 311–312.

25. U.N., PwF 9847, Richard Eastcott, Jr., 28 March 1795.

26. Honiton: H.O. 42 / 61, William Tucker, 4 April 1801, enclosing copy of anonymous letter of 2 April 1801. Exmouth: H.O. 42 / 61, James Coleridge, 29 March 1801.

27. H.O. 42 / 61 / 554, handbill signed by William Johns et al., enclosed in F. St. Aubyn and J. Williams, 5 April 1801, and Devon Q.S. Rolls, 1802, deposition of John Liddon, 20 Sept. 1800.

28. D.R.O., 1262M / L50, deposition of Henry Legassicke, 12 May 1801.

29. For the "theater" of gentry hegemony see E. P. Thompson, "Patrician Society, Plebeian Culture," *Journal of Social History,* 7 (Summer 1974), 389–390; Douglas Hay, "Property, Authority and the Criminal Law," in Hay et al., *Albion's Fatal Tree,* pp. 26–56; and E. P. Thompson, "Eighteenth Century English Society: Class Struggle without Class?" *Social History,* 3 (May 1978), 158–163. For Modbury: D.R.O., 1262M / L53, Modbury, 2 May [1801], signature obliterated. Totnes: H.O. 42 / 62 / 350, Giles Welsford, 1 May 1801. Bellamarsh: *NCh,* 8 Aug. 1795. Dock: H.O. 42 / 61, letter of 2 April 1801 [name cut off, docketed "Account of Riot at Plymouth (Dock) of 31 March 1801 by Mr. J. E. to Mr. W. E."] and H.O. 42 / 61 / 554, handbill enclosed in F. St. Aubyn and J. Williams, 5 April 1801. Crediton: H.O. 42 / 34, anonymous handbill in George Bent, 5 April 1795, reprinted in Hay et al., *Albion's Fatal Tree,* pp. 311–312.

30. D.R.O., 1262M / L52, Henry Studdy, 7 April 1801.

31. Indictments of rioters are found in Devon Q.S. Rolls, Midsummer and Michaelmas, 1795, Easter, 1801, and Epiphany, 1802; and Assize 24 / 43, Devon, Summer 1795; Assize 21 / 18, Devon, Summer 1796; and Assize 25 / 1 / 13 and 25 / 3 / 2, Devon, Summer 1801.

32. D.R.O., 1262M / L53 [notes], 5–6 May [1801]. I have traced the baptisms, marriages, and burials of four of the six indicted Modbury rioters of 1801—John Cove (1751–1814), Richard Shepherd (1756–1829), Nicholas Wakeham (1757–?), and Roger Chipman (1770–1820)—in the Modbury parish register transcripts in the Exeter City Library. I have found mention of the baptism (1760) of one of the Bellamarsh rioters of 1795, and the marriages of two others (1785, 1794) in the Islington parish register transcripts, Exeter City Library.

33. See A. S. Kussmaul, "The Ambiguous Mobility of Farm Servants," *Economic History Review,* 2nd ser., 34 (1981), 222–229.

34. Rioters' identities are drawn from the sources cited in n. 31. Compare Bohstedt, "Riots," pp. 200–201.

35. W. G. Hoskins, *Industry, Trade, and People in Exeter, 1688–1800, with Special Reference to the Serge Industry* (Manchester: Manchester University Press, 1935), p. 127; H.O. 42 / 61, J. H. Rodd, 5 April 1801, and

resolutions of the General Committee [of Dartmouth], John Hine, chairman, n.d.; and H.O. 42 / 61 / 351, J. G. Simcoe, 27 March 1801; and D.R.O., 1262M / L52, Henry Studdy, 7 April 1801.

36. H.O. 42 / 62, John Underhay to Lord Fortescue, 31 May 1801. D.R.O., 1262M / L61, George Sanders and Peter Pridham to Lord Fortescue, 20 April 1801. H.O. 42 / 61, Thomas Kitson, 25 April 1801.

37. H.O. 42 / 62 / 254, miscellaneous documents from Giles Welsford [1801]; and Devon County Record Office, Totnes Land Tax Assessments, 1800.

38. From a contemporary handbill, reprinted in *Western Antiquary*, 8 (1888–1889), 171.

39. John Cove occupied a house in Modbury large enough to pay a land tax of four shillings. His wife, Joanna, died of illness on 10 March 1801, only three weeks before the Modbury food riot for which John was convicted. Exeter City Library, Parish Register Transcripts, and Devon County Record Office, Land Tax Assessments and 269A / PO2, Modbury Overseers of the Poor, Accounts, Out-Relief. The Overseers' accounts list payments to Cove for shoes ranging from £23 to £80 annually between 1795 and 1803. Total payments after the riot were £31 in the year 1801–1802 and £40 in 1802–1803.

40. Honiton: H.O. 42 / 50, Courtenay Hidley, 10 May 1800. *LCo,* 2 April 1795; H.O. 42 / 61, John B. Cholwich, 24 March 1801, and James Coleridge, 29 March 1801, in J. G. Simcoe, 29 March 1801; Devon County Record Office, 269A / PO2, Modbury Overseers of the Poor, Accounts, Out-Relief. It is possible that Cove received payment on account of his wife's illness (n. 39).

41. H.O. 42 / 61, James Coleridge, 29 March 1801, in J. G. Simcoe, 29 March 1801.

42. E. W. Martin, *The Shearers and the Shorn: A Study of Life in a Devon Community* (London: Routledge and Kegan Paul, 1965), p. 51.

43. Twenty-nine of thirty-five riots took place in medium-sized towns. Two riots took place in Exeter (population 17,398), and four in parishes with populations under one thousand. Eight food riots took place in greater Plymouth. All population figures in this chapter are taken from the *Abstract of the Answers and Returns Made Pursuant to an Act Passed in the Forty-First Year of His Majesty, King George III...* [the census of 1801], 2 vols. (London, 1801), I: Enumeration, and the *Abstract of the Answers and Returns Made Pursuant to an Act Passed in the Fifty-First Year of His Majesty, King George III...* [the census of 1811] (London, 1811), part I: Enumeration. The only riotous towns that grew more than 10 percent between 1801 and 1811 were Brixham (18.3 percent), Honiton (15.1 percent), and Sidmouth (34.8 percent). The riot at Bellamarsh mill has been excluded because the rioters assembled from five parishes.

44. H.O. 42 / 61, John Pulling to William Pulling, Sat. eve [4 April 1801]; D.R.O., 1262M / L53, minutes [of magistrates' investigation], n.d.; 1262M / L59, J. I. Fortescue, 4 April 1801.

45. Indeed so stable was Devon society that it continued to be a repository of folk traditions well into the nineteenth century. For example, for Whitsuntide revels, see Charles Worthy, *Devonshire Parishes, or the Antiquities, Heraldry and Family History of Twenty-Eight Parishes in the Archdeaconry of Totnes*, 2 vols. (Exeter, 1887–1889), I, 274–275. For wife sales and witchcraft, see Sabine Baring-Gould, *Devonshire Characters and Strange Events* (London: J. Lane, 1908), pp. 58–83.

46. Hoskins, *Industry, Trade and People*, pp. 138–139; George Rudé, *The Crowd in History, 1730–1848* (New York: John Wiley & Sons, 1964), pp. 40–41; Walter James Shelton, *English Hunger and Industrial Disorders: A Study of Social Conflict during the First Decade of George III's Reign* (London: Macmillan, 1973), p. 32; and *LCh*, 6–9 Sept. 1766.

47. Bohstedt, "Riots," p. 155.

48. Thompson, "Moral Economy," pp. 135, 83–88, 96–97; Alan Everitt, "The Marketing of Agricultural Produce in England," in Joan Thirsk, ed., *The Agrarian History of England and Wales*, vol. 4, *1500–1640* (Cambridge: Cambridge University Press, 1967), pp. 486–488.

49. The argument here is that if a market town had a more formal local government, such as a municipal corporation, and if that corporation represented at least the town's elite, rather than being arbitrarily chosen manorial officials, then the town officials were more likely to be sensitive to public clamor, even if the "elected" officials were merely co-opted by fellow members of the town corporation rather than chosen by the public.

50. Everitt, "Marketing"; John Chartres, "Markets and Marketing in Metropolitan Western England in the Late Seventeenth and Eighteenth Centuries," in Michael Havinden, ed., *Husbandry and Marketing in the Southwest, 1500–1800* (Exeter: University of Exeter, 1973), pp. 63–74; Thompson, "Moral Economy," pp. 84–87; Daniel Lysons and Samuel Lysons, *Magna Britannia*, 6 vols. (London, 1806–1822), VI, *Devonshire*, 21, 108, 127, 129–130, 136, 143, 150, 364, 376.

51. The difference between towns and parishes is as follows. A parish is a unit of civil administration, and most important here, the unit that had its population measured in the early censuses of 1801 and 1811. It covered an area with distinct boundaries. It might have many people or few; they might live in scattered settlements or clumped together. A town is a more informal generic designation for a settlement with enough people living closely together to be visibly recognizable as a town. Depending on its age and history, it might or might not have a church, a market, or a local government, which might be, for instance, a chartered municipal corporation or a manorial institution descended from the manors of medieval times. A market was established in a town, at least officially, by the specific prescription of a royal or manorial charter. Market towns and populous parishes were not simply the same communities, at least not for "quiet" parishes. Of *nonriotous* parishes, eight were "large" (population over fifteen hundred) market towns, thirteen were "large" nonmarket towns, and ten were "small" market towns. Nearly four hundred other

communities were nonriotous small nonmarket parishes. Of *riotous* parishes, nineteen were "large" market towns, two were small market towns, two were "large" nonmarket towns, and five were small nonmarket parishes. (Obviously, some parishes were not towns at all.)

In 1801 Devon had forty-two parishes with populations of 1,500 or over. The median population of twenty-one riotous parishes was 3,080; of twenty-one nonriotous parishes, 1,698. The typical nonriotous parish was a wide, sprawling, isolated rural parish on the edge of Dartmoor, such as Moreton Hampstead.

52. The economic basis of the regional divisions is explained in more detail in Bohstedt, "Riots," pp. 156–158. North, east, and south Devon were also administrative districts (Lysons and Lysons, *Magna Britannia*, VI, xxxi).

53. Robert Fraser, *A General View of the County of Devon* (London, 1794), p. 12, and Charles Vancouver, *General View of the Agriculture of the County of Devon* (London, 1808), p. 107, and compare pp. 109 and 224.

54. South Hams: H.O. 42 / 52, J. H. Rodd, 28 Oct. 1800. East Devon: U.N., PwF 9847, Richard Eastcott, Jr., 28 March 1795; E. A. G. Clark, *The Ports of the Exe Estuary, 1660–1860: A Study in Historical Geography* (Exeter: University of Exeter, 1960), p. 84; and Vancouver, *Devon*, pp. 230–231. Cullompton: U.N., PwF 298, letter from "a gentleman of fortune and respectability" to Nathaniel Battin, 30 June 1795. Tor Bay fleets: Paul Treby, letter of February 1795, in *Ann. Ag.*, 24 (1795), 238, and H.O. 42 / 35, William Elford, 6 April 1795; H.O. 42 / 50, William Elford, 25 June 1800; and H.O. 42 / 61, Giles Welsford, 4 April 1801.

55. Barnstaple, Bideford, Brixham, Dartmouth, Exeter, Ilfracombe, Plymouth, and Topsham had riots. The other two ports, Kingsbridge and Teignmouth, had milder forms of unrest.

56. Newton and Honiton: *EFP*, 26 March 1801; *SYM*, 6 July 1795. Sidmouth: H.O. 42 / 35, petition to the magistrates from the Volunteers of Sidmouth, c. 20 Sept. 1800, enclosed in "the statement of the Rev. Marker ...," 22 Dec. 1800. South Hams: H.O. 42 / 61, J. H. Rodd, 5 April 1801. Exeter: H.O. 42 / 61, James Coleridge, 29 March 1801, enclosed in J. G. Simcoe, 29 March 1801; Clifford papers, GCLM, George Burrington, 29 March 1801; D.R.O., 1262M / L48, J. G. Simcoe, 28 March 1801. Brixham: D.R.O., 1262M / L52, Henry Studdy, 7 April 1801. For further evidence of the influence of rumor and example, see Bohstedt, "Riots," pp. 175–177.

57. Joan Thirsk, "The Farming Regions of England," in Thirsk, ed., *Agrarian History of England and Wales*, IV, 71–78, and Fraser, *Devon*, map facing p. 10; and Vancouver, *Devon*, pp. 97, 400–401.

58. The ratio is based upon figures in the *Abstract of the Answers and Returns* [the census of 1811], I: Enumeration. This ratio cannot be used as a precise measure of occupations. Rather it is a conversion into simple proportions of the local census reporter's *impression* of how much his parish was engaged primarily in agriculture or in trade and industry.

The median ratios for market towns and "large" parishes were 2.0 and 1.75. Two-thirds of the riotous towns were above that median, while two-thirds of the nonriotous places were below that median. See Bohstedt, "Riots," pp. 165–167, for a more detailed discussion.

59. Thompson, "Patrician Society," p. 385.

60. William Marshall, *The Rural Economy of the West of England* (London, 1796), I, 107–108. The context implies that Marshall meant pilferage rather than mob pillage. See Chap. 8 for farm workers' movements, including the meeting and riot in Crediton, Devon, in 1795.

61. Martin Dunsford, *Historical Memoirs of the Town and Parish of Tiverton in the County of Devon*, 2nd ed. (Exeter, 1790), pp. 205–258; H.O. 42 / 25 / 492, address of woolcombers of Devon and Exeter, Willington, and Taunton, meeting at Bradninch, 24 April 1793; H.O. 42 / 30 / 327, John Cutler to Judge Buller, 26 May 1794.

62. J. L. Hammond and Barbara Hammond, *The Skilled Labourer, 1760–1832* (1919; reprint ed., New York: Harper & Row, 1970), p. 197; W. G. Hoskins, *Industry, Trade, and People*, pp. 54–61; Joyce Youings, *Tuckers Hall Exeter: The History of a Provincial City through Five Centuries* (Exeter: University of Exeter; Incorporation of Weavers, Fullers, and Shearmen, 1968), pp. 175–176; and H.O. 42 / 34, printed handbill of the journeymen fullers of Exeter, 28 March 1795.

63. Hoskins, *Industry, Trade, and People*, pp. 74–85; and H. J. Hanham, "Ashburton as a Parliamentary Borough, 1640–1868," *Transactions of the Devonshire Association*, 98 (1966), 222–223, 242–243.

64. Tiverton: Dunsford, *Tiverton*, p. 245, n. 195; Modbury: D.R.O., 1262M / L53, William Foot, 23 May 1801; Ashburton: 1262M / L13, Robert Abraham, Jr., 5 June 1797; Crediton: *LEM*, 1–3 April 1801.

65. U.N., PwF 297–298, letter from "a gentleman of fortune and respectability at Cullompton," 30 June 1795, in Nathaniel Battin, 2 July 1795; H.O. 42 / 61, J. G. Simcoe, 27 March 1801; D.R.O., 1262M / L44, Henry Skinner, 4 Sept. 1800, and John Kennaway, 9 Sept. 1800; Uffculme: D.R.O., 1262M / L58, John Pearse Manley, 19 May 1801. Bohstedt, "Riots," pp. 200–202.

One might expect that friendly societies would furnish yet another basis for plebeian cohesion and, hence, riot. Friendly societies were clubs that pooled their members' small weekly dues to provide insurance against sickness, unemployment, and funeral expenses. They were also social organizations and were one of the important precursors of modern trade unions. Devon did have an unusually high proportion of friendly society members in its population around 1800; see F. M. Eden, *Observations on Friendly Societies* (London, 1801), p. 7. During the eighteenth century the societies of woolen workers became open to all trades within their communities as the industry declined; see Margaret D. Fuller, *West Country Friendly Societies: An Account of Village Benefit Clubs and Their Brass Pole Heads* (Reading, Berkshire: University of Reading, Museum of English Rural Life, 1964), pp. 4–5. Detailed figures of friendly society membership were collected from parish overseers in 1802; see *P. P.* 1803–1804 (175), XIII, "Abstract of Returns Relative to the Expence and Maintenance of the Poor," pp. 97–116. An analysis of these figures shows that riotous

Devon parishes did not have a greater *proportion* of their inhabitants enrolled in friendly societies than comparable nonriotous "large" parishes and market towns. But they did have greater *absolute numbers* of friendly society members. Perhaps when combined with other factors, such as the size of the town and nonagricultural employment, friendly society membership helped field a "critical mass" of organized common people for riot, and more so in manufacturing parishes than in agricultural parishes.

66. Compare the Tillys' model in Charles Tilly, Louise Tilly, and Richard Tilly, *The Rebellious Century, 1830–1930* (Cambridge, Mass.: Harvard University Press, 1975), pp. 248–252, 264–270, and see also Rudé, *Crowd in History*, pp. 5, 268.

67. The ten towns were: Ashburton (2 riots), Barnstaple (1), Bideford (2), Dartmouth (2), Exeter (2), Honiton (3), Okehampton (2), Plymouth (3), Tiverton (1), and Totnes (2). Bideford was not a parliamentary borough; three "pocket boroughs," Bere Alston, Plympton Erle, and Tavistock, had no riots. Ashburton and Honiton were not municipal boroughs; the two municipal boroughs that did not have riots, South Molton and Torrington, seem to have been preserved in large part through the benevolence of Lords Fortescue and Rolle, respectively.

68. Lewis B. Namier, *The Structure of Politics at the Accession of George III*, 2d ed. (London: Macmillan, 1957), pp. 140–144 and chap. 6, discusses the pervasiveness of official and personal patronage in the boroughs of Devon and Cornwall.

69. Hanham, "Ashburton," pp. 222–230.

70. See Lewis Namier and John Brooke, *The House of Commons, 1754–1790*, 3 vols. (London: Her Majesty's Stationery Office, 1964), I, 48–49 and 55–56, and their surveys of Devon constituencies, I, 251–262. Also for Okehampton: T. H. B. Oldfield, *An Entire and Complete History, Personal and Political, of the Boroughs of Great Britain* (London, 1792), p. 226; Exeter: Alexander Jenkins, *The History and Description of the City of Exeter...* (Exeter, 1806), p. 222; Barnstaple and Honiton: T. H. B. Oldfield, *The Representative History of Great Britain and Ireland* (London, 1816), III, 300; Tiverton: Hoskins, *Industry, Trade, and People*, pp. 44–46; Dunsford, *Tiverton*, pp. 245–258, and compare pp. 238–242 for the violent political conflict of 1754.

71. For instance, at Nantwich in the 1840s, working men refrained from criticizing abuses in the management of local charities for fear of jeopardizing their poor relations. See "The Reminiscences of Thomas Dunning," in *Testaments of Radicalism: Memoirs of Working Class Politicians, 1790–1885*, ed. David Vincent (London: Europa Publications, 1977), p. 144.

72. Exeter: Youings, *Tuckers Hall*, pp. 138, 158–160; for the social composition of the town corporations in Devon, see "First Report of the Commission on Municipal Corporations," *P. P.* 1835, XXIII, 429–645.

73. Plymouth: *LMCh*, 9 April 1795 and *SYM*, 6 April 1795. Exeter: H.O. 42 / 34, handbill of 28 March 1795; *EFP*, 16 April 1795; Exeter Q.S. Minute Book, 1788–1798, 1800–1801, and Q.S. Rolls, Midsummer and

Michaelmas 1795 and Midsummer 1800 to Michaelmas 1801. The county Quarter Sessions also symbolically punished three vendors for engrossing or regrating small quantities of food in 1796 and 1800 (Devon Q.S. Rolls, Easter 1796 and Michaelmas 1800). Four other vendors were tried at the Quarter Sessions and Assizes for especially provacative price fixing; one vendor had attempted to collaborate on raising butter prices right in the face of a clamorous crowd (Assize 24 / 43, Devon, Summer 1800; and Devon Q.S. Rolls, Michaelmas 1800).

74. Exeter: U.N., PwF, Richard Eastcott, Jr., 28 March 1795; Honiton: H.O. 42 / 50, Courtenay Hidley, 10 May 1800.

75. For instance, in Totnes, Barnstaple, and Ashburton: *SYM*, 30 March 1795, 31 March 1800, and 2 Feb. 1801; and in Crediton and Exeter: *EFP*, 15 Jan. and 26 March 1801.

76. Ashburton: H.O. 42 / 34, William Sunter to Robert MacKreth, 4 May 1795; Tiverton: H.O. 42 / 61, John B. Cholwich, 24 March 1801; Plymouth: *EFP*, 2 April 1801, and *LEM*, 1–3 April 1801; Exeter: U.N., PwF 9847, Richard Eastcott, Jr., 28 March 1795.

77. D.R.O., 1262M / L52, N. Brooking, Mayor of Dartmouth, 9 April 1801 and J. Willcock, 1, 15 April 1801, and 1262M / L60, J. Willcock, Mayor, and Thomas Grant, 30 March 1801.

78. Compare Hay, "Property," pp. 40–49. Four men were indicted for rioting in the Exeter *area* on 23 March 1801. One was convicted and imprisoned for six months, one bill was ignored, one was respited *per curia*, and one was not proceeded against. Charges against two Ashburton rioters were also dropped (Assize 24 / 43 and Assize 25 / 1, Devon, Summer 1801, Lent 1802, and Summer 1802). Several rioters, however, including two in Totnes, were let off with public apologies (Bohstedt, "Riots," pp. 400–402).

79. Brixham: D.R.O., 1262M / L52, J. G. Simcoe to Lord Fortescue, 13 April 1801, and 1262M / L53, Lord Fortescue, 26 May 1801; dockyard: H.O. 42 / 61 / 735, 741, Lord Fortescue, 28 and 30 April 1801.

80. On the crusade against Jacobinism, see J. R. Western, "The Volunteer Movement as an Anti-Revolutionary Force, 1793–1801," *English Historical Review*, 71 (Oct. 1956), 603–614, especially 605. Much of Western's evidence, however, came from Scotland and from the papers of Henry Dundas, Pitt's chief political lieutenant. For the sponsors' views, see, for instance, D.R.O., 1262M / L5, muster roll of the Bideford Volunteers, 5 Aug. 1794; and H.O. 50 / 332, articles and muster roll of the Brixham Volunteer Corps, 30 April 1798. The Fortescue county lieutenancy papers (D.R.O., 1262M) are full of letters from gentlemen jockeying for prestige and precedence as Volunteer officers.

81. Tavistock: *EFP*, 2 July 1795; Honiton: *SYM*, 6 July 1795; Cullompton: U.N., PwF 298, letter from a "gentleman of fortune and respectability" to Nathaniel Battin, 30 June 1795; Teignmouth: D.R.O., 1262M / L13, especially James Waye, 11 and 13 June 1797, J. Newcombe, 8 and 13 June 1797; Axminster: D.R.O., Q.S. Rolls, 1802, deposition of John Liddon, 20 Sept. 1800.

82. Exeter: D.R.O., 1262M / L44, R. Eales, 3 Dec. 1800; East Devon

and Sidmouth: H.O. 42 / 55, "the statement of the Rev. Marker ...," 22 Dec. 1800; Sidbury: H.O. 42 / 55, Lord Rolle, 22 Dec. 1800; Branscombe, Seaton and Beer: H.O. 42 / 55, Thomas Puddicombe, 21 Dec. 1800, and Lord Rolle, 24 Dec. 1800; D.R.O., 1262M / L46, copy of the evidence of Mr. Daniel French...Thomas Bidry...and John Wood [Dec. 1800].

83. Exeter: D.R.O., 1262M / L59, R. Eales, 23 March 1801; Newton: H.O. 42 / 61, R. Eales, 30 March 1801; Totnes: Clifford papers, GCLM, Thomas Kitson, 28 March 1801; Dartmouth: 1262M / L52, Henry Studdy, 30 March 1801. For many other examples, see Bohstedt, "Riots," pp. 123–130, 177–181, 234–237.

84. Bohstedt, "Riots," pp. 246–257. There is little evidence that Volunteers were screened to guarantee the political purity of the corps in Devon, despite the gentry's occasional worries that men of "democratic" or "republican" principles were enrolling (p. 229).

85. Western, "Volunteer Movement," p. 609; Bohstedt, "Riots," pp. 221–223, 261; and D.R.O., 1262M / L41, and 1262M / L12, James Waye, 11 June 1797. Privates typically received one to two shillings per week. See pay lists in W.O. 13.

86. Elected officers were commissioned by the crown after approval by local authorities and the lord lieutenant. See Bohstedt, "Riots," p. 213. See pp. 218–221, 229, for specific citations in D.R.O., 1262M / L9, L41, and L21.

87. D.R.O., 1262M / L9, F. Buller, 28 Feb. and 15 March 1796.

88. Clifford papers, Volunteers 1794, correspondence to Lord Clifford from Lord Fortescue and others, 1794–1801, petition of the Teignmouth Company of Volunteers, 7 Sept. 1795; and D.R.O., 1262M / L9, James Waye, 5 Sept. and 14 Oct. 1795, and Lord Fortescue, 8, 26, Oct. 1795, and 1262M / L41, Lord Fortescue, 7 Jan. 1800; D.R.O., 1262M / L9, Colonel Rolle [1794].

89. Clifford papers, GCLM, copy of Lord Clifford, 1 April 1801.

90. Of course there is little explicit evidence of such calculations, although the Totnes, Brixham, and Exeter crowds resolved in advance to make their coercion orderly. Bohstedt, "Riots," p. 361, and D.R.O., 1262M / L61, George Sanders and Peter Pridham, 20 April 1801, and 1262M / L59, R. Eales, 23 March 1801.

91. Plymouth: *SYM*, 6 April 1795, and H.O. 42 / 61, handbill, 2 April 1801, enclosed in J. G. Simcoe, 5 April 1801; Exeter: *EFP*, 2 April 1801, and H.O. 42 / 61, Charles Fanshawe, 26 March 1801; Tiverton: H.O. 42 / 61, John B. Cholwich, 24 March 1801.

92. D.R.O., 1262M / L60, J. Willcock, Mayor, and Thomas Grant, 30 March 1801; 1262M / L52, J. Willcock, 1, 15, April 1801.

93. H.O. 42 / 61, borough of Clifton Dartmouth Hardness resolutions of the General Committee..., n.d.; and D.R.O., 1262M / L52, N. Brooking (Mayor), 9 April 1801, and Henry Studdy, 7 April 1801.

94. The best accounts are D.R.O., 1262M / L52, Henry Studdy, 7 April 1801; H.O. 42 / 61, depositions of Phillip Gillard et al., in Richard Eales, 21 April 1801; D.R.O., 1262M / L61, George Sanders and Peter Pridham, 20 April 1801; and *SYM*, 11 May 1801.

95. H.O. 42 / 61, T. Kitson, 25 April 1801.

96. Note 11, and H.O. 42 / 61, John Pulling [4 April 1801].

97. Exmouth and Ottery: H.O. 42 / 61, James Coleridge, 29 March 1801, in J. G. Simcoe, 29 March 1801; Uffculme: D.R.O., 1262M / L58, John Pearse Manley, 18 May 1801; Newton Abbot: Clifford papers, GCLM, Lord Clifford to General Simcoe, 1 April 1801. For agreements in other parishes, see *EFP*, 8 Jan., 19 and 26 March, and 11 May 1801.

98. The exception that proves the rule—of the connection between the rioters' discipline and the supporting framework of community politics—was the riot at the Bellamarsh mill. The rural mill was attacked by a crowd recruited from five parishes rather than from a single community. The people of the nearest town, Chudleigh, did not participate. The rioters destroyed the mill's machinery and badly beat up the miller. Their object seemed to be not to domesticate the miller but to put him out of business, for he had a large trade in ship's biscuits for the navy and hence drained the countryside of food. The proprietor himself reported that local opinion held that he had "done much injury to the community." This case spilled over the framework of local politics and over the classic "protocol of riot." The victim's business was oriented toward a distant market, and there was no local framework that might call him to account. The crowd came from a wide area and so was sheltered by relative anonymity. D.R.O., 1262M / L5, Lord Clifford [April 1795]; *LG*, 26 May 1795; *LCh*, 18 April 1795; H.O. 42 / 34, G. W. Byne, 6 May 1795; and *NCh*, 8 Aug. 1795.

99. Compare Thompson, "Moral Economy," pp. 120–126.

100. Exeter and Crediton: Clifford papers, GCLM, Lieutenant Colonel Beckwith, 27 March 1801; and *LEM*, 1–3 April 1801. For declarations: H.O. 42 / 61 / 649, Fortescue's circular signed by R. Eales, 18 April 1801; and D.R.O., 1262M / L63, handbill printed by the mayor of Dartmouth, 23 April 1801. Totnes and Dartmouth: M.A.F. 10 / 283; and H.O. 42 / 62 / 130, William Adams [1 June 1801].

101. M.A.F. 10 / 279 and 285. Towns reporting "ruined" markets include Bideford: D.R.O., 1262M / L52, J. Willcock, 15 April 1801, and Paul Orchard, 15 April 1801; the Chudleigh area: D.R.O., 1262M / L52, Lord Clifford, 4 April 1801; and Plymouth dock: *LCo*, 13 April 1795.

102. H.O. 42 / 61, John Pulling [6 April 1801], and F. St. Aubyn and J. Williams, 16 April 1801.

103. T. A. Critchley, *The Conquest of Violence: Order and Liberty in Britain* (New York: Schocken Books, 1970), especially pp. 14, 25, 66–71; Malcolm I. Thomis, *The Town Labourer and the Industrial Revolution* (London: B. T. Batsford, 1974), pp. 20–47.

104. Jerome H. Skolnick, *The Politics of Protest* (New York: Ballantine Books, 1969), p. 5.

105. Compare John Stevenson, "Social Control in England, 1790–1829," in *Social Control in Nineteenth-Century Britain*, ed. A. J. Donajgrodski (London: Croom Helm, 1977), on the breakdown of traditional "police" control and for the early evolution of the modern police; F. C. Mather, *Public Order in the Age of the Chartists* (Manchester: Manchester University

Press, 1959); and J. Hart, "Reform of the Borough Police," *English Historical Review*, 70 (1955), 411–427.

106. *EFP*, 9 April 1801 and H.O. 42 / 61, Mr. Marsden, 20 April 1801. The third occasion was the Crediton farm laborers' meeting (*LCh*, 22 April 1795).

One hour after the Riot Act proclamation commanding rioters to disperse had been read, any rioter remaining on the scene was legally a felon and could be summarily dealt with by lethal force, with legal immunity from the consequences for magistrates and soldiers. Leon Radzinowicz, *A History of English Criminal Law and its Administration from 1750*, 4 vols. (London: Stevens and Sons, 1948–1968), vol. 4, *Grappling for Control*, p. 131. Very few rioters in England (none in Devon) in this period were prosecuted under the Riot Act. Common law indictments for riot or for specific criminal acts were preferred.

107. The constables of Plymouth and Dock were paid. D. Roy Tucker "Quarter Sessions and County Council Government in Devon in the Nineteenth Century," *Transactions of the Devonshire Association*, 84 (1952), 182, 188. Constables collaborated with rioters in Totnes, for instance (H.O. 42 / 62 / 348, Thomas Kitson, 1 May 1801). For instances of special constables' helping magistrates: *LCo*, 22 April 1795 (Crediton), and *EFP*, 2 April 1801 (Plymouth and Exeter).

108. Sheepwash: D.R.O., 1262M / L59, J. Inglett Fortescue, 4 April 1801; Newton: 1262M / L53, Mr. Taylor, 1 May 1801.

109. At Tavistock and Honiton, see n. 81; at Bideford: D.R.O., 1262M / L52, Paul Orchard, 15 April 1801; at Dock: H.O. 42 / 61, "Account of riot at Plymouth [Dock] by Mr. J. E. to Mr. W. E.," 2 April 1801; and Plymouth: *LEM*, 1–3 April 1801.

110. D.R.O., 1262M / L52, memo of riots at Modbury [should be Newton], April 1801. On five occasions, the Yeomanry were called out, mostly for patrol duty. Only at Plymouth did they help to disperse crowds—peacefully (*EFP*, 16 April 1795 and 2 April 1801 and *LEM*, 1–3 April 1801). Compare Radzinowicz, *History*, IV, 114.

111. D.R.O., 1262M / L5, Lord Clifford [April 1795]; and *LCo*, 22 April 1795.

112. In 1795 most militia regiments were embodied (placed on active service) and deployed along the south and east coasts, generally not in their "home" counties. Militiamen joined at least sixteen food riots in 1795! For citations, see Bohstedt, "Riots," p. 62. Also *EFP*, 19 Sept. 1793 and 13 Aug. 1795; and D.R.O., 1262M / L13, R. Eales, 27 July 1797; W.O. 40 / 17, letter from the mayor, recorder, and aldermen of Barnstaple, 17 March 1800.

113. D.R.O., 1262M / L63, memorandum, "Force in the Western District," 3 April 1801. I have counted seven hundred Invalids as though they were evenly divided between Plymouth and Pendennis, Cornwall.

114. See R. N. Worth, *History of the Town and Borough of Devonport, Sometime Plymouth Dock* (Plymouth, 1870), pp. 54, 90, 93; Henry Francis Whitfeld, *Plymouth and Devonport: In Times of War and Peace* (Plymouth,

1900), pp. 190, 261; H.O. 42 / 61 / 735, 741, Lord Fortescue, 28 and 30 April 1801; R. A. Morriss, "Labour Relations in the Royal Dockyards, 1801–1805," *Mariner's Mirror*, 62 (1976), 337–346. For the public house scandal, see Bohstedt, "Riots," pp. 276–277; for the commissioner's uncooperativeness, see H.O. 42 / 61 / 690, J. Williams and F. St. Aubyn, 23 April 1801, and enclosures.

115. See for instance, H.O. 42 / 61, J. Williams and F. St. Aubyn, 16 April 1801, Mr. Marsden, 20 April 1801, and Lord Fortescue, 14 April 1801; and *LP*, 15–17 April 1801.

116. *EFP*, 2 April 1801 and *LEM*, 1–3 April 1801.

117. See n. 116; *LMCh*, 3 April 1801; H.O. 42 / 61, J. Williams and F. St. Aubyn, 31 March 1801 [two letters], and [name cut off], docketed "Mr. J. E. to Mr. W. E.," 2 April 1801.

118. H.O. 42 / 61 / 398, F. St. Aubyn and J. Williams, 31 March to 1 April 1801; *EFP*, 9 April 1801; *SYM*, 13 April 1801.

119. H.O. 42 / 61 [name cut off], docketed "Mr. J. E. to Mr. W. E.," 2 April 1801, and J. Williams and F. St. Aubyn, 31 March 1801; Morriss, "Labour Relations," p. 339, and Bohstedt, "Riots," p. 281.

120. Clifford papers, Volunteers 1794, letters to Lord Clifford from Lord Fortescue and others, 1794–1801, Lord Fortescue, 2 April 1801; H.O. 42 / 61, Lord Fortescue, 4 April 1801. For threats against an artillery officer and a magistrate who had made stern statements against rioters, see H.O. 42 / 61, J. P. Bastard, 18 April 1801, memorandum of Mr. Joy's evidence, and anonymous letter, Honiton, 2 April 1801, enclosed in William Tucker, 4 April 1801.

121. Quoted in *SYM*, 23 Nov. 1795.

122. For instance, Fortescue succeeded in preventing the Quarter Sessions from raising the daily wage for farm laborers until after the Crediton laborers' demonstration in 1795. He also opposed the idea of a county relief subscription in late 1800. More positively, however, he led the passage and implementation of the relief resolutions of 8 April 1801. See Bohstedt, "Riots," pp. 419, 432, and 435; and Clifford papers, Volunteers 1794, Accounts 1794, Lord Fortescue, 12 and 18 April 1795; D.R.O., 1262M / L45, James Buller, 25 Nov. 1800, and Lord Fortescue, 29 Nov. 1800; and H.O. 42 / 61 / 503, Lord Fortescue, 9 April 1801.

123. Rolle: Benson Freeman, *The Yeomanry of Devon, 1794–1927* (London: St. Catherine's Press, 1927), p. 24; landownership: W. G. Hoskins, *Devon*(London: Collins, 1954), pp. 87–88; W. G. Hoskins, "The Ownership and Occupation of the Land in Devonshire, 1650–1850" (Ph.D. diss., London University, 1938), pp. 86–88; and Oldfield, *Representative History* (1816), III, 283. Simcoe had purchased parts of the manors of Dunkeswell and Hemiock, the former in 1784 (Lysons and Lysons, *Magna Britannia*, VI, 170, 267). For local charitable activity, see, for instance, Lord Fortescue's personal accounts, D.R.O., 1262M / E21 / 2, and FE1.

124. H.O. 42 / 61, J. G. Simcoe, 5 April 1801; Lord Fortescue, 5 April 1801; and D.R.O., 1262M / L52, Lord Rolle, 4 April 1801.

125. D.R.O., 1262M / L5, Lord Clifford [between 6 and 13 April 1795], and [14 April 1795].

126. *SYM,* 23 March 1795; D.R.O., 1262M / L53, J. B. Karslake, 4 May 1801; 1262M / L61, J. B. Karslake, 29 April 1801; and R. Eales, 24 April 1801; 1262M / L52, Lord Rolle, 14 April 1801; and H.O. 42 / 61, Lord Rolle, 1 April 1801.

127. In 1795, Fortescue preferred that farm workers' wages be raised by voluntary initiatives and examples rather than by direction of Quarter Sessions (Clifford papers, Volunteers 1794, Accounts 1794, Lord Fortescue, 12, 18 April 1795). See Chap. 8.

128. Clifford papers, GCLM, Lord Clifford, 1 April 1801.

129. H.O. 42 / 55, Lord Rolle, 22 Dec. 1800; D.R.O., 1262M / L46, Lord Rolle, 28 Dec. 1800.

130. D.R.O., 1262M / L58, Lord Rolle, 19 Jan. 1801; 1262M / L45, J. G. Simcoe, 8 Jan. 1801; *SYM,* 5 and 12 Jan. 1801; *EFP,* 1 Jan. 1801.

131. H.O. 42 / 61, J. G. Simcoe, 27 March 1801. Compare D.R.O., 1262M / L44, J. V. Nutcombe, 19 Sept. 1800.

132. H.O. 42 / 61, R. Eales, 30 March 1801, in Lord Rolle, 1 April 1801; and D.R.O., 1262M / L59, R. Eales, 1 April 1801.

133. D.R.O., 1262M / L59, John B. Cholwich, 24 March 1801.

134. See the letter circulated by the Duke of Portland, Home Secretary, to lords lieutenant and magistrates in September 1800 in response to widespread food rioting (H.O. 43 / 12, Duke of Portland to G. Coldham, 10 Sept. 1800).

135. Clifford papers, GCLM, Lord Clifford, 31 March 1801, and notes in Lord Clifford's hand; and 2 April 1801.

136. For instance, Thompson, "Moral Economy," pp. 83–94.

137. H.O. 42 / 34, Lord Fortescue, 11 April 1795; H.O. 42 / 61, Lord Fortescue, 21 April 1801, and 5 April 1801.

138. Letters of J. G. Simcoe in H.O. 42 / 61, 5 and 7 April 1801; D.R.O., 1262M / L59, 24 March 1801; 1262M / L48, 28 March 1801; 1262M / L52, 2 April 1801; and Clifford Papers, GCLM, 24 March 1801.

139. H.O. 42 / 61, J. G. Simcoe, 7 April 1801. The Duke of Portland rejected Simcoe's proposals. See H.O. 42 / 61 / 496, Duke of Portland, 9 April 1801.

140. H.O. 42 / 61, J. G. Simcoe, 5 and 7 April 1801; and D.R.O., 1262M / L52, J. G. Simcoe, 13 April 1801.

141. The instructions are found in H.O. 42 / 61, memorandum of 30 March 1801, H.O. 1262M / L59, and in D.R.O., 1262M / L59 and L63.

142. D.R.O., 1262M / L59, Lord Fortescue to Henry Studdy and P. J. Taylor, 14 April 1801; and 1262M / L63, circular to Volunteer Corps, 17 April 1801. Compare Bohstedt, "Riots," pp. 238–241.

143. H.O. 42 / 61, J. G. Simcoe, 5 April 1801.

144. H.O. 42 / 61, list of corps embodied in Lord Fortescue, 30 April 1801. See also Bohstedt, "Riots," pp. 392–393.

145. Letters of Lord Fortescue in D.R.O., 1262M / L63, 8 April 1801; H.O. 42 / 62 / 342, 28 April 1801; D.R.O., 1262M / L59, 17 April 1801; H.O. 42 / 61, 4 and 12 April 1801.

146. Except for riots in Plymouth and Dock on 13 and 15 April.

147. See Clifford papers, GCLM, Lieutenant Colonel Beckwith, 27 March 1801; H.O. 42 / 34, W. Symons, 6 April 1795; H.O. 42 / 61, Mayor Langmead, 15 April 1801; and *LEM*, 1–3 April 1801.

148. *EFP*, 2 April 1801; D.R.O., 1262M / L52, J. Willcock, 1 April 1801, and Lord Rolle, 4 April 1801; H.O. 42 / 61, Lord Fortescue, 4 and 5 April 1801.

149. Hay, "Property, Authority, and the Criminal Law," pp. 40–56.

150. Bohstedt, "Riots," pp. 400, 405–409. Arrests in Exeter: H.O. 42 / 61, R. Eales, 30 March 1801.

Recent emphases on the dialogic function of riot may underestimate the real costs, in the form of legal punishments, levied on the rioters. See, for instance, Peter Clark, "Popular Protest and Disturbance in Kent, 1558–1640," *Economic History Review*, 2nd ser., 29 (August 1976), 365–382, and John Walter and Keith Wrightson, "Dearth and the Social Order in Early Modern England," *Past and Present*, 71 (May 1976), 28–33, 36, 40–42.

151. See n. 98. Three other men were indicted. One could not be found, and the other two were condemned and then reprieved so as to suffer transportation (*EFP*, 16 April 1795; H.O. 42 / 34, G. W. Byne, 6 May 1795; Assize 24 / 43, Devon, Summer 1795; and *LCh*, 1–4 Aug. 1795). For Campion's execution, see *EFP*, 6, 13 Aug. 1795; *Western Antiquary*, 8 (1888–1889), 171; and W.O. 1 / 1085, M. Dyons, 5 Aug. 1795. Shortly after the riot, the proprietor of the mill wrote to the government begging that troops be kept in the area, or else his life and property would be in danger from armed mobs of villagers in the neighborhood who meant to take retribution if Campion should hang (W.O. 1 / 1085 fol. 39, Geo. W. Byne, 7, 9 May 1795, and H.O. 42 / 34, G. W. Byne, 6 May 1795).

152. H.O. 42 / 61, Lord Fortescue, 4 April 1801. H.O. 43 / 12 / 497, Duke of Portland, 7 April 1801; and H.O. 42 / 61, J. G. Simcoe, 5 April 1801.

153. D.R.O., 1262M / L53, copy of letter in William Foot, 23 May 1801, and D.R.O., 1262M / L53 ["Minutes" of the magistrates' investigation, c. 1 May 1801], and attached letter, dated Modbury, 2 May [1801], signature obliterated; and H.O. 42 / 62 /.339, Lord Fortescue, 28 April 1801.

154. H.O. 42 / 61, Lord Fortescue, 14 and 30 April 1801, and Thomas Kitson, 25 April 1801.

155. H.O. 42 / 62 / 348, Thomas Kitson, 12 May 1801; and H.O. 43 / 13 / 107, Duke of Portland, 22 July 1801.

156. Bohstedt, "Riots," pp. 430–434; and, for example, H.O. 42 / 34, W. Symons, 6 April 1795; H.O. 42 / 61, W. Bastard, 10 April 1801, mayor and magistrates of Plymouth, 11 April 1801, and Lord Fortescue, 12 April 1801.

157. H.O. 42 / 61 / 503 [resolutions of the Devonshire magistrates], 8 April 1801, in Lord Fortescue, 9 April 1801; and H.O. 42 / 61, printed orders to the overseers from the county bench, in Lord Fortescue, 19 April 1801.

158. D.R.O., 1262M / L53, J. G. Simcoe, 3 and 23, May 1801, and Lord

Fortescue, 6 May 1801. Before long, the peace preliminaries with France were signed, so it is hard to tell how far the plan to raise more Yeomanry went.

159. D.R.O., 1262M / L53, Colonel G. Montague, 4 May 1801, and Lord Fortescue, 21 May 1801.

160. Hence it seems more likely that ancient paternalistic regulation of markets derived from popular price-fixing traditions than vice versa.

161. See, for instance, Thompson, "Moral Economy," 107–115; John Stevenson, *Popular Disturbances in England, 1700–1870* (London: Longman's, 1979), pp. 102–106, and the sources cited there.

162. Compare Roger Wells, "The Revolt of the South-West, 1800–1801: A Study in English Popular Protest," *Social History*, 6 (October 1977), 713–744.

3. Manchester, a Town of Strangers

1. E. P. Thompson, *The Making of the English Working Class* (New York: Vintage Books, 1966), pp. 9–13.

2. Monsieur de Givry, quoted in W. H. Chaloner, "Manchester in the Latter Half of the Eighteenth Century," *Bulletin of the John Rylands Library*, 42 (1959–60), 42. For the population of Manchester and Salford, see Alfred P. Wadsworth and Julia de Lacey Mann, *The Cotton Trade and Industrial Lancashire, 1600–1780* (Manchester: Manchester University Press, 1931), pp. 509–510; C. W. Chalklin, *The Provincial Towns of Georgian England: A Study of the Building Process, 1740–1820* (London: Edward Arnold, 1974), pp. 336–338.

3. Dr. Thomas Henry, "Observations on the Bills of Mortality for the Towns of Manchester and Salford," read in January, 1786, printed in *Memoirs of the Literary and Philosophical Society of Manchester*, III (Warrington, 1790), 160–161.

4. [Robert Southey], *Letters from England: By Don Manuel Alvarez Espriella*, 3rd ed. (London, 1814), II, 85.

5. Cotton statistics: B. R. Mitchell, with Phyllis Deane, *Abstract of British Historical Statistics* (Cambridge: Cambridge University Press, 1971), p. 178.

On Manchester's industrialization: Bryan Roberts, "Agrarian Organization and Urban Development," in *Manchester and São Paulo: Problems of Rapid Urban Growth*, ed. John D. Wirth and Robert L. Jones (Stanford: Stanford University Press, 1978), p. 89; Chalklin, *Provincial Towns*, pp. 35–38; W. H. Chaloner, "Robert Owen, Peter Drinkwater and the Early Factory System in Manchester, 1788–1800," *Bulletin of the John Rylands Library*, 37 (September 1954), 85–91; John Kennedy, "Observations on the Rise and Progress of the Cotton Trade in Great Britain," *Memoirs of the Literary and Philosophical Society of Manchester*, 2nd ser., 3 (1819), 127–129; and John Kennedy, "A Brief Memoir of Samuel Crompton; with a Description of His Machine Called the Mule, and of the Subsequent

Improvement of the Machine by Others," *Memoirs of the Literary and Philosophical Society of Manchester*, 2nd ser., 5 (1831), 337–344.

6. Kennedy, "Rise and Progress," pp. 127–128.

7. For cotton mills in 1790: A. E. Musson and Eric Robinson, *Science and Technology in the Industrial Revolution* (Toronto: University of Toronto Press, 1969), pp. 400–403. For 1795, Stanley D. Chapman lists insurance policies over £5000 for seventeen cotton manufacturing firms with mills in Manchester and Salford, as well as other places; see Stanley D. Chapman, "Fixed Capital Formation in the British Cotton Industry, 1770–1815," *Economic History Review*, 2nd ser., 23 (1970), 256–257. For 1800: Chaloner, "Latter Half of the Eighteenth Century," p. 48. By 1800 there were said to be thirty-two steam engines at work in the Manchester trade; Edward Baines, Jr., *History of the Cotton Manufacture in Great Britain* (London, 1835), p. 226. For 1802: W. H. Chaloner, "The Birth of Modern Manchester," in *Manchester and Its Region*, ed. C. F. Certer (Manchester: Manchester University Press, 1962), p. 133. That figure apparently comes from G. A. Lee's "statement to the 1816 Select Committee on Children employed in the Manufactories," cited in Frances Collier, *The Family Economy of the Working Classes in the Cotton Industry, 1784–1833* (Manchester: Manchester University Press, 1964), p. 15, n. 2. For 1803: R. S. Fitton and A. P. Wadsworth, *The Strutts and the Arkwrights, 1758–1830: A Study of the Early Factory System* (Manchester: Manchester University Press, 1958), note, p. 192. In May 1802 McConnel and Kennedy reported there were about twenty new factories "building this summer." G. W. Daniels, "The Cotton Trade during the Revolutionary and Napoleonic Wars," *Transactions of the Manchester Statistical Society* (1915–1916), p. 63. For 1809: G. W. Daniels, "Valuation of Manchester Cotton Factories in the Early Years of the Nineteenth Century," *Economic Journal*, 25 (Dec. 1915), 626. For 1811: G. W. Daniels, "Samuel Crompton's Census of the Cotton Industry in 1811," *Economic History* (Jan. 1930), p. 109. For 1815–1820: J. H. Clapham, "Some Factory Statistics of 1815–16," *Economic Journal*, 25 (Sept. 1915), 476–477. For trade fluctuations, see Michael M. Edwards, *The Growth of the British Cotton Trade, 1780–1815* (Manchester: Manchester University Press, 1967), pp. 11–19.

8. "Minutes of Evidence, Committee on the Petition of Several Weavers &c.," *P. P.* 1810–1811 (232), IX, 2. The population statistic is from Chalklin, *Provincial Towns*, p. 336.

9. I have calculated ratios of capital to labor for the lists of factories for 1809 and 1811 (see n. 7), based on the ratio for one of the largest Manchester firms in 1816, McConnel and Kennedy. These figures suggest there were some 13,250 spinning-mill workers in 1809 and 13,800 in 1811, when 95 percent of the spindles were said by Samuel Crompton to be mule spindles (Daniels, "Cotton Factories," and Daniels, "Crompton's Census"). A list of 1803 gave 8,475 workers in cotton and woolen mills of more than 20 workers, and an 1816 list found 12,940 workers employed in mills in and about Manchester (*MM*, 11 Jan. 1803, quoted in Fitton and Wadsworth, *Strutts*, note, p. 192, and Clapham, "Factory Statistics," p.

477). Another observer in 1816 estimated that 23,053 workers were employed in mills in Manchester, Salford, Chorlton, and Hulme (Clapham, "Factory Statistics," p. 476).

10. *P. P.* 1810–1811 (232), IX, 2.

11. Chaloner, "Latter Half of the Eighteenth Century," p. 49, and Musson and Robinson, *Science and Technology,* pp. 393–458; John Aikin, *A Description of the Country from Thirty to Forty Miles round Manchester* (London, 1795), p. 178; Chaloner, "Birth," p. 134; Chalklin, *Provincial Towns,* p. 38.

12. H.O. 42 / 19, Thomas Butterworth Bayley and Henry Norris to Henry Dundas, 19 July 1791. Bayley repeated his lament the following year in connection with his report on the hostility to and the burning of Grimshaw's power-loom factory (Scottish Record Office, Edinburgh, The Melville papers, GD 51 / 1 / 362 / 1, T. Bayley to Henry Dundas, 18 March 1792).

13. *MM,* 8 Aug. 1786, quoted in A. P. Wadsworth, "The First Manchester Sunday Schools," *Bulletin of the John Rylands Library,* 33 (March 1951), 299.

14. Ibid., p. 307, quoting *MM,* 10 Aug. 1784.

15. James Wheeler, *Manchester: Its Political, Social, and Commercial History, Ancient and Modern* (London, 1836), p. 22.

16. *MM,* 29 June 1802. They added that the number of disorderly persons committed to the New Bayley Prison was greater than ever.

17. Kennedy, "Rise and Progress," pp. 124–125, 129.

18. *Proceedings of the Board of Health in Manchester* (Manchester, 1805), pp. 12–13, 18–19.

19. Percival: Ibid., p. 34; Aikin, *Description,* p. 192; Southey, *Letters from England,* II, 88–96.

20. Edward Baines, *History, Directory, and Gazeteer of the County Palatine of Lancaster* (Liverpool, 1825), II, 119.

21. *Board of Health,* p. 12; Sir Frederic Morton Eden, *The State of the Poor,* 3 vols. (London, 1797), II, 350.

22. See John Aikin, *Description,* p. 191; James Ogden, *A Description of Manchester* (Manchester, 1783), quoted in N. J. Frangopulo, *Rich Inheritance: A Guide to the History of Manchester* (Wilmslow: Richmond Press, 1962), p. 40; Joseph Aston, *The Manchester Guide* (Manchester, 1804), p. 55.

23. Thomas Carlyle's phrase is discussed in Harold Perkin, *The Origins of Modern English Society, 1780–1880* (London: Routledge and Kegan Paul, 1969), pp. 183–195.

24. For Manchester's government, see Arthur Redford and Ina Stafford Russell, *The History of Local Government in Manchester,* 3 vols. (London: Longman's, Green and Co., 1939–1940), I, chaps. 2 and 3. This outline of Manchester's Court Leet is drawn from Redford and Russell, *Local Government,* I, chaps. 3 and 4; Sidney Webb and Beatrice Webb, *The Manor and the Borough,* 2 vols. (1908; reprint ed., Hamden, Conn.: Archon Books, 1963), I, 99–113; Leon Soutierre Marshall, *The Development of Public*

Opinion in Manchester, 1780–1820 (Syracuse, N.Y.: Syracuse University Press, 1946), chap. 5; and Aston, *Manchester Guide,* pp. 50–56.

25. *A Report of the Committee of the Associated Ley-Payers in the Township of Manchester* (Manchester, 1794), pp. 30–31.

26. Redford and Russell, *Local Government,* I, 68. John Scholes, *Scholes's Manchester and Salford Directory,* 2nd ed. (Manchester, 1797). Thomas Battye charged that the special constables were chosen from "the very dregs of society." Thomas Battye, *The Red Basil Book* (Manchester, 1796), p. 88.

27. See Chap. 5.

28. Sidney Webb and Beatrice Webb, *The Parish and the County* (1906; reprint ed., Hamden, Conn.: Archon Books, 1963), pp. 75–76.

29. Redford and Russell, *Local Government,* I, 91, 254–255; see Archibald Prentice, *Historical Sketches and Personal Recollections of Manchester* (London and Manchester, 1851), p. 34. Prentice makes unsubstantiated charges that Nadin had made great profit from his office, and that he survived by "seasonable Loans" to magistrates, a dubious charge, given the wealth of the magistrates.

30. "Manchester in 1788: Address to the Jury of the Court Leet by William Roberts, Esqr.," reprinted in *The Court Leet Records of the Manor of Manchester,* ed. J. P. Earwaker (Manchester, 1889), IX, 242.

31. See, for instance, Earwaker, ed., *Court Leet Records,* IX, 92–98 (1794), 134 (1797), 146 (1799), 156–165 (1800), and 172–186 (1801). The fines for smoke were often respited to allow the mill owners to correct the nuisance (Webb and Webb, *Manor and Borough,* note, p. 105).

32. Earwaker, ed., *Court Leet Records,* IX and X. Compare Redford and Russell, *Local Government,* I, 134.

33. *MM,* 30 April 1793; Lancashire Q.S. Indictments and Recognizances, Summer 1795; and Q.S. Order Book, October 1795.

34. Webb and Webb, *Manor and Borough,* pp. 104, 108. Redford and Russell, *Local Government,* I, 82.

35. *Report of the Associated Ley-Payers,* p. 1, quoted in G. B. Hindle, *Provision for the Relief of the Poor in Manchester, 1754–1826,* Remains Historical and Literary...of Lancaster and Chester, 3rd ser., vol. 22 (Manchester: Chetham Society, 1975), p. 43, and see also pp. 27–37; and Redford and Russell, *Local Government,* II, 96.

36. Redford and Russell, *Local Government,* I, 181.

37. Hindle, *Provision for the Poor,* pp. 36, 60, 71, 75; Redford and Russell, *Local Government,* II, 97; and Thomas Battye, *Strictures upon the Churchwardens and Overseers of Manchester* (Manchester, 1801), pp. 17–18. Compare Chap. 5.

38. *MM,* 17 Feb. 1795.

39. The precept, though evidently not the practice, was not to appoint active merchants and magistrates. Compare Arnold Thackeray, "Natural Knowledge in Cultural Context: The Manchester Model," *American Historical Review,* 79 (June 1974), 680. Thackeray suggests that justices of

the peace were men of "independent fortune" and not merchants, at least not active merchants, but he does not really analyze their careers or family backgrounds. For Bayley, see n. 40. For Drinkwater, see Chaloner, "Early Factory System," p. 84. For Norris, Richardson, and Fletcher, Elizabeth Raffald, *The Manchester and Salford Directory* (Manchester, 1781). I am grateful to Professors Charles Tilly and Frank Munger for helping me to use the Manchester directories. For Leaf, see ibid., Edmond Holme, *A Directory for the Towns of Manchester and Salford, for the Year 1788* (Manchester, [1788]) and *P. P.* 1802–1803 (114), III, 47. Check was checked cloth; fustian was a stout fabric made of cotton and flax. For Simpson, see Holme, *Directory; Scholes's Manchester and Salford Directory* (1788); Gerard Bancks, *Bancks's Manchester and Salford Directory* (Manchester, 1800). Farington was listed as a merchant in a list of subscribers to the Internal Defense Fund (*MM*, 30 Sept. 1794). For Silvester, see *Scholes's Directory* (1794), and Arthur Redford, *Manchester Merchants and Foreign Trade, 1794–1858* (Manchester: Manchester University Press, 1934), pp. 6, 52, and 63.

40. Biographical information on Bayley is drawn from Webb and Webb, *Parish and County,* pp. 366–368; Thomas Percival, "Biographical Memoirs of Thomas Butterworth Bayley, Esq.," (1802), in Percival's *Works* (1807), II, 289–305; Ernest Axon, *The Bayley Family of Hope and Manchester* (Manchester, 1894), pp. 13–19; Caroline Robbins, *The Eighteenth-Century Commonwealthman* (Cambridge, Mass.: Harvard University Press, 1961), p. 354; Michael Ignatieff, *A Just Measure of Pain: The Penitentiary in the Industrial Revolution, 1750–1850* (New York: Pantheon Books, 1978), pp. 63, 77; Hindle, *Provision for the Poor,* p. 29; and *Board of Health,* pp. 1 and 53. The quotations are from Percival, "Biographical Memoirs," pp. 290–294 and 301–302.

41. The criticisms, written in 1779 and 1780, came from the Reverend Thomas Seddon. They are quoted in Axon, *Bayley Family,* pp. 14–15. For Percival, see his "Biographical Memoirs," pp. 302–303.

42. Percival, "Biographical Memoirs," p. 299.

43. Aston, *Manchester Guide,* p. 155; and Hindle, *Provision for the Poor,* p. 111.

44. Hindle, *Provision for the Poor,* chap. 6.

45. Except for the revival of the Manchester Soup Charity in the winter of 1808–1809, following the weavers' strike of 1808, and in February 1811, and some provision of coals in 1803 (Hindle, *Provision for the Poor,* pp. 102 and 122). The best description of Manchester's network of philanthropy is Hindle, *Provision for the Poor,* especially chap. 8.

46. Report of the Manchester Committee for Sunday Schools (1792), quoted in Wadsworth, "Sunday Schools," pp. 312, 319.

47. William E. A. Axon, *The Annals of Manchester: A Chronological Record From the Earliest Times to the End of 1885* (Manchester, 1886), pp. 121–124, 134. "Tory" and "Church and King" are nearly synonymous. Tories were those who supported the Tory government. Their right wing, the "Church and King" advocates, staunchly opposed all threats to the Established Church or the political status quo.

For Phillips and Hanson, see Chaps. 5 and 6. Another exception was Richard Ford, the commander of the Light Horse Volunteers, the merchants' Yeomanry, who seems to have been a liberal in the early 1790s. Artisans formed the St. George's Corps of Independent Volunteers, but the corps seems to have fallen apart (Axon, *Annals*, p. 133).

48. H.O. 42 / 95, R. A. Farington to Lord Hawkesbury, 28 May 1808; and *MM*, 31 May 1808.

4. Cavalry and Soup Kitchens

1. J. Phillip Dodd, "South Lancashire in Transition: A Study of the Crop Returns for 1795–1801," *Transactions of the Historic Society of Lancashire and Cheshire*, 117 (1965), 95; Alan Booth, "Food Riots in the North-West of England, 1790–1801," *Past and Present*, 77 Nov. 1977), 87.

2. Prices: *Ann. Ag.*, 24 (1795), 620; 25 (1796), 128, 233, 348. Anxiety: H.O. 42 / 35, Thomas Richardson to Earl of Derby, 29 July 1795, and Derby's covering letter, 1 Aug. 1795. Oats, said Derby, had risen to an "enormous price."

3. *MM*, 4 Aug. 1795.

4. H.O. 42 / 35, enclosures in Earl of Derby, 1 Aug. 1795; Booth, "Food Riots," pp. 86–87 (wheaten bread); for white bread, see E. P. Thompson, "The Moral Economy of the English Crowd in the Eighteenth Century," *Past and Present*, 50 (Feb. 1971), 80–82.

5. The following account of the 1795 rioting is based upon: *MM*, 4 Aug. 1795; *YC*, 3 Aug. 1795; H.O. 42 / 35, Nathan Crompton to Martin Marshall, 30 July 1795; and Lancashire Q.S. Indictments and Recognizances, Oct. 1795, and Order Book, 1796.

6. *The Court Leet Records of the Manor of Manchester*, ed. J. P. Earwaker (Manchester, 1889), IX, 100, 108.

7. Nine of the twelve people charged with rioting on the two days were women. One Charles Nicholls, a whitesmith, was charged in both days' rioting. The other two men were laborers. One of the women was identified as a chapman. Otherwise, Thursday's women were "single-women," Friday's, wives and widows (Lancashire Q.S. Indictments and Recognizances, Oct. 1795).

This account differs from Booth's emphases on the orderly character of the riots in the northwest, their resort to forced sale, and the lack of outright seizure. Booth did not distinguish different patterns in different towns (Booth, "Food Riots," pp. 93, 95).

8. Booth, "Food Riots," p. 90, table.

9. *MG*, 1 Feb. 1800. Justice Bayley was reported to have prevented a riot on February 1 (*MM*, 11 Feb. 1800). The London press included Manchester in a list of riotous towns at this time and added that the military had intervened, but it seems most unlikely that a riot occurred in Manchester (*LObs*, 16 Feb. 1800; *LEM*, 14–17 Feb. 1800).

10. *MG*, 24 May 1800; *MM*, 3 June 1800.

11. *MM,* 17 June 1800; *MG,* 26 July 1800; *MM,* 29 July 1800.

12. Booth, "Food Riots," pp. 93–95. Arthur Redford emphasizes the short distances involved in most migration to the industrial towns. Arthur Redford, *Labour Migration in England, 1800–1850,* 2nd ed. (Manchester: Manchester University Press, 1964), pp. 64–65. For the "moral economy," see Thompson, "Moral Economy."

13. Rioters at one mill in 1757 were said to have demanded and obtained corn at the "old price," though they were driven off by gunfire. This account of riots of 1757 and 1762 is drawn from J. P. Earwaker, ed., *The Constables' Accounts of the Manor of Manchester* (Manchester, 1892), III, appendices III-V, 359–372, which reprints contemporary newspaper accounts; Francis Nicholson and Ernest Axon, "The Hatfield Family of Manchester and the Food Riots of 1757 and 1812," *Transactions of the Lancashire and Cheshire Antiquarian Society,* 28 (1910), 81–114; Tim Bobbin, pseud. [John Collier], *Truth in a Mask: Or Shude-Hill Fight; Being a Short Manchesterian Chronicle of the Present Times* (1757), in *The Works of John Collier (Tim Bobbin) in Prose and Verse,* ed. Henry Fishwick (Rochdale, 1894), pp. 191–205; and Leon Soutierre Marshall, *The Development of Public Opinion in Manchester, 1780–1820* (Syracuse: Syracuse University Press, 1946), p. 247 n. 1.

14. After the Shude Hill fight in 1757, the gentlemen of Manchester advertised their determination to execute the laws against forestallers, engrossers, and regraters (Earwaker, ed., *Constables' Accounts,* III, 366).

Several historians have concluded that food riots were relatively rare in the north: Max Beloff, *Public Order and Popular Disturbances, 1660–1714* (London: Frank Cass & Co., 1938, 1963), p. 74; Walter J. Shelton, *English Hunger and Industrial Disorders: A Study of Social Conflict during the First Decade of George III's Reign* (London: Macmillan Press, 1973), p. 37 for 1766, but compare note, p. 21; R. B. Rose, "Eighteenth Century Price Riots and Public Policy in England," *International Review of Social History,* 6 (1961), p. 286; and J. Stevenson, "Food Riots in England, 1792–1818," in *Popular Protest and Public Order: Six Studies in British History, 1790–1920,* ed. R. Quinault and J. Stevenson (London: George Allen & Unwin, 1974), pp. 36, 45. George Rudé believed food riots were more likely to occur in the north and west than in the south and east; see *The Crowd in History: A Study of Popular Disturbances in France and England, 1730–1848* (New York: John Wiley & Sons, 1964, p. 37. Alan Booth has shown that there were more food riots in the northwest than previous studies had suggested, though I have been unable to verify from contemporary sources the riots he lists for Manchester in 1797, 1798, and 1799 (Booth, "Food Riots," pp. 84, 89–90).

15. Alfred P. Wadsworth and Julia de Lacey Mann, *The Cotton Trade and Industrial Lancashire, 1600–1780* (Manchester: Manchester University Press, 1931), p. 356; John Aikin, *A Description of the Country from Thirty to Forty Miles round Manchester* (London, 1795), p. 203, and the "Bramall" letter in Nicholson and Axon, "Hatfield Family," p. 85.

16. Booth, "Food Riots," p. 85; John Holt, *General View of the Agriculture of the County of Lancaster* (London, 1794), p. 13; Dodd, "Crop

Returns," p. 90; John Holt, *General View of the Agriculture of Lancaster* (London, 1795), p. 206; Redcliffe N. Salaman, "The Oxnoble Potato: A Study in Public-House Nomenclature," *Transactions of the Lancashire and Cheshire Antiquarian Society*, 54 (1954), 74; Aikin, *Description*, pp. 18, 203, and 204: part of Manchester's potato supplies came by land from north Cheshire and southwest Lancashire; *MM*, 6 Dec. 1800.

17. Aikin, *Description*, p. 201. This discussion of Manchester's markets is based on Arthur Redford and Ina Stafford Russell, *The History of Local Government in Manchester*, 3 vols. (London: Longman's, Green and Co., 1939–1940), I, 147; Joseph Aston, *The Manchester Guide* (Manchester, 1804), pp. 263–267; James Ogden, *A Description of Manchester* (Manchester, 1783), p. 72. Apples, a very important food for the poor, were brought from the cider counties of the southwest (Aikin, *Description*, p. 204). The apple market also included other fresh fruits. In 1781 Elizabeth Raffald's *Directory* listed no fewer than 54 flour dealers, 26 grocers, 34 butchers, and 14 bakers.

18. Both the Tory *Manchester Mercury* and the Whig-Reformer *Manchester Gazette* condemned speculators throughout the food crises of these years. The *Gazette* pointed out that farmers had ample opportunity to fix price agreements in their agricultural societies and other meetings, while artisans' combinations (informal trade unions) were punishable by imprisonment. The *Gazette* also called for government regulation of the corn trade: "So far as regards the interference of authority with private property, we must observe, that individuals have only a qualified property in the articles of general use and necessity" (*MG*, 16 Aug. and 1 Nov. 1800). That was precisely the attitude of eighteenth-century rioters and magistrates in traditional communities!

19. "Manchester in 1788. Address to the Jury of the Court Leet by William Roberts, Esqr.," reprinted in Earwaker, ed., *Court Leet Records*, IX, 242.

20. Declaration by the boroughreeve and constables of Manchester (*MM*, 30 July and 6 Aug. 1799); and Earwaker, ed., *Court Leet Records*, IX, 124 (1797), 134, and 153–155.

21. *MM*, 4 Aug. 1795. Privately, Bayley did agree with the Duke of Bridgewater's judgment that the scarcity was aggravated by "undue monopoly" (H.O. 42 / 50, T. B. Bayley to the Duke of Portland, 23 June 1800).

22. *MG*, 14 Dec. 1799.

23. Ibid., 27 Sept. 1800.

24. *MM*, 14 Dec. 1802, and compare *MM*, 17 May 1803.

25. Apparently enclosed in H.O. 42 / 50, T. B. Bayley, 23 June 1800, and quoted in J. L. Hammond and Barbara Hammond, *The Skilled Labourer, 1760–1832* (New York: Harper and Row, 1970), p. 65.

26. H.O. 42 / 53, paper taken from the toll gates of the New Bridge, Manchester, 29 Nov. 1800, enclosed in T. B. Bayley, 30 Nov. 1800.

27. H.O. 42 / 61, enclosed in T. B. Bayley, 11 April 1801.

28. H.O. 50 / 48, T. Bayley, 3 Nov. 1800, and see Chap. 5.

29. Compare Booth, "Food Riots," p. 104.

30. The *Manchester Gazette* of 18 April 1801 published the resolutions of this meeting. The article said the gathering consisted of "inhabitants of Oldham, Rochdale, Royton, Middleton, Chadderton, etc.," but Manchester was almost certainly represented, for both radicals and organized textile workers had begun to concert their actions across the cotton district. See Chap. 6.

31. Booth, "Food Riots," p. 104.

32. Michael M. Edwards, *The Growth of the British Cotton Trade, 1780–1815* (Manchester: Manchester University Press, 1967), pp. 12, 14; G. W. Daniels, "The Cotton Trade during the Revolutionary and Napoleonic Wars," *Transactions of the Manchester Statistical Society* (1915–1916), pp. 58, 59, 62; Duncan Bythell, *The Handloom Weavers: A Study in the English Cotton Industry during the Industrial Revolution* (Cambridge: Cambridge University Press, 1969), p. 275.

33. "Minutes of Evidence Taken before the Committee on the Cotton Weavers' Petitions," *P.P.*, 1802–1803 (114), III, pp. 31–63, especially James Holcroft's testimony, pp. 31–39, and the address of the committee of tradesmen against the Combination Act in *MG*, 14 Dec. 1799.

34. Booth, "Food Riots," p. 98; Thompson, "Moral Economy," pp. 115–116; Natalie Zemon Davis, *Society and Culture in Early Modern France* (Stanford: Stanford University Press, 1975), p. 148; and J. L. Hammond and Barbara Hammond, *The Village Labourer*, 4th ed. (London: Longman's, Green and Co., 1927), p. 117.

35. This statement draws on tabulations from my national sample of 617 riots. Some description of the rioters is available for 163 food riots. Of the 73 food riots in which women are identified, they acted alone in 9 cases, with children in 5, with other unidentified rioters in 13, and with both children and other unidentified rioters in 11 cases. Hence in 35 riots women participated with other (male) groups.

36. For women who were spinners and weavers, Chap. 6; for women in friendly societies, see *MM*, 2 July 1799.

37. This paragraph and the next are based upon reports in *MM*, 4, 11 Aug. 1795 and 17 June 1800; and *YC*, 3 Aug. 1795.

38. The magistrates' handbill of 21 Nov. 1799 is reproduced in G. B. Hindle, *Provision for the Relief of the Poor in Manchester, 1754–1826* (Manchester: Chetham Society, 1975), facing p. 89. Food riots had already occurred in Oldham: Edwin Butterworth, *Historical Sketches of Oldham* (Oldham, 1856), p. 144; and *MG*, 23 Nov. 1799.

39. H.O. 42 / 50, T. B. Bayley, 8 May 1800. This letter suggests that at this time, Bayley was more concerned about the weavers' campaign than by the hunger unrest.

40. *MM*, 4, 11, 18 Aug., and 22, 29 Dec. 1795.

41. On soup kitchen technology, see *The Reports of the Society for Bettering the Condition and Increasing the Comforts of the Poor*, I (London, 1798), 148–150, 164–169, and Fritz Redlich, "Science and Charity: Count Rumford and His Followers," *International Review of Social History*, 16

(1971), 184–216. I am indebted to Mr. Kenneth E. Carpenter for this reference.

42. *MG,* 14, 21 Dec. 1799. Chorlton Street was in a neighborhood of cellar slums identified as a fever epidemic area in 1796: *Proceedings of the Board of Health in Manchester* (Manchester, 1805), p. 17. See also *MG,* 30 Nov. 1799, and 29 March and 31 May 1800; and Hindle, *Provision for the Poor,* pp. 95–96, 99, 121–122.

43. On "police," see Leon Radzinowicz, *A History of English Criminal Law and Its Administration from 1750,* 4 vols. (London: Stevens and Sons, 1968), IV, 34–40, and *The Compact Edition of the Oxford English Dictionary* (Oxford: Oxford University Press, 1971), s.v. "police." See Hindle, *Provision for the Poor,* for the subscriptions. The relief fund of January 1795 was ended in a few months; formation of the fund in January 1799 may have been stimulated by food riots or unrest in December 1798. See W. E. A. Axon, *The Annals of Manchester: A Chronological Record from the Earliest Times to the End of 1885* (Manchester, 1886), p. 126. I have not been able to find primary sources confirming these riots, however. They are not mentioned in the *Mercury* or the *Gazette.*

44. *MM,* 4 Aug. 1795.

45. Quoted in Hindle, *Provision for the Poor,* p. 120.

46. *MG,* 6 Dec. 1800.

47. Hindle, *Provision for the Poor,* pp. 92–93. Compare the *Reports of the Society for Bettering the Condition of the Poor,* I, 169 and 216.

48. *MG,* 28 Dec. 1799. The outright sale of soup had been provided for when the Soup Charity was revived in November (*MG,* 9 Nov. 1799). The Committee for the General Relief of the Poor in December 1800 reverted to the more controlled policy of visiting poor families to ascertain needs for bedding and clothing, though rice and coal were sold at the public shops.

49. *MG,* 3 May 1800.

50. H.O. 42 / 110, address of February 1811, quoted in Hammond and Hammond, *Skilled Labourer,* pp. 83, 89–90.

51. Declaration of the magistrates in Lancaster, 7 Oct. 1800, in *MM,* 6 Dec. 1800. They also resolved to suppress riots.

52. *MM,* 1 Sept. 1795.

53. *MM,* 27 Oct. 1795 (my italics).

54. Butterworth, *Oldham,* pp. 137–139 and 144–145.

55. In July 1795 a crowd of women and boys in Oldham demolished the windows of the provision dealers. The next morning Justice Joseph Pickford of Royton arrived and, with the aid of the Light Horse Volunteers, took several prisoners. That led to a violent rescue attempt in which several prisoners were injured by the troops (Butterworth, *Oldham,* p. 138). Pickford was the magistrate who in the previous year had not only refused to intervene in the "Church and King" mob attack on Royton's Reformers, but had then charged the Reformers with riot. See Samuel Bamford, *The Autobiography of Samuel Bamford,* 3rd ed., 2 vols. (London: Frank Cass and Co., 1967), I, *Early Days,* pp. 47–48.

In the same month in the sprawling parish of Rochdale, a food riot ended in bloodshed; the Volunteers had been ordered by the magistrates to fire on a crowd of rioters who refused to disperse. Two old men were killed outright (*MM*, 11 Aug. 1795). It may be that the disorganized violence and bitter class antagonisms resulting from *rural* industrialization and rapid population growth made Rochdale into a rural industrial slum and swamped the social networks in a way parallel to that of Manchester. But the unnecessary killings of 1795 certainly left the people's rage hanging over the magistrates, and the enduring bitterness may account for the unusual violence in Rochdale during the weavers' strike of 1808 (see Chap. 6).

In Ashton in February 1800, the rioters were so well organized that they brought a scale with them to measure out the grain at the warehouse they attacked. They sold the grain and gave the money to the owner, according to his own testimony. Then they stoned the Volunteers and Justice W. R. Hay, who tried to disperse them (*MM*, 11 Feb. 1800, and P. L. 27 / 7, Lancashire Assize Depositions, Spring 1800). The many depositions in this case suggest how easy it was for witnesses in a smaller town to identify rioters.

56. Alan Booth emphasizes the orderly behavior of the Lancashire food rioters, but he does not distinguish between Manchester and the smaller towns ("Food Riots," pp. 93–95).

5. Entrepreneurial Politics

1. See J. P. Earwaker, ed., *The Court Leet Records of the Manor of Manchester* (Manchester, 1889), vols. 8–10, for lists of town officials. For the "suspects," see Archibald Prentice, *Historical Sketches and Personal Recollections of Manchester* (London and Manchester, 1851), pp. 423–424. I have traced occupations in the Manchester directories of the period.

2. Joseph Aston, *The Manchester Guide* (Manchester, 1804), p. 52.

3. On patronage, see Harold Perkin, *The Origins of Modern English Society, 1780–1880* (London: Routledge and Kegan Paul, 1969), pp. 44–57, and Sir Lewis Namier, *The Structure of Politics at the Accession of George III*, 2nd ed. (London: Macmillan and Co., 1963), pp. 88–89, 95–96, 104, 119, 129–134. Favors to an entire community might include political support of a local industry or donations of land or money to community causes.

4. By contrast with Nottingham, for instance. See Malcolm I. Thomis, *Politics and Society in Nottingham, 1785–1835* (Oxford: Basil Blackwell, 1969), pp. 122–126.

5. Leon Soutierre Marshall, *The Development of Public Opinion in Manchester, 1780–1820* (Syracuse: Syracuse University Press, 1946), pp. 81–82, 108.

6. Arthur Redford, *Manchester Merchants and Foreign Trade, 1794–1858* (Manchester: Manchester University Press, 1934), pp. 3–5; Witt Bowden, *Industrial Society in England towards the End of the Eighteenth Century*, 2nd ed. (London: Frank Cass & Co., 1965), p. 167.

7. This account is based on Marshall, *Public Opinion*, pp. 184–185;

Frida Knight, *The Strange Case of Thomas Walker* (London: Lawrence & Wishart, 1957), pp. 26–30, 32–33; Redford, *Manchester Merchants,* pp. 6–7; Bowden, *Industrial Society,* pp. 169–193; and John Money, *Experience and Identity: Birmingham and the West Midlands, 1760–1800* (Manchester: Manchester University Press, 1977), pp. 33–46.

8. Francis Espinasse, *Lancashire Worthies,* 2nd ser. (London, 1877), pp. 308–309, which points out that Walker supported even the Corn Law of 1815; Marshall, *Public Opinion,* pp. 186–187; Redford, *Manchester Merchants,* pp. 11–13. Conversely, the majority of Manchester's leading merchants and manufacturers, especially the cotton spinners, were free-traders but also Tories.

9. Bowden, *Industrial Society,* p. 168, quoting Board of Trade 6 / 140, doc. 45.

10. Pauline Handforth, "Manchester Radical Politics, 1789–1794," *Transactions of the Lancashire and Cheshire Antiquarian Society,* 66 (1956), 88–89; and *MM,* 20 Jan. 1789. The Pittite future magistrates were Peter Drinkwater and John Simpson. Among the many future Tory borough-reeves were C. F. Brandt, Edward Place, George Barton, Nathan Crompton, Edward Hobson, William Fox, John Kearsley, John Poole, and Joseph Thackeray. The radicals named here appear time and again in the petitions of the 1790s, and they were among the thirty-four leading opposition "suspects" named by the Loyal Association in 1793.

11. See Arnold Thackeray, "Natural Knowledge in Cultural Context: The Manchester Model," *American Historical Review,* 79 (June 1974), 679, 681, 694, 705; for the Test Act controversy in Manchester, I have drawn upon G. M. Ditchfield's excellent article, "The Campaign in Lancashire and Cheshire for the Repeal of the Test and Corporation Acts, 1787–1790," *Transactions of the Historic Society of Lancashire and Cheshire,* 126 (1977), 108–138.

12. *MM,* 9 Feb. 1790, and for Percival, see Ditchfield, "Campaign," p. 118. The Test and Corporation Acts created hazards for Dissenters taking up municipal or crown offices, including the magistracy, but not parochial or manorial offices in Manchester. See Albert Goodwin, *The Friends of Liberty: The English Democratic Movement in the Age of the French Revolution* (London: Hutchinson and Co., 1979), p. 77. Hence, Ditchfield's argument that repeal would have made a real difference in local politics fits corporate towns best. In Manchester, the steward of the manor's charge to the grand jury concerning town officials' beliefs shifted from complete religious toleration in 1788 to a requirement for political loyalism in 1793. See Arthur Redford and Ina Stafford Russell, *The History of Local Government in Manchester,* 3 vols. (London: Longman's, Green and Co., 1939–1940), I, 196.

13. Thomas Walker, *A Review of Some of the Political Events Which Have Occurred in Manchester during the Last Five Years* (London, 1794), p. 11; Ditchfield, "Campaign," p. 125.

14. Circulars quoted in Ditchfield, "Campaign," p. 123, and in Knight, *Thomas Walker,* p. 39.

15. The Tories had requested a "Public Meeting of the Inhabitants

...who are Members of the Established Church." The Dissenters protested that by the resolution of a previous town meeting in 1788, the boroughreeve could sanction and convene only "general" meetings. *MM*, 2, 9, 16, and 23 Feb. 1790; and Walker, *Review*, pp. 11–14.

16. Knight, *Thomas Walker*, p. 40–43.

17. Ditchfield, "Campaign," p. 126.

18. Walker, *Review*, pp. 15, 19.

19. Handforth, "Radical Politics," pp. 90–91; Walker, *Review*, pp. 15–16.

20. *MM*, 20 Jan. 1789 and 9 Feb. 1790; Redford and Russell, *Local Government*, I, 192–193.

21. Knight, *Thomas Walker*, pp. 48, 51–57, 59; Handforth, "Radical Politics," pp. 92–93; and *The Whole Proceedings on the Trial of an Action Brought by Thomas Walker, Merchant, against William Roberts, Barrister-at-Law, for a Libel...* (taken in shorthand by Joseph Gurney; Manchester, 1791).

22. Walker, *Review*, p. 23.

23. Knight, *Thomas Walker*, p. 64; Donald Clare, "The Local Newspaper Press and Local Politics in Manchester and Liverpool, 1780–1800," *Transactions of the Lancashire and Cheshire Antiquarian Society*, 73–74 (1963–1964), p. 112; Handforth, "Radical Politics," p. 97; Goodwin, *Friends of Liberty*, pp. 201–203, 235; Walker, *Review*, p. 33; *MH*, 9 June 1792; Knight, *Thomas Walker*, p. 86; *The Whole Proceedings on the Trial of an Indictment against Thomas Walker of Manchester, Merchant [et al.]...for a Conspiracy...* (Manchester, 1794), especially p. 78.

24. The political mobilization of the nation in this period has been discussed inter alia in Austin Mitchell, "The Association Movement of 1792–93," *Historical Journal*, 4 (1961), 56–77; Donald E. Ginter, "The Loyalist Association Movement of 1792–93 and British Public Opinion," *Historical Journal*, 9 (1966), 179–190; Eugene Charlton Black, *The Association: British Extraparliamentary Political Organization, 1769–1793* (Cambridge, Mass.: Harvard University Press, 1963); and E. P. Thompson, *The Making of the English Working Class* (New York: Vintage Books, 1966), pp. 102–116; and Goodwin, *Friends of Liberty*, pp. 263–267.

25. The Society's letter was published in the *Manchester Herald*. I quote from Knight, *Thomas Walker*, p. 77.

26. Walker, *Review*, p. 37; compare *MM*, 5 June 1792.

27. Aston, *Manchester Guide*, pp. 122, 131.

28. Until December 1795, when Bayley and other magistrates bound over several rioters (below). Bayley did not sign any of the partisan petitions after the 1789 petition against Pitt.

29. Walker, *Review*, pp. 40, 55; Knight, *Thomas Walker*, p. 86.

30. George Stead Veitch, *The Genesis of Parliamentary Reform* (London: Constable & Co., 1913), p. 235; and Mitchell, "Association Movement," p. 58.

31. *MM*, 11 Dec. 1792.

32. According to the *Manchester Chronicle*, quoted in Knight, *Thomas Walker*, p. 93.

33. W. Cooke Taylor, *Life and Times of Peel*, I (1846), 10, quoted in Espinasse, *Lancashire Worthies*, pp. 110–111. But see also the account in *MM*, 18 Dec. 1792, where Peel is reported to have warned of sedition, at which the audience expressed a "conspicuous" determination to preserve "liberty."

34. One of the two was of course Thomas Walker. "The magistrates of Salford Hundred" were listed collectively, but it is doubtful that Thomas B. Bayley was a signer (*MM*, 18 Dec. 1792).

35. Compare George Rudé, *The Crowd in the French Revolution* (Oxford: Oxford University Press, 1959), p. 239.

36. I use the concept of "licensing" suggested in Thompson, *Making of the Working Class*, pp. 68, 71–75.

37. Walker, *Review*, pp. 56, 57, 59.

38. Knight, *Thomas Walker*, pp. 93–94.

39. Thompson, *Making of the Working Class*, p. 113.

40. Walker, *Review*, pp. 65–67.

41. Ibid., pp. 56–59. However, when Unite saw two of the beadles nearby, he cried out to the mob, "Come away from the house! *D--n* his house don't come near it!"

42. Ibid., pp. 64, 73–74.

43. Hooligans: Knight, *Thomas Walker*, pp. 93–94; "destitute of property": Walker, *Review*, p. 59.

44. Mitchell, "Association Movement," p. 68.

45. Compare E. P. Thompson, "'Rough Music': Le charivari anglais," *Annales: Economies, Societés, Civilisations*, 27 (1972), 291.

46. See n. 3.

47. *MM*, 18 Dec. 1792.

48. Handforth, "Radical Politics," pp. 101–104, and Knight, *Thomas Walker*, pp. 119–178. The Loyalists' list of suspects is given in Prentice, *Historical Sketches*, p. 423.

49. Walker, *Review*, p. 16. The parent Church and King Club of 1790 continued to meet annually to commemorate the defeat of the Dissenters (*MM*, 10 March 1795, 8 March 1796, 19 Feb. 1799, 8 Feb. 1803, 14 Feb. 1804).

50. *MM*, 11, 18 Dec. 1792, and Prentice, *Historical Sketches*, p. 422, quoting the Loyal Association's minutes of 21 Dec. 1792.

51. Mitchell, "Association Movement," p. 65.

52. Handforth, "Radical Politics," p. 101; Prentice, *Historical Sketches*, pp. 422–423; Walker, *Review*, pp. 85–86; Mitchell, "Association Movement," pp. 66, 73; and see *MM*, 3, 15 May 1798.

53. *MM*, 7 Oct. and 11 Nov. 1794. Manchester and Lancashire had just raised several corps of a different kind of Volunteers, the Fencibles, who were sent to Ireland and the West Indies. William E. A. Axon, *The Annals of Manchester: A Chronological Record from the Earliest Times to the End of 1885* (Manchester, 1886), pp. 121, 123. Compare *MM*, 26 Aug. and 30 Sept. 1794. The gentlemen's patriotic purses were temporarily exhausted, and there was no need to arm any more workers since Loyalists were already enrolled in the clubs.

54. Prentice, *Historical Sketches,* p. 426, quoting Loyal Association minutes.

55. H. O. 50 / 27, Earl of Derby, 6 March 1797, and enclosures. *MM,* 3, 10 April and 8 May 1798.

56. *MM,* 20 Feb. 1798.

57. *MM,* 24 April 1798.

58. H.O. 50 / 48, Thomas B. Bayley, 3 Nov. 1800 (his italics).

59. John Western argued that the raising of the Volunteers was part of the government's campaign to mobilize popular Loyalism in the 1790s. See his "The Volunteer Movement as an Anti-Revolutionary Force, 1793–1801," *English Historical Review,* 71 (1956), 603–614. The Volunteers in Manchester were the third phase of the local mobilization, following mobs and associations.

60. An appeal for a supplementary Volunteer subscription avoided provocative rhetoric and drew the support of Reformers George Lloyd and George Philips and Old Whigs Bayley and Percival (*MM,* 24 July 1798). The relatively nonpartisan Bayley was one of the colonels of the new battalions.

61. C. W. Chalklin, *The Provincial Towns of Georgian England: A Study of the Building Process, 1740–1820* (London: Edward Arnold, 1974), pp. 279–280; Michael M. Edwards, *The Growth of the British Cotton Trade, 1780–1815* (Manchester: Manchester University Press, 1967), p. 12; G. B. Hindle, *Provision for the Relief of the Poor in Manchester, 1754–1826* (Manchester: Chetham Society, 1975), p. 59.

62. The eight are the seven who signed the *Report* of 1794 plus another who signed a letter to the press as chairman of the ALP. Only one, Thomas Greendrod, is not listed in the directories at all. See *A Report of the Committee of the Associated Ley-Payers in the Township of Manchester* (Manchester, 1794).

63. *MM,* 17 March 1795.

64. Thomas Bateman, Richard Roberts, and William Seddon were the "suspects," and George Lloyd and John Mitchell, M.D., were the veteran reformers. The petitions of 1795 are discussed below.

65. *Associated Ley-Payers,* p. ii.

66. Ibid., pp. xx and 31; Hindle, *Provision for the Poor,* p. 62. According to Marshall, *Public Opinion,* p. 87, the churchwardens threatened to levy new assessments on the small landlords of "miserable" cottages, and that made the Associated Ley-Payers shift their attention from the rates to the other abuses in disbursements. On small landlords, see Chalklin, *Provincial Towns,* p. 174. But Chalklin emphasizes that most housing construction up to 1800 in Manchester was the work of *large* developers (pp. 89–98).

67. *Associated Ley-Payers,* p. 31. See Hindle, *Provision for the Poor,* pp. 59–66.

68. *Associated Ley-Payers,* p. 10.

69. Ibid., pp. 9–10, 30–31; Knight, *Thomas Walker,* p. 118.

70. *MM,* 22 July 1794; and Hindle, *Provision for the Poor,* p. 66.

71. Redford and Russell, *Local Government*, I, 88–89.

72. See Hindle, *Provision for the Poor*, pp. 65–70, Sidney Webb and Beatrice Webb, *The Parish and the County* (1906; reprinted, Hamden, Conn.: Archon Books, 1963), p. 75.

73. For Battye see Hindle, *Provision for the Poor*, chap. 5.

74. Thomas Battye, *The Red Basil Book, or Parish Register of Arrears* (Manchester [1796]), p. iv. Basil is tanned sheepskin used in bookbinding.

75. Thomas Battye, *A Reply to Mr. Unite's Address to the Ley-Payers of Manchester, 2nd Ed. with Considerable Additions* [14 Dec. 1794], p. 21.

76. Battye, *Red Basil Book*, pp. 42–43, 77, and compare Thomas Battye, *A Disclosure of Parochial Abuses, Artifice, and Peculation, in the Town of Manchester...*, 2nd ed. (Manchester, 1796), pp. 2, 5, 36. Sir Frederic Morton Eden, *The State of the Poor*, 3 vols. (London, 1797), II, 342.

77. *MM*, 25 Nov. 1794.

78. The boroughreeve and the two constables had all been members of the original Committee of the Loyal Association. *MM*, 17 March 1795.

79. *SYM*, 21 Sept. 1795.

80. *MM*, 14 April 1795 and compare 25 Aug. 1795, and 2 Feb. 1796; Redford and Russell, *Local Government*, I, 190; Earwaker, ed., *Court Leet Records*, IX, 121, 122, 125, 132; and Hindle, *Provision for the Poor*, pp. 70–71.

81. *MM*, 27 Jan., 3 Feb. 1795; Marshall, *Public Opinion*, pp. 253–254 n. 63; the members of the Manchester Literary and Philosophical Society are given in the *Memoirs of the Literary and Philosophical Society of Manchester*, vols. 1–5 (1785–1798). Robert Peel was not a signer of the peace petition as Marshall incorrectly said on p. 126.

82. *MM*, 10, 17 Feb. 1795.

83. Thompson, *Making of the Working Class*, pp. 144–146.

84. *MM*, 17, 24 Nov., 1 Dec. 1795.

85. *MM*, 8 Dec. 1795, and Prentice, *Historical Sketches*, p. 426.

86. Ibid., p. 427, and *MM*, 15 Dec. 1795.

87. I have conflated the declarations of the Loyal Associators at Mr. James Howarth's The Lamb, and the Loyal Association at Mr. Thomas Betley's The Waggon Horses. One address appears to paraphrase the other closely (*MM*, 8 Dec. 1795). These were not among the dozen Loyal Associations listed in April 1795 as cooperating with the parent society, so they seem to represent even newer extensions of the Loyalists' strength.

88. Prentice, *Historical Sketches*, p. 427.

89. *MM*, 8, 15 Dec. 1795.

90. *LMCh*, 26 Dec. 1795, and *MM*, 22 Dec. 1795.

91. *MM*, 8, 15, and 22 Dec. 1795, and 26 Jan. 1796; *LMCh*, 26 Dec. 1795 and 26 Jan. 1796.

92. *MM*, 3 Feb. 1795 and 15, 22 Dec. 1795.

93. *MM*, 8, 15 Dec. 1795.

94. The *Mercury's* understated report is almost laughable: "an unexpected influx of people entered the ground: a little interruption consequently commenced, and we are extremely sorry to hear, that it

terminated in a degree of violence which ought always to be discountenanced" (8, 15 Dec. 1795).

95. *LT*, 14 Dec. 1795; *MM*, 15 Dec. 1795.

96. Walker, *Review*, pp. 33, 93; *LMCh*, 5 Aug. 1794; *MM*, 12 Aug. 1794.

97. Walker, *Review*, p. 98.

98. *LMCh*, 7 March 1796; *Reg. Times*, VIII (1796), 150; *LCh*, 3–5 March 1796; *MM*, 8 March 1796; *CI*, 14 May 1796.

99. Redford and Russell, *Local Government*, I, 214–219.

100. See the *Directories* for 1794, 1797, and 1800 for infirmary boards and police commissioners.

101. Goodwin, *Friends of Liberty*, p. 228.

6. The Mobilization of the Weavers

1. Duncan Bythell, *The Handloom Weavers: A Study in the English Cotton Industry during the Industrial Revolution* (Cambridge: Cambridge University Press, 1969), chap. 8; J. L. Hammond and Barbara Hammond, *The Skilled Labourer, 1760–1832* (New York: Harper and Row, 1970), chap. 4; and H. A. Turner, *Trade Union Growth, Structure and Policy* (Toronto: University of Toronto Press, 1962), pp. 44–107.

2. Joseph Aston, *A Picture of Manchester* (Manchester, 1816), p. 19.

3. Alfred P. Wadsworth and Julia de Lacey Mann, *The Cotton Trade and Industrial Lancashire, 1600–1780* (Manchester: Manchester University Press, 1931), p. 383.

4. *MM*, 22 Feb., 22 March 1803, 15 May, 9 June 1804, 5 March 1805; Sidney Webb and Beatrice Webb, *The History of Trade Unionism*, rev. ed. (London: Longman's, Green and Co., 1920), pp. 56–57, 75–76; Arthur Redford, *Manchester Merchants and Foreign Trade, 1794–1858* (Manchester: Manchester University Press, 1934), p. 67; Francis Espinasse, *Lancashire Worthies*, 2nd ser. (London, 1877), p. 96; and Edward Baines, *History of the Cotton Manufacture in Great Britain* (London, 1835), pp. 265–285.

5. See Chap. 3, and W. H. Chaloner, "Manchester in the Latter Half of the Eighteenth Century," *Bulletin of the John Rylands Library*, 42 (1959–1960), 48.

6. H. Catling, *The Spinning Mule* (Newton Abbot: David and Charles, 1970), p. 149.

7. The Rules of the Friendly Associated Cotton Spinners of Manchester in 1792 stated that "no member...shall learn any person to spin cotton (except his *or her* own child...)," quoted in Witt Bowden, *Industrial Society in England towards the End of the Eighteenth Century*, 2nd ed. (London: Frank Cass and Co., 1965), p. 300, and also that new spinners arriving in Manchester should pay the society's entrance fee or else "he *or she* shall be deemed unworthy the Notice of any member." Quoted in Neil Smelser, *Social Change in the Industrial Revolution: An Application of Theory to the British Cotton Industry* (Chicago: University of Chicago Press, 1959), p. 320. My italics.

8. Ivy Pinchbeck, *Women Workers and the Industrial Revolution, 1750–1850* (London: George Routledge & Sons, 1930), p. 186; Frances Collier, *The Family Economy of the Working Classes in the Cotton Industry, 1784–1833* (Manchester: Manchester University Press, 1964), pp. 60, 67, and 69.

9. William Lazonick, "The Subjection of Labor to Capital: The Rise of the Capitalist System," *Review of Radical Political Economics*, 10 (Spring 1978), 8–10.

10. Collier, *Family Economy*, p. 5. Hand-mule spinners had formed combinations in Stockport in 1785 and 1792. R. G. Kirby and A. E. Musson, *The Voice of the People: John Doherty, 1798–1854, Trade Unionist, Radical and Factory Reformer* (Manchester: Manchester University Press, 1975), p. 13.

11. Quoted in Bowden, *Industrial Society*, p. 300. Combinations were unions of workers, which might be ad hoc or permanent. They were forbidden by particular statutes governing specific trades before the general prohibition enacted by the Combination Acts of 1799 and 1800. The Combination Acts were not systematically enforced before or after 1800, but the threat of capricious enforcement was always a real one. Magistrates and employers found it easier to break workers' combinations by applying other statutes or the common law, especially prohibitions against breaking contracts and leaving work undone, both of which could be invoked against strikes, as well as "master and servant" legislation. See A. Aspinall, ed., *The Early English Trade Unions: Documents from the Home Office Papers in the Public Record Office* (London: Batchworth Press, 1949), Introduction; Webb and Webb, *History of Trade Unionism*, pp. 250–251; and C. R. Dobson, *Masters and Journeymen: A Prehistory of Industrial Relations, 1717–1800* (London: Croom Helm, 1980), 135–141.

12. *MM*, 24 Feb., 3 March, 8 Sept. 1795; G. W. Daniels, "The Cotton Trade during the Revolutionary and Napoleonic Wars," *Transactions of the Manchester Statistical Society* (1915–1916), p. 59; C. H. Lee, *A Cotton Enterprise, 1795–1840: A History of M'Connell & Kennedy Fine Cotton Spinners* (Manchester: Manchester University Press, 1972), p. 118.

13. *MM*, 8 Sept. 1795.

14. Bowden, *Industrial Society*, p. 301.

15. *MM*, 6, 13 Feb. and 3 April 1798; *AR*, 26 March 1798; *LMCh*, 27 March 1798; *LObs*, 1 April 1798.

16. In the machine-breaking riots of 1779, magistrates in smaller towns had compromised with rioters out of both sympathy and prudence. Arthur G. Rose, "Early Cotton Riots in Lancashire, 1769–1779," *Transactions of the Lancashire and Cheshire Antiquarian Society*, 73–74 (1963–1964), 91. The magistrates of Manchester had not of course shown the same alacrity in dispersing the "Church and King" crowds of 1792 and 1795.

17. *MM*, 15 March 1796, 3 Nov. 1801, 13 Nov. 1804, 29 Jan. 1805; Lee, *Cotton Enterprise*, p. 118; Daniels, "Cotton Trade," pp. 63, 65; Kirby and Musson, *Voice*, pp. 15–16.

18. Ibid., p. 13; Redford, *Manchester Merchants*, pp. 66–67.

19. [E. C. Tufnell] *Character, Object, and Effects of Trades' Unions, with*

Some Remarks on the Law Concerning Them (London, 1834), pp. 13–17; "Select Committee on Artizans and Machinery," *P. P.* 1824 (51), V, 573–574 and 604–609; Turner, *Trade Union Growth,* p. 67; Hammond and Hammond, *Skilled Labourer,* p. 93; Kirby and Musson, *Voice,* pp. 14–15. I follow Hammond and Hammond's estimate of the numbers turned out, though Tufnell estimated 30,000 workers were turned out. One of a group of striking spinners was convicted at the Manchester Quarter Sessions for hooting and assaulting a spinner who continued to work (*MM,* 7 Aug. 1810).

20. Bythell, *Handloom Weavers,* p. 43.

21. Arthur Redford, *Labour Migration in England, 1800–1850,* 2nd ed. (Manchester: Manchester University Press, 1964), pp. 134–152.

22. H.O. 42 / 47, J. Singleton, 27 May 1799; and "Committee on the Cotton Weavers' Petitions," *P. P.* 1808 (177), II, 13, 27; Pinchbeck, *Women Workers,* p. 164; "Minutes of Evidence Taken...Relating to...Disputes between Masters and Workmen Engaged in the Cotton Manufacture," *P. P.* 1802–1803 (114), III, 13.

23. John Holt, *General View of the Agriculture of the County of Lancaster* (London, 1794), p. 73; Bythell, *Handloom Weavers,* pp. 45–48.

24. E. P. Thompson, *The Making of the English Working Class* (New York: Vintage Press, 1966), p. 278.

25. Gilbert J. French, *The Life and Times of Samuel Crompton,* 2nd ed. (Manchester, 1860), pp. 275–278, quoted in S. D. Chapman, *The Cotton Industry in the Industrial Revolution* (London: Macmillan Press, 1972), p. 60; Smelser quotes estimates ranging from 108,000 in 1788 to 200,000 in 1810 (*Social Change,* p. 137).

26. Bythell, *Handloom Weavers,* pp. 48–49.

27. For the concept of "proto-industrialization" see Franklin F. Mendels, "Recent Research in European Historical Demography," *American Historical Review,* 70 (1975), 1065–1073; Mendels, "Proto-Industrialization: The First Phase of the Industrialization Process," *Journal of Economic History,* 32 (March 1972), 241–261; and Charles Tilly and Richard Tilly, "Agenda for European Economic History," *Journal of Economic History,* 31 (1971), 184–198.

28. *P. P.* 1808 (177), II, 22, 25; "Report of the Commissioners on the Hand-Loom Weavers," *P. P.* 1841 (296), X, 44–47.

29. The numbers of hand-loom weavers began to decline only after the mid-1820s (Bythell, *Handloom Weavers,* p. 53; Chapman, *Cotton Industry,* p. 60). For urban variants of the monstrous supply curve of labor well into the nineteenth century, see Raphael Samuel, "Workshop of the World: Steam Power and Hand Technology in mid-Victorian Britain," *History Workshop,* 3 (1977), 47, and Henry Mayhew, "The Slopworkers and Needlewomen," in *The Unknown Mayhew,* ed. Eileen Yeo and E. P. Thompson (New York: Pantheon Books, 1971), pp. 116–180.

30. George W. Daniels, *The Early English Cotton Industry with Some Unpublished letters of Samuel Crompton* (Manchester: Manchester University Press, 1920), pp. 44–45. Bythell (*Handloom Weavers,* pp. 182–183) and

Turner (*Trade Union Growth*, p. 80) point to the "shop union" of eighteenth-century weavers as the germ of trade union development, but Wadsworth and Mann emphasize that the "shop" in question was the warehouse of the merchant-manufacturer, not a loom shop where weavers were assembled, and so the foundation for collective action was much less solid than Bythell and Turner suppose. See Wadsworth and Mann, *Cotton Trade*, pp. 345, 361–369, 373.

31. Paul Mantoux, *The Industrial Revolution in the Eighteenth Century*, English rev. ed. (New York: Harper and Row, 1961), p. 442.

32. But "the populace so far from aiding the endeavors used to put out the fire, rather impeded them." Scottish Record Office, the Dundas papers, GD 5 / 1 / 362 / 1, T. Bayley to Henry Dundas, 18 March 1792; *MM*, 20 March 1792; and "Report of the Committee on Cartwright's Petition," *P. P.* 1808, II, 138. Compare Bythell, *Handloom Weavers*, p. 198.

33. Bythell, *Handloom Weavers*, pp. 52–53; Wadsworth and Mann, *Cotton Trade*, p. 374.

34. Turner, *Trade Union Growth*, p. 60.

35. "Abstract of Answers and Returns. . . Relative to the Expence and Maintenance of the Poor in England," *P. P.* 1803–1804, XIII. F. M. Eden believed in 1801 that more than one-fourth of the societies in the manufacturing districts were not registered. See Bowden, *Industrial Society*, pp. 297–298.

36. Wadsworth and Mann, *Cotton Trade*, pp. 361–362 and 375; *MH*, 2, 23 June 1792; *MG*, 27 Feb. 1800; *MM*, 19 July 1796, 6 March–1 May 1798, 12 Oct., 14 Dec. 1802, and 17 May 1803.

37. F. M. Eden, *Observations on Friendly Societies* (London, 1801), p. 23.

38. Aspinall, *Early Trade Unions*, p. 215.

39. Ibid., p. 214. Not, as Bythell suggests, that weavers were prominent members of all such societies in Lancashire (*Handloom Weavers*, p. 182).

40. F. M. Eden, *The State of the Poor*, 3 vols. (London, 1797), II, especially pp. 350–359.

41. Manchester and Salford reported 212 friendly societies with nearly 13,000 members in 1802–1803, while towns like Ashton-under-Lyne, Bolton, and Oldham reported 4,000 or more members in populations one-fifth or less the size of Manchester's. The ratio of friendly-society members to total population in 1801 was 1:4, or greater, for Ashton, Bolton, Oldham, Newton, and Bury, but only 1:7 for Manchester and Salford. Figures are from returns in *P. P.* 1803–1804, cited in n. 35, and the census of 1801, *Abstract of Answers and Returns Made Pursuant to an Act Passed in the Forty-first Year of His Majesty, King George III*. . . (London, 1801), vol. 1.

42. See "Evidence on the Weavers' Petition," *H. C. J.*, 8 May 1800; and *P. P.* 1802–1803 (114), III, 3–13, 17, 46–47, 54–55.

43. Collier, *Family Economy*, p. 5; Bythell, *Handloom Weavers*, pp. 177–178.

44. Bythell, *Handloom Weavers*, p. 38.

45. Wadsworth and Mann, *Cotton Trade*, pp. 319–320; and Daniels, *Early Cotton Industry*, p. 143.

46. Bythell, *Handloom Weavers*, pp. 58 and 61.

47. *H. C. J.*, 8 May 1800; *P. P.* 1803 (114), and *P. P.* 1808 (177).

48. As were the woolen hand-loom weavers of both the older districts of East Anglia, the West Country, and the West Riding, on whom E. P. Thompson's discussion of the weavers' lost culture is based (*Making of the Working Class*, chap. 9).

49. H.O. 42 / 47, John Singleton, 27 May 1799; William Radcliffe, *Origin of the New System of Manufacture, Commonly Called 'Power Loom Weaving'* (Stockport, 1828), p. 12 and n. 41.

50. H.O. 42 / 47, The Association of the Weavers to the public, Bolton, 13 May 1799, broadside in J. Singleton, 27 May 1799; "Address to the Nobility, Gentry, and People of Great Britain," in *MG*, 21 Dec. 1799, and *LMCh*, 26 Dec. 1799; and compare testimony in *H. C. J.*, 8 May 1800, especially that of James Holcroft.

51. Bythell, *Handloom Weavers*, pp. 98 and 275. Series of reported wages during the wars by weavers seeking parliamentary relief show a much greater drop in the 1790s than do series reported in the 1820s and 1830s. Compare *P. P.* 1808 (177) for several series reported by witnesses who were weavers. John Foster's figures show wages dropping more than 60 percent between 1792 and 1799. See *Class Struggle and the Industrial Revolution: Early Industrial Capitalism in Three English Towns* (New York: St. Martin's Press, 1974), p. 45.

52. From weekly prices in the *London Gazette*.

53. "Testimony of John Settle, and James Holcroft," *H. C. J.*, 8 May 1800.

54. Samuel Bamford, *The Autobiography of Samuel Bamford*, 2 vols., 3rd ed. (London: Frank Cass and Co., 1967), I, *Early Days*, p. 118; and Sydney J. Chapman, *The Lancashire Cotton Industry: A Study in Economic Development* (Manchester: Manchester University Press, 1904), p. 181.

55. Compare Edwin Butterworth, *Historical Sketches of Oldham* (Oldham, 1856), p. 136, and Daniels, "Cotton Trade."

56. *P. P.* 1803 (114), III, 32; *H. C. J.*, 1 May 1800.

57. *MM*, 10 April 1798; Daniels, "Cotton Trade," pp. 63, 77.

58. Radcliffe, *Origin*, p. 69; *H. C. J.*, 8 May 1800.

59. *P. P.* 1808 (177).

60. *LMCh*, 26 Dec. 1799.

61. P.C. 1 44 / A155, Thomas Bancroft, 29 April 1799.

62. Compare Hammond and Hammond, *Skilled Labourer*, pp. 59–61.

63. Michael M. Edwards, *The Growth of the British Cotton Trade, 1780–1815* (Manchester: Manchester University Press, 1967), p. 13; Daniels, "Cotton Trade," p. 61; H.O. 42 / 47, J. Singleton, 27 May 1799.

64. Weavers' petition of 29 June 1799, in Radcliffe, *Origin*, p. 76.

65. Ibid., and H.O. 42 / 47, John Singleton, Wigan, 28 April and 27

May 1799; and Thomas Bancroft, Bolton, 11 April 1799; and P.C. 1 44 / A155, Thomas Bancroft, Bolton, 29 April 1799.

66. P.C. 1 44 / A155, Thomas Bancroft, 29 April 1799.

67. Ibid.

68. Aspinall, *Early Trade Unions*, p. 30; H.O. 42 / 47, Thomas Bancroft, 11 and 14 April 1799; and H.O. 42 / 40, papers connected with John Cheetham and the United Englishmen of Manchester.

69. H.O. 42 / 47, Thomas Bancroft, 11 April 1799; P.C. 1 44 / A155, Thomas Bancroft, 29 April 1799; and H.O. 42 / 47, J. Singleton, Wigan, 28 April and 27 May 1799.

70. H.O. 43 / 11 / 222–223, Duke of Portland to Thomas Bancroft, 8 Aug. 1799 (in Aspinall, *Early Trade Unions*, pp. 25 and 27).

71. J. L. Hammond and Barbara Hammond, *The Town Labourer, 1760–1832: The New Civilization* (London: Longman's, Green and Co., 1966), p. 123. Compare Dobson, *Masters and Journeymen*, pp. 135–141.

72. P.C. 1 45 / A164, T. B. Bayley, 7 Nov. and 16 Nov. 1799, with handbill and enclosures.

73. Aspinall, *Early Trade Unions*, pp. 28–30.

74. By contrast, there is no mention of the spinners' strikes in the Home Office papers of the period.

75. P.C. 1 45 / A164, T. B. Bayley, 16 Nov. 1799.

76. H.O. 42 / 48, Manchester magistrates' handbill, 28 Nov. 1799 (also in *MG*, 14 Dec. 1799); and handbill of 21 Nov. 1799, in G. B. Hindle, *Provision for the Relief of the Poor in Manchester, 1754–1826* (Manchester: Chetham Society, 1975), facing page 89. For the soup kitchens, see *MG*, 14, 21 Dec. 1799, and above, Chap. 4.

77. Mantoux, *Industrial Revolution*, p. 459 n. 1, citing Webb mss, Textiles, IV, 1.

78. *H. C. J.*, 5 March 1800. The Volunteers of Bolton were irritated because their colonel had gone to London to testify against the first weavers' petition. See H.O. 42 / 50, T. B. Bayley, 8 May 1800.

79. Hammond and Hammond, *Skilled Labourer*, p. 62, quoting a letter of 1798.

80. H.O. 42 / 50, T. B. Bayley, 8 May 1800.

81. *MG*, 14 Dec. 1799.

82. *MG*, 21 Dec. 1799.

83. P.C. 1 45 / A164, T. B. Bayley, 16 Nov. 1799. For a parallel later contrast between craft societies and more "politically" inclined unskilled workers' unions, see Hugh Armstrong Clegg, Alan Fox, and A. F. Thompson, *A History of British Trade Unions since 1889*, vol. 1, *1889–1910* (Oxford: Clarendon Press, 1964), pp. 6–8, 38, 92, 94.

84. 39 and 40 Geo. III, c. 90. Compare Hammond and Hammond, *Skilled Labourer*, pp. 63–65, for details of the Act, and *P. P.* 1802–1803 (114), III, 10–60, for testimony on its operation.

85. "Testimony of James Ramsbotham, Cotton Manufacturer, and James Holcroft, Weaver," *P. P.* 1802–1803 (114), III, 34, 44.

86. Chap. 5, and Alan Booth, "Food Riots in the North-West of England 1790–1801," *Past and Present*, 77 (Nov. 1977), 101 n. 106.

87. H.O. 42 / 50, T. B. Bayley, 23 June 1800. Compare Hammond and Hammond, *Skilled Labourer*, p. 65.

88. H.O. 42 / 53, T. B. Bayley, 30 Nov. 1800. On November 3, Bayley reported "throughout this Country there is a general Rumour of rising, *If* Parliament does *not* reduce the Price of Grain, etc." He added that "the Democrats" were trying "to excite a general Outcry against the War, and the Ministry;—as the Causes of the Dearness of Provision" (H.O. 50 / 48).

89. H.O. 42 / 53, Thomas Bancroft, 10 Nov. 1800; H.O. 42 / 52, T. B. Bayley, 21 Oct. 1800; H.O. 42 / 62 / 112, J. Singleton, 27 May 1801.

90. H.O. 42 / 61, T. B. Bayley, 4 April 1801.

91. I have accepted many of the critical observations of E. P. Thompson on the spies' reports of sedition, though not all of his inferences as to the scale and significance of the revolutionary underground. See Thompson, *Making of the Working Class*, pp. 488–494.

92. H.O. 42 / 53, Thomas Bancroft, 19 Nov. 1800; H.O. 42 / 61, Thomas Bancroft, 9 Feb. 1801, and J. Singleton, 24 March 1801.

93. H.O. 42 / 62, W. R. Hay, 18 May, 7 June 1801.

94. *MM*, 11, 18 Aug. and 1, 8, 15, 22 Sept. 1801; P.L. 28 / 4, Lancashire Summer Assizes, 1801, Gaol Delivery Book; H.O. 42 / 61, R. Fletcher, 6 April 1801. "Letter to the Friends of Freedom in the Town and Neighborhood of Bolton," 16 March 1813, in *The Blackfaces of 1812* (Bolton, 1839; reprint ed., New York: Arno Press, 1972), p. 16.

95. One of the seven men arrested was John Buckley. A John Buckley of Whitefield had been one of the weavers' delegates who signed the Association's declaration of 13 May 1799. See "Letter of William Moor," 15 March 1831, in *The Blackfaces of 1812*, pp. 18–19, and H.O. 42 / 61, Thomas Bancroft, 14 March 1801.

96. *MM*, 24 March 1801; H.O. 42 / 61, T. B. Bayley, 4 and 11 April 1801, enclosing examination of Charles Bent; and H.O. 48 / 10 / 89, opinion of the law officers in reply to Bayley's letter of 11 April 1801. Another proposal at the meeting was that those who did not like the conduct of the Union Societies should pool their money to buy provisions. For the Union Societies' cooperative see above, Chap. 4, and *MG*, 27 Sept. 1800.

97. *MG*, 18 April 1801. The *Gazette* said ten thousand attended from Oldham, Rochdale, Royton, Middleton, and Chadderton. Colonel Fletcher estimated the crowd was three thousand at any one time, but that four thousand people had come and gone during the meeting. Fletcher's spies had seen a paper posted on a tree that contained the following headings: equal representation, universal suffrage, reduction of the national debt, lowering of provisions (H.O. 42 / 61, R. Fletcher, 6 April 1801). The resolutions were circulated as a printed handbill in Manchester (H.O. 42 / 62 / 145, R. Fletcher, 6 June 1801). This handbill was printed by William Cowdroy, printer of the *Manchester Gazette*, a man with radical associations. H.O. 42 / 62 / 73, Thomas Bancroft 17 May 1801; Leon S. Marshall, *The Development of Public Opinion in Manchester, 1790–1820*

(Syracuse: Syracuse University Press, 1946), p. 126; H.O. 42 / 62, Ralph Fletcher, 8 June 1801; and *MG*, 30 May 1801.

98. H.O. 48 / 10 / 153–155; H.O. 42 / 62: folio 7, Major Gore, 3 May 1801, enclosing letter of W. R. Hay, 4 May 1801; and folio 15, Colonel Entwisle (Jr.), 4 May 1801 (reply: H.O. 43 / 13 / 52).

99. H.O. 42 / 62 / 145, R. Fletcher, 6 June 1801; folio 110, T. Bancroft 27 May 1801; folio 112, John Singleton, 27 May 1801.

100. H.O. 42 / 62, T. Bancroft, 27 May 1801; *LP*, 1–3 June 1801; *LMCh*, 3 June 1801. One or two other "public" meetings may also have been held, though they were not known to the magistrates for some time (H.O. 42 / 62, T. Bancroft, 17 May 1801).

101. See *MG*, 6 Dec. 1800.

102. H.O. 42 / 61, T. Bancroft, 2 May 1801.

103. H.O. 42 / 61, Ralph Fletcher, 6 April 1801. Compare Hammond and Hammond, *Skilled Labourer*, p. 67.

104. Compare F. K. Donnelly and J. L. Baxter, "Sheffield and the English Revolutionary Tradition, 1791–1820," *International Review of Social History*, 20 (1975), 418, referring to 1816–1817.

105. Historians eager to find evidence of a significant revolutionary movement in England must compare their findings with the Irish Rebellion of 1798, when a much more formidably organized revolutionary movement was relatively quickly crushed by a poorly led military force. Thomas Pakenham, *The Year of Liberty: The Story of the Great Irish Rebellion of 1798* (London: Hodder and Stoughton, 1969).

106. "It appears to me that the minds of the lower classes have been dreadfully warped from their Allegiance, but that there is a good deal of boast when they talk of Revolutions" (H.O. 42 / 62, T. Bancroft, 17 May 1801). "Reveries of rebellion" is adapted from E. P. Thompson, "The Crime of Anonymity," in Douglas Hay et al., *Albion's Fatal Tree: Crime and Society in Eighteenth-Century England* (New York: Pantheon Books, 1975), p. 308.

107. For instance, of the thirty men who signed the first address of 1799, three were from Manchester and Salford, while seven or eight were from Bolton (H.O. 42 / 47, address of 13 May 1799, Bolton, in J. Singleton, 27 May 1799). Of the fourteen who signed the public reply to the magistrates of Manchester, seven were from Bolton (*MG*, 21 Dec. 1799). The other addresses, also from Bolton, are in Radcliffe, *Origin*, pp. 76–77, and *MG*, 3 May 1800.

108. See, for example, C. H. Saxelby, ed., *Bolton Survey* ([Bolton]: Bolton Branches of the Geographical and Historical Association and the Bolton Field Naturalists Society, 1953), pp. 90–91.

109. Mantoux, *Industrial Revolution*, p. 442.

110. See n. 41.

111. H.O. 42 / 61, Mr. Yates to Robert Peel, 14 March 1801; and Thomas Ainsworth, 12 March 1801.

112. *MG*, 3 May 1800.

113. *P. P.*, 1808 (177), II, 3–16.

114. P.C. 1 44 / A155, T. Bancroft, 29 April 1799. That offer was

declined by the weavers' leaders, who said a general (regional) remedy was necessary.

115. See Chap. 4. Bolton seems to have been a transitional case; labor organization seems to have made food riot obsolete, for Bolton alone among the main cotton towns did not have a food riot in this period.

116. *H. C. J.*, 18 Feb. 1802.

117. Redford, *Manchester Merchants*, pp. 65–66; *MM*, 2 March 1802, 22 Feb. and 1 March 1803, and 14 and 28 Feb., 29 May, and 5 June 1804.

118. *H. C. J.*, 1803, passim; Hammond and Hammond, *Skilled Labourer*, pp. 68–69, 73–74; *P. P.* 1803 (114), III; and *H. C. J.*, 26 Feb. 1807.

119. Marshall, *Public Opinion*, p. 131; Daniels, "Cotton Trade," p. 77; *MG*, 21 Nov. 1807; and Edwards, *Growth of Cotton Trade*, p. 17.

120. *MG*, 26 Dec. 1807; *MM*, 29 Dec. 1807; and H.O. 42 / 91, R. A. Fletcher, 27 Dec. 1807.

121. H.O. 42 / 95, R. Fletcher, 24 Feb. 1808; "Handbill of the Bolton Weavers' Committee, 29 January 1808," in *Historical Gleanings of Bolton and District*, ed. B. T. Barton (Bolton, 1881), pp. 38–39.

122. Daniels, "Cotton Trade," p. 77.

123. Ibid., pp. 75–76, and *P. P.* 1808 (177), II, passim. The arguments of the proponents were not as confused as Bythell says (*Handloom Weavers*, p. 170). They simply advocated an alternative economic analysis to laissez faire. Unrestricted competition meant monstrous hours and deplorable wages for the weavers, for "men of little capital" entered the trade, cut wages, and ended in failure, dumping their goods on the market below cost. A minimum wage would thus have stabilized production by preventing that. Moreover, a rise of 30 percent in wages would mean a rise of only 10 percent in the market price of the goods, which some London merchants testified would not hurt sales. Such a minimum wage would have reduced the hours and raised the wages of weavers, who would individually have had to produce less to reach survival wages, and that would have eased the glut on the market. Indeed, a minimum wage might have induced a more rapid displacement of hand-loom weaving by more efficient machine production. However, whether magistrates or manufacturers would have been willing to expend the same energy to enforce such a minimum as they did to chase radicals and markets, respectively, is a larger question bound up with the whole structure of class.

124. The debate anticipated the laissez faire conclusion of the committee, published in 1809, that a minimum wage was unworkable and undesirable (quoted in Bythell, *Handloom Weavers*, p. 154). But see n. 123.

125. *A Complete Collection of State Trials...*, compiled by T. B. Howell and continued by Thomas Jones Howell, vol. 31, *1809–1813* (London, 1823), col. 17.

126. H.O. 42 / 95, J. Silvester, 31 May 1808, and R. A. Farington, 24 May 1808; *State Trials*, 31, col. 11–17; *MM*, 31 May 1808.

127. *State Trials*, 31, cols. 11–14, 17; H.O. 42 / 95, R. A. Farington, 25 and 26 May 1808; *AR*, 25 May 1808; *LObs*, 29 May 1808.

128. *State Trials*, 31, cols. 15–17; H.O. 42 / 95, R. A. Farington, 25 and 26 May 1808; *MM*, 31 May 1808; *AR*, 25 May 1808; *LObs*, 29 May 1808; and Archibald Prentice, *Historical Sketches and Personal Recollections of Manchester* (London and Manchester, 1851), p. 31.

129. R. A. Farington, J. Silvester, and Ralph Wright were the three active magistrates whose reports are cited in nn. 126–139. Farington did mention a rise in flour and oatmeal prices as "an unfortunate circumstance" (H.O. 42 / 95, 26 May 1808).

130. Henry Norris, ex-merchant, who lived outside Manchester, was the only magistrate in the area to express sympathy for the weavers' plight, but he did not appear to have been directly involved in the events in Manchester (H.O. 42 / 95, Henry Norris, 30 May 1808). Thomas Battye had remarked in 1796 that most of the Manchester magistrates were merchants, "newly manufactured justices." *The Red Basil Book, or Parish Register of Arrears* (Manchester, 1796), p. 54. The artisans who protested the Combination Act in 1799 complained that, "The magistrates before whom we are to be convicted, are many of them Merchants or Manufacturers, consequently interested" (P.C. 1 45 / A164, handbill in T. B. Bayley, 16 Nov. 1799). J. Silvester was chairman of the Manchester Commercial Society in 1801. See Redford, *Manchester Merchants*, p. 63.

131. See Chap. 3, n. 39.

132. H.O. 42 / 95, J. Silvester, 31 May 1808; R. A. Farington, 1 June 1808; and Ralph Wright, 31 May 1808. Compare radical handbills in Aspinall, *Early Trade Unions*, pp. 98–99, 100–101.

133. H.O. 42 / 95, R. A. Farington, 25, 28, 31 May and 1 June 1808.

134. H.O. 42 / 95, handbill of Manchester magistrates, 26 May 1808.

135. H.O. 42 / 95, R. A. Farington 28, 31 May and 9 June 1808.

136. Notice by the boroughreeve and constables of Manchester, 28 May 1808 in *MM*, 31 May 1808.

137. H.O. 42 / 95, R. A. Farington, 28 May and 1 June 1808; and J. Silvester, 2 June 1808.

138. Ibid., R. A. Farington, 9 and 11 June 1808; Lancashire Record Office, Salford Hundred Q.S., QSB / 1, July 1808 (Recognizances), and QJI, July 1808 (Indictments). I am very grateful to Prof. Frank Munger for these Quarter Session references. Apparently the eight or nine prisoners convicted from Manchester had had their trials continued from the July to the October Quarter Sessions. The *Manchester Mercury* (25 Oct. 1808) reported that four were sentenced to one month in jail, and four others, from one to two weeks.

139. Bythell, *Handloom Weavers*, p. 192; *MM*, 8 Dec. 1795, 20 and 27 Nov. 1798, 24 and 31 July 1804, 26 May and 15 Dec. 1807, and 31 May 1808.

140. *State Trials*, 31, col. 21.

141. See Chap. 3.

142. *State Trials*, 31, passim; and Bythell, *Handloom Weavers*, p. 192.

143. *MG*, 23 July 1808; *LMCh*, 18 Nov. 1809; Prentice, *Historical Sketches*, p. 33.

144. *AR*, 1 June 1808; H.O. 42 / 95, J. Silvester, 2 June 1808.

145. H.O. 42 / 95, R. A. Farington, 4 and 9 June 1808; and *AR*, 7 June 1808.

146. *AR*, 1 June 1808 and Chronicle for 1808, p. 64; H.O. 42 / 95, J. Silvester, 2 June 1808, and R. A. Farington, 9 June 1808.

147. Partly because the committee of manufacturers that made the offer of 20 percent could not "bind" the other manufacturers to give either the raise or employment (Aspinall, *Early Trade Unions*, p. 97).

148. *MM*, 28 June 1808; H.O. 42 / 95, R. A. Farington, 9 and 16 June 1808, and Lord Ribblesdale, 10 June [1808].

149. *AR*, 21 June 1808 and Chronicle for 1808, p. 64; *MM*, 28 June 1808; *LObs*, 26 June 1808; *LMCh*, 25 June 1808; and H.O. 42 / 95, R. A. Farington, 27 June 1808.

150. *MM*, 26 July 1808, and Lancashire Record Office, Q. S. Indictments, Summer 1796.

151. The Irish: H.O. 42 / 95, J. Silvester, 2 June 1808; Ralph Wright, 27 May 1808; and R. A. Farington, 28 May and 4 June 1808. In July 1807 an Orange Friendly Society was attacked by a body of Roman Catholic Irishmen, and several people were severely wounded (*MM*, 14, 21 July 1807). I am grateful to Prof. Frank Munger, whose sources are the recognizances in the Lancashire Q. S. files, for the information about the rioters' neighborhoods. Friendly societies: H.O. 42 / 95, R. A. Farington, 9 and 14 June 1808.

152. See Hammond and Hammond, *Skilled Labourer*, pp. 78–79, for a synopsis of the strike actions.

153. Stockport: H.O. 42 / 95, C. Prescot and J. Philips, 28 May 1808; and *LMCh*, 1 June 1808, which reports that individual "spies" dragged weavers out of their shops by the hair; Bolton: James Christopher Scholes, *History of Bolton, with Memorials of the Old Parish Church* (Bolton, 1892), p. 290. The Bolton weavers did scuffle with law officials, however. (Lancashire Record Office, QJI, Q. S. Indictments, July 1808).

154. P.L. 27 / 8, and T.S. 11 / 4173; *LMCh*, 9 Sept. 1808; H.O. 42 / 95, Mayor of Wigan, 15 June 1808.

155. *LMCh*, 9 Sept. 1808; Butterworth, *Oldham*, p. 158.

156. *LMCh*, 9 June and 9 Sept. 1808, and P.L. 27 / 8, depositions; Bythell, *Handloom Weavers*, note, p. 190; and *MM*, 7 June 1808.

157. H.O. 42 / 95, Thomas Drake and John Entwisle, 4 and 8 June 1808; P.L. 27 / 8, depositions; and *LMCh*, 3 June and 9 Sept. 1808. For 1795, see *MM*, 11 Aug. 1795.

158. H.O. 42 / 95, Henry Norris, 30 May 1808, and Mayor of Wigan, 15 June 1808.

159. H.O. 42 / 95, Sir Richard Clayton, 26, 31 May and 1 June 1808. He had apparently confronted rioters in a similar fashion during the machine-breaking riots of 1779 (Rose, "Early Cotton Riots," p. 80).

7. Reprise: 1812

1. E. P. Thompson, *The Making of the English Working Class* (New York: Vintage Books, 1966), p. 570. The anxiety felt by middle-class families in Manchester is conveyed in the letters of the Hatfield family. Francis Nicholson and Ernest Axon, "The Hatfield Family, of Manchester, and the Food Riots of 1757 and 1812," *Transactions of the Lancashire and Cheshire Antiquarian Society*, 28 (1910), 96–100. The general outline of Luddism in this chapter draws upon Thompson, *Making of the Working Class*, pp. 552–602; J. L. Hammond and Barbara Hammond, *The Skilled Labourer, 1760–1832* (New York: Harper and Row, 1919), chap. 10; and Frank Ongley Darvall, *Popular Disturbances and Public Order in Regency England* (London: Oxford University Press, 1934), chaps. 1, 3, 5.

2. This paragraph is based on John Dinwiddy, "Luddism and Politics in the Northern Counties," *Social History*, 10 (Jan. 1979), 33–63. The quotation from John Knight is on p. 63.

3. Ibid., p. 42.

4. Compare Thompson, *Making of the Working Class*, p. 492.

5. The requisition was signed by many of the Tory activists of the 1790s (*MM*, 31 March 1812).

6. John Edward Taylor, *Notes and Observations, . . . on the Papers Relative to the Internal State of the Country, Recently Presented to Parliament: [and] . . . Reply to Mr. Francis Phillips' Exposure of the Calumnies Circulated by the Enemies of Social Order against the Magistrates and the Yeomanry Cavalry of Manchester and Salford* (London, 1820), p. 147.

7. *LT*, 11 April 1812.

8. *MG*, 9 May 1812.

9. *LT*, 11 April 1812. The reference was to Whig sympathizers for Catholic emancipation. Archibald Prentice, *Historical Sketches and Personal Recollections of Manchester* (London and Manchester, 1851), p. 48.

10. Prentice, *Historical Sketches*, pp. 49–51; *LT*, 11 April 1812; and Dinwiddy, "Luddism and Politics," p. 43.

11. *MM*, 14 April 1812. A later commentator sniffed that the rioters were "contemptible in numbers, object and character." Francis Phillips, *An Exposure of the Calumnies Circulated by the Enemies of Social Order against the Magistrates and the Yeomanry Cavalry of Manchester and Salford* (London, 1819), pp. 4 and 57.

12. *MG*, 11 April 1812.

13. *MG*, 18 April 1812.

14. Taylor, *Notes and Observations*, pp. 144–147; and Prentice, *Historical Sketches*, p. 51.

15. See Dinwiddy, "Luddism and Politics," pp. 46–48, 63.

16. Ibid., pp. 62–63.

17. Joseph Aston, *A Picture of Manchester* (Manchester, 1816), pp. 204–205; *LT*, 11 April 1812.

18. Dinwiddy, "Luddism and Politics," p. 43.

19. Darvall, *Popular Disturbances,* pp. 96–98.

20. Ibid., p. 99.

21. Dinwiddy, "Luddism and Politics," p. 45.

22. Thompson, *Making of the Working Class,* p. 568 and the sources cited there.

23. *MG,* 18 April 1812.

24. *MG,* 25 April 1812; *MM,* 21 April 1812.

25. T.S. 11 / 3582, case against Hannah Smith.

26. *LT,* 23 April 1812; and *MM,* 26 May 1812.

27. *LT,* 27 April 1812.

28. *LT,* 25 April 1812.

29. Taylor, *Notes and Observations,* p. 5.

30. *MG,* 9 May 1812.

31. John Howarth, a smith who was executed for food rioting in 1812, had been arrested in 1801 for raving about the Jacobins. He had been freed on condition that he act as a spy. See "Letter of William Moor" (1831), in *The Blackfaces of 1812* (Bolton, 1839; reprinted., New York: Arno Press, 1972), pp. 18–19; *LT,* 26 May 1812.

32. *MG,* 25 April 1812; and *LT,* 28 April 1812. Likewise a county lieutenancy meeting prepared only coercive measures and no relief program (*MG,* 23 May 1812).

33. G. B. Hindle, *Provision for the Relief of the Poor in Manchester, 1754–1826* (Manchester: Chetham Society, 1975), p. 103.

34. *MM,* 2 and 9 Jan. 1812; *MG,* 30 May 1812; Hammond and Hammond, *Skilled Labourer,* p. 296.

8. The Agrarian Equipoise

1. H.O. 42 / 55, Lord Rolle, 24 Dec. 1800, enclosing anonymous letter to farmer Sansom.

2. H.O. 42 / 87, J. Symons, 12 Oct. 1806.

3. See E. P. Thompson, "The Crime of Anonymity," in Douglas Hay et. al., *Albion's Fatal Tree: Crime and Society in Eighteenth-Century England* (New York: Pantheon Books, 1975), pp. 296–297.

4. *CI,* 2 July and 10 Sept. 1796; H.O. 42 / 62 / 578, 580, Mr. Sitwell, 7 Dec. 1801.

5. W.O. 40 / 17, Thomas Sill, 27 Jan. 1796.

6. Population in 1801 from the *Abstract of the Answers and Returns Made Pursuant to an Act Passed in the Forty-first Year of His Majesty, King George III . . .* [the census of 1801]. See Chap. 2, at n. 58.

7. The great towns of more than 20,000 inhabitants may be grouped as follows (with the number of riots in my national sample): "New" towns, primarily products of rapid industrial growth: Manchester (11 riots), Birmingham (10), Sheffield (5), Leeds (3). "Old" towns, often parliamentary boroughs (abbreviated pb: with electorate): Nottingham, pb: 2,000 (13 riots), Bristol, pb: 5,000 (8), Norwich, pb: 3,000 (8),

Newcastle, pb: 2,500 (5), Bath, pb: 30 (5). "Mixed" towns, comprising both a parliamentary borough and a dynamic local economy: Liverpool, pb: 2,000 (16 riots), Plymouth, pb: 200 (9), Portsmouth, pb: 100 (5), Hull, pb: 1,200 (4). The sizes of the electorates are based on Sir Lewis Namier and John Brooke, *The House of Commons, 1754–1790*, 3 vols. (New York: Oxford University Press, 1964), I. Large parliamentary boroughs often provided both supporting networks for collective violence and occasions for its practice at elections. See Chaps. 2 and 9.

8. Thirty-six riots took place in "agrarian villages," of which seventeen were led by identifiable nonagricultural workers such as the tinners of Cornwall or the colliers of the Forest of Dean. The remaining *nineteen* riots are "agrarian riots." In addition, twenty riots took place in places of unknown population, of which thirteen were led by nonagrarian rioters, leaving *seven* "agrarian riots." Finally, fourteen riots in larger, or nonagricultural towns were led by rioters identified as "country people" or agricultural laborers.

9. In England and Wales, only 38.5 percent of the population in 1801 lived in the 283 towns and cities of 2,000 or more. That proportion rises only to 43.7 percent if 223 other "towns" of fewer than 2,000 are included. See W. A. Armstrong, "La population de l'Angleterre et du pays de galles (1789–1815)," *Annales de Demographie Historique*, 2 (1965), 148. For national occupational proportions, see B. R. Mitchell and Phyllis Deane, *Abstract of British Historical Statistics* (Cambridge: Cambridge University Press, 1962), p. 60. Nor does my national sample seem significantly biased against the inclusion of agrarian riots.

10. Assize 5 / 115 / I, Herefordshire, Summer 1795, Indictments and Depositions, and H.O. 42 / 35, Lord Bateman, 13 July 1795.

11. *CI*, 12 Dec. 1795; *NCh*, 12 Dec. 1795 and 2 April 1796.

12. *NCh*, 24 Oct. 1795, and *CI*, 24 Oct. 1795.

13. Dereham and Kinginhall, Norfolk: *LSt*, 20 July 1800, and H.O. 42 / 33, Robert John Buxton, 4 Dec. 1794; Sandford, Oxfordshire: H.O. 42 / 51, C. Willoughby, 17 Sept. 1800.

Seizures and sales outside the market took place at Standerwick (*LCh*, 23–25 July 1795), and Hetherset, Norfolk (*LMCh*, 24 July 1795). Only at St. Ives, a large market town, did country people take part in a forced sale. They had gathered for the hiring fair, not apparently for marketing (*LP*, 8–11 Aug. 1800).

14. William Marshall, *The Rural Economy of the West of England*, 2 vols. (London, 1796), I, 107–108. D.R.O., 1262M / L46, Lord Rolle, 28 Dec. 1800, and Robert Fraser, *A General View of the Agriculture of the County of Devon* (London, 1794), p. 17; and E. P. Thompson, "The Moral Economy of the English Crowd in the Eighteenth Century," *Past and Present*, 50 (Feb. 1971), 119.

15. 7s.–8s. / bushel is 56s.–64s. / quarter (8 bushels, approximately a quarter ton). From 1791 to 1794 wheat prices ranged from about 43s. to 52s. 3d. (Mitchell and Deane, *British Historical Statistics*, p. 488).

16. H.O. 42 / 35, C. Willoughby, 28 June and 5 July 1795. N. Kent,

Hints to Gentlemen of Landed Property (1775), pp. 263–265, quoted in W. Hasbach, *A History of the English Agricultural Labourer* (London: P. S. King & Son, 1908), p. 127.

17. Emergency relief scales were also sometimes tied to wheat prices and family sizes (*LCo*, 3 Nov. 1795).

18. Winkleigh: H.O. 42 / 62 / 84, information of Richard Davey, 2 April 1801; Branscombe: D.R.O., 1262M / L46, Lord Rolle, 28 Dec. 1800; Surrey: H.O. 42 / 52, Mr. Nitford, 8 Oct. 1800.

19. Thompson, "Moral Economy," p. 135.

20. *NCh*, 14 Nov. 1795; Thompson, "Moral Economy," p. 119; and see N. Kent, *Hints*, quoted in Hasbach, *History*, p. 127.

21. As in Diss, above, and Ely (*CI*, 26 Sept. 1795).

22. H.O. 42 / 34, J. Lloyd to H. Leycester, 11 April 1795.

23. On the "desperation of impotence," see Thompson, "Crime of Anonymity," pp. 272, 275, 306.

24. Norfolk: Diss, Hetherset, Dereham, and Kinginhall (see notes 13 and 14), Sharington Common near Holt (*NCh*, 26 Dec. 1795, and H.O. 42 / 37, Henry Jodrell to Lord Townshend, 22 Dec. 1795, enclosed in Lord Townshend, 23 Dec. 1795), and Old Buckenham (H.O. 42 / 71, Thomas Beevor, 17 June 1800). In addition, riotous assemblies were reported in Hingham, East and West Rudham, and Saxlingham (see notes 25 and 109, and *NCh*, 25 July 1795). For Yeaxley, see *LCh*, 16–18 July 1795.

25. For 1792: H.O. 42 / 22 / 520, Mr. Alderson [Nov. 1792]; Saxlingham: H.O. 42 / 36, copy of a printed paper delivered as a speech by James Besey, 18 Oct. 1795, enclosed in R. Fellowes, 19 Oct. 1795; Larlingford: H.O. 50 / 26, Robert John Buxton, 23 Nov. 1796.

26. Naomi Riches, *The Agricultural Revolution in Norfolk*, 2nd ed. (New York: Augustus M. Kelley, 1967), pp. 64–69, 77, 133, 136, 143–144, and 152. "There is an honesty, I had almost said an honour, about [Norfolk farm-labourers] when working by the day, which I have not been able to discover in the day-labourers of any other county." William Marshall, *Rural Economy of Norfolk* (1787), I, 41, quoted in Hasbach, *History*, note, p. 145. Compare J. D. Chambers and G. E. Mingay, *The Agricultural Revolution, 1750–1880* (New York: Schocken Books, 1966), pp. 59, 61, 78, and 99.

27. W.O. 40 / 17, passim. Of thirty-one civilian-military brawls in the national sample, nineteen were started by the soldiers, and three by civilians. Nine are of unclear origin.

28. Robert W. Malcolmson, *Popular Recreations in English Society, 1700–1850* (Cambridge: Cambridge University Press, 1973), pp. 54–55. The fair in late summer was often the place where young male and female workers sought to change employers. That moment of transition and freedom, and perhaps prosperity from pay bonuses, was also a time when the farm servants were dressed in their finest clothes to impress prospective employers and incidentally, prospective sexual partners. In these "sexual markets," soldiers were natural rivals to young male workers in trying to capture the fancy of available young women.

29. W.O. 40 / 17, petition from the inhabitants of Abingdon, 11 Feb. 1795, G. Watts to Mr. Dundas, 8 April 1795, and Mr. Loveden, 8 April 1795. Compare U.N., PwF 6161, Lord Llandaff, 1 Aug. 1795.

30. Farnham: W.O. 40 / 17, R. C. Smith, 22 and 24 May 1800, Colonel Cartwright, 27 May 1800, and *CI*, 7 June 1800; Claxton: *LMCh*, 16 March 1807.

31. Unless otherwise specified, the sources for this account of the riots against the Supplementary Militia Act are: Caistor, Horncastle, Alford, and Boston, Lincolnshire: H.O. 50 / 26, passim; and Lindsey County Library, Banks Collection (Hereafter LCL Banks), 3 / 1 / 1–27. Northamptonshire: (Clipstone) *LObs*, 13 Nov. 1796; (Kettering, Wellingborough, and Northampton) H.O. 50 / 26, George Robinson et al., 11 Nov. 1796, in Earl of Northampton, 11 and 13 Nov. 1796. Norfolk: (Norwich and Larlingford) H.O. 50/26, Marquis Townshend, 17 and 20 Nov. (enclosing William Adair, 17 Nov. 1796), and 24 Nov. (enclosing Robert John Buxton, 23 Nov. 1796), and 27 Nov. 1796. Cumberland: (Penrith) H.O. 50 / 26, W. Lowthorpe to Lord Lonsdale, 22 Dec. 1796, in Lord Lonsdale, 28 Dec. 1796; (Cockbridge) H.O. 42 / 40, H. Salterthwaite, 4 Jan. 1796, in Lord Lonsdale, 8 Jan. 1797; (Carlisle) *LMCh*, 12 Jan. 1797. Barmouth, Merionethshire: H.O. 50 / 26, Edward Corbet, 23 Nov. 1796. Wing, Buckinghamshire: H.O. 50 / 26, Marquis of Buckingham, 17, 18, and 22 Dec. 1796. Oswestry, Shropshire: H.O. 50 / 26, John Mytton et al., 3 Dec. 1796. Ulverston, Lancashire: H.O. 42 / 40, Thomas Sutherland, 11 Feb. 1797, and P.L. 27 / 7, Lancashire Assize Depositions, Feb. 1797. Stowe on the Wold, Gloucestershire: H.O. 42 / 39, Lord Berkeley, 12 Dec. 1796. Bakewell, Derbyshire: H.O. 42 / 40, Magistrates of High Peak Hundred, 26 Jan. 1797. Denbigh, Denbighshire: H.O. 42 /34, John Lloyd, 1 and 6 April 1795. See also J. R. Western, *The English Militia in the Eighteenth Century: The Story of a Political Issue, 1660–1802* (London: Routledge & Kegan Paul, 1965), pp. 290–302; and David Neave, "Anti-Militia Riots in Lincolnshire, 1757 and 1796," *Lincolnshire History and Archaeology,* 11 (1976), 21–27. The county lieutenancy was the group of officials responsible for administering the county's militia. They were headed by the lord lieutenant.

32. Horncastle: H.O. 50 / 26, Thomas Coltman, 5 Nov. 1796; Boston: H.O. 50 / 26, mayor and magistrates of Boston, 10 Nov. 1796; Spilsby: LCL Banks, 3 / 1 / 6, the Reverend Edward Walls, 7 Nov. 1796, which also mentions a village brickmaker; Ulverston: H.O. 42 / 40, Thomas Sutherland, 11 Feb. 1797, and P.L. 28 / 3, Lancashire Gaol Delivery Book, Lent, 1797; other sources as in note 31. Only at Oswestry is there specific evidence of nonagrarian rioters: "colliers, lime-men, and others." In Wales, Methodists were blamed in Barmouth and Dissenters in Denbigh.

33. The preceding statements are based on Western, *English Militia,* pp. 258, 264, 281, and 283. In Dorset, for instance, one man in eight available was required to serve, but in Lancashire only one in forty-three and in Cumberland and the West Riding, one in twenty-eight (p. 246). For Halifax, see H.O. 50 / 26, Henry Wickham et al., 17 Dec. 1796.

34. For Lincolnshire wheat prices, calculated from the weekly reports

in the *London Gazette*, see Talbott Miller, "The Riots against the Militia Laws in Lincolnshire, 1796" (B.A. thesis, Harvard University, 1974), p. 30a; see also LCL Banks, 3 / 2 / 20, Thomas Coltman, 29 March 1797. Although Lincolnshire was a large county, it witnessed only three food riots in 1795, two of which were minor. For wages see A. L. Bowley, "The Statistics of Wages in the United Kingdom during the Last Hundred Years. (Part 1): Agricultural Wages," *Journal of the Royal Statistical Society*, 61 (1898), 706.

35. No general meetings of the lieutenancy to carry out that procedure were announced in the *Lincoln, Rutland, and Stamford Mercury* from 1789 to 1794 (Miller, "Riots," p. 27). Compare LCL Banks, 3 / 1 / 27, Banks's "Diary of the Riots in Lindsey, 1796," fol. 1.

36. LCL Banks, 3 / 1 / 27, Banks's "Diary," fols. 3, 21, and 25.

37. H.O. 50 / 26, Duke of Ancaster, 3 Nov. 1796; LCL Banks, 3 / 1 / 27, "Diary," fols. 26–27. The clerk was so incompetent that one of the first acts of the magistrates to restore order was to replace him.

38. H.O. 50 / 26, Sir Joseph Banks [7 Nov. 1796]; LCL Banks, 3 / 1 / 27, "Diary," fols. 1, 6–10; and *LiRSM*, 14, 21, 28 Oct., and 4, 11 Nov. 1796.

39. Western, *English Militia*, pp. 140–154, 291–94; Neave, "Anti-Militia Riots," pp. 21–22.

40. For 1795, see LCL Banks, 3 / 1 / 27, "Diary," fol. 1; for 1796, see ibid., fol. 2.

41. The crowds were armed in Penrith, Cockbridge, Kettering, Ulverston (see n. 31), and in Lincolnshire (see n. 60). In the national sample, rioters were reported to be armed in only 212 of 617 riots. For Denbigh, see H.O. 42 / 34, John Lloyd, 1 and 6 April 1795.

42. See n. 31.

43. In Cockbridge and Penrith, the magistrates were able to identify the parishes from which the rioters came, and in Ulverston, to get sufficient information to identify eight rioters and convict four (see n. 31).

44. H.O. 50 / 26, Thomas Coltman, 7 Nov. 1796. Caistor and Horncastle: H.O. 50 / 26, Thomas Coltman, 5 Nov. 1796, and LCL Banks, 3 / 1 / 2, Thomas Coltman, 3 Nov. 1796. Spilsby: LCL Banks, 3 / 1 / 6, Rev. Edward Walls, 7 Nov. 1796; and Neave, "Anti-Militia Riots," p. 23. The crowd seemed to be trying to avoid explicit extortion, a felony. Alford: LCL Banks, 3 / 1 / 27, and H.O. 50 / 26, F. Wilson, 9 Nov. 1796, in Thomas Coltman, 9 Nov. 1796. For "sturdy begging," see John Bohstedt, "Riots in England, 1790–1810, with Special Reference to Devonshire" (Ph.D. diss., Harvard University, 1972), pp. 3–4.

45. LCL Banks, 3 / 1 / 5, Joseph Banks, 7 Nov. 1796.

46. H.O. 50 / 26, Thomas Coltman, 7 Nov. 1796; Ibid., Lord Clive, 3 Dec. 1796; and see also Ibid., Duke of Portland to Duke of Ancaster, 9 Nov. 1796.

47. Ibid., Joseph Banks, 11 Nov. 1796.

48. LCL Banks, 3 / 1 / 27, "Diary," fol. 11.

49. Neave, "Anti-Militia Riots," p. 24.

50. LCL Banks, 3 / 1 / 37, Thomas Coltman, 30 March 1797.

51. Ibid., and H.O. 50 / 26, J. Banks, 13 Nov. 1796.

52. LCL Banks, 3 / 1 / 24A and 32, Thomas Coltman to Joseph Banks, 21 and 28 Nov. 1796, and LCL Banks 3 / 1 / 19, Joseph Banks, 13 Nov. [1796].

53. LCL Banks, 3 / 1 / 10a, Mrs. F. Dashwood (aged 80), to Thomas Coltman, 9 Nov. 1796, in T. Coltman to Joseph Banks, 10 Nov. 1796. Compare Western, *English Militia*, pp. 290, 301.

54. LCL Banks, 3 / 1 / 27, "Diary," fol. 7, and 3 / 1 / 16, "Extract from the Clerk's Letter Respecting the Caistor Transaction." For allowances, see Western, *English Militia*, pp. 286–290. For parallel resistance to naval impressment because of low naval wages, see Norman McCord and David E. Brewster, "Some Labour Troubles of the 1790s in North East England," *International Review of Social History*, 13 (1968), 377.

55. LCL Banks, 3 / 1 / 6, the Reverend Edward Walls, 7 Nov. 1796.

56. Boston: Ibid., 3 / 1 / 14, John Linton, 11 Nov. 1796. Horncastle: Ibid., 3 / 1 / 5 [Joseph Banks], 7 Nov. 1796.

57. Except perhaps in Norfolk (B.L., Add. MSS. 35667, J. Dixon, 17 Nov. 1796, and H.O. 50 / 26, note on W. Beckwith, 19 Nov. 1796, in Lord Newark, 22 Nov. 1796).

58. H.O. 42 / 40, Thomas Sutherland, 11 Feb. 1797.

59. H.O. 50 / 26, Francis Wilson, vicar of Alford, 9 Nov. 1796, in Thomas Coltman, 9 Nov. 1796.

60. LCL Banks, 3 / 1 / 27, "Diary," fol. 6.

61. Ibid., 3 / 1 / 5, Joseph Banks, 7 Nov. 1796.

62. Ibid., 3 / 1 / 2, Thomas Coltman, 3 Nov. 1796. See also 3 / 1 / 10a, Mrs. Dashwood, 9 Nov. 1796, in Thomas Coltman, 10 Nov. 1796. H.O. 50 / 26, Joseph Banks to John King, 14 Nov. 1796.

63. So Banks believed, in regard to popular fears that the supplementary militia would be channeled into the old militia. For in the case of the army, the government had "before now been guilty of Breeches of Faith" (LCL Banks, 3 / 2 / 4, Joseph Banks to Thomas Coltman, 29 Dec. 1796). From 1798 on, the supplementary militia was indeed used as a kind of recruiting antechamber for the army (Western, *English Militia*, pp. 265–269). For 1756, see Western, *English Militia*, pp. 122, 150, and 298. For an explanation of the Act of 1796, see *LiRSM*, 21 Oct. 1796.

64. Western, *English Militia*, pp. 303–338, especially p. 338.

65. See H.O. 50 / 26, Joseph Banks, 7 Nov. 1796.

66. LCL Banks, 3 / 1 / 17, Richard Ellison to Joseph Banks [12 Nov. 1796].

67. H.O. 50 / 26, Duke of Portland to Duke of Ancaster, 9 Nov. 1796.

68. LCL Banks, 3 / 2 / 7, Richard Ellison et al. to Home Office, 8 Feb. 1797.

69. Ibid., 3 / 1 / 12, Joseph Banks to John King, 11 Nov.1796.

70. Miller, "Riots," p. 91, and *LiRSM*, 18, 25 Nov., 2, 9 Dec. 1796. LCL Banks, 3 / 1 / 39, handbill, "Defence against Foreign Invasion" (italics and capitals as in original).

71. Ibid., 3 / 2 / 7, Richard Ellison et al., 8 Feb. 1797.

72. H.O. 50 / 26, Joseph Banks to John King, 15 Nov. 1796; and LCL Banks, 3 / 1 / 21, Joseph Banks to Richard Ellison, 16 Nov. 1796, and 3 / 1 / 23, copy of Joseph Banks and Lord Gwyddir to Duke of Portland, 21 Nov. [1796], and draft notes.

73. LCL Banks, 3 / 2 / 4 and 8, Joseph Banks, 29 Dec. 1796 and 11 Feb. [1797]; H.O. 50 / 26, Duke of Ancaster, 31 Dec. 1796, and H.O. 50 / 27, Richard Ellison et al., 8 Feb. 1797. Banks told the Home Office that "Ellison abuses you all like pickpockets" (LCL Banks, 3 / 2 / 10, Joseph Banks to John King, 16 Feb. 1797).

74. LCL Banks, 3 / 2 / 5 and 6, Samuel Buck to Richard Ellison, 28 Jan. and 7 Feb. 1797.

75. Yorkshire: Ibid., 3 / 2 / 11, Samuel Buck, 21 Feb. 1797; Lincoln-shire: Ibid., 3 / 2 / 12–19, letters of Feb.–March 1797, especially J. King to J. Banks, 20 March 1797; 3 / 2 / 24, draft notes of J. Banks, 31 March 1797; and 3 / 2 / 72, J. Banks, 3 April 1797. Bawtry, Nottinghamshire: H.O. 50 / 27, Peter Hammond, 4 March 1797. Buckinghamshire: H.O. 50 / 26, Marquis of Buckingham, 25 Nov. 1796; and LCL Banks, 3 / 2 / 24, Banks's notes, 31 March 1797.

76. For contemporary references that contrasted docile "peasants" with aggressive urban wage earners, see Witt Bowden, *Industrial Society in England towards the End of the Eighteenth Century*, 2nd. ed. (London: Frank Cass & Co., 1965), note, p. 298. C. R. Dobson counted 6 labor disputes involving farm workers among 383 disputes for all trades between 1717 and 1800. See his *Masters and Journeymen: A Prehistory of Industrial Relations, 1717–1800* (London: Croom Helm, 1980), pp. 24–25. The two episodes in which farm workers' movements involved force occurred in Crediton, Devon, in 1795, and Steeple, Essex, in 1800.

77. Elizabeth W. Gilboy, *Wages in Eighteenth Century England* (Cambridge, Mass.: Harvard University Press, 1934), pp. 50–70, 80–81, 88–89, 180, and 214.

78. H.O. 42 / 22 / 151, Mr. Bush to Evan Nepean, 11 Oct. 1792; Ellis Charles Raymond Hadfield, *The Canals of Southern England* (London: Phoenix House, 1955), pp. 77–78, quoted in E. L. Jones, "The Agricultural Labour Market in England, 1793–1872," *Economic History Review*, 2nd ser., 17 (Dec. 1964), 323; and A. H. John, "Farming in Wartime: 1793–1815," in *Land, Labour, and Population in the Industrial Revolution*, ed. E. L. Jones and G. E. Mingay (New York: Barnes and Noble, 1967), p. 33.

79. Jones and Mingay, eds., *Land, Labour, and Population*, pp. 31–32; Jones, "Labour Market," p. 323, and J. D. Chambers, "Enclosure and Labour Supply in the Industrial Revolution," *Economic History Review*, 2nd ser., 5 (1953), reprinted in E. L. Jones, ed., *Agriculture and Economic Growth in England, 1650–1815* (London: Methuen & Co., 1967), pp. 112–113.

80. Compare A. F. J. Brown, *Essex at Work, 1700–1815* (Chelmsford: Essex County Council, 1969), pp. 132–133, and T. L. Richardson, "The Agricultural Labourer's Standard of Living in Kent, 1790–1840," in *The Making of the Modern British Diet*, ed. Derek J. Oddy and Derek S. Miller (London: Croom Helm, 1976), pp. 103–116.

81. Hasbach, *History*, pp. 121–129.

82. Glenn Hueckel, "English Farming Profits during the Napoleonic Wars, 1793–1815," *Explorations in Economic History*, 13 (1976), 339.

83. H.O. 42 / 24 / 178, resolutions of the Alnwick labourers, enclosed in fol. 173, J. Blackett, 21 Feb. 1793. Compare fol. 176, Colonel John Reed, 8 Feb. 1793.

84. E. J. Hobsbawm and George Rudé, *Captain Swing* (New York: Pantheon Books, 1968), pp. 40–47.

85. E. J. Hobsbawm, "Customs, Wages, and Work-load," in *Labouring Men: Studies in the History of Labour*, ed. E. J. Hobsbawm (London: Weidenfeld and Nicolson, 1964), pp. 347–348; for the Heacham laborers, see *NCh*, 14, 21, and 28 Nov. 1795. Their declaration, reprinted from the *Annals of Agriculture*, 25 (1795), 503, is in J. L. Hammond and Barbara Hammond, *The Village Labourer* (London: Longman's, Green and Co., 1966), pp. 133–135. Alnwick: H.O. 42 / 24 / 176, John Reed, 8 Feb. 1793.

86. Alnwick: source cited in n. 83. For the strikes of sailors and other workers on the Tyne and the Wear in 1792, see McCord and Brewster, "Some Labour Troubles," pp. 367–376. Thatcham: Hobsbawm and Rudé, *Captain Swing*, p. 82. Monkton: Dobson, *Masters and Journeymen*, p. 117.

87. Bowden, *Industrial Society*, p. 299. Compare Howard Newby, *The Deferential Worker: A Study of Farm Workers in East Anglia* (Madison: University of Wisconsin Press, 1979),pp. 46–47; and Hobsbawm and Rudé, *Captain Swing*, pp. 61–63.

88. And except for tiny Rutland. See table 4.

89. Dobson, *Masters and Journeymen*, pp. 116–117.

90. Clifford papers, Volunteers 1794, A / cs 1794, Lord Fortescue, 18 April 1795; and D.R.O., 1262M / L5, Lord Clifford, [between 6 and 13 April 1795].

91. H.O. 42 / 34, the Reverend George Bent, 4 April 1795. The handbill is reprinted in E. P. Thompson, "The Crime of Anonymity," pp. 311–312.

92. D.R.O., 1262M / L5, Lord Clifford, 27 April 1795. See D.R.O., 1262M / L5, Lord Clifford to Lord Fortescue, [14 April 1795]; *LCo*, 16 and 22 April 1795; *EFP*, 23 April 1795; and Devon Q. S. Rolls, Midsummer 1795. The woman, Mary Plympsell, had previously been arrested for riot in 1793 (Assize 24 / 43, Devon, Summer 1793). Bowley reported a figure of 7s. a week, or 1s. 2d. a day for Devon in 1795 (Bowley, "Agricultural Wages," p. 704). By 1804, however, one observer reported to the Board of Agriculture that wages in Devon were 6s. per week, plus beer. Quoted in Hueckel, "English Farming Profits," p. 339.

93. *CI*, 13 Aug. 1796.

94. *LP*, 1–4 Aug. 1800.

95. Quoted in Dobson, *Masters and Journeymen*, p. 145. Compare Kenyon's famous charge to the grand jury at the Shropshire Assizes, reprinted in *Ann. Ag.*, 25 (1795), 110–111.

96. *LMCh*, 11 Oct. 1800; *LP*, 13–16 and 20–23 June, and 1–4 Aug. 1800; Assize 35 / 240, Essex, Summer Assizes, 1800, Felony Indictments and Gaol Calendar; and Brown, *Essex*, pp. 131–132. Brown also mentions

the arrest in 1793 of Isaac Seer, the "first known farmworkers' leader" in Essex, for visiting farms with other men in an attempt to spread their strike.

97. Assize 35 / 234, Kent, Lent, 1794. In September 1800, several Norfolk laborers were imprisoned for a year by the Assizes for having assembled and conspired to force their employers to raise wages. See E. P. Thompson, "Foreword," in A. J. Peacock, *Bread or Blood: A study of the Agrarian Riots in East Anglia in 1816* (London: Victor Gollancz, 1965), p. 10.

98. H.O. 42 / 25 / 194b, 194d, and 194h, Phil Monoux, Sandy near Biggleswade, 21 and 28 March 1793, and enclosure, letter from Baldock, 26 March 1793. One laborer was subsequently sentenced to a year's imprisonment for threatening to pull down a house (Dobson, *Masters and Journeymen*, p. 117).

99. H.O. 42 / 34, Marquis of Salisbury to Duke of Portland, 24 March and 12 April 1795, and H.O. 42 / 35, William Baker, 10 July 1795, and enclosure.

100. U.N., PwF 233, William Baker, 11 July 1795, and H.O. 42 / 35, Sir A. Hume, 11 July 1795.

101. H.O. 42 / 37, undated letter from Sir A. Hume, "Saturday night," [12 July 1795], minuted "found in 1795."

102. H.O. 42 / 35, William Baker, 13 July 1795; and U.N., PwF 235, William Baker, 14 July 1795. E. P. Thompson has recounted a similar episode of "bargaining" by anonymous letter in Uley, Gloucestershire, in 1795. See "Crime of Anonymity," pp. 292–294.

103. *LCh*, 8–10 March 1796, and *GM*, May 1795 and March 1796, and E. P. Thompson, "Crime of Anonymity," pp. 296–297. Baker wrote that "the damage...is not so considerable as the motive and circumstances...are atrocious" (H.O. 42 / 51, William Baker, 12 Sept. 1800). It was in Cheshunt, a few miles south of Hoddesdon, that a violent anonymous protest against enclosure appeared in 1799 (E. P. Thompson, "Crime of Anonymity," pp. 313–314).

104. H.O. 42 / 49, enclosure in Mr. Wilshere to Marquess of Salisbury, 13 Feb. 1800. H.O. 42 / 50, William Baker, 17 Aug. 1800.

105. *Ann. Ag.*, 26 (1796), 178, quoted in Hammond and Hammond, *Village Labourer*, p. 140.

106. H.O. 42 / 22 / 224, Lord Townshend, 11 Nov. 1792.

107. H.O. 42 / 53, Marquis of Buckingham, 2 Nov. 1800; my italics. That was precisely one of the abuses condemned by the Poor Law commissioners in 1834.

108. Lewes: H.O. 42 / 61, Henry S. Sherdwell, 15 Feb. 1801. Ardingly: *LP*, 23 April 1800. It is not clear whether "augmented" meant raised or supplemented by relief. Eatonbridge: Six laborers were fined 1s. and sent to jail until the fine was paid (Assize 35 / 235, Kent, Lent 1795). Fakenham: H.O. 42 / 49, Lord Townshend, 5 March 1800.

109. East and West Rudham: *LMCh*, 23 March 1795. Heacham: see n. 85. Hadleigh Common and the magistrates: *LCo*, 18 Oct. 1795, and Hammond and Hammond, *Village Labourer*, p. 137; *LMCh*, 13 May 1795

(Hampshire and Berkshire). In the latter case, at Speenhamland, the justices suggested that farmers increase wages in proportion to high prices—an apparent reversal of the famous Speenhamland policy. On Whitbread's Bills, see Hammond and Hammond, *Village Labourer*, pp. 138–139.

110. W.O. 40 / 17, J. Lee, 5 Feb. 1800. The poem is reprinted in full in Thompson, "Crime of Anonymity," pp. 338–339.

111. Chidingfold: H.O. 42 / 61, Lord Midleton, 19 and 20 Feb. 1801. Sharborough Castle and Lingfield: H.O. 42 / 61, Thomas Turton, 7 Feb. 1801. Gosden: *LP*, 9–11 Feb. 1801.

112. Mark Blaug, "The Myth of the Old Poor Law and the Making of the New," *Journal of Economic History*, 23 (June 1963), pp. 167–172.

113. Compare Brown, *Essex*, pp. 130–131.

114. Chambers and Mingay, *Agricultural Revolution*, p. 83.

115. Enclosure riots occurred at the following places: Sheffield (1791): H.O. 42 / 19, letters of John Wilkinson and V. M. Eyres, 23, 25, 29, 30, 31 July, and 1, 4, 6, 25 Aug. 1791; *LT*, 30 July, and 1, 4, 23 Aug. 1791, and 28 March 1792; *LiRSM*, 19 and 26 Aug. 1791; *YC*, 2, 9, 16, 23 Aug. and 6 Sept. 1791, and 27 Mar. and 8 May 1792. Pitchford near Shrewsbury (1791): *LMCh*, 19 Sept. 1791. Streatham (1794): *LCh*, 6–8 May 1794. Maulden, Bedfordshire (1796): W.O. 40 / 17, James Webster, 2, 8, and 12 Aug. 1796. Bintry, Norfolk (1797): *LObs*, 29 Jan. 1797, and Assize 35 / 237, Norfolk, Lent 1797. Wilbarston, Northamptonshire (1799): *AR*, 25 July 1799, and *LMCh*, 31 July 1799. Beckley (Otmoor), Oxfordshire (1800): Oxfordshire County Record Office, Q.S. Rolls, Michaelmas 1800 (docs. 5–10). Burgh, Norfolk (1802): *RM*, 11 Oct. 1802. Headington, Oxfordshire (1806): Assize 5 / 126 and 4 / 22, Oxford, Summer 1806, and Lent and Summer 1807; and Llandeniolen, Caernarvonshire (1809): H.O. 42 / 98, Lord Bulkeley, 9 Oct. 1809, and enclosures. Of these, Hammond and Hammond mentioned Maulden, Wilbarston, and Otmoor (*Village Labourer*, pp. 73, 83–96). They thus exaggerated the riotous resistance by using a good proportion of the cases without saying so. Disturbances over enclosures that did not become riots occurred in Mere and Gillingham, on the Wiltshire-Dorset border (Assize 25 / 7 / 20 and 23 / 9, Wiltshire and Dorset, Summer 1810), and Somerleyton near Lowestoft (W.O. 40 / 17, Robert Reeve, depositions, 17 Sept. 1802; Robert Sparrow, 17 and 21 Sept. 1802; and R. Turner, 19 Sept. 1802).

116. An important summary of recent research is William Lazonick, "Karl Marx and Enclosures in England," *Review of Radical Political Economics*, 6 (1974), 1–59. This paragraph also draws upon G. E. Mingay, *Enclosure and the Small Farmer in the Age of the Industrial Revolution* (London: Macmillan, 1968), especially pp. 24–32; and Chambers and Mingay, *Agricultural Revolution*, pp. 82, 86–87; Riches, *Norfolk*, p. 59. W. E. Tate, "Opposition to Parliamentary Enclosures in Eighteenth Century England," *Agricultural History*, 19 (1948), 137, quoted in Chambers and Mingay, *Agricultural Revolution*, p. 87, emphasized the rarity of protest from propertied villagers.

117. Chambers, "Labour Supply," p. 117.

118. For allotments, see D. C. Barnett, "Allotments and the Problem of Rural Poverty, 1780–1840," in *Land, Labour, and Population*, ed. Jones and Mingay, pp. 162–186. The quotation is from Hobsbawm and Rudé, *Captain Swing*, p. 35.

119. Streatham Common: *GM*, 4 May 1794, p. 571. Maulden: The quotations are from W.O. 40 / 17, James Webster, 2, 8, and 12 Aug. 1796, and Hammond and Hammond, *Village Labourer*, p. 96 n. 4. Thomas Carter was charged (and acquitted) with cutting down three yards of the duke's enclosure fence in January 1801 (Assize 35 / 241, Bedfordshire, Summer 1801). Compare Hammond and Hammond, *Village Labourer*, p. 96.

120. Sources in n. 115. It is quite likely the two incidents were connected. Mere and Gillingham are only three miles apart, and the dates of the incidents are 10 and 12 March 1810.

121. For which see Richard Burn, *Justice of the Peace*, 18th ed. (London, 1797), IV, s.v. "forcible entry." Such incidents seem to have taken place at Eccleshall, Staffordshire (Staffordshire Record Office, Q.S. Rolls, Michaelmas 1796) and at Evesham, Worcestershire (Assize 5 / 120 / III–IV, Recognizances and Indictments, Worcestershire, Lent and Summer 1800, Assize 4 / 22, p. 141, Lent 1800 and Assize 9 / 1, Estreats, Summer 1800).

122. W. E. Tate, "Opposition," pp. 141–142, quoted in Chambers and Mingay, *Agricultural Revolution*, p. 87 and see p. 84; Eric J. Evans, "Some Reasons for the Growth of English Rural Anti-Clericalism c.1750–c.1830," *Past and Present*, 66 (Feb. 1975), 94–100.

123. Maulden: W.O. 40 / 17, James Webster, 2 Aug. 1796. Wilbarston: *GM*, Sept. 1799, p. 801, *LMCh*, 31 July 1799.

124. Though every student must hear the old chestnut, "Queen Anne: 'What would it cost to enclose St. James Park?' Minister: 'Only a crown, Mum!'"

125. Sources as in n. 115.

126. Bintry: Assize 35 / 237, Norfolk, Lent 1797; the rioters were acquitted. Headington: Assize 5 / 126, Oxfordshire, Summer 1806. Wilbarston: *AR*, 25 July 1799 and *LObs*, 4 Aug. 1799. Sheffield: see n. 115.

127. A. S. Kussmaul, "The Ambiguous Mobility of Farm Servants," *Economic History Review*, 2nd ser., 34 (1981), 222–229.

128. Hammond and Hammond, *Village Labourer*, pp. 83–96. Compare Oxford County Record Office, Q.S. Rolls, Michaelmas 1800 (docs. 5–10), and Hobsbawm and Rudé, *Captain Swing*, pp. 141–142.

129. *YC*, 2 Aug. 1791 and 8 May 1792; *LT*, 1 and 4 Aug. 1791 and 28 March 1792; H.O. 42 / 19, John Wilkinson, 23 July 1791, and V. M. Eyres, 30 and 31 July and 25 Aug. 1791; J. L. Hammond and Barbara Hammond, *The Town Labourer, 1760–1832: The New Civilization* (London: Longman's, Green and Co., 1966), pp. 55.

130. F. K. Donnelly and J. L. Baxter, "Sheffield and the English Revolutionary Tradition, 1791–1820," *International Review of Social History*, 20 (1975), 398–423, especially 400.

131. J. Wheat, 18 Oct. 1792, quoted in Allan W. L. Seaman, "Reform

Politics at Sheffield, 1791–1797," *Transactions of the Hunter Archaeological Society*, 7 (1956), 216.

132. H.O. 42 / 19, John Wilkinson, 23 July 1791.

133. The Loyal Independent Sheffield Volunteers fired on a crowd, killing two citizens and wounding several. The Home Secretary, the Duke of Portland, wrote to the Reverend John Wilkinson of his "great concern at the unhappy consequences," but conceded that the measures taken appeared to have been "unavoidable" (H.O. 43 / 7 / 111, Duke of Portland, 10 Aug. 1795). Compare *YC*, 17 Aug. 1795; *LMCh*, 10 Aug. 1795; and Donnelly and Baxter, "Sheffield," pp. 402–403, where the apt parallel with Peterloo is drawn.

134. *LiRSM*, 26 Aug. 1791; *YC*, 16 and 23 Aug., and 6 Sept. 1791.

135. Kussmaul, "The Ambiguous Mobility of Farm Servants," 222–235.

9. Riots and Community Politics in Historical Perspective

1. For Yorkshire and Lancashire, see Roger A. E. Wells, *Dearth and Distress in Yorkshire, 1793–1802*, Borthwick Papers no. 52 (York: Borthwick Institute of Historical Research, University of York, 1977), pp. 16–22, 24–26, 28–29; and Alan Booth, "Food Riots in the North-West of England, 1790–1801," *Past and Present*, 77 (Nov. 1977), 91, 93–99. Other examples are drawn from H.O. 42, and *CI, LMCh*.

2. C. R. Dobson, *Masters and Journeymen: A Prehistory of Industrial Relations, 1717–1800* (London: Croom Helm, 1980), chap. 6; Newcastle / Tyneside: Norman McCord and David E. Brewster, "Some Labour Troubles of the 1790s in North East England," *International Review of Social History*, 13 (1968), 370–375; Chester: H.O. 42 / 74, John Bennett, 29 Dec. 1803.

3. H.O. 42 / 51, W. W. Watson to Duke of Portland, 31 Aug., 1, 3, and 7 Sept. 1800.

4. *CI*, 23 April 1796, and *NCh*, 23 April 1796; Sidney Webb and Beatrice Webb, *English Local Government*, 11 vols. (1903–1929; reprint ed., Hamden, Conn.: Archon Books, 1963), III, *The Manor and the Borough*, 536, 553; for charity, see *NCh*, 1795 and 1800.

5. J. K. Edwards, "The Economic Development of Norwich, 1750–1850, with Special Reference to the Worsted Industry" (Ph.D. diss., University of Leeds, 1963), p. 449; "Senex," *East Anglian*, 31 Jan. and 14 Feb. 1832, quoted in Edwards, "Economic Development," p. 240; and *P. P.* 1840, XXIII, 306, 311–312.

6. On Norwich politics, see C. B. Jewson, *The Jacobin City: A Portrait of Norwich in Its Reaction to the French Revolution, 1788–1802* (Glasgow: Blackie & Son, 1975); B. D. Hayes, "Politics in Norfolk, 1750–1832" (Ph.D. diss., Cambridge University, 1957); *NCh*, 1790, 1796, 1802; and Albert Goodwin, *The Friends of Liberty: The English Democratic Movement in the Age of the French Revolution* (London: Hutchinson & Co., 1979), pp.

154–158, 275; and H.O. 42 / 22 / 413–414 and 520, reports from Norwich by Mr. Alderson, 17 and 26 Nov. 1792.

7. This paragraph summarizes some of the findings of John Money, *Experience and Identity: Birmingham and the West Midlands, 1760–1800* (Montreal: McGill-Queen's University Press, 1977), especially chaps. 3–7, and pp. 263–267 and 278–283.

8. Ibid., pp. 220–223, 261–267; R. B. Rose, "The Priestley Riots of 1791," *Past and Present*, 18 (Nov. 1960), 71–72, 78–82; *BG*, 6 April 1801; H.O. 42 / 35, magistrates of Birmingham, 23 June 1795; and H.O. 42 / 52, magistrates of Birmingham, 3 Oct. 1800. For the artisans, see Birmingham Reference Library, Ms. diary of Edward Pickard. I am grateful to Mr. E. P. Thompson for this reference. For the food riots, see, for instance, *LMCh*, 25 June 1795, and *LP*, 14–17 Feb., 12 and 15–17 Sept. 1800.

9. *LMCh*, 25 June 1795, and Birmingham Reference Library, Ms. diary of Edward Pickard; *BG*, 10, 17 Aug. 1795, 6 April 1801; and *LObs*, 23 Sept. 1810.

10. H.O. 42 / 35, Mr. Legge, 8 July 1795; Birmingham Reference Library, Ms. diary of Edward Pickard; *BG*, 21 Sept. 1795, and 15, 29 Sept. 1800.

11. Malcolm I. Thomis, *Politics and Society in Nottingham, 1785–1835* (Oxford: Basil Blackwell, 1969), chaps. 7–8, and pp. 51–52 and 101–102; *LCh*, 26–29 June 1790; *CI*, 3 Aug. 1793, 19 July 1794; *YC*, 7 July 1794.

12. *LEM*, 1 and 5–8 Sept. 1800; *LSt*, 17 Sept. 1800; H.O. 42 / 51, T. and E. Golby, 7 Sept. 1800, in William Walford, Banbury, 17 Sept. 1800, and George Coldham, 6 Sept. 1800; H.O. 43 / 12, Duke of Portland, 10 Sept. 1800.

13. This unique letter was confiscated from the pocket of a "great leader" of a contingent of Middleton Cheney "stocking weavers" who rioted in Banbury. Middleton Cheney was some sixty miles from Nottingham (H.O. 42 / 51, T. and E. Golby, 7 Sept. 1800, enclosed in William Walford, Banbury, 17 Sept. 1800).

14. J. Stevenson, "The London 'Crimp' Riots of 1794," *International Review of Social History*, 16 (1971), 40–58; John Stevenson, *Popular Disturbances in England, 1700–1870* (New York: Longman's, 1979), pp. 53–67, 74–90, 164–166, 173–175, 184–190; M. Dorothy George, *London Life in the Eighteenth Century* (Harmondsworth: Penguin Books, 1925, reprint ed., 1965), pp. 166, 199, 208; Dobson, *Masters and Journeymen*, pp. 38–46.

15. *LiRSM*, 23 July 1790; *LMCh*, 16 Aug. 1808; people accused of "unnatural crimes," including the "Vere-street gang": *LMCh*, 10 July 1810; *LCh*, 28 Sept., and 9 and 18 Oct. 1810; and *LObs*, 14 Oct. 1810.

16. For the "Old Price" riots, see many reports in *LT*, *LMCh*, *LCh*, *LObs*, Sept.–Dec. 1809. "Cock-and-hen" clubs: *LT*, 24 June 1793; and *LMCh*, 29 Dec. 1798. Donnybrooks: *LObs*, 19 Aug. 1804; and *LMCh*, 23 Sept. 1809.

17. My national sample (see Table 1) includes 5 food riots in London between 1790 and 1810, among 123 London riots of all kinds. Stevenson

has found 20 "price" riots in London between 1790 and 1821 among 224 riots of all kinds (*Popular Disturbances,* p. 307). Stevenson and Rudé have suggested explanations for the rarity of food riots in London that I paraphrase in the following discussion. J. Stevenson, "Food Riots in England, 1792–1818," in *Popular Protest and Public Order: Six Studies in British History, 1790–1920,* ed. R. Quinault and J. Stevenson (London: George Allen & Unwin, 1974), p. 51; and George Rudé, *Paris and London in the 18th Century: Studies in Popular Protest* (London: Collins-Fontana, 1970), pp. 55–57.

18. Calculated from figures given in Stevenson, *Popular Disturbances,* p. 92.

19. Stevenson, "Food Riots," p. 51.

20. The Norwich Court of Guardians, for instance, bought wheat in Hamburg (P.C. 1 / 29 / A64, Jeremiah Ives, 24 Aug. 1795). The Manchester Union of Friendly Societies ordered grain direct from a Hamburgh house in the winter of 1801 (*MM,* 14 Dec. 1802).

21. For the political and economic springs of London protest, see George Rudé, *Wilkes and Liberty: A Social Study of 1763 to 1774* (Oxford: Oxford University Press, 1962); Rudé, *Paris and London,* chaps. 8–12; and Stevenson, *Popular Disturbances,* chaps. 4, 8, and 9; and John Stevenson, ed., *London in the Age of Reform* (Oxford: Basil Blackwell, 1977). Nicholas Rogers, "Aristocratic Clientage, Trade and Independency: Popular Politics in Pre-Radical Westminister," *Past and Present,* 61 (Nov. 1973), 96–104.

22. George Rudé, "The Growth of Cities and Popular Revolt, 1750–1850: With Particular Reference to Paris," in *French Government and Society, 1500–1850: Essays in Memory of Alfred Cobban,* ed. J. F. Bosher (London: Athlone Press of the University of London, 1973), pp. 172–173, 190.

23. Harold Perkin, *The Origins of Modern English Society, 1780–1880* (London: Routledge and Kegan Paul, 1969), pp. 188–192.

24. See, for instance, Gwyn A. Williams, *Artisans and Sans-Culottes: Popular Movements in France and Britain during the French Revolution* (New York: W. W. Norton and Co., 1969), p. 11.

25. R. J. White, *Waterloo to Peterloo* (London: Heinemann, 1957), p. 191.

26. Charles Tilly, "Collective Violence in European Perspective," in *Violence in America: Historical and Comparative Perspectives,* ed. Hugh Davis Graham and Ted Robert Gurr (New York: Bantam Books, 1969), p. 16; George Rudé, *The Crowd in History: A Study of Popular Disturbances in France and England, 1730–1848* (New York: John Wiley & Sons, 1964), pp. 226–227, 239; Stevenson, *Popular Disturbances,* pp. 309–311.

27. Rudé, *Crowd in History,* pp. 68, 268. Compare Stevenson, *Popular Disturbances,* pp. 112, 135.

28. Charles Tilly, Louise Tilly, and Richard Tilly, *The Rebellious Century, 1830–1930* (Cambridge, Mass.: Harvard University Press, 1975), pp. 49–50, and see Chap. 8, above.

29. McCord and Brewster, "Some Labour Troubles," pp. 377–383; Stevenson, *Popular Disturbances,* p. 148.

30. Stevenson, *Popular Disturbances,* p. 147; and *CI,* 22 Oct. 1796, and *LMCh,* 17 July 1795. For similar disputes among local militia units see *LObs,* 25 June 1809 and 3 June 1810; and *NC,* 26 May 1810.

31. See Chap. 2.

32. Compare Charles Tilly, "Food Supply and Public Order in Modern Europe," in *The Formation of National States in Western Europe,* ed. Charles Tilly (Princeton: Princeton University Press, 1975), especially pp. 387, 431; and Louise A. Tilly, "The Food Riot as a Form of Political Protest in France," *Journal of Interdisciplinary History,* 2 (1971), 25–26, 35–45, 56–57. The argument may well work better for food riots in Continental societies, which, by comparison with those in England, had more people living in local peasant subsistence economies, less-developed national markets at the beginning of the eighteenth century, and more ambitious governmental programs of market regulation—and perhaps more mouths to feed, given the importance of large land armies on the Continent.

33. John Stevenson has emphasized that in 1795–1796, "at least fifty food disturbances took place at communication centers, either coastal ports, canal or river ports, or towns within easy carting distance of major population centers." See "Food Riots in England, 1792–1818," in *Popular Protest and Public Order: Six Studies in British History, 1790–1920* (London: George Allen and Unwin, 1974), p. 43. But that is not a large proportion of the number of food riots in that period: my national sample shows 120 food riots in 1795–1796. Many of the towns Stevenson includes would have had riots for reasons other than their being communication centers (see Chap. 2), and his figure of fifty probably includes "disturbances" that would not be included in my national sample, although Stevenson does not define his criteria.

34. Markets: Alan Everitt, "The Marketing of Agricultural Produce," in *The Agrarian History of England and Wales,* ed. Joan Thirsk, vol. 4, *1500–1640* (Cambridge: Cambridge University Press, 1967), pp. 467–478, 568–573. Early food riots: Peter Clark, "Popular Protest and Disturbance in Kent, 1558–1640," *Economic History Review,* 2nd ser., 29 (Aug. 1976), 368–370; John Walter and Keith Wrightson, "Dearth and the Social Order in Early Modern England," *Past and Present,* 71 (May 1976), 26–27. The national market: C. W. J. Granger and C. M. Elliott, "A Fresh Look at Wheat Prices and Markets in the Eighteenth Century," *Economic History Review,* 2nd ser., 20 (1967), 262. Granger and Elliott qualify their conclusions: "...the basic conclusion that the three series [London, Eton, Winchester] are not badly out of step...This implies a fairly well-developed market over the area concerned...it is more normal to treat the different markets as one...in wheat at least, the autonomy of markets can be seriously overstated."

35. H.O. 42 / 51, W. W. Watson, 7 Sept. 1800.

36. Walter James Shelton, *English Hunger and Industrial Disorders: A Study of Social Conflict during the First Decade of George III's Reign* (London: Macmillan, 1973), pp. 4–5, 7–8; Compare Money, *Experience and Identity,* pp. 249–250. The shock was registered and perhaps assauged by twenty-

four death sentences imposed on rioters by special commissions in 1766, though most were reprieved (Rudé, *Crowd in History*, pp. 43–44).

37. Rudé, *Crowd in History*, p. 268.

38. See Chap. 4 and Jewson, *Jacobin City*, pp. 64, 66.

39. See, for instance, Stevenson, *Popular Disturbances*, pp. 266, 293.

40. Rudé, *Crowd in History*, pp. 66–68; E. J. Hobsbawm, *Labouring Men: Studies in the History of Labor* (London: Weidenfeld & Nicholson, 1964), pp. 8–9, 16, 130, 144.

41. Dobson, *Masters and Journeymen*, chap. 1, especially p. 22.

42. Stevenson, *Popular Disturbances*, p. 130.

43. Dobson, *Masters and Journeymen*, p. 27; and Hobsbawm, *Labouring Men*, pp. 7–14.

44. Hobsbawm, *Labouring Men*, pp. 7, 10–12. For Shepton Mallet, see J. de L. Mann, *The Cloth Industry in the West of England from 1640 to 1880* (Oxford: Oxford University Press, 1971), pp. 124–125.

45. As for instance in the mechanization of worsted spinning in Yorkshire, which displaced the spinsters (spinners) in the Norfolk countryside who had formerly supplied the Norwich weaving industry with yarn (Edwards, "Economic Development of Norwich," pp. 160–185).

46. Dobson, *Masters and Journeymen*, pp. 27, 29.

47. Ibid., pp. 27–28.

48. I have counted 44.5 labor riots, that is, 41 riots in which labor issues were uppermost, and 7 (divided by 2) in which labor issues were coequal with other causes, usually food prices. The riot over apprenticeship took place at Banbury: H.O. 42 / 26 / 36, Robert Spillman, 25 Aug. 1793; see also Chap. 1. For Tyneside and Lancashire, see McCord and Brewster, "Some Labour Troubles," pp. 367–377, and Chaps. 6 and 9, above.

49. Sidney Webb and Beatrice Webb, *The History of Trade Unionism*, rev. ed. (London: Longman's, Green and Co., 1920), chap. 1 and p. 26.

50. Dobson, *Masters and Journeymen*, pp. 25, 30, 36–46, 74–92; Chap. 2; McCord and Brewster, "Some Labour Troubles," pp. 367–375; Hobsbawm, *Labouring Men*, p. 13. Compare Stevenson, *Popular Disturbances*, p. 131.

51. Franklin F. Mendels, "Proto-Industrialization: The First Stage of the Industrialization Process," *Journal of Economic History*, 32 (March 1972), 241–261.

52. Roy A. Church and S. D. Chapman, "Gravener Henson and the Making of the English Working Class," in *Land, Labour and Population in the Industrial Revolution*, ed. E. L. Jones and G. E. Mingay (New York: Barnes and Noble, 1967), p. 145; Edwards, "Economic Development," pp. 40–42; George, *London Life*, pp. 174–202, 210. For the London tailors, for instance, see T. M. Parssinen and I. J. Prothero, "The London Tailors' Strike of 1834 and the Collapse of the Grand National Consolidated Trades' Union: A Police Spy's Report," *International Review of Social History*, 22 (1977), pp. 68–71.

53. Frank Ongley Darvall, *Popular Disturbances and Public Order in Regency England* (London: Oxford University Press, 1934; reprint ed., 1969), pp. 26–27.

54. Ibid., pp. 39–42, and Church and Chapman, "Gravener Henson," p. 145.

55. Darvall, *Popular Disturbances,* p. 44.

56. Thomis, *Politics and Society,* pp. 38–39, 81; Darvall, *Popular Disturbances,* 44–47, 64; J. L. Hammond and Barbara Hammond, *The Skilled Labourer, 1760–1832* (London: Longman's, Green and Co., 1919), pp. 258–259.

57. Darvall, *Popular Disturbances,* p. 209, states that by February 1812, more than 1,000 frames had been broken in the 3 Midland counties. See Malcolm I. Thomis, *The Luddites: Machine-Breaking in Regency England* (Newton Abbot: David and Charles, 1970), pp. 177–182, for a list of incidents in the Midlands. In that list Thomis includes only 14 incidents in Nottingham itself, each involving 1, 2, or several frames. Compare A. Temple Patterson, *Radical Leicester: A History of Leicester, 1780–1850* (Leicester: University College, 1954), pp. 58, 105. On the "roughneck" explanation for the geography of Luddism, compare Patterson, *Radical Leicester,* pp. 59, 106; Thomis, *Politics and Society,* p. 86; and Church and Chapman, "Gravener Henson," pp. 140–142.

58. E. P. Thompson, *The Making of the English Working Class,* 2nd ed. (Harmondsworth: Penguin Books, 1968), pp. 928–930; Hammond and Hammond, *Skilled Labourer,* pp. 227–236; Darvall, *Popular Disturbances,* pp. 43, 77–79, 85, 87, 327–330; and Thomis, *Politics and Society,* pp. 86–87, 90–91.

59. Darvall, *Popular Disturbances,* p. 168.

60. Compare E. P. Thompson, *The Making of the English Working Class* (New York: Vintage Books, 1966), pp. 543, 548–552. Thompson places more emphasis upon ideological change and the abrogation of paternalistic legislation (c. 1800–1814) than I believe is warranted by the chronology of the development of the framework knitting industry.

61. E. J. Hobsbawm and George Rudé, *Captain Swing* (New York: Pantheon Books, 1968), pp. 207, 219, 243–246.

62. See Robert Moore, *Pitman, Preachers and Politics: The Effects of Methodism in a Durham Mining Community* (Cambridge: Cambridge University Press, 1974). The organizations of the "labor aristocracy" represent other such networks of collective identity that may have contributed broad social reinforcement to trade unions. See R. Q. Gray, "Styles of Life, The 'Labor Aristocracy,' and Class Relations in Later 19th Century Edinburgh," *International Review of Social History,* 18 (1973), 428–452, and Geoffrey Crossick, *An Artisan Elite in Victorian Society: Kentish London, 1840–1880* (London: Croom Helm, 1978).

63. John Brewer, *Party Ideology and Popular Politics at the Accession of George III* (Cambridge: Cambridge University Press, 1976), chaps. 8–9, especially pp. 190–191; John Money, "Taverns, Coffee Houses and Clubs: Local Politics and Popular Articulacy in the Birmingham Area, in

the Age of the American Revolution," *The Historical Journal*, 14 (1971), pp. 15–47; and Money, *Experience and Identity*, pp. 279–283.

64. The phrase is Rudé's. George Rudé, *The Crowd in the French Revolution* (Oxford: Oxford University Press, 1959), p. 239. Compare Thompson, *Making of the Working Class* (1966), p 75.

65. Thomis, *Politics and Society*, p. 180; Stevenson, *Popular Disturbances*, p 186; Jewson, *Jacobin City*, pp. 49–50, and *CI*, 19 July 1794; F. K. Donnelly and J. L. Baxter, "Sheffield and the English Revolutionary Tradition, 1791–1820," *International Review of Social History*, 20 (1975), 400, 412–415.

66. Eleven "Church and King" riots are included in my national sample of 617 riots, 1790–1810. See Table 1.

67. John Dinwiddy, "Luddism and Politics in the Northern Counties," *Social History*, 10 (January 1979), 33–63. Jewson, *Jacobin City*, pp. 32, 40, 46–51, 66, 80; and Goodwin, *Friends of Liberty*, pp. 212–213, 275–276, 279–280, 377–378.

68. The title of chap. 13 (1850–1870) in Stevenson, *Popular Disturbances*.

69. Michael E. Rose, "The Anti-Poor Law Movement in the North of England," *Northern History*, 1 (1966), 74–86, 90; Nicholas C. Edsall, *The Anti-Poor Law Movement, 1834–1844* (Manchester: Manchester University Press, 1971), pp. 45–100, 255–260.

70. For the riot in Bristol in 1831, see Susan Thomas, *The Bristol Riots* (Bristol: Bristol Historical Association, 1974), and for the Todmorden anti-Poor Law riots of 1838, see Edsall, *Anti-Poor Law Movement*, pp. 157–160, and excerpts from the "Fifth Annual Report of the Poor Law Commissioners" (1839), pp. 31–34, reprinted in G. D. H. Cole and A. W. Filson, *British Working Class Movements: Select Documents, 1789–1875* (London: Macmillan, 1967), pp. 337–340.

71. See Perkin, *Origins of Modern English Society*, chaps. 7–9.

72. Charles Tilly, "Collective Violence in European Perspective," pp. 4–5. Donald Richter, "Public Order and Popular Disturbances in Great Britain, 1865–1914," (Ph.D. diss., University of Maryland, 1964). Moreover, Richter's study rests primarily upon printed sources, and so is a sample of all disturbances.

73. Stevenson, *Popular Disturbances*, pp. 279–282; and Walter L. Arnstein, "The Murphy Riots: A Victorian Dilemma," *Victorian Studies*, 19 (Sept. 1975), 51–71.

74. Tilly, "Collective Violence," p. 43.

75. See Standish Meacham, *A Life Apart: The English Working Class, 1890–1914* (Cambridge, Mass.: Harvard University Press, 1977), pp. 44–45, 48–54. The idea that collective violence depends upon "solidarity" and that urbanization disrupts the bases of solidarity, after which new kinds may be rebuilt, is suggested by Charles Tilly, Louise Tilly, and Richard Tilly, *The Rebellious Century, 1830–1930* (Cambridge, Mass.: Harvard University Press, 1975), pp. 83–84.

76. Thompson, *Making of the Working Class*, pp. 9, 11.

77. R. S. Neale, *Class in English History, 1680–1850* (Oxford: Basil Blackwell, 1981), pp. 19–24. Neale goes on to say that for Marx, "This sense of the historical role of the *class* requires a perception of the antagonism which inheres in class relations as defined. Along with this must go an understanding of the fact that every *class* struggle is a political struggle and that every political struggle must be aimed at the overthrow, almost certainly the revolutionary overthrow, of the existing political state" (p. 23). Indeed, many Marxist scholars have virtually equated class consciousness and revolutionary consciousness. I would argue, however, that in the nineteenth century, English workers could and did become conscious of themselves as a class within a class system of power and property that exploited them, without either becoming *practically* revolutionary *or* accepting the existing system and its "bourgeois" values as legitimate. Rather, in many instances they held to a radical critique of the system as an ideal, while working pragmatically for less than ideal improvements—but such is most political life.

78. Theda Skocpol, "France, Russia, China: A Structural Analysis of Social Revolution," *Comparative Studies in Society and History*, 18 (1976), 175–210; and Theda Skocpol, *States and Social Revolutions: A Comparative Analysis of France, Russia, and China* (Cambridge: Cambridge University Press, 1979).

79. Thomas Pakenham, *The Year of Liberty: The Story of the Great Irish Rebellion of 1798* (London: Hodder & Stoughton, 1969).

80. Among the literature on hegemony, the pieces most pertinent to this discussion are E. P. Thompson, "Patrician Society, Plebeian Culture," *Journal of Social History*, 7 (Summer 1974), 387–405; E. P. Thompson, "Eighteenth-Century English Society: Class Struggle without Class?" *Social History*, 3 (1978), 133–165; and Douglas Hay, "Property, Authority, and the Criminal Law," in Douglas Hay et al., *Albion's Fatal Tree: Crime and Society in Eighteenth Century England* (New York: Pantheon, 1975), especially pp. 49, 56, 61–63; and E. P. Thompson, *Whigs and Hunters: The Origins of the Black Act* (New York: Pantheon, 1975), p. 262.

81. Besides the works cited in note 80, see Douglas Hay, "Poaching and the Game Laws on Cannock Chase," and E. P. Thompson, "The Crime of Anonymity," in Hay et al., *Albion's Fatal Tree*, pp. 189–308.

82. Thompson, "Patrician Society, Plebeian Culture," p. 405.

83. Perkin, *Origins of Modern English Society*, pp. 183–195; and Thompson, *Making of the Working Class*, pp. 107–115, 177–178.

84. This view would support those who see artisan radicalism, not factory proletarianization, as the chief source of Victorian socialism and laborism. See, for example, Gareth Stedman Jones, *Outcast London* (Oxford: Oxford University Press, 1971), pp. 339–341, and the sources he cites. Thus the decline of riots as viable means of local political bargaining would add the social role of displaced citizen to the more familiar ideological and craft bases of artisan radicalism.

Index